Sew Any Fabric

Foreword by Nancy Zieman

Claire Shaeffer

Published by

kp krause publications
An F&W Publications Company

700 East State Street • Iola, WI 54990-0001
715-445-2214 • 888-457-2873
www.krause.com

Please call or write for our free catalog of publications. To place
an order or obtain a free catalog, please call 800-258-0929.

Library of Congress Catalog Number: 2003108199
ISBN: 0-87349-643-4

Photos page 5 courtesy of Lacy Lovelies Fashion Fabrics (left)
and Simplicity Patterns (right).
Photo page 8 courtesy of Lyn Lackey and Bernina of America.
Photo page 108 courtesy of PtakCouture.com.

Edited by Nicole Gould.
Designed by Marilyn McGrane.

Printed in the United States of America

Acknowledgments

I wish to thank the many friends, colleagues, home-sewers, and businesses who took the time to answer questions, make suggestions, and provide photographs for this book.

- Special thanks to Nancy Zieman for writing the Foreword.
- Barbara Atkins, Diane Faulkner, Linda Fitzerald, Lissa Gay, Vicki Haseman, Ann Jacobi, Dawn Jardine, Bill Jones, Judy Kirpich, Ngai Kwan, Barbie McCormick, Carolyn Morris, Linda Nicolson, Debbie Ramseyer, Abby Riba, Judith Scroggin-Gridley, Welmoed Sisson, and Wanda Stephen for their help with the Sewability classifications.
- Phyllis Tortora and Billie Collier for technical information about textiles.
- Susan Brenne, Ruth Ciemnoczolowski, Marsha Cohen, Tina Colombo, Rochelle Harper, and Penny Schwyn for sharing their knowledge of various fabrics.
- My colleagues in the Professional Association of Custom Clothiers (PACC) for their continued support and the wealth of information which they have shared so generously.
- Cheri Collins for developing the stabilizer chart.
- Joy Landeira for general suggestions and criticism.
- Barb Alexander and Lee MacKenzie at Batik Butik, Susan Andriks, Art of Photography, Elaine Bakken, Kathy Barnard at Martha Pullen, Dacia Bates and Sandi Bolton at Lacy Lovelies, Bernina of America, Regina Causemann at Burda, Kathleen Cheetham at Petite Plus Patterns, Nancy Cornwell, Ila Erickson, Nancy Erickson, Frank Biemer and Fairfield Processing Co., Inc., Susan Fears, Raffaella Galeotafiore at Solotu Design Studio, Maria Guzman, Pam Howard, Pamela Isaacs-Erny at Off-the-Cuff Designs, Lyn Lackey, Jo Leichte at Bernina, Carol Kimbell, Carol Lambeth, Joi Mahon, Kathy Marrone and Jennifer Fragleasso at The McCall Pattern Co., Karen Maslowski, Linda MacPhee at MacPhee Outerwear Workshop Ltd., Make It Yourself With Wool, Eric McMaster and Kimberly Wick at KWIK•SEW®, Monica McMurry, Tammy O'Connell of Jitney Patterns, Pamela Ptak, Mary Ray, Rochelle Harper Patterns, Debi Shaeffer, Judy Raymond and Maureen Dudley at Simplicity Patterns, Paul Shanley and Diane Tatara at Wild Ginger Software®, Maj Smith, Gabrielle Stanley, Lena Stepanenko, Linda Stewart at Joy and Co., Marinda Stewart, Francine Walls, and Gloria Young for providing photographs.
- Jim Guin at American & Efird, Inc., Wade Roberts at Gutermann, and Vicky Smith at YLI for providing threads and information about them.
- Fabric Collections, Fashion Sewing Group, Freudenberg Nonwovens, Greenberg & Hammer, Inc., HTC, Inc., Palmer/Pletsch Inc., Richard Brooks, and Staple Sewing Aids Corp. for providing interfacing swatches and information about them.
- My editor Niki Gould and the staff at Krause Publications for making my writing look good.

Foreword

Claire may not realize this, but her first book, *Claire Shaeffer's Fabric Sewing Guide*, has been a ready reference book on my desk for years. Now that I've had the opportunity to read her updated book *Sew Any Fabric*, I have added this second book to my bookshelf, which houses books that I use on a frequent basis when preparing for TV shows, writing articles, and answering viewer questions. I especially appreciate the user-friendly format, easy-to-follow directions, and practical information. It is a valuable resource for all sewing enthusiasts. I know that you, too, will keep this book handy and use it frequently.

Nancy Zieman
President, Nancy's Notions Producer/Host, Public Television's
Sewing With Nancy

Table of Contents

Introduction • 6

Part One • The Fabrics • 8

Part Two • Sewing Techniques • 108

**Part Three
Fabric / Fiber
Dictionary
118**

**Part Four
Appendices
138**

**Resource List
154**

**Bibliography
155**

**Index
156**

Introduction

A quick reference, *Sew Any Fabric* was designed to accommodate the busy, hectic schedules of the twenty-first century. This indispensable guide was written for everyone: home sewers and professionals alike who are sewing new fabrics, looking for fresh ideas, improving their skills, or learning to sew; but it was written especially for anyone who wants good results, but doesn't have a lot of time to get them.

Sew Any Fabric's user-friendly format focuses on 88 of today's most popular fabrics while the Fabric/Fiber Dictionary defines and describes an additional 600 fabrics which can be sewn in a similar manner. Organized for easy reference, this must-have guide provides the practical, up-to-date information you need to sew any fabric successfully and confidently.

Part One - *The Fabrics* is arranged in an easy-to-use, A-to-Z format. Each fabric is described in a short, concise chapter which includes a brief definition, its Sewability classification, a list of similar fabrics, suggestions for using the fabric, garment types, and appropriate design details; a Sewing Checklist; and Workroom Secrets.

The fabric definition describes the fabric and its most important features. This is particularly important for fabrics which are similar, have the same name, or are part of a large group. For example, terry cloth can be a woven or knit, stretch or non-stretch, and each is slightly different.

The unique Sewability classification tells you how easy the fabric is to sew. I have divided the fabrics into six groups: Very Easy, Easy, Average, Above Average, Challenging, and Very Challenging so you will know what to expect if you haven't sewn the fabric before.

Very Easy	Easy	Average	Above Average	Challenging	Very Challenging

The Sewing Checklist summarizes the basic details for the fabric: Essential Supplies, Machine Setup, and Sewing Basics. The Sewing Checklist is a thimbleful of sewing know-how—everything you need to know in 30 seconds or less. Here, I have selected the most frequently used methods which will produce quality results when you have a busy schedule and limited time.

The Workroom Secrets provide additional information, helpful hints, secrets of the trade, and specific suggestions which apply to that particular fabric. Many of these are based on my experiences as a college instructor for more than twenty years.

Fundamental sewing procedures which are common to all fabrics are described in the first chapter—Any Fabric. These include selecting needles, threads, and notions; layout, cutting, and marking techniques; stabilizing seams and edges; tissue and sandwich stitching; eliminating or changing a seamline; and reducing the sleeve cap.

Part Two - *The Sewing Techniques* provides descriptions and easy-to-follow, step-by-step details for sewing the seams, hems, edge finishes, and closures which I have recommended in the fabric chapters. To maximize your time, these directions feature quality techniques with little hand sewing. To expand your knowledge of garment construction, consult my earlier books: *Claire Shaeffer's Fabric Sewing Guide*, *Couture Sewing Techniques*, *High Fashion Sewing Secrets*, and *The Complete Book of Sewing Short Cuts*.

Part Three - *The Fabric/Fiber Dictionary* describes an additional 600 fabrics. In addition to the definition, I have included a cross reference to a similar fabric(s) in Part One - The Fabrics.

Part Four - *The Appendices* are a mini-encyclopedia filled with additional material regarding sewing machine needles, threads, needle/thread guide, interfacings, stabilizers, fiber identification, sewing terms, and a resource list. Here, you will find useful answers to frequently asked questions.

How to Use This Book

Sew Any Fabric is an indispensable guide for sewers at all skill levels.

Begin with the first chapter—Any Fabric. I exercised a little poetic license here since "Any" isn't really the first alphabetically; but the information in this chapter applies to every fabric, every time you sew. It is so important that I didn't want you to miss it.

Review the chapter on the fabric you plan to sew. For some fabrics, you will want to read about similar fabrics as well.

If your fabric is not listed as a chapter in Part One - The Fabrics, look for it in the index; many will be listed as a Similar Fabric. Others will be described in Part Three - The Fabric/Fiber Dictionary with a cross reference for sewing suggestions.

Review the step-by-step directions for various sewing techniques—seams, hems, edge finishes, and closures—in Part Three - The Sewing Techniques. Make some samples to fine-tune old skills, learn new skills, or determine which techniques you like best.

If you are a novice or need a quick refresher course, review the Appendices. You will find the additional material particularly useful.

Check out the needle, thread, and interfacing charts. Similar products are grouped together so you are not limited if your favorites are not available.

Look for unfamiliar sewing terms in the Glossary - Appendix F.

To reap the most from this book, read it every time you sew. Make notes in it. Highlight the things you like; cross out what you don't. Experiment with new fabrics; and add your own experiences.

Sew Any Fabric was written for you. From the beginning, this book has focused on basic, quality techniques, how they are applied to today's most popular fabrics, and how you can apply what you already know to sew any fabric successfully. Use it to develop your confidence and skills.

There will always be new fabrics to inspire, excite, and delight you. Some fabrics will be more challenging than others; but, with the knowledge you have acquired in the past, you can meet these challenges and unravel their secrets to sew any fabric successfully.

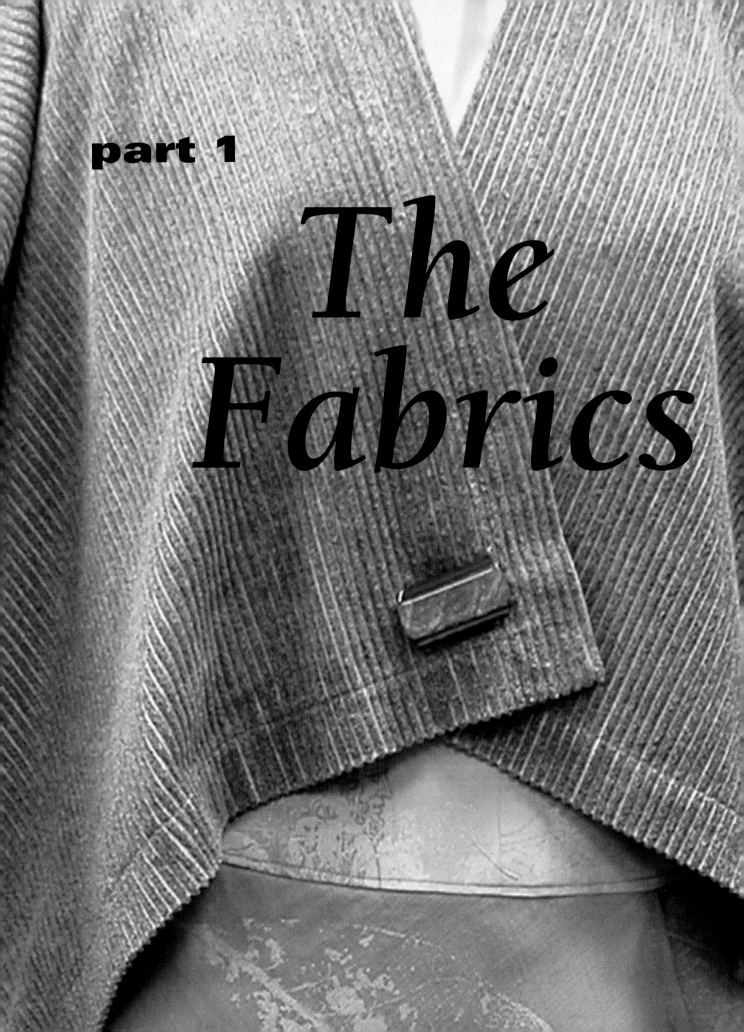

part 1

The Fabrics

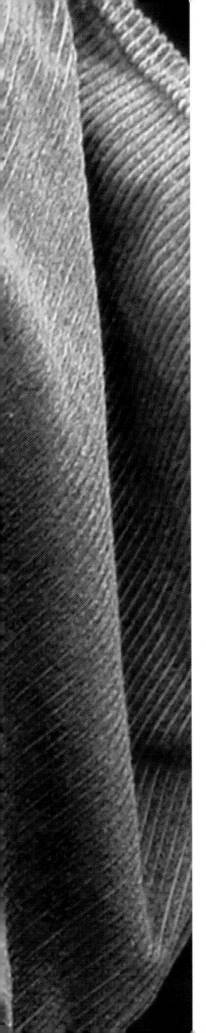

Any Fabric

There are many variables when sewing different fabrics and, sometimes, when sewing the same fabric; but there are some basic principles and techniques which will ensure success when sewing any fabric.

I begin *Sew Any Fabric* with Any Fabric, even though it is not first alphabetically. Here, I describe in detail the tools, supplies, and techniques which I personally use and recommend throughout the book. If you are a novice, you will learn various techniques which you can apply to all fabrics. If you haven't sewn for a while, I'll introduce you to my favorite notions and a few new techniques. If you are more experienced, you will find a quick review of techniques which I have taught for many years.

There are hundreds of different fabrics available today, but many are sewn using similar techniques. *Sew Any Fabric* focuses on the 88 most popular or frequently sewn fabrics. In each chapter, I have included a list of Similar Fabrics which are sewn in a similar manner as well as suggestions in the Fabric and Fiber Dictionary to guide you when sewing an additional 600 fabrics.

Almost every fabric can be used for a variety of designs from everyday casual garments to high fashion evening wear. The photographs and list of Design Elements provide a guide for creating designs and choosing patterns.

I have selected a variety of designs to inspire and excite you. Some are my own while others came from students, colleagues, designers, and pattern companies. Most are simply styled to showcase the fabric attractively. A few are innovative originals; but many similar patterns are available at your local retailers.

Photo courtesy of KWIK•SEW®

Worsted • *Simply styled, this chic jacket has a relaxed fit and easy-to-sew collar.*

The models are just as diverse as the designs. Some are professionals while others are home-sewers like you and me. Some models are pencil thin; others, pleasingly plump. Some are very young; others, not so young.

- When sewing a difficult or new fabric, choose an easy-to-sew design with minimal seaming.
- Sew with a positive attitude.
- To save time, stitch it right the first time.
- Test, test, test; when in doubt practice before stitching the garment.
- Start all new projects with a new machine needle.
- Change needles frequently; synthetic fibers dull needles faster than natural fibers.
- Use polyester thread for more elastic seams
- Wind the bobbin slowly. When wound on high, the thread heats up and stretches. Then, when sewn into the seam, it relaxes, and the seam puckers. Puckered seams cannot be pressed out.
- Hold the fabric firmly in front and back of the foot when stitching.
- Stitch with the fabric bulk to the left of the needle.
- To reduce skipped stitches and other stitching problems when straight stitching, use a foot such as a wide straight-stitch foot to hold the fabric firmly.
- Stitch directionally with the grain; generally, this is from wide to narrow on the garment section.
- Stitch in the direction of the nap, as if you were petting an animal.
- Begin stitching at the point of difficulty (e.g., when stitching reverse corners, begin at the corner; when stitching a notched collar, begin at the notch).
- Stitch with the longer or stretchier fabric on the bottom.
- Stitch with the bias on the bottom.
- Sew flat; set the pockets before sewing the side seams.
- Sew inside loops, circles, sleeves, pant legs, and collars carefully to avoid inadvertently stitching through unwanted layers.
- When topstitching, stitch with the right-side up unless directed otherwise.
- Understitch faced edges.
- The most common causes of stitching problems are a dirty machine; an incorrectly threaded machine; and a damaged, wrong size, or wrong type needle.
- Pressing is an essential phase of sewing. Good pressing can enhance a poorly stitched garment; poor pressing can destroy a well-made design.

The Sewing Machine

Your most important tool is a quality sewing machine. It does not have to be the latest model or the most expensive machine. I have several machines ranging from my first machine which only straight stitches to a top of the line, computer model that will stitch fabulous embroideries as well as beautiful garments; I use them all.

If you don't have a machine, talk to your local dealer; ask him or her to help you select a machine. If you have a machine that has not been used for a while, have it cleaned and serviced.

Essentials Supplies

The Sewing Checklist in each chapter provides a concise outline of tools, supplies, and techniques for that particular fabric.

Before sewing any fabric, review the list of Essential Supplies. You will already have most of these items; if you don't, purchase them when you buy your fabric.

Needles

Even the most expensive machine will not perform well if you are using dull, bent, or damaged needles or the wrong size or type needles. My machines are not fussy about the brand, so I use needles from many needle manufacturers. Your machine may be more particular.

Needles are described by size and name. The name describes the needle type; i.e., universal, sharp (microtex, denim, quilting), stretch, topstitching, ballpoint. See Appendix A – Sewing Machine Needles for a more complete description of needle types.

In this book, I begin with the needle type which will give the best results. In *Claire Shaeffer's Fabric Sewing Guide*, I listed the needle which was most readily available first; now it is often second on the list.

The needle size describes the diameter of the needle shank: the smaller the number, the smaller the needle. I recommend a range of sizes because most fabrics vary in weight and thickness. I always begin with the smallest size—no need to make a large hole when a small one will do—and make a test seam. If there are skipped stitches, I use a larger needle and/or different needle type.

Generally, for topstitching, machine buttonholes, and embroidery, a larger needle or a topstitching needle will accommodate a heavier thread better.

Threads

Always choose a quality thread. Nothing is more frustrating than thread that breaks frequently.

When selecting cotton, cotton covered polyester, and polyester threads, look for terms such as *long-staple*. Premium cotton threads will be labeled *mercerized*, *Egyptian or Peruvian cotton*, or *extra long staple*.

For natural fiber fabrics (cotton, wool, silk, and linen), I prefer cotton threads which cause fewer stitching problems. But cotton threads are not as elastic, strong, or durable as polyester threads; and, when sewing some fabrics—leather, suede, and waterproof fabrics—cotton threads will mildew or rot.

Sewing threads are available in several weights from fine to heavy-weight. All-purpose threads are medium-weight and most common. See Appendix B – Threads for more information about threads

Many threads do not have the thread size indicated. One reason is that cotton and polyester threads are sized differently; i.e., all-purpose cotton thread (50/3) and polyester thread (100/3) are about the same size.

The thread size (50/3) describes the thread weight (50) and the number of plies (3) which have been twisted together to make the thread. Generally, a higher number indicates a finer thread.

All-purpose or regular threads can be used on most fabrics for general sewing, seaming, buttonholes, and topstitching. They are available in cotton (50/2, 50/3), cotton covered polyester, polyester (100/3), and silk (50, A). Polyester thread is most elastic; cotton, least.

Fine or lightweight threads are preferred for seaming, buttonholes, and topstitching on lightweight fabrics. These threads include fine cotton machine embroidery thread (60/2, 70/2), lightweight polyester, extra-fine cotton covered polyester, lightweight silk (200,100), and lightweight serger threads (120/2).

Machine embroidery/topstitching threads or heavy threads are used for topstitching, machine embroidery, quilting, sewing buttons, strong seams, and joining heavy fabrics. Generally for seaming, I prefer threads which are 40 weight and unglazed, such as cotton and polyester threads for topstitching and machine quilting thread. When heavier threads are not available, substitute two strands of all-purpose thread.

Specialty threads include machine embroidery, textured, serger, glazed, water soluble basting, fusible, and invisible threads.

• *Machine embroidery threads* are available in several weights: 60, 50, 40, and 30. They are designed for topstitching and embroidering and frequently have a nice sheen.

• *Textured threads* include texturized or woolly nylon and woolly polyester. Soft and elastic, these threads leave fewer pressing imprints and add elasticity to seams, hems, and twin needle stitching when used on the bobbin or overlock machine. To use in the needle, use a needle threader to insert the thread.

• *Serger threads* (60/3, 70/3) provide a soft edge finish for serging lightweight fabrics. Lightweight serger threads (80/2, 100/2, 120/2) are less likely to leave a pressing imprint on light and medium-weight silks and rayons. They can also be used for general sewing on delicate fabrics.

• *Water soluble basting thread* dissolves when pressed with steam or washed. Use it in the bobbin.

• *Fusible thread* melts when pressed with heat and moisture. Use it in the bobbin. I often use it to create self-basting zippers.

• *Glacé or hand quilting thread* (40/3) is a glazed cotton thread designed for hand sewing. Use it in the bobbin for gathering and ease. These threads can leave a residue in the bobbin case when used extensively.

• *Invisible* or monofilament nylon and polyester threads are available in clear and smoke. Designed to blend in invisibly, some are softer than others.

The Needle/Thread Guide in Appendix C is a handy reference for selecting the appropriate needle/thread combination.

Cutting Equipment

Scissors and Shears

When selecting cutting equipment, quality is better than quantity. Begin with a good pair of 7" (17.5cm) or 8" (20cm) shears. Add serrated shears for cutting lightweight or squirmy fabrics, stainless steel shears for fabrics such as microfibers and polyesters which dull the blades easily, and 5" (12.5cm) trimmers for clipping and trimming.

Rotary Cutter and Mat

A rotary cutter requires a cutting mat to avoid damaging your cutting table. It is particularly useful when cutting straight edges. But, like needles and pins, the blades dull quickly when cutting some fabrics.

Marking Tools

For most fabrics, I use clips, chalk, pins, erasable pens, or safety pins; but intricate seams and some fabrics require thread, tailor's tacks, or tracing wheel and tracing carbon.

• *Short ⅛" clips* are the quickest and easiest marking method.

• *Chalk* is available in several forms: clay, wax, chalk wheels, chalk pencils, and disappearing chalk. I use only white and prefer chalk wheels, disappearing chalks, or even a soap sliver. Use wax chalk only on wool and hair fibers; it will stain other fabrics, especially hemp, linen, cotton, and silk.

• *Straight pins* are suitable for fabrics which will not be marred, but they may fall out.

• *Safety pins* are a good choice for sheers and loosely woven fabrics.

• *Erasable pens* (air erasable and water soluble) are handy marking tools, but they will stain some fabrics permanently.

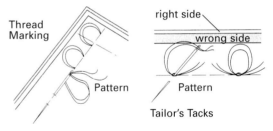

Thread Marking

right side

wrong side

Pattern

Pattern

Tailor's Tacks

• *Thread and tailor's tacks* are the best choice when stitching accuracy is critical and other methods might damage the fabric. Thread marking is a row of long basting stitches while tailor's tacks are used for marking matchpoints and dart ends.

• *Tracing wheel and tracing carbon* are another good choice for marking intricate seams. I use only white to avoid permanent stains.

Miscellaneous

There are many tools and supplies which will help you to sew more skillfully as well as more quickly. Some are traditional sewing tools and notions, while others are simple household items. Here are my favorites:

Pins

My favorite pins are flower pins, super fine pins, regular silk pins, and safety pins. I keep my "used" pins in separate boxes from the new pins; so, when sewing delicate fabrics, I can use only new pins. I discard all pins that fall on the floor.

• *Regular silk pins* have a diameter of .7-.85mm and are suitable for most fabrics.

• *Flower pins* are extra long and have large flat heads. Most have a diameter of .65mm. I use them when I need a long pin or a pin with a large head. They are also useful for marking and when cutting with a rotary cutter because you can put the ruler on top of the pinned fabric and the ruler will lie flat.

• *Extra fine pins* have a diameter of .6mm.

• *Super fine pins* have a diameter of .5mm. Super fine pins are the smallest available and the least likely to leave pin scars on delicate fabrics. Surprisingly, these pins also work well on many densely woven fabrics. I use several brands—IBC, Iris, and a Japanese import from Professional Sewing Supplies. (See Resource List.)

If you don't have super fine pins, use fine handsewing needles (sizes 9 to 12).

• *Safety pins* have several uses: marking the right side of fabrics which look the same on both sides and marking construction symbols on fabrics such as chiffon and lace. Use small safety pins on fine fabrics and larger ones on other fabrics.

Trimmed with a fashionable faux fur collar, this casual jacket is a good choice for novices and experts alike.

Photo courtesy of KWIK•SEW®

Weights and temporary adhesive sprays

When pins will damage the fabric, use weights and temporary adhesive sprays to hold the pattern pieces in place for cutting out. If you don't have pattern weights, use dinner knives, lead drapery weights, or large washers.

I also use 202—a temporary adhesive spray for patterns. It has less adhesive than many temporary sprays, but other spray adhesives will also work. When pinning is the only answer, extend the grainline on the pattern pieces so you can pin at the top and bottom in the seam allowances.

Shim

Sometimes called a Hump Jumper or Jean-a-ma-Jig, a shim is a device to level the machine foot and help prevent skipped or uneven stitching when stitching over bulky seams. If you do not have a shim, make one by folding a piece of cardboard. To use the shim, slide it under the back of the presser foot as you stitch onto the seam. Then, as you stitch off, reposition the shim under the front of the foot.

Extra bobbin case

This luxury item is a real headache reducer. I use mine when ease-basting, gathering, topstitching, embroidering, or using textured and heavy threads so I won't have to change the tension on my primary bobbin case.

Basting aids

I do not like to rip so I use a variety of basting aids to avoid ripping. My favorites include washable glue sticks, quilting clothes pins, and hand basting; but I also use washable double-stick basting tape, spray adhesives, fusible thread, spring hair clips and paper clips. The quilting clothes pins are particularly useful for basting materials such as leather, faux fur, and quilted fabrics which have thick layers or will be damaged by pins.

Elastics

Braided, clear, and non-roll are the elastics which I use most often.

• *Braided elastic* narrows when stretched, making it easy to insert into casings.

• *Clear elastic* is 100 percent polyurethane and stretches 300 percent. It narrows when stretched and is not damaged when it is stitched through for gathers or stays.

• *Non-roll elastic* is firm and strong enough to support elastic waists on heavy knits and heavy skirts.

Stabilizers

Generally I prefer a water soluble stabilizer, but I also use spray starch, liquid stabilizers, tissue paper, lightweight tearaways, and burn away stabilizers.

I use them to stitch machine buttonholes, for tissue stitched seams and sandwich stitching. (See Appendix E – Stabilizers.)

Stay tape

Many seams and edges need to be stabilized to prevent them from stretching out of shape. You can purchase lightweight stay tapes or rayon seam binding, but I generally use a narrow strip of lightweight selvage or a silk organza strip which has been pressed to remove all stretch.

Fray retardants

Use fray retardants, seam sealants, and a solution of diluted white glue to reduce fraying. Apply carefully to avoid applying too much and leaving a permanent stain.

Tape

On fabrics, use drafting tape or pink hair set tape which does not leave a sticky residue.

Use regular transparent tape to wrap the toes of the presser foot to avoid snagging loosely woven and open knit fabrics.

Interfacings

When choosing interfacings, consider the fabric care, the amount and direction of stretch, quality, weight, hand, and color; the fiber content; garment quality, type, design, use, and desired finished appearance; your sewing skills, time available, and personal preference.

In the Interfacing Checklist (Appendix G), the most common interfacings are listed by weight. Similar products are grouped together so you can make substitutions when needed.

Lining and Underlinings

Linings and underlinings are optional for many fabrics and designs. Traditional tailored garments are always lined, but a contemporary design in the same fabric might be unlined.

Machine Setup

For each fabric, I've described the stitch lengths, tension, and machine feet which I use to make my first test seam. These are guides; you may prefer longer stitches or shorter ones, depending on your fabric and machine.

Feet: I use a variety of special feet to eliminate many frustrating stitching problems. My favorites include: the wide straight stitch foot, roller foot, even-feed foot, and the zipper foot.

The wide straight stitch foot is my favorite for straight stitching; it holds the fabric firmly, and reduces stitching problems and puckered seams. The roller and even feed (walking) feet reduce underlayer creep. If you don't have these feet, use the zigzag or all-purpose foot which came with your machine. There are also many other special feet which you will find useful. Put your favorites on a wish list to help your family and friends select a gift you will enjoy.

Sewing Basics

There are many techniques which range from quick and easy to haute couture. In this book, I have listed techniques which will produce quality garments with the least amount of time and effort. They are easy to use and will provide good results for novices and experts alike.

Workroom Secrets

Fabric Prep: Most fabrics need to be preshrunk or relaxed before cutting. Use the fiber content, yarn structure, fabric weave and color, manufacturer's recommendations, and planned garment construction as a guide to decide whether the garment will be laundered or dry-cleaned.

Garments which will be laundered can be machine or hand washed and machine or line dried. Wash and dry the uncut fabric the way you plan to wash the garment. Cotton fabrics have progressive shrinkage and must be preshrunk at least three times to prevent shrinkage in the finished garment. Generally, dark and bright colors will fade more than pastels. Vinegar and salt, which were recommended for many decades, will not set the dyes.

If the garment will be dry-cleaned, steam it well or ask your dry-cleaner to do so. Generally, I hang the fabric over the shower rod; fill the bathtub with hot water; and leave it until dry. I also use a hand steamer or good steam iron.

To hand wash, I generally use shampoo with a neutral pH.

Layout/Cutting: Lay out the pattern so the grainline on the pattern is parallel to the selvage. For a nap layout, position the pattern pieces so that all tops are in the same direction. For a layout without nap, the pattern tops can be placed in either direction. When using a single layer layout, make a set of duplicate pattern pieces; label them "left" and "right" to avoid cutting errors. For the layout, place the pattern pieces face up on the right side of the fabric.

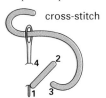
cross-stitch

If the fabric looks the same on both sides, decide which side you like better. Then mark the right side with a thread cross-stitch, drafting tape, or small safety pins; or mark the back with chalk.

Seams: For most fabrics, I prefer seams that are easy to sew, flat, and inconspicuous and I often look to quality ready-to-wear for construction ideas. Most ready-made garments are assembled with plain seams which are pressed open with the edges serged separately or pressed closed with the edges trimmed and serged together. For the latter, seams are often stitched with a 4- or 5-thread safety-stitch serger. Some traditional seams like the flat-fell seam are generally replaced by the easy-to-stitch, flatter topstitched seam.

In addition to the plain seam, there are many other seams which are well designed for specific designs, purposes, and fabrics. These are described in Sewing Techniques (page 108).

Seaming Techniques: I use and frequently recommend several seaming techniques which make it easier to sew most fabrics, reduce stitching problems, and improve the finished design. The most useful of these—tissue stitching, sandwich stitching, and taping—can be applied anytime you sew; while eliminating or adding seams and changing seamlines require some advance planning before the garment is cut.

• *Tissue stitching* – To prevent stitching problems, stitch with a stabilizer such as tissue, water soluble stabilizer, or burn-away stabilizer between the fabric and feed dogs.

• *Sandwich stitching* – Stitch with the seam sandwiched between two strips of stabilizer.

• *Taping seams* – Many fabrics need to be stabilized at seams, edges, foldlines, and openings to preserve the garment shape and prevent stretching when the garment is worn.

Using the pattern pieces as a guide, mark the finished length on the stay. Wrong side up, center the stay over the seamline; baste, then stitch permanently. When taping a folded edge, center the stay over the fold; pin. Use a long running stitch to sew it inconspicuously in place.

For stretch fabrics, use clear elastic instead of a regular stay to maintain the shape without losing the elasticity.

• *Eliminating or adding seamlines* – Eliminating a seam which joins the garment and facing will reduce bulk at the edge when sewing heavy or bulky fabrics. Adding a seam is often required when sewing narrow fabrics or for design.

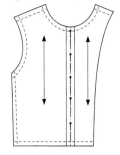

To eliminate a seam, match and pin the pattern pieces together on the seamline. Cut out the garment section in one piece.

Eliminating Seams

To add a seam, draw the new seam on the pattern, cut the pattern apart, and add a seam allowance to each edge.

• *Changing seamlines* – Seams on the straight grain pucker more than seams on a slight bias. Redraw the cutting line so it is a very slight A-line or pegged. At the hemline, mark a point ½" (1.2 cm) from the original cutting line; connect the point and cutting line at the hip. Very few fabrics can be cut off-grain successfully.

Redraw Seamlines

Hems and Edge Finishes:
For many designs, I prefer a plain hem which is finished by hand or machine; but there are many other hems and edge finishes which are more appropriate for some fabrics, specific designs, and special purposes. These are described in Sewing Techniques (page 112).

Closures:
Review the techniques for Closures and Fasteners in Sewing Techniques (page 116).

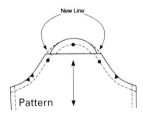

Sleeves:
Many fabrics are difficult to shrink, and a sleeve cap with more than 1¼" ease can be difficult to sew into the armhole attractively.

To reduce the sleeve cap ease, make a horizontal fold across the top of the cap; a ⅛" (3mm) fold will reduce the ease ⅜" to ½" (1-1.2cm). Redraw the cutting lines without reducing the sleeve width.

Pressing:
I frequently spend more time pressing than stitching.

To avoid spitting and spewing, be sure the iron has warmed up and steams properly before beginning. Press all seams flat; then press them open.

When pressing fabrics with multiple fiber types, set the heat for the most sensitive fabric.

When pressing fabrics with surface texture, bound pockets, and bound buttonholes, cover the pressing surface with a thick terry towel.

When in doubt, cover the fabric with a press cloth. Cover a seam roll with wool; arrange the seam on it. Press the seam open; then spank with a clapper until the seam is flat. Do not move the garment until dry.

Tools and supplies:

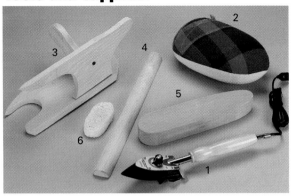

• *Irons:* In addition to a regular steam iron, I use a hand steamer to shrink and steam fabrics and garments and a small hobby iron to press hard-to-reach seams. (1)

• A *ham* is a firmly shaped pressing cushion which allows you to press curved sections easily. A ham holder is a nice addition so you can set the ham on its end or side. (2)

• A *point presser* is a wooden tool which allows you to press seams open on collars, cuffs, and garment edges. Some are straight with a point at the end while others, such as the Tailor Board, have a variety of curved edges. This is an investment item and worth every penny. (3)

• A *Seam Stick™* is a half-round hardwood stick. I use it for pressing seams open; I have a second stick to use on top as a clapper when pressing difficult fabrics. (4)

• A *wooden clapper* is used to spank seams and edges to flatten them. (5)

• A *clean cellulose sponge* is indispensable for applying water directly to fabrics which will not waterspot and to a press cloth on others. Wet the sponge and shake so that it will not drip. (6)

• *Press cloths* are essential. Dry or damp, they protect the fabric from the heat of the iron and unwanted waterspots. Use white or light-colored cloths on light-colored fabrics and dark cloths on dark fabrics. Launder them frequently to avoid transferring soil to your new designs. You can purchase press cloths or make your own.

Lightweight cotton muslin which has been machine washed several times is a good all-purpose press cloth.

Two layers of silk organza make a nice see-through cloth.

Wool press cloths are essential when pressing wool and hair fibers. Cover the ironing board with a large piece of wool and use a smaller piece to cover the fabric.

• Use a *50/50 solution of white vinegar/water* to set pleats, creases, and seams on microfibers, polyesters, and other difficult-to-press fabrics. Always test first to be sure that the solution does not spot the fabric or change the colors.

• Use a *bar of Ivory soap* for sharper creases and seams on wool fabrics. For creases and folded edges, rub the soap on the wrong side, and press. For seams, rub the stitching line on each side; then press the seam open.

Garment Care:
All garments will maintain their pristine appearance longer if dry-cleaned. If you plan to launder the finished design, all components must be washable; preshrink all fabric before cutting.

Acetate

Acetate is a manufactured cellulosic fiber. The first fabric to melt, not scorch, under the iron, acetate has a high luster, looks and feels luxurious, drapes beautifully, and absorbs moisture. It is inexpensive and used for a wide range of fabrics from jersey and double knits to brocade and lace. It is shrink-, moth-, and mildew-resistant and is frequently used for lining materials in combination with other fibers and by itself.

Antique satin and antique taffeta are two of the most popular, and most difficult to sew. They are frequently used for bridal gowns because, compared to silk, they are inexpensive and retain their white color. For more information when sewing, see Satin and Taffeta.

Comfortable to wear, acetate fabrics are warm in winter and cool in summer. They resist staining, shrinking, pilling, moths, and mildew, but are easily damaged by hot irons, waterspots, and ripping.

Sewing Checklist

Essential Supplies

Needles: Woven fabrics – sharp (HM), universal (H). **Knit fabrics** – stretch (HS), universal (H), ballpoint (H-SUK). Sizes – lightweight, 60/8-70/10; medium-weight, 70/10-80/12; heavy-weight, 80/12-90/14.

Thread: Lightweight fabrics – lightweight (cotton, polyester, cotton covered polyester, silk), all purpose thread. **Medium-weight fabrics** – all purpose thread. **Heavy-weight fabrics** – all purpose, machine embroidery/topstitching threads. **Very heavy fabrics** – machine embroidery/topstitching threads.

Miscellaneous: Fine pins, water soluble stabilizer.

Cutting: Lightweight fabrics – serrated shears. **Other fabrics** – sharp shears, rotary cutter/mat.

Marking: Chalk, clips, erasable pens.

Interfacings/Linings/Underlinings: All types, depending on the fabric structure and garment design. When sewing white, underline with baby flannel or cotton batiste to make it opaque.

Machine Setup

Stitch Length: Lightweight fabrics – 1.5-1.75mm (15-18spi). **Medium-weight fabrics** – 2-2.5mm (10-12spi). **Heavy fabrics** – 2.5-3mm (8-10spi). **Very heavy fabrics** – 3-4mm (6-8spi) **All weights** – zigzag (W,.5-L,2).

Tension: Depends on the fabric.

Feet: Straight stitch, roller, zigzag.

Sewing Basics

Test Garment: Rarely required.

Fabric Prep: Steam or dry-clean.

Layout: Nap – single layer when matching patterns.

Seams/Hems: Depends on the fabric weight, structure, and transparency and the garment quality, design, use, and care.

Seam/Hem Finishes: All types – avoid bulky finishes such as Hong Kong on lightweight fabrics; they will show on the finished garment.

Closures: Buttonholes (machine, inseam), buttons or loops, ties, zippers (hand, machine, invisible).

Pressing: Medium heat; press cloth and steam.

Garment Care: Dry-clean.

Trade Names: Celanese, Celebrate®, Chromspun®, Estron®, MicroSafe™.

Acetate Fabrics: Antique satin, antique taffeta, brocade, crepe, double knits, faille, jersey, lace, moiré, satin, taffeta, tricot.

Uses: Bridal and evening gowns, sportswear, loungewear, foundation garments, lingerie, dresses, blouses, skirts, linings.

Design Details: Avoid seams on the straight grain. When this is not possible, redraw the seamlines so they are slightly off grain. (See Any Fabric page 14.)

Burn Test: Acetate fuses and melts. It burns quickly and is not self-extinguishing. It smells like vinegar and leaves an irregular shaped, hard, brittle charcoal. Acetate will dissolve in acetone.

Workroom Secrets

Fabric Prep: Prep depends on manufacturer's recommendation, garment design, quality, and use. Acetate is washable, but many dyes and finishes used on it are not.

Pressing: Test press. Acetate is easily damaged by improper pressing, hot irons, and waterspots. Some will even spot when steamed.

Garment Care: Dryclean. Most colors will fume fade when exposed to atmospheric fumes.

Sophisticated and elegant, this dress is from the Custom Couture Collection by Claire Shaeffer. (Vogue Pattern 7658, courtesy of The McCall Pattern Co.)

Acrylic

Acrylic is a synthetic fiber produced from a liquid which has been made from coal, air, water, oil, and limestone. Fibers can be modified to create a variety of fibers from smooth, cotton-like yarns to bulky, fur types. The most popular fabrics are raschel and sweatshirt knits, faux fur fabrics, and water-repellent fabrics.

Known for warmth without weight, acrylic fabrics can be woven or knitted. They are resilient, quick drying, and resistant to wrinkling, sunlight, weather, oil, chemicals, moths, and mildew. They wick well and can be heat-set into permanent pleats and creases.

Acrylics pill, shrink badly, retain static electricity, and absorb little moisture. They absorb and hold perspiration odors.

They dull needles and scissors quickly; woven fabrics fray badly. They do not ease well and soil easily. Skipped stitches and puckered seams are frequently a problem. They are easily damaged by hot irons, steam, and hot dryers.

Trade Names: Acrilan®, BioFresh, Bounce-Back, Creslan®, Du-Rel®, Duraspun®, Fi-Lana®, Micro-Supreme®, Pil-Trol™, So-Lara®, Orlon®, Ware-Dated®, WeatherBloc, Zefran.

Uses: Dresses, skirts, sportswear, activewear, nightwear, infants' and children's garments, curtains.

Burn test: An acrylic burns rapidly with a hot flame, sputters, and smokes. It is not self-extinguishing, and leaves a crisp black mass. It smells like hot vinegar.

Workroom Secrets

Fabric Prep: Depends on manufacturer's recommendation, garment design, quality, and use. Most can be machine washed and dried on low. Remove from the dryer immediately and hang to prevent wrinkling.

Layout/Cutting: Use a single layer and duplicate pattern pieces when matching patterns or cutting bulky fabrics. Use flower pins to hold the pattern pieces in place.

Seams: Stay seams at shoulders to avoid unwanted stretch and to maintain the garment shape.

Pressing: Test press. Acrylics are easily damaged by improper pressing, hot irons, and steam. When in doubt, use a lower temperature or press cloth.

Stitching: Start all new projects with a new needle. Change needles frequently; synthetic fibers dull needles faster than natural fibers.

Garment Care: Check the manufacturer's suggestions. Better garments will maintain their pristine appearance longer when dry-cleaned. To remove perspiration odors, use detergents that destroy odor-causing bacteria.

Developed as a substitute for wool, acrylic fibers are warm, comfortable to wear, and easy to sew. (Photo courtesy of KWIK-SEW®.)

Sewing Checklist

Essential Supplies

Needles: Woven fabrics – sharp (HM), universal (H). **Knit fabrics** – stretch (HS), universal (H), ballpoint (H-SUK). Sizes – lightweight, 60/8-70/10; medium-weight – 70/10-80/12; heavy-weight – 80/12-90/14; very heavy-weight – 90/14-100/16.

Thread: Lightweight fabrics – lightweight (cotton, polyester, cotton covered polyester, silk), all purpose thread. **Medium-weight fabrics** – all purpose thread. **Heavy-weight fabrics** – all purpose, machine embroidery/topstitching threads. **Very heavy fabrics** – machine embroidery/topstitching threads.

Miscellaneous: Flower pins, safety pins, water soluble stabilizer.

Cutting: Sharp shears, rotary cutter/mat.

Marking: Chalk, clips, erasable pens, safety pins, flower pins.

Interfacings/Linings/Underlinings: Depends on the fabric weight, garment type, quality, and structure; same care properties.

Machine Setup

Stitch Length: Lightweight fabrics – 1.5-1.75mm (15-18spi). **Medium-weight fabrics** – 2-2.5mm (10-12spi). **Heavy-weight fabrics** – 2.5-3mm (8-10spi). **Very heavy fabrics** – 3-4mm (6-8spi). **All weights** – zigzag (W,.5-L,2).

Tension: Depends on the fabric.

Feet: Straight stitch, zigzag, roller foot.

Sewing Basics

Test Garment: Rarely required.

Fabric Prep: Machine wash/dry, steam, or dry-clean.

Layout: Knits – always nap. **Wovens** – depends on fabric design and pattern. Use single layer and duplicate pattern pieces when matching patterns or cutting bulky fabrics.

Seams/Hems: All types – depends on the fabric weight, structure, and transparency; and garment quality, design, use, and care.

Closures: Buttonholes (machine, inseam), buttons or loops, ties, zippers (hand, machine, invisible).

Pressing: Medium heat; press cloth and steam.

Garment Care: Machine wash/dry or dry-clean, depending on garment structure and quality.

Batiste

Batiste is a semisoft, lightweight, plain-weave fabric. Usually cotton or cotton/poly blend, it is durable, comfortable to wear, washable, and presses easily. It wrinkles and shrinks, has little elasticity, and varies in transparency, depending on the color and quality. When used as underlining, it will cling to cotton undergarments.

Similar Fabrics: Airplane cloth, broderie anglaise, calico, cambric, dimity, cotton dobby, dotted Swiss, eyelet, eyelash voile, gauze, gingham, handkerchief linen, jaconet, lawn, mull, nainsook, pima cotton, pongee, rayon challis, shirtings, souffle, tissue gingham, Tana lawn, voile.

Uses: Blouses, dresses, lingerie, infants' and children's wear, handkerchiefs, underlinings, and interfacings.

Design Elements: Gathers, pleats, tucks, lace trims, lace insertions.

Sewing Checklist

Essential Supplies

Needles: Sharp (HM, HJ), universal (H); sizes 60/8-70/10.

Thread: Lightweight (cotton, cotton covered polyester), all-purpose (cotton, polyester, cotton covered polyester). Topstitching – lightweight or all purpose threads. Serger – lightweight serger thread.

Miscellaneous: Super fine pins, small safety pins, spray starch, acid-free tissue, stabilizers – water soluble, liquid, lightweight tear-away.

Cutting: Serrated shears, rotary cutter/mat.

Marking: Chalk, clips, pins, safety pins, erasable pens.

Interfacings: Lightweight sew-ins, very lightweight fusibles, self-fabric, organdy.

Linings/Underlinings: Optional, washable.

Machine Setup

Stitch length: 2-2.5mm (10-12spi).

Tension: Lightly balanced.

Feet: Wide straight stitch, all-purpose, roller foot. Small hole throat plate.

Sewing Basics

Fabric Prep: Shrinks, machine wash/dry all cotton fabrics three times.

Layout: Without nap – double layer.

Seams: Plain (pressed open or closed), narrow, French, faux French, safety-stitch serged.

Hems: Narrow or wide, depending on design; single or double fold; hand (blindstitch, slipstitch); topstitch.

Seam/Hem Finishes: Folded, turned and stitched, pinked, serged, zigzag.

Edge Finishes: Facings (self-fabric, bias), bindings, edge-to-edge linings, lace trim.

Closures: Buttonholes (machine, hand), buttons/loops, ties, zippers (hand, machine).

Pressing: Medium to high heat, damp cloth, or steam.

Workroom Secrets

Layout/Cutting/Marking: Batiste does not require a nap layout except when fabrics have a one-way printed design.

Stitching: Begin with a new sharp (HM) needle. Use a straight stitch foot and small hole throat plate to reduce stitching problems. Hold fabric firmly in front and behind the presser foot when stitching. Use a shorter stitch length when stitching curves. Begin stitching on a stabilizer; then stitch onto the fabric. When needed, tissue stitch seams to reduce puckering.

Seams: Use French seams for christening garments, fine blouses, and dresses. For softer, more drapeable French seams, sew the seams by hand, not machine; or use narrow seams finished with serging or zigzag instead of French seams. To make enclosed seams at edges less conspicuous, trim seam allowances evenly to ⅛" to ¼" (3-6mm).

Buttonholes: Before machine stitching, spray area with starch to add body or use water soluble stabilizer. Stitch using a new sharp needle and fine machine embroidery thread.

Edge Finishes: To avoid unattractive facing shadows, replace traditional facings with underlinings, bindings, or edge-to-edge linings.

Pressing: Test press on fabric scrap; lightweight, thin batiste fabrics require a lower setting.

Garment Care: Machine wash and dry casual designs and children's wear. Hand wash fine garments. Before storing, wash but do not starch or iron. Wrap in acid-free tissue.

Ideal for sleepwear, batiste is easy to sew and comfortable to wear. (McCall's Pattern – 3854, NY NY Junior®; courtesy of The McCall Pattern Co.)

Beaded and Sequined Fabric

Beaded and sequined fabrics are embellished with decorative threads, beads, and sequins which are sewn, fused, or glued on a variety of background fabrics such as taffeta, wool knits, open raschel knits, satin, chiffon, organza, lace, tulle, silk shantung, and cotton blends. Embellishments are applied in dense all-over patterns, random individual motifs, and border designs. Some have fabric patterns which require matching.

Designs can be applied individually or in strips. They are frequently applied with a chain stitch, which when inadvertently pulled from one end, will unravel a large section. Most have a nap. They dull scissors and needles quickly and are easily damaged by moisture and excess heat.

Workroom Secrets

Fabric Prep: Most do not shrink; press from the wrong side with a warm, dry iron. Most will be damaged if laundered.

Layout/Cutting/Marking: For easy clean-up, cover the floor and cutting table with a clean sheet. Use a nap layout, and spread fabric in a single layer with the right-side up. Use duplicate pattern pieces. When laying out sequined fabrics, the "nap" should go down so the sequins feel smooth when you run your hand from the neck to the hem. To reduce fraying, do not cut until you are ready to sew; after cutting, handle the fabric as little as possible or bind the edges with 1" (2.5cm) drafting tape. Use clips sparingly.

Stitching: Needles dull quickly; change them frequently. Baste as needed to avoid ripping.

Seams: Choose a seam appropriate for the garment quality and use. Use plain seams for quick and easy designs and sequin appliqué seams for quality garments.

Seam/Hem Finishes: For an elegant finish on unlined garments and to eliminate scratchy seams, use a Hong Kong binding with silk chiffon or lightweight lining, or use a tricot binding.

Interfacings: Avoid fusibles.

Underlinings: Use to add body to lightweight or soft fabrics.

Linings: Line garments to cover scratchy seams.

Designed by Maj Smith, this fabulous wedding gown is embellished with a variety of beads, trims, and lace. (Photo courtesy of Maj Smith.)

Pressing: Test press. Many beaded, sequined, and embellished fabrics are easily damaged by steam and high heat. Cover the pressing surface with a thick terry towel to avoid flattening or damaging embellished fabrics.

Garment Care: To protect skirts and pants from clip hanger marks, sew in ribbon hanger loops at the waist.

Beaded and Sequined Types: Beaded wovens, knits, chiffons, and tulle; all-over sequined designs.

Uses: Evening/formal wear, jackets, coats, dresses, blouses, bustiers, skirts, pants, trims.

Design Elements: Minimal seaming, flared skirts, bindings, pockets (inseam), sequin appliqué seams. Avoid intricate designs, pleats.

Sewing Checklist

Essential Supplies
Needles: Sharp (HM, HJ), stretch (HS), universal (H); sizes 60/8-90/14, depending on the background fabric.
Thread: All-purpose or lightweight (cotton, polyester, cotton covered polyester).
Cutting: Stainless steel or old sharp shears, weights, duplicate pattern pieces.
Marking: Chalk, clips, erasable pens, tailor's tacks, thread, safety pins.
Miscellaneous: Weights, ¼" (6mm) ribbon, extra machine needles.
Interfacings/Underlinings: Avoid fusibles; use silk organza, chiffon, lightweight sew-in interfacings such as Sewin' Sheer.
Linings/Underlinings: Generally for outerwear, formal designs, and scratchy fabrics.

Machine Setup
Stitch Length: 2-2.5mm (10-12spi).
Tension: Lightly balanced; light pressure.
Feet: Zipper, wide straight stitch, zigzag.

Sewing Basics
Test Garment: Recommended for quality garments.
Fabric Prep: Press wrong side with a dry iron.
Layout: Nap – single layer right-side up, duplicate pattern pieces.
Seams: Plain (pressed open), sequin appliqué.
Seam/Hem Finishes: Serged, zigzag, bound, Hong Kong.
Hems: Hand (blindstitch, blind catchstitch, catchstitch), interfaced, double-stitched, faced.
Edge Finishes: Facings (lining, bias), bands, bindings, edge-to-edge linings.
Closures: Buttons/loops, buttonholes (machine, bound, inseam), ties, snaps, zippers (hand, machine, invisible).
Pressing: Medium heat, press cloth.
Garment Care: Dry-clean.

Boiled Wool

Boiled wool is made of 100 percent merino wool which has been dyed, knitted, shrunk, and fulled. Available in two weights, medium and heavy, it has the suppleness and comfort of a knit and the stability, shape retention, and warmth of a woven fabric. It is reversible, durable, and resistant to abrasion, wind, and rain. It does not wrinkle or fray, but it is bulky and may pill.

Similar Fabrics: Blanket cloth, Chinella®, double knit, duffel, friezé, loden, mackinac, wadmal.

Uses: Tailored designs, unlined or reversible garments, casual jackets, coats, capes, ponchos, skirts, sweaters, pants, vests.

Design Elements: Minimal seaming, topstitching, foldover braid, bindings, embroidered designs, pockets (all types).

Sewing Checklist

Essential Supplies
Needles: Universal (H); sizes 70/10-90/14, depending on the fabric weight.
Thread: All purpose (cotton, polyester, cotton covered polyester). Topstitching – machine embroidery/topstitching (cotton, polyester, cotton covered polyester, silk), all purpose.
Cutting: Sharp shears.
Marking: Chalk, clips, erasable pens, pins.
Miscellaneous: Flower pins, shim, safety pins, water soluble stabilizer, cut away stabilizer.
Interfacings: Optional, fusible or sew-in.
Linings/Underlinings: Optional, same care as garment.

Machine Setup
Stitch length: 2.5-3mm (8-10spi).
Tension: Lightly balanced.
Feet: Zigzag, wide straight stitch.

Sewing Basics
Test Garment: Rarely needed.
Fabric Prep: Preshrink with steam or dry-clean, handwash.
Layout: Nap – double layer; heavy-weight – single layer.
Seams: Plain (pressed open or closed), topstitched, nonwoven lapped, decorative serged, bound, strap.
Hems: Hand (blind stitch, catchstitch), topstitched.
Seam/Hem Finishes: Serged, zigzag, unfinished.
Edge Finishes: Bindings, foldover braid, facings, linings.
Closures: Buttonholes (machine, corded, bound, inseam), buttons/loops, frogs, toggles, ties, zippers (hand, machine, invisible, decorative).
Pressing: Medium heat, damp cloth, or steam.
Garment Care: Dry-clean, hand wash.

Workroom Secrets

Fabric Prep: To make the garment washable, purchase an additional ¼ yard and hand wash before cutting.
Layout/Cutting/Marking: Mark right side of each section with safety pins. Spread heavier fabrics in a single layer, right-side up. Use duplicate pattern pieces.
Seams: Press seams and darts open or to one side; then topstitch to hold them flat. To topstitch inconspicuously, press seams open and topstitch each side close to the seamline, using inside of straight stitch presser foot as a guide. Trim close to the topstitching. For a sportier look, emphasize the seamlines by topstitching about ¼" (6mm) away. To embellish the design, topstitch using decorative stitches and contrast thread.
Stitching: Use a shim to balance the foot when crossing bulky seams.
Edge Finishes: Bind edges with foldover braid, ribbon, bias bindings, faux suede, or leather.
Buttonholes: For machine stitched buttonholes, place water soluble stabilizer on top of the fabric to prevent the stitches from embedding in the fabric. For more defined buttonholes, cord them and/or stitch with machine embroidery thread (30/2, 40/2).
Zippers: Stabilize the opening with lightweight selvage or tape to prevent stretching.
Embroidery: Use water soluble stabilizer on top of the fabric and several layers of lightweight tearaway stabilizer on the wrong side.

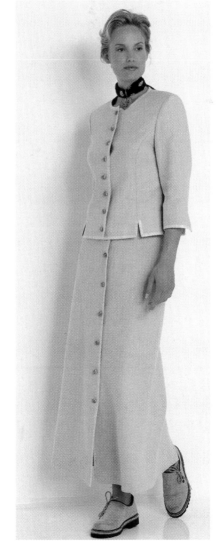

Boiled wool is the perfect choice for this classic cardigan and skirt. (Burda pattern – 8831; courtesy of Burda.)

Bouclé

Bouclé is a firmly woven, textured material woven with bouclé yarns in wool or wool blends. It resists wrinkles, does not crease well, and may be bulky, pill, or snag. Available in all weights from lightweight to heavy, its textured surface helps to hide stitching irregularities.

Workroom Secrets

Fabric Prep: Preshrink with steam or dry-clean. Do not wash unless you want to change the character of the fabric.

Layout/Cutting/Marking: Use small safety pins to mark right side of the fabric and construction symbols. Use flower pins to hold pattern pieces in place.

Stitching: Use polyester threads for more elastic seams. To prevent underlayer creep, use a roller or even-feed foot, hold the fabric firmly in front and behind the presser foot, or tissue stitch seams. Understitch by hand for a soft, inconspicuous finish.

Buttonholes: For more defined buttonholes, cord the buttonholes and/or stitch with machine embroidery thread (30/2, 40/2).

Zippers: Stabilize opening with lightweight selvage or stay tape to prevent stretching.

Pockets: Stabilize pocket openings to prevent stretching. To reduce bulk, line patch pockets and flaps with a lightweight lining.

Interfacing: When working with lightweight bouclé, use a textured weft fusible to give the fabric loft.

Underlinings: Underline pants and skirts to preserve the shape.

A good choice for less experienced seamsters, bouclé has a textured surface which will hide sewing irregularities. (Photo courtesy of KWIK·SEW®.)

Pressing: Test press. Bouclé fabrics are easily damaged by improper pressing. When steaming, watch for shrinking. Before pressing, cover the ironing board with a piece of wool. When pressing the right side, use a self-fabric press cloth. To press seams, cover a seam roll with wool; then arrange the seam on it. Press the seam open; then spank with a clapper until the seam is flat. Do not move the garment until dry. To restore the textured surface after pressing, let the iron hover ½" (1.2cm) above the surface and steam generously.

Similar Fabrics: Astrakhan, bouclette, chenille, chinchilla, curl, éponge, gimp, poodle cloth, ratiné, textured wools.

Uses: Dressy jackets, coats, skirts, dresses.

Design Elements: Simple designs, shaped seams, gathers, soft pleats. Avoid sharp creases.

Sewing Checklist

Essential Supplies

Needles: Universal (H), sharp (HM, HJ); sizes 70/10-90/14, depending on fabric weight.

Thread: All purpose (cotton, polyester, cotton covered polyester). Topstitching – all purpose, machine embroidery/topstitching thread.

Cutting: Sharp shears, rotary cutter/mat.

Marking: Chalk, clips, tailor's tacks, flower pins, safety pins.

Miscellaneous: Flower pins, safety pins, stay tape, water soluble stabilizer.

Interfacings: Sew-in, hair canvas, fusibles, weft-insertion.

Linings/Underlinings: Generally for quality garments.

Machine Setup

Stitch length: 2-3mm (8-12spi).

Tension: Lightly balanced.

Feet: Roller, wide straight stitch, even-feed, zigzag.

Sewing Basics

Test Garment: Recommended, fabric is easily damaged by ripping.

Fabric Prep: Steam or dry-clean to shrink.

Layout: Nap – double or single layer, depending on fabric thickness.

Seams: Plain, pressed open.

Hems: Hand (blindstitch, blind catchstitch, catchstitch).

Seam/Hem Finishes: Serged, zigzag, bound, Hong Kong, pinked; if lined, none.

Edge Finishes: Facings, bindings, edge-to-edge lining.

Closures: Buttonholes (machine, corded, bound, inseam), buttons/loops, zippers (hand, machine, invisible).

Pressing: Cool to medium heat, damp cloth or steam, wool press cloth.

Fabric Care: Dry-clean.

Broadcloth and Chambray

Broadcloth and chambray are semi-soft, firmly woven, plain weave cottons or cotton/polyester blends. Well-suited for beginners, they are durable, washable, comfortable to wear, and easy to sew and embroider.

Broadcloth has fine ribs. Solid colors look the same on both sides. Prints are brighter on the right side.

Chambray has a colored warp and white filling and looks the same on both sides. The heather appearance of chambray will hide most stitching irregularities.

Similar Fabrics: Batik, calcutta cloth, cotton flannel, denim look-alikes, gingham, madras, muslin, percale, oxford cloth, piqué, sheeting, shirtings, silk broadcloth, waffle cloth, wash-and-wear cottons.

Uses: Casual garments, Western designs, children's clothes, shirts, sportswear.

Design Elements: Tailored details, topstitching, patch pockets, shirt and dolman sleeves, pleats, tucks, decorative snaps, embroidery. Avoid seams on the straight grain when sewing cotton/polyester blends.

Sewing Checklist

Essential Supplies

Needle types: Sharp (HJ), universal (H); sizes 70/10-80/12.

Thread: All purpose (cotton, polyester, cotton covered polyester). Topstitching – all purpose, machine embroidery/topstitching thread.

Cutting: Sharp shears, rotary cutter/mat.

Marking: Chalk, clips, erasable pens, pins.

Miscellaneous: Water soluble, lightweight tearaway, cutaway stabilizers; safety pins.

Interfacings: Optional; washable, fusible, sew-in, self-fabric.

Linings/Underlinings: Rarely.

Machine Setup

Stitch Length: 2-2.5mm (10-12spi).

Tension: Balanced.

Feet: Wide straight stitch, zigzag.

Sewing Basics

Test Garment: Not required.

Fabric Prep: Preshrink; machine wash/dry.

Layout: Without nap – double layer, right sides together.

Seams: Plain (pressed open or closed), topstitched, faux flat fell, lapped, safety-stitch serged.

Hems: Hand (blindstitch), topstitched, shirttail.

Seam/Hem Finishes: Serged, zigzag, pinked.

Edge Finishes: Facings, bindings, bands, ribbing.

Closures: Buttonholes (machine), buttons/loops, decorative snaps, zippers (machine).

Pressing: Medium to high heat, damp cloth or steam.

Garment Care: Machine wash/dry.

Workroom Secrets

Fabric Prep: Machine wash/dry three times to shrink. To avoid excess fraying, serge the ends separately or stitch them together before shrinking.

Layout/Cutting/Marking: Most fabrics do not require a nap layout. The exception is prints which have a one-way design. Chambray and solid colored broadcloths look the same on both sides. Mark the wrong side with a chalked "X" or use small safety pins to mark the right side. When sewing cotton/polyester blends, redraw any seams on the straight grain to avoid puckering. (See Any Fabric page 14.)

Seams: To avoid fraying when laundered, finish seams by serging them together or use topstitched, lapped seams, or safety-stitch serged. To simulate flat fell seams, use topstitched seams, which are much easier to sew.

Topstitching: Printed broadcloth and chambray are easy fabrics to topstitch because any irregularities will be hidden in the print or the heather appearance of the chambray. To highlight the topstitching, use contrast and/or machine embroidery thread (30/2, 40/2).

Pressing: Use a lower temperature or a press cloth when pressing cotton blends.

Embroidery: Use water soluble stabilizer on top of the fabric; or on the wrong side, use cutaway stabilizer or several layers of lightweight tearaway.

This handsome broadcloth shirt is ideal for year-round comfort. (Photo courtesy of Lacy Lovelies Fashion Fabrics.)

Brocade

Brocade is an elegant, decorative fabric. Woven on a jacquard loom with an extra set of yarns, it is available in several weights and fibers. It has a low relief pattern on the face and long floats on the back. It may be bulky, difficult to ease, ravel badly, and snag easily. Its decorative pattern helps to hide stitching irregularities.

Workroom Secrets

Layout/Cutting/Marking: Use a nap layout even though a nap is not noticeable. When matching fabric patterns, use a single layer layout and duplicate pattern pieces. Avoid erasable pens; they may stain permanently.

Stitching: Begin with a new needle. When stitching fabrics with metallic threads, use a new needle with a sharp point (HM or HJ). To avoid snagging the wrong side of fabric when stitching, use a roller foot.

Linings: Linings eliminate the need for seam finishes and protect long thread floats on wrong side from snags.

Underlinings: Generally brocades do not need underlining, but lighter weight materials such as cloqué, plissé, and some matelassés may.

Buttonholes: To prevent machine stitches from embedding in the fabric, stitch with water soluble stabilizer on top of the fabric. For more defined buttonholes, stitch over cording and/or stitch with machine embroidery thread (30/2, 40/2).

Pressing: Test press to determine the appropriate heat, moisture, and pressure for the fiber content. When steaming, watch for shrinking. Always use a press cloth when pressing the right side. To avoid flattening the fabric, press on a soft surface such as a thick towel. To prevent seam and hem impressions, use a seam roll and brown paper strips under the edges of the seam.

Garment Care: Dry-clean to maintain the garment's pristine appearance. Store special-occasion garments on well-padded hangers. The colors on upholstery fabrics may run when dry-cleaned.

Understated and elegant, this design is fabricated in a beautiful brocade. (Photo courtesy of Simplicity Patterns.)

Similar Fabrics: Brocatelle, broché, cloqué, cotton suiting, imperial brocade, matelassé, tapestry, upholstery, upholstery satin, venetian, plissé.

Uses: Special occasion and formal wear, dressy suits, coats, dresses, draperies, handbags.

Design Elements: Simple designs to showcase the fabric, minimal seaming, all type pockets. Avoid intricate seams, fussy details.

Sewing Checklist

Essential Supplies

Needles: Sharp (HM, HJ), universal (H); sizes 70/10-90/14, depending on fabric weight.

Thread: All purpose (cotton, polyester, cotton covered polyester). Serger – lightweight serger thread, textured thread.

Cutting: Sharp shears, rotary cutter/mat, duplicate pattern pieces when cutting a single layer.

Marking: Chalk, clips, pins, tailor's tacks, thread.

Miscellaneous: Super fine pins, weights, covered snaps, thick towel, brown paper, water soluble stabilizer.

Interfacings: Sew-in, hair canvas.

Linings/Underlinings: Generally for quality garments.

Machine Setup

Stitch length: 2-3mm (8-12spi).

Tension: Lightly balanced.

Feet: Wide straight stitch, roller, even-feed, zigzag.

Sewing Basics

Test Garment: Recommended.

Fabric Prep: Preshrink with steam or dry-clean.

Layout: Nap – double layer; single layer if matching pattern or cutting heavy fabric.

Seams: Plain (pressed open), piped.

Hems: Hand (blindstitch, catchstitch), interfaced, double-stitched.

Seam/Hem Finishes: Serged, zigzag; if lined, none.

Edge Finishes: Facings (self-fabric, lining), bindings, foldover braid, edge-to-edge linings.

Closures: Buttonholes (machine, bound, corded, inseam), buttons/loops, zippers (hand, machine, invisible), covered snaps.

Pressing: Low to medium heat, steam.

Garment Care: Dry-clean.

Charmeuse

Charmeuse is a soft, light- to medium-weight satin faced fabric with a dull back. Generally woven in silk, rayon, or polyester, fabrics with a tighter weave fray less and are more durable and more resistant to seam slippage while those with a looser weave have longer floats, more luster, and drape better. It snags easily, ravels badly, and is easily marred by pins, rough hands and sewing surfaces, abrasion, ripping, and improper pressing.

Similar Fabrics: Antique satin, charvet silk, crepe backed satin, jacquard, sandwashed silk, sandwashed rayon, sandwashed Tencel®, sueded charmeuse, tissue faille.

Uses: Dressy garments, special occasion and evening wear, blouses, dresses, pants, lingerie, linings, underlinings.

Design Elements: Gathers, soft pleats, ruffles, flares, drapes, cowl necklines, bias cuts. Avoid close fitting designs and seams on the straight grain.

Sewing Checklist

Essential Supplies
Needles: Sharp (HM, HJ), universal (H); sizes 60/8-70/10.
Thread: Lightweight (cotton, cotton covered polyester, polyester, silk), all purpose. Topstitching – lightweight thread (cotton, silk). Serger – lightweight serger thread, textured thread.
Cutting: Serrated shears, rotary cutter/mat.
Marking: Chalk, clips, tailor's tacks, thread.
Miscellaneous: Super fine pins, fine needles (sizes 9-12), weights, nylon stocking scrap, water-soluble stabilizer, tissue.
Interfacings: Lightweight fusibles and sew-ins, silk organza, lightweight silks, polyester chiffon, marquisette, soft organza.
Linings: Optional, depending on garment type.
Underlinings: Self fabric, chiffon, organza; use to add body and reduce seam slippage on close fitting designs.

Machine Setup
Stitch length: 2-2.5mm (10-12spi).
Tension: Lightly balanced.
Feet: Wide straight stitch, roller foot; small hole throat plate.

Sewing Basics
Test Garment: Recommended.
Fabric Prep: Steam, dry-clean, wash, depending on fiber.
Layout: Nap – double layer.
Seams: Plain (open or closed), topstitched, French, faux French.
Hems: Hand (blindstitch, catchstitch), shirttail, machine rolled.
Seam/Hem Finishes: Serged, pinked, hand overcast; if lined, none.
Edge Finishes: Facings, bindings.
Closures: Buttonholes (machine, hand, bound, inseam); buttons/loops; zippers (machine, hand, invisible).
Pressing: Cool to medium heat; steam, press cloth.
Garment Care: Dry-clean.

Workroom Secrets
Layout/Cutting/Marking: Before cutting, scrape your nail across the satin floats. If yarns separate, fabric will ravel badly and seams will pull out when stressed. Cut seam widths wider. Use weights or pin only in the seam allowances. Set pins parallel to selvage. Mark lightly. Avoid erasable pens and colored chalk; they may stain permanently.

Stitching: Hand baste to ensure stitching accuracy and reduce ripping. Begin with a new needle with a sharp point (HM). To check for burrs, stitch through a scrap of nylon stocking. Use a wide straight stitch foot. Begin stitching on water soluble stabilizer, then stitch onto the fabric. Press with steam to remove the stabilizer. To reduce puckered seams, hold fabric firmly in front and back of foot when stitching.

Seams: Avoid seams on the straight grain. (See Any Fabric page 14.) When pin basting, use fine needles.

Seam/Hem Finishes: To reduce thread imprints when serging, use textured thread in the loopers.

Buttonholes: Stitch machine buttonholes with fine machine embroidery thread.

Zippers: Use lightweight zippers.

Pressing: Test press; charmeuse is easily damaged by hot irons and waterspots.

Garment Care: Dry-clean to maintain the garment's pristine appearance.

Designed by Linda Stewart, this stunning charmeuse wedding gown is underlined with self-fabric and accented with silk organza. (Photo courtesy of Linda Stewart Couture Designs for Joy and Company and Art of Photography, Kingsport, Tennessee.)

Chenille

Chenille can be one of several different fabrics: (1) a fabric woven with chenille yarns, (2) a multi-layer fabric that has been stitched and slashed, or (3) a tufted pile fabric. This section focuses on tufted fabrics. When sewing the others, see Bouclé or Broadcloth.

Chenille is available in the form of bedspreads as well as traditional yardage. Made by punching tufts into a woven fabric, it has an uneven surface with thick and thin areas. It is easier and quicker to sew than other pile fabrics.

Workroom Secrets

Fabric Prep: To preshrink, machine wash/dry three times.

Layout/Cutting/Marking: To position the fabric design attractively, spread in a single layer right-side up. Mark using clips. Generally, chenille does not require a nap layout.

Stitching: To simulate quality ready-to-wear, reduce or eliminate hand sewing as much as possible. To stitch over uneven layers, use a zipper foot or shim. To baste, use flower pins or quilting clothes pins.

Seams: Bound seams are a nice finish on unlined jackets and coats. Stitch right sides together. Trim seam to ¼" or ⅜" (6-10mm), and bind seam with bias-cut lining fabric, tricot, or lightweight cotton. Fold seams toward back when joining to another section. Bound seams are also attractive when stitched on the right side. To stitch decorative bound seams, begin wrong sides together; trim and bind with contrast bias or ribbon. When joining chenille to a smooth fabric, stitch with the chenille on the bottom.

Seam/Hem Finishes: Before finishing, brush edges with a stiff brush to remove tufts close to the edges; then serge or zigzag. On unlined jackets and coats, bind seam/hem edges to prevent shedding. Use serged, topstitched, strap, and bound seams to finish unlined jackets attractively.

Hems: Topstitch hems with a single or twin needle. For a decorative hem, use a contrast facing on the right side to trim.

Edge Finishes: Replace self-fabric facings with lightweight bindings, bands, ribbings, or smooth fabric facings.

Zippers: Exposed zippers are less likely to catch the tufts. To stitch the zipper, begin with the zipper and chenille right sides together; stitch a ¼" (6mm) seam. Press the chenille away from the zipper and topstitch ¼" (6mm) from the seam.

Garment Care: Turn garment inside out to wash. Use a fabric softener to reduce lint.

A patchwork of textures gives new interest to this simple classic shirt. (Photo courtesy of KWIK·SEW®.)

Similar Fabrics: Sculptured velour, Hi-Lo fleece.

Uses: Elegant casual designs, jackets, swimsuit coverups, tee tops, shorts, pants, bathrobes, children's wear.

Design Details: Minimal seaming, wrap fronts, elastic casings, ribbing trims.

Sewing Checklist

Essential Supplies

Needles: Sharp (HM, HJ), universal (H); sizes 70/10-90/14.

Thread: All-purpose (cotton, polyester, cotton covered polyester). Serger – lightweight serger.

Cutting: Large, sharp shears, duplicate pattern pieces.

Marking: Chalk, clips, erasable pens, safety pins.

Miscellaneous: Stiff bristle brush, flower pins, safety pins, quilting clothes pins, shim.

Interfacings: Fusibles applied to facing or nonwovens.

Linings/Underlinings: Rarely used.

Machine Setup

Stitch Length: 2.5-3mm (8-10spi); topstitching: 3-3.5mm (7-8spi)

Tension: Lightly balanced; light pressure.

Feet: Roller, wide straight stitch, zigzag.

Sewing Basics

Test Garment: Rarely needed.

Fabric Prep: Machine wash/dry.

Layout: Nap – single layer, wrong-side up; matching – single layer, right-side up; duplicate pattern pieces.

Seams: Plain (pressed open or closed), decorative bound.

Hems: Hand: (blindstitch), machine stitched.

Seam/Hem Finishes: Serged, zigzag, bound (tricot, lightweight lining).

Edge Finishes: Facings (self-fabric, smooth fabric, bias, contrast trim), bindings, elastic casings.

Closures: Buttonholes (machine, inseam), buttons/loops, ties, zippers (machine, invisible, exposed), hooks/eyes.

Pressing: Medium to high heat; steam.

Garment Care: Machine wash/dry.

Chiffon

Chiffon is a lightweight, transparent, plain-weave fabric made with fine, highly twisted yarns. Soft and drapeable, it is easily damaged by ripping and improper pressing. Silk chiffon is softer and more difficult to control than polyester chiffon.

Similar fabrics: Beaded chiffon, crepeline, embroidered chiffon, chiffon/satin stripe, georgette, mousseline, soft organza, triple layer chiffon.

Uses: Dressy garments, blouses, dresses, pants, lingerie, special occasion and evening wear, wraps, linings, underlinings, stay tapes.

Design Elements: Gathers, soft pleats, ruffles, flares, drapes, cowl necklines, bias cuts. Avoid close fitting designs.

Sewing Checklist

Essential Supplies

Needles: Sharp (HM, HJ), universal (H); sizes 60/8-70/10.

Thread: Lightweight (cotton, cotton covered polyester, silk), all purpose. Topstitching – lightweight or all purpose. Serger – lightweight serger thread, textured thread.

Cutting: Serrated shears, rotary cutter/mat, tissue.

Marking: Chalk, clips, tailor's tacks, thread.

Miscellaneous: Super fine pins, fine needles (sizes 9-12), flesh-colored chiffon, nylon stocking scrap, water soluble stabilizer, tissue.

Interfacings: Lightweight sew-ins, Sewin' Sheer™, soft organza, lightweight silk, marquisette, polyester chiffon.

Linings/Underlinings: Optional, depends on garment type and quality.

Machine Setup

Stitch Length: 2-2.5mm (10-12spi).

Tension: Lightly balanced.

Feet: Wide straight stitch, roller foot; small hole throat plate.

Sewing Basics

Test Garment: Highly recommended.

Fabric Prep: Silk, steam or dry-clean; polyester, machine wash/dry.

Layout: Nap – double layer.

Seams: Plain (pressed open, closed), topstitched, French, faux French, bound.

Hems: Narrow (machine-rolled, merrow, pin, zigzag, shirttail), hand (blindstitch).

Seam/Hem Finishes: Serged, hand overcast, bound.

Edge Finishes: Facings (bias, tulle, ribbon), bindings, edge-to-edge linings.

Closures: Buttonholes (machine, hand, inseam, bound), buttons/loops, zippers (hand), covered snaps, hooks/eyes.

Pressing: Cool to medium heat; steam, press cloth.

Garment Care: Dry-clean.

Workroom Secrets

Test Garment: To avoid ripping and over-handling, make a test garment before cutting the fabric to refine the fit and practice your sewing skills.

Layout/Cutting/Marking: Spread tissue paper on the cutting table; then lay out the fabric and pattern. Pin through all layers only in the seam allowances to avoid damaging the fabric. Cut through all layers, using sharp serrated shears or a rotary cutter/mat.

Basting: Hand baste to ensure stitching accuracy and prevent ripping. Pin baste with fine (9-12) needles. Mark the right side of each section with a cross-stitch.

Stitching: Begin with a new, sharp needle (HM). Check for burrs on the needle by stitching through a scrap of nylon stocking. Use a wide straight stitch or roller foot to reduce stitching problems; or use a zigzag foot, and move needle to the right-hand position. Sandwich stitch seams. Sandwich and pin the chiffon seam between strips of water soluble stabilizer. Stitch; then steam lightly to remove the stabilizer. To stitch curves, shorten the stitch length. Do not backstitch; knot the thread ends.

Seams: French seams will drape more softly when hand sewn. To finish plain seams, trim to ¼" (6mm); then hand overcast or zigzag (W,3-L,2) over the raw edges. To make the seams invisible, trim to ¼" (6mm) and bind with flesh-colored chiffon.

Darts: Trim the dart take-up to ¼" (6mm) and overcast by hand.

Buttonholes: When possible, use button loops instead of buttonholes. To stitch machine buttonholes, sandwich the chiffon between two layers of water soluble stabilizer. Stitch with a fine, sharp needle (HM) and lightweight embroidery thread.

Pressing: Test press; chiffon is easily damaged by improper pressing and too much heat.

This elegant dress, features a velvet bodice and a chiffon sari skirt. (Photo courtesy of Gabrielle Stanley.)

China Silk

China silk is a semi-soft, firmly woven, plain weave silk fabric that looks the same on both sides. It is easily damaged by hot irons, pins, needles, and ripping. Light colors are transparent.

Workroom Secrets

Fabric Prep: If you plan to launder the garment, hand wash the silk before cutting. Submerge in a basin of hot water for about 20 minutes; hang to drip dry. While still damp, use warm iron to remove any wrinkles. When making lingerie, machine wash/dry to preshrink. To avoid excess fraying, stitch the ends together before laundering.

Layout/Cutting/Marking: To avoid confusing the right and wrong sides, mark the right side with a cross-stitch. Spread fabric in double layer; pin selvages together. Lay out the pattern; and pin only in the seam allowances. Cut, using sharp, serrated shears or a rotary cutter/mat.

Basting: Hand baste to ensure stitching accuracy and prevent ripping. Pin baste with super fine pins or fine needles (sizes 9-12).

Stitching: Begin with a new, sharp (HM) needle. Use a wide straight stitch or roller foot to reduce stitching problems; or use a zigzag foot, and move the needle to the right-hand position. Sandwich stitch seams. Sandwich and pin the silk seam between strips of water soluble stabilizer. Stitch; then steam press to remove the stabilizer. When stitching curves, shorten the stitch length. Do not backstitch; knot the thread ends.

Seams: To avoid fraying when laundered, use French seams or finish seams by serging or zigzagging them together. To simulate flat fell seams on tailored designs, use topstitched seams which are much easier to sew.

Hems: Generally, narrow hems are more attractive than wide ones.

Edge Finishes: Replace facings with bindings, edge to edge linings, or underlinings to avoid unattractive facing shadows. When facings cannot be avoided, cut them straight or make them an element of the design.

Buttonholes: To machine stitch buttonholes, sandwich the silk between two layers of water soluble stabilizer. Stitch with a fine, sharp (HM) needle and lightweight embroidery thread.

Pressing: Test press. China silk is easily damaged by improper pressing and too much heat.

Designed by Deborah Shelton Harris for Sew Beautiful magazine, this classic heirloom design is a French-sewn flapper design featuring china silk and lace. (Photo courtesy of Martha Pullen Company and photographer Jennifer and Company.)

Similar Fabrics: Fuji silk, honan silk, jap silk, silk broadcloth.

Uses: Blouses, lingerie, linings.

Design Elements: Gathers, pleats, tucks, lace trims, lace insertions, topstitching, shirt and dolman sleeves.

Sewing Checklist

Essential Supplies

Needles: Sharp (HM, HJ), universal (H); sizes 60/8-70/10.

Thread: Lightweight (cotton, polyester, cotton covered polyester, silk), lightweight serger thread, all purpose. Topstitching – lightweight or all purpose thread. Serger – lightweight serger thread.

Cutting: Serrated shears, rotary cutter/mat, tissue.

Marking: Chalk, clips, tailor's tacks, thread.

Miscellaneous: Super fine pins/needles, weights, water-soluble stabilizers, tissue.

Interfacings: Featherweight sew-ins or fusibles, organza, lightweight silks.

Linings/Underlinings: Rarely, except for modesty, color, or design.

Machine Setup

Stitch Length: 2-2.5mm (10-12spi).

Tension: Lightly balanced.

Feet: Wide, straight stitch, roller foot; small hole throat plate.

Sewing Basics

Test Garment: Depends on design.

Fabric Prep: Preshrink with steam, wash/dry, or dry-clean.

Layout: Without nap – double layer.

Seams: Plain (pressed open or closed), topstitched, French, faux French.

Hems: Narrow hems – machine-rolled, merrow, satin stitch, lettuce, shirttail; plain hems – topstitch or hand (blindstitch, catchstitch).

Seam/Hem Finishes: Serged, zigzag, pinked, hand overcast.

Edge Finishes: Facings (self-fabric, bias), bindings, edge-to-edge linings, lace trims.

Closures: Buttonholes (machine, hand, inseam), buttons/loops, zippers (hand, machine stitched), covered snaps, hooks/eyes.

Pressing: Low to medium heat; steam, press cloth.

Garment Care: Dry-clean to maintain the garment's pristine appearance. Wash/dry casual designs and lingerie if fabric was pretreated.

Corduroy

Corduroy is a pile fabric, woven with an extra set of filling yarns to make vertical wales or ribs, which range from very thin to thick and heavy. Generally a cotton or cotton-blend, it does not ease well, is difficult to press sharply, and may add weight to larger figures.

Similar Fabrics: Corduroy chenille, featherwale, high-low, pinwale, midwale, thick and thin corduroy, uncut or no-wale corduroy.

Uses: Casual or tailored designs, coats, jackets, shirts, skirts, dresses, jumpers, pants, vests, childrens and infants wear.

Design Elements: Crisp silhouettes, shaped seams, soft pleats or shirring, all type pockets.

Sewing Checklist

Essential Supplies
Needles: Sharp (HJ, HM), universal (H); sizes 70/10-100/16.

Thread: All purpose (cotton, polyester, cotton covered polyester). Topstitching – machine embroidery/topstitching threads, 2 threads all-purpose thread. Serger – all purpose, serger threads.

Cutting: Sharp shears, rotary cutter/mat, duplicate pattern pieces when using a single layer.

Marking: Chalk, clips, erasable pens, pins, tailor's tacks, thread.

Miscellaneous: Shim, stiff brush, needle board, Velvaboard, velveteen press cloth, water soluble stabilizer.

Interfacings: Usually, sew-in or fusible.

Linings: Generally for outer-wear and quality designs.

Machine Setup
Stitch length: 2-2.5mm (10-12spi).

Tension: Lightly balanced; light pressure.

Feet: Roller, even-feed, zigzag, zipper.

Sewing Basics
Test Garment: Depends on design, quality.

Fabric Prep: Steam, dry-clean, or wash/dry, depending on the design quality, and use.

Layout: Nap – wrong sides together; heavy or patterned fabrics – single layer right-side up.

Seams: Plain (pressed open or closed), topstitched.

Hems: Hand (blindstitch, blind catchstitch), double-stitched, topstitched.

Seam/Hem Finishes: Serged, zigzag, pinked; if lined, none.

Edge Finishes: Facings (self-fabric, lining), bindings (self-fabric, contrast, faux leather or suede), ribbing.

Closures: Buttonholes (machine, bound, inseam), buttons/loops, lacings, zippers (machine, invisible, decorative), decorative snaps.

Pressing: Medium to high heat, steam; velveteen press cloth, needleboard, or Velvaboard.

Garment Care: Dry-clean or wash/dry.

Workroom Secrets

Layout/Cutting/Marking: Check for permanent crease at fold; refold as needed to position crease inconspicuously. For better wear, lay out so nap runs down. For richer color, lay out so nap runs up. Remove pins immediately after cutting to avoid permanent imprints.

Stitching: Stitch with the nap, instead of the grain. Use a shim to stitch over thick seams easily.

Seams: Substitute topstitched seams for flat felled seams; the latter are too bulky for most corduroys. Use a stiff brush to remove loose pile at raw edges.

Buttonholes: For more defined machine buttonholes, cover fabric with water soluble stabilizer, use corded buttonholes, and/or stitch with machine embroidery thread (30/2, 40/2).

Topstitching: A nice detail for sportswear, use two strands of regular thread when topstitching thread is unavailable. Topstitch with the nap.

Linings: Outerwear garments are more comfortable and easier to slip into when lined.

Pressing: Test press. To avoid flattening the pile, cover the ironing board with a piece of velveteen or use a needle-board or a Velvaboard. Use a velveteen press cloth to press right side.

Garment Care: To protect skirts and pants from clip hanger marks, sew in ribbon hanger loops at the waist. To retain the garment's pristine appearance, dry-clean. When laundering, turn the garment inside out. To freshen the pile, hang in a steam-filled bathroom for 30 minutes. Do not handle or wear until completely dry.

The lace trim on this dress transforms the plain, traditional corduroy into an adorable, go-anywhere design. (Photo courtesy of Simplicity Patterns.)

Cotton

Sometimes called "the fiber of a thousand faces," cotton is known for its comfort, appearance, versatility, and performance. Available in a wide variety of fabric weights, surface patterns, and weaves, cotton is a component of many fabrics. It is frequently blended with polyester to make easy-care, wrinkle-resistant fabrics. The quality depends on the fineness and length of the fiber.

Comfortable to wear, easy to dye, and versatile, cotton is known for its absorbency and resistance to abrasion, static electricity, pilling, and moths. It ravels, soils easily, burns rapidly, shrinks, and has little elasticity.

Workroom Secrets

Fabric Prep: Depends on manufacturer's recommendation, garment design, quality, and use. A washable fiber, cotton will shrink. It has progressive shrinkage and may shrink when washed several times. Many cotton fabrics can be washed and dried while others will become limp, lose any special finishes, or shrink badly. When in doubt, wash a small piece before washing the entire piece.

Layout/Cutting/Marking: Many fabrics have no nap or one-way pattern and do not require a nap layout. Examine the fabric carefully before using a without nap layout. When both sides look alike, mark the right side with chalk, safety pins, or a thread cross-stitch. Fabrics such as velvet, velveteen, corduroy, jacquards, some napped fabrics, and many prints require a nap layout.

Pressing: Use a lower temperature or a press cloth when pressing cotton blends and lightweight fabrics.

Garment Care: Cotton can be laundered or dry-cleaned, depending on the dyes, finishes, fabric structure, garment design, quality, and use. Better garments will maintain their pristine appearance longer when dry-cleaned.

Designed by Paul Shanley, this fabulous cotton shirt was created with PatternMaster Tailor Made™ software. (Photo courtesy of Wild Ginger Software®.)

Cotton Fabrics: Batiste, broadcloth, calico, cambric, canvas, challis, chambray, chino, chintz, cluny lace, corduroy, covert, crepe, damask, denim, dimity, dotted swiss, double-faced cottons, double knit, drill, duck, durable press cottons, embroidered cottons, eyelet, flannel, gabardine, gauze, guipure lace, gingham, homespun, hopsacking, interfacings, jersey, lawn, madras, monk's cloth, muslin, net, organdy, oxford cloth, percale, pique, plissé, pongee, poplin, ratiné, rib knits, raschel knits, sailcloth, sateen, seersucker, sheets, suede cloth, terry, ticking, velour, velvet, velveteen, voile, whipcord.

Uses: All type garments.

Burn Test: Cotton burns rapidly with a yellow flame, leaving an afterglow and light colored, feathery ash. It smells like paper or rags.

Sewing Checklist

Essential Supplies

Needles: Woven fabrics – sharp (HM), universal (H). **Knit fabrics** – stretch (HS), universal (H), ballpoint (H-SUK). Sizes – lightweight, 60/8-70/10; medium-weight, 70/10-80/12; heavyweight, 80/12-90/14.

Thread: Lightweight fabrics – lightweight (cotton, polyester, cotton covered polyester, silk), all purpose thread. **Medium-weight fabrics** – all purpose thread. **Heavyweight fabrics** – machine embroidery/topstitching threads or all purpose. **Very heavy fabrics** – machine embroidery/topstitching threads.

Miscellaneous: Fine pins, water soluble stabilizer, safety pins.

Cutting: Lightweight fabrics – serrated shears. Other fabrics – sharp shears; rotary cutter/mat; duplicate pattern pieces when using a single layer.

Marking: Chalk, clips, erasable pens, pins, safety pins.

Interfacings/Linings/Underlinings: Depends on the fabric weight, garment type, quality, and structure; same care properties.

Machine Setup

Stitch Length: Lightweight fabrics – 1.5-1.75mm (15-18spi). **Medium-weight fabrics** – 2-2.5mm (10-12spi). **Heavy-weight fabrics** – 2.5-3mm (8-10spi). **Very heavy fabrics** – 3-4mm (6-8spi). **All weights** – zigzag (W,.5-L,2.5).

Tension: Depends on the fabric.

Feet: Straight stitch, zigzag, roller foot.

Sewing Basics

Test Garment: Depends on fabric/garment/quality.

Fabric Prep: Machine wash/dry, steam, or dry-clean.

Layout: Depends on fabric.

Seams/Hems: All types, depending on the fabric weight, structure, and transparency and garment quality, design, use, and care.

Closures: Buttonholes (machine, hand, inseam), buttons/loops, ties, zippers (hand, machine, invisible).

Pressing: High heat; damp press cloth and steam.

Garment Care: Machine wash/dry; dry-clean.

Crêpe de Chine

Crêpe de Chine is a fine, light to medium-weight silk crepe with a dull luster that drapes gracefully. Easily marred by machine needles, pins, ripping, and improper pressing, it is slippery and challenging to sew.

Crêpe Types/Similar Fabrics: Brazilian crepe, crepe backed satin, crepe marocain, crepon, flat crepe, moss crepe, polyester crepe, rayon crepe.

Uses: Dressy designs, soft blouses, shirts, skirts, dresses, pants, jackets, lightweight coats, lingerie, and linings.

Design Elements: Gathers, soft pleats, ruffles, flares, drapes, cowl necklines, collars, bias cuts, elastic casings. Avoid close fitting designs and seams on the straight grain; include underlinings for structured silhouettes.

Sewing Checklist

Essential Supplies

Needles: Sharp (HM), universal (H); sizes 60/8-70/10.
Thread: Lightweight (cotton, cotton covered polyester, silk), all purpose (cotton, polyester, silk). Topstitching – lightweight, all purpose. Serger – lightweight serger thread, textured thread.
Cutting: Serrated shears, rotary cutter/mat.
Marking: Chalk, clips, super fine pins, tailor's tacks, thread, tracing wheel/white tracing carbon.
Miscellaneous: Super fine pins, weights, lightweight zippers, wigan or muslin, water soluble stabilizer, tissue.
Interfacings: Featherweight and very lightweight sew-ins, very lightweight and low-temp fusibles, organza, soft organza, lightweight silks.
Linings/Underlinings: Optional, depending on design and quality.

Machine Setup

Stitch length: 2-2.5mm (10-12spi).
Tension: Lightly balanced.
Feet: Wide straight stitch, roller foot, zigzag; small hole throat plate.

Sewing Basics

Test Garment: Optional, depending on design and fabric quality.
Fabric Prep: Steam or dry-clean; for lingerie, wash/line dry.
Layout: Without nap – double layer.
Seams: Plain (pressed open, closed), topstitched, French, faux French.
Hems: Hand (blindstitch), shirttail, machine rolled, pin, interfaced, topstitched.
Seam/Hem Finishes: Serged, zigzag, pinked, hand overcast; if lined, none.
Edge Finishes: Facings, bias bindings, bands, casings, ribbings.
Closures: Buttonholes (machine, bound, inseam), buttons/loops, zippers (hand, machine, invisible).
Pressing: Medium heat, dry iron, damp and dry press cloths.
Garment Care: Dry-clean; hand-launder if pre-treated.

Workroom Secrets

Fabric Prep: Generally it is best to steam or dry-clean to preshrink. Hand or machine wash in cool water when making lingerie. When washed, it will shrink as much as 15 percent and dark colors will fade.

Layout/Cutting/Marking: Use soft cotton or silk thread to mark the right side with a cross-stitch. Use weights or place pins only in the seam allowances. Set pins parallel to the selvage. Mark lightly. Avoid erasable pens and colored chalk; they may stain permanently.

Stitching: Begin with a new needle with a sharp (HM) point. To reduce puckered seams, use a wide straight stitch foot; and hold the fabric firmly in front and back of the foot when stitching.

Seams: Avoid seams on the straight grain. Plain seams pressed open drape better than self-finished seams such as French and faux French. Hand baste to ensure stitching accuracy and reduce ripping. Tissue stitch or sandwich stitch seams to reduce stitching problems. When pin basting, use fine needles or super fine pins. (See Any Fabric page 13.)

Hems: On lightweight crêpe de Chine, narrow machine rolled hems allow skirts to float and billow more than double fold shirttail hems. Finish hems on medium and heavy-weight crepes with a single fold 2" (5cm) plain hem. Interface with wigan or muslin for a soft roll at the hemline. Hand sew with blindstitches. Finish hems on casual designs with topstitching. Finish the raw edge; then topstitch with a single or twin needles. Finish hems on dressy garments by hand with a blindstitch.

Seam/Hem Finishes: To reduce thread imprints when serging, use textured thread in the loopers. Avoid bound and Hong Kong finishes, which are too bulky for most crêpe de Chine designs.

Buttonholes: Machine stitch with fine embroidery thread.

Zippers: Use lightweight zippers. To avoid stretching the opening, stabilize with a lightweight stay.

Pressing: Test press; crêpe de Chine waterspots and is easily damaged by hot irons and improper pressing.

Garment Care: Dry-clean to maintain the garment's pristine appearance.

Sophisticated and elegant, this crêpe de Chine blouse is from the Custom Couture Collection by Claire Shaeffer. (Vogue Pattern 7718, courtesy of The McCall Pattern Co.)

Damask

Damask is a reversible fabric made on a jacquard loom. It features elaborate designs woven in cotton, linen, silk, wool, worsted, rayon, and manufactured fibers. Flatter than brocade, it does not ease well, wrinkles, and is easily damaged by wax, colored chalk, and erasable pens.

Workroom Secrets

Fabric Prep: To preshrink, dry-clean or steam dark colors which will fade badly and become white at edges. Wash/dry light colors if you plan to wash the garment. Purchase an additional ¼ to ½ yard for washable garments.

Marking: Avoid wax or colored chalks and erasable pens, which may stain permanently.

Stitching: To machine stitch through multiple thicknesses, rub seams with a bar of Ivory soap to lubricate the needle or pound with a cloth-covered hammer to soften fibers. When crossing bulky seams, use a shim to level the foot and prevent skipped stitches. (See Any Fabric page 12.)

Seams: Use sturdy topstitched seams and hems for unlined and washable designs. To flatten seams, topstitch. For dressier designs, topstitch close to the seam. For sportswear, topstitch ¼" (6mm) away or use a wide twin needle to simulate flat fell seams. For an elegant finish on unlined designs, finish seams with tricot binding or Hong Kong binding. Use strap or lapped seams only for reversible garments.

Topstitching: Lengthen the stitch (3-4mm). Use a topstitching needle which has a deeper groove when using heavier threads. Use a twin needle (HJ) to double stitch. When topstitching edges, use a zipper foot so the foot will remain level.

Interfacing: Consider bias-cut linen or self-fabric when interfacing.

Sleeves: Shrink and shape sleeve caps before setting into the garment. Reduce the ease as needed to ease fullness smoothly. (See Any Fabric page 14.)

Buttonholes: Machine stitch buttonholes with a sharp needle (HM). Lengthen the stitch length slightly. Spray the fabric with spray starch to add a little crispness.

Pressing: To avoid slicking the fabric, press from the wrong side. Use a press cloth when pressing the right side.

Embroidery: Damask is an easy fabric to embroider. Use water soluble stabilizer on top of the fabric with tearaway or cutaway stabilizer on the wrong side.

Garment Care: Dry-clean to maintain the garment's pristine appearance.

This understated design is a good choice to showcase the damask fabric. (Butterick Pattern – 5990; courtesy of The McCall Pattern Co.)

Similar Fabrics: Linen, cotton jacquard, linen-look raw silk, silk linen, double-faced fabrics.

Uses: Reversible or unlined garments, tailored designs, casual jackets, coats, skirts, pants.

Design Elements: Minimal seaming, crisp silhouettes, topstitching.

Sewing Checklist

Essential Supplies

Needles: Sharp (HM, HJ), universal (H); sizes 70/10-90/14; twin needle (ZWI HJ 4.0/100).

Thread: All purpose (cotton, polyester, cotton covered polyester). Topstitching – all purpose, machine embroidery/topstitching (cotton, polyester, silk-D, acrylic).

Cutting: Sharp shears, rotary cutter/mat.

Marking: Chalk, clips, erasable pens, pins.

Miscellaneous: Shim, safety pins, spray starch, stabilizers – water soluble, burn-away, tearaway, cut away.

Interfacings: Optional; fusible, sew-in, linen, or self-fabric.

Linings/Underlinings: Optional; same care as garment.

Machine Setup

Stitch Length: 2.5-3mm (8-10spi).

Tension: Lightly balanced.

Feet: Wide straight stitch, roller, zigzag.

Sewing Basics

Test Garment: Optional, depending on design and garment quality.

Fabric Prep: Preshrink. Steam, dry-clean, hand or machine wash, depending on design.

Layout: With nap – double layer; patterned fabrics – single layer, duplicate pattern pieces.

Seams: Plain (pressed open or closed), topstitched, bound, strap, lapped.

Seam/Hem Finishes: Serged, zigzag, tricot bound, Hong Kong.

Hems: Hand (blindstitch, catchstitch, double-stitched), topstitched, twin needle, wrong-side out.

Edge Finishes: Facings, bindings, linings.

Closures: Buttonholes (machine, corded, bound, inseam); buttons/loops, ties, zippers (hand, machine, invisible).

Pressing: Medium to high heat, damp cloth or steam.

Garment Care: Machine wash/dry or dry-clean.

Denim

Denim is a densely woven, crisp, twill-weave cotton or cotton/blend fabric with colored threads in warp and white threads in the filling. It is washable, durable, and comfortable to wear. Bulky and difficult to ease, it abrades easily, fades, crocks, and shrinks. It is available in a variety of weights (6-16 oz.) and is frequently blended with spandex for additional comfort and shape retention.

Similar Fabrics: African mudcloth, awning, broché, brushed denim, canvas, cavalry twill, chino, cotton twill, coutil, drill, duck, dungaree, jean, metallic denim, pillow ticking, poplin, sailcloth, stonewashed denim, tarpaulin, washed denim.

Uses: All type garments from jeans to evening wear.

Design Elements: Topstitching, faux fur/fur linings, rivets, decorative snaps, all type zippers.

Sewing Checklist

Essential Supplies

Needles: Sharp (HJ), universal (H); sizes 70/10-110/18. Topstitching – topstitching (N), sharp (HJ), sizes 90/14-100/16 or twin needle (ZWI HJ 40/100).

Thread: All purpose (polyester, cotton covered polyester, polyester). Topstitching – machine embroidery, topstitching (cotton covered, polyester), silk buttonhole twist, metallic, 2 strands all purpose.

Cutting: Sharp shears, rotary cutter/mat.

Marking: Chalk, clips, erasable pens, pins.

Miscellaneous: Shim, hammer, Ivory soap, spray bottle, cut-away stabilizer.

Interfacings: Washable, fusible, or sew-in.

Linings/Underlinings: Optional, same care as garment.

Machine Setup

Stitch length: 2-3mm (8-12spi).

Tension: Adjust as needed.

Feet: Wide straight stitch, roller, even-feed, zigzag.

Sewing Basics

Fabric Prep: Machine wash/dry for everyday garments; dry-clean or steam quality garments to avoid abrasion streaks.

Layout: Without nap – double layer; brushed denim/one way patterns – nap.

Seams: Plain (pressed open or closed), topstitched, lapped, strap.

Hems: Hand (blindstitch, double-stitched), topstitched, single or double fold, fused.

Seam/Hem Finishes: Serged, zigzag.

Edge Finishes: Facings (self-fabric, lightweight or contrast fabric), bindings, bands, ribbing, lining.

Closures: Buttonholes (machine, bound, inseam), buttons/loops, snaps, zippers (machine, hand, decorative), lacings.

Pressing: High heat, damp cloth or steam; reduce heat for blends and stretch fabric or use a press cloth.

Garment Care: Machine wash/dry; dry-clean.

Workroom Secrets

Fabric Prep: Wash and machine dry several times to preshrink, remove excess dye, and soften the fabric. To avoid white abrasion streaks on denim, dry clean or soak in very hot water 20 minutes; drip dry; repeat several times.

Stitching: Use polyester thread for more elastic seams and to reduce seam failure. To machine stitch through multiple thicknesses easily, rub seams and hems with a bar of Ivory soap to lubricate the needle or pound with a cloth-covered hammer to soften fibers. When crossing bulky seams, use a shim to level the presser foot and prevent skipped stitches.

Topstitching: Lengthen the stitch (3-4mm). Use a topstitching needle which has a deeper groove. Use a twin needle (HJ) to double stitch. Use cotton covered polyester thread which will fade with the denim.

Seams: Use faux flat-fell seams to duplicate the look of real flat fell seams which are generally too bulky.

Hems: To prevent curling, serge the raw edge. Fuse hem in place; and topstitch with a wide twin needle. If a twin needle is not available, edgestitch; then topstitch again ¼" to ⅜" (6mm-1cm) away.

Embroidering: When embroidering, avoid tearaway stabilizers which may distort the stitches when removed.

Garment Care: To reduce abrasion, turn the garment wrong-side out before washing. Remove everyday garments from the dryer while damp; shake vigorously, smooth, and hang to dry. For better garments, iron until dry or dry-clean. When pressing, spritz with water to dampen. Dry-clean to maintain the garment's pristine appearance.

This smashing asymmetrical skirt is particularly attractive in denim. (Burda pattern – 8492, courtesy of Burda.)

Double Cloth

Double cloth is a reversible fabric which can be separated into two pieces of cloth with completely different weaves, colors, or patterns. Generally wool or a wool blend, these fabrics range from lightweight, soft fabrics to heavy, crisp materials.

Double cloth fabrics are particularly attractive when used for unlined garments, but they can also be used for traditional designs. When used for reversible garments, one side will always be more attractive than the other.

Workroom Secrets

Layout/Cutting/Marking: Mark right side of each section with safety pins.

Seams: Double-cloth seams are attractive and inconspicuous.

1. Baste 1⅛" (2.8cm) from the edge to avoid an unattractive demarcation line when separating fabrics for double-cloth seams.

2. Separate the layers to the basting.

3. Right sides together, stitch the seams on the outer layer. Press open, and trim to a scant ½" (1.2cm).

4. On the inner layer, trim the seam allowances to ⅜". Fold the edges under, and slipstitch the folds together. Press.

5. Topstitch, if desired.

Hems: Use double-cloth hems on the edges of quality garments.

1. Baste 1⅛" (2.8cm) from the edge. Separate to the basting.

2. Trim the hem allowance to ¼ to ½" (6mm-1.2cm). Fold the edges in; slipstitch the folded edges together.

3. Topstitch, if desired.

Edge Finishes: Stay openings with a narrow strip (¼"/6mm) of lightweight fusible to prevent stretching. Trim the seams to a scant ¼" (6mm).

Topstitching: Use decorative stitches and/or contrast thread to highlight the topstitching for a more decorative finish. Topstitch seams and darts to hold them flat. To topstitch inconspicuously, topstitch each side close to the seamline. To topstitch edges, use a zipper foot. Topstitch a generous ¼" (6mm) from the edge to enclose the seam allowances. Use a shim when crossing bulky seams.

Buttonholes: Machine stitch buttonholes with water soluble stabilizer on top of the fabric to prevent the stitches from embedding in the fabric.

Embroidery: Use water soluble stabilizer on top of the fabric and several layers of lightweight tearaway stabilizer on the wrong side.

Warm and comfortable, use double cloth to make this go-anywhere poncho reversible. (Photo courtesy of KWIK-SEW®.)

Similar Fabrics: Blanket cloth, boiled wool, double knit, loden.

Uses: Unlined or reversible garments, tailored designs, dresses, skirts, jackets, coats, capes, ponchos.

Design Elements: Crisp, tailored details, topstitching, braid trims, bindings.

Sewing Checklist

Essential Supplies

Needles: Universal (H), sharp (HM, HJ); sizes 70/10-90/14.

Thread: All purpose (cotton, polyester, cotton covered polyester). Topstitching – machine embroidery/topstitching (cotton, polyester, cotton covered polester, silk), all purpose.

Cutting: Sharp shears, rotary cutter/mat.

Marking: Chalk, clips, pins, tailor's tacks, thread.

Miscellaneous: Flower pins, shim, safety pins, stabilizers – water soluble, cut away, lightweight tearaway.

Interfacings/Linings/Underlinings: Rarely.

Machine Setup

Stitch Length: 2.5-3mm (8-10spi).

Tension: Lightly balanced; light pressure.

Feet: Wide straight stitch, zipper, zigzag.

Sewing Basics

Test Garment: Recommended.

Fabric Prep: Preshrink with steam or dry-clean.

Layout: Nap – light to medium-weight, double layer; heavy-weight – single layer.

Seams: Plain (pressed open or closed), topstitched, abutted, decorative serged, strap, double-cloth seam.

Hems: Double-cloth hem, hand (catchstitch, double-stitched), topstitched.

Seam/Hem Finishes: Serged, zigzag, Hong-Kong binding.

Edge Finishes: Foldover braids, bindings, facings to trim, double-cloth hem.

Closures: Buttonholes (machine, corded, inseam), toggles, frogs, zippers (hand, machine, invisible).

Pressing: Medium heat, steam; wool press cloth.

Garment Care: Dry-clean.

Double-Faced Fabric

Double-faced or two-faced fabrics are reversible fabrics with two attractive sides. They can look the same on both sides or have different colorways or patterns. Unlike double cloth, they cannot be separated into two pieces of cloth.

They are well suited for reversible and unlined jackets and coats, and available in a variety of fibers and fabrications. These fabrics range from lightweight, soft fabrics to heavy, crisp materials. The focus in this chapter is on reversible garments.

Double-Faced Fabrics: Blanket cloth, boiled wool, crêpe de Chine, damask, double knit, duplex prints, faux suede, granite cloth, hemp, jacquard patterns, linen, satin backed crepe, wool crepe, woven plaids and stripes.

Uses: Reversible or unlined garments, dresses, skirts, jackets, coats, capes, ponchos.

Design Elements: Simple designs, minimal seams, wrap styles, tailored details, topstitching, dropped shoulders, shirt and kimono sleeves, foldover braids, bindings.

Sewing Checklist

Essential Supplies
Needles: Woven fabrics – sharp (HM), universal (H). **Knit fabrics** – stretch (HS), universal (H), ballpoint (H-SUK). Sizes – lightweight, 60/8-70/10; medium-weight, 70/10-80/12; heavy-weight, 80/12-90/14.
Thread: Lightweight fabrics – lightweight (cotton, polyester, cotton covered polyester, silk), all purpose thread. **Medium-weight fabrics** – all purpose thread. **Heavy-weight fabrics** – all purpose, machine embroidery/topstitching threads. **Very heavy-weight fabrics** – machine embroidery/topstitching threads.
Cutting: Lightweight fabrics – serrated shears, other fabrics – sharp shears; rotary cutter/mat.
Marking: Chalk, clips, erasable pens, tailor's tacks, thread.
Miscellaneous: Fine pins, safety pins, water soluble stabilizer.
Interfacings: Depends on the fabric weight, garment type, quality, and structure; same care properties.

Machine Setup
Stitch Length: Lightweight wovens – 1.5-1.75mm (15-18spi). **Medium-weight wovens** – 2-2.5mm (10-12spi); **Heavy-weight wovens** – 2.5-3mm (8-10spi). **Very heavy-weight wovens** – 3-4mm (6-8spi).
Tension: Depends on the fabric.
Feet: Straight stitch, zigzag, roller foot.

Sewing Basics
Test Garment: Depends on design, fabric, and quality.
Fabric Prep: Machine wash/dry, steam, or dry-clean.
Layout: Depends on fabric.
Seams: Plain, strap, bound, French, faux French, stand-up French, decorative French.
Hems: Hand (blindstitch, catchstitch), shirttail, wrong-side out, topstitched.
Seam/Hem Finishes: Serged, zigzag, turned under, tricot binding, Hong Kong finish.
Closures: Buttonholes (machine, inseam), lacings, button links, toggles, frogs, fabric and ribbon ties.
Pressing: Depends on fiber and fabric structure.
Garment Care: Machine wash/dry; dry-clean.

Workroom Secrets
Fabric Prep: Depends on fiber, garment design, quality, and use.
Layout/Cutting/Marking: Examine the fabric to determine if it has a nap. When in doubt, use a nap layout. When both sides look the same, mark the side which you have selected as the "right" side at the outset, using safety pins. All reversible garments are more attractive on one side.
Seams/Reversible Garments: For reversible garments, use seams such as strap, lapped, decorative French, decorative bound, and stand-up French seams which will be attractive on both sides. Decorative French seams are a good choice for lightweight fabrics. There are two versions: stand-up French and topstitched French. To sew stand-up French seams, consider a wider finished seam. Stitch first with right sides together; then stitch with wrong sides together so the finished seam is on the outside. When joining the seamed section to another section, fold the French seam down or toward the back. To sew a topstitched French seam, stitch the seam as usual; press it to one side, and edgestitch flat against the garment.
Seams/Unlined Garments: For unlined garments which are not reversible, you can use any of the seams for reversible garments, but the best choice is generally the simplest and easiest: a narrow seam. To sew, stitch a plain seam, then trim and serge or zigzag the edges together; or stitch a safety-stitch seam. Another attractive seam for jackets and coats is a plain seam with a contrast Hong Kong finish.
Seam/Hem Finishes: A neat finish for reversible designs is to fold under the raw edge of hems or seams, and edgestitch flat. Use bound and Hong Kong finishes only when the fabric is medium to heavy-weight.
Edge Finishes: Facings (self, contrast, trim), foldover braids, and bindings work well on reversible garments as well as unlined items.
Interfacings: Self-fabric is often a good choice.
Garment Care: Double-faced fabrics can be laundered or dry-cleaned, depending on the dyes, finishes, fabric structure, garment design, quality, and use. Better garments will maintain their pristine appearance longer when dry-cleaned.

Crepe-back satin—Can't decide which side to use? Use them both to create a stunning design. (Burda Pattern – 8859, courtesy of Burda.)

Double Knit

Double knit are medium to heavy-weight warp knits and have little stretch. Generally, made of wool, wool blends, or polyester, they hold their shape well and do not run or ravel.

Workroom Secrets

Fabric Prep: To preshrink wool and wool blends, steam or dry-clean; for polyester, hand wash or machine wash/dry. Purchase an additional ¼ yard when washing wool/wool blend garments.

Layout/Cutting/Marking: Mark right side with small safety pins.

Seams: Stabilize seams with stay tape at shoulders, neck, and waist to prevent stretching. (See Any Fabric page 13.)

Topstitching: To highlight the structural details, topstitch seams and edges ¼" (6mm) to ½" (1.2cm) from stitching line or edge. To topstitch inconspicuously, press seams open; topstitch each side close to the seamline.

Hems: When hemming with a blindstitch, take an occasional backstitch. On quality designs, interface hems; on heavy fabrics, double- or triple-stitch hems with the additional rows in the middle of the hem allowance. For a decorative hem, topstitch several rows, or use a twin needle. To prevent rippling, fuse a strip of lightweight knit interfacing to the hem allowance.

Facings: Understitch or topstitch to prevent facings from rolling to the outside.

Buttonholes: Stabilize machine buttonholes with a small strip of fusible interfacing; position the strip with the least amount of stretch parallel to the opening. Use water soluble stabilizer on top of the fabric to prevent the stitches from embedding in the fabric.

Zippers: Stay the opening with lightweight selvage to prevent stretching. Hand stitch zippers on quality designs. On heavy fabrics, machine stitch the opening; then sew zipper in by hand. (See Sewing Techniques page 117.)

Underlining: To maintain the shape, use partial underlining for skirt backs and knees of pants.

Pressing: To set creases, saturate a brown paper grocery bag with water. Place the bag over the fabric and iron until the paper is dry.

Garment Care: Dry-clean to maintain the garment's pristine appearance.

A favorite for casual and dressy designs alike, double knits are comfortable to wear and easy to sew. (Photo courtesy of KWIK·SEW®.)

Similar Fabrics: Blanket cloth, Chinella®, double cloth, duffel, frieze, loden, mackinac, wadmal.

Uses: Unlined or reversible garments, casual or tailored designs, jackets, coats, capes, ponchos, skirts, pants.

Design Elements: Tailored details, structured silhouettes, minimal seaming, decorative seaming, topstitching, foldover braids, bindings, pockets (all types).

Sewing Checklist

Essential Supplies

Needles: Universal (H); sizes 70/10-90/14.

Thread: All purpose (cotton, polyester, cotton covered polyester). Topstitching – machine embroidery/topstitching (cotton, polyester, cotton covered polyester), silk buttonhole twist, all purpose threads.

Cutting: Sharp shears.

Marking: Chalk, clips, pins, erasable pens.

Miscellaneous: Flower pins, weights, shim, stay tape, safety pins, stabilizers – water soluble, tearaway, cut away.

Interfacings: Garment details, fusible or sew-in.

Linings: Optional, depending on design, quality, and use; same care as garment.

Machine Setup

Stitch Length: 2.5-3mm (8-10spi).

Tension: Lightly balanced.

Machine Feet: Roller, wide straight stitch, even-feed, zigzag.

Sewing Basics

Test Garment: Optional.

Fabric Prep: Preshrink with steam, dry-clean, or handwash.

Layout: Nap – double layer; heavy – single layer using duplicate pattern pieces.

Seams: Plain (pressed open or closed), taped, topstitched.

Seam/Hem Finishes: Serged, zigzag; if lined, none.

Hems: Hand (blindstitch, blind catchstitch, catchstitch, double-stitched), interfaced, topstitched, twin needle, wrong-side out.

Edge Finishes: Facings (self-fabric, lining), bindings, foldover braid, linings.

Closures: Buttonholes (hand, machine, corded, bound, inseam); buttons/loops, zippers (hand, machine, invisible).

Pressing: Medium heat, damp cloth or steam.

Garment Care: Dry-clean or machine wash/dry, depending on fiber content, design, quality, and use.

Embroidered Fabric

Embroidered fabrics are embellished with decorative threads, beads, sequins, glitter, paillettes, ribbons, and sparkling chips. Sewn or glued on a variety of background fabrics such as taffeta, wool knits, open raschel knits, satin, chiffon, lace, tulle, silk shantung, cotton and cotton blends, embellishments are applied in dense all-over patterns, random individual motifs, and border designs.

Similar Fabrics: All-over sequined designs, cracked ice, embroidered laces and border designs, beaded knits, chiffons, eyelet, sari cloth, tulle.

Uses: Evening/formal wear, jackets, coats, dresses, blouses, bustiers, skirts, pants, children's garments.

Design Elements: Minimal seaming, bindings, pockets (inseam). Avoid intricate designs.

Sewing Checklist

Essential Supplies

Needles: Sharp (HM, HJ), stretch (HS) universal (H); sizes 60/8-90/14, depending on the background fabric.

Thread: All-purpose or lightweight (cotton, polyester, cotton covered polyester, silk).

Cutting: Stainless steel shears, flower pins, weights.

Marking: Chalk, clips, tailor's tacks, thread, safety pins.

Miscellaneous: Old sharp shears, weights, ¼" (6mm) ribbon, duplicate pattern pieces, water soluble stabilizers.

Interfacings: Sew-ins.

Linings/Underlinings: Generally for outerwear, formal designs, and scratchy fabrics.

Machine Setup

Stitch Length: 2-2.5mm (10-12spi).

Tension: Lightly balanced; light pressure.

Feet: Zipper, wide straight stitch, zigzag.

Sewing Basics

Test Garment: Recommended.

Fabric Prep: Steam or dry-clean; wash cottons and cotton blends.

Layout: Nap – single layer right-side up, duplicate pattern pieces.

Seams: Plain (pressed open), sequin appliqué.

Seam/Hem Finishes: Serged, zigzag, bound.

Hems: Hand (blindstitch, blind catchstitch, catchstitch), interfaced.

Edge Finishes: Facings (self-fabric, lining, bias), bands, bindings, edge-to-edge linings.

Closures: Buttons/loops, buttonholes (machine, bound, inseam, corded), ties, snaps, zippers (hand, machine, invisible).

Pressing: Medium heat, press cloth, steam.

Garment Care: Dry-clean; launder if the fabric was pretreated.

Workroom Secrets

Fabric Prep: Steam or dry-clean, depending on background fabric. Hand or machine wash cotton and cotton blends, depending on the garment design.

Layout/Cutting/Marking: For easy clean-up, cover the floor and cutting table with a clean sheet. Spread fabric in a single layer with the right-side up. To reduce fraying, do not cut until you are ready to sew; after cutting, handle the fabric as little as possible. Use clips sparingly. Avoid erasable pens; they may stain permanently.

Stitching: Baste as needed to avoid ripping.

Seam/Hem Finishes: For an elegant finish in unlined garments, use a Hong Kong binding with silk chiffon.

Underlinings: To add body to lightweight or soft embroidered fabrics, use silk organza, polyester chiffon, or lightweight sew-in interfacings.

Linings: Line the garment or bind seams with tricot or chiffon.

Pressing: Test press. Many embroidered and embellished fabrics are easily damaged by steam and high heat. Use a press cloth when pressing the right side. Cover the pressing surface with a thick terry towel to avoid flattening or damaging the embellishments on the fabric.

Garment Care: To protect skirts and pants from clip hanger marks, sew in ribbon hanger loops at the waist.

Designed by Raffaella Galeotafiore, this elegant gown features an allover embroidery pattern with small motifs reapplied at the upper edge of the bodice. (Photo courtesy of Raffaella Galeotafiore and Solotu Design Studio.)

Faux Fur Fabric

Faux fur fabrics are pile fabrics on a woven or knitted backing. Available in a variety of weights, thicknesses, pile depths, and fur-like designs, some are lightweight and easy to handle while others are heavy and stiff. Most are bulky and heat sensitive, but mistakes, distortions, and crooked seams are easy to hide. They are not as warm as real fur, but they are less expensive to clean, non-allergenic, and mothproof.

Workroom Secrets

Pattern Prep: To reduce bulk, eliminate non-fitting seams at center back and straight seamlines at the front edges. (See Any Fabric page 14.) On the collar pattern, add a seam at center back. The hair can run away from the center, toward it, or toward the floor.

Layout/Cutting/Marking: Some faux furs do not have a nap, but most do. Drape the fabric over a chair and stand back to study it. Look for any special design elements which will influence the cutting. Mark the pile direction and any pelt markings with chalk on the wrong side. Lay out fabric in a single layer, wrong-side out. Use duplicate pattern pieces, and pin pattern in place with flower pins. Before cutting, double check to be sure there is a pair of each section. Use scissor points or a mat knife to cut just the backing. Do not clip-mark when using narrow zigzag seams.

Seams: For narrow fur seams, trim seam allowances to ¼" (6mm). Brush or tape pile away from the edge. Right sides together, stitch (W,4-L,3) on seam allowance. Press. To reduce bulk on plain seams, stitch the seam. Then trim away the pile on the seam allowances with appliqué scissors. Steam the seam open. Glue or catch-stitch the raw edges to the backing if it will not stay flat. Use a dog comb to pull pile out of seam.

Hems: To reduce bulk, face hem with lining fabric.

Pressing: Test press. Many faux furs are very heat and moisture sensitive. Do not let the iron touch the pile of the fabric. To avoid flattening the pile, cover the pressing surface with a thick towel or Velvaboard®.

Garment Care: To avoid flattening the pile with clip hangers, sew in ribbon hanger loops at the waist.

Easy to sew and fun to wear, everyone will enjoy this fanciful faux fur. (Photo courtesy of KWIK·SEW®.)

Similar Material: Fur, wool fleece, fleece.
Uses: Jackets, skirts, pants, vests, coats, capes, ponchos, linings, hats, muffs, pillows, bedspreads, dog beds.
Design Elements: Simple uncluttered designs, minimal seaming, inseam pockets. Avoid intricate details, pleats, gathers, double-breasted styles.

Sewing Checklist

Essential Supplies
Needles: Universal (H); sizes 80/12-100/16.
Thread: All purpose (cotton, polyester, cotton covered polyester).
Cutting: Sharp shears, mat knife, duplicate pattern pieces.
Marking: Chalk, clips, erasable pens, pins, safety pins.
Miscellaneous: Flower pins, wire dog comb, thick towel, Velvaboard®, mat knife, duplicate pattern pieces, drafting tape, ¼" (6mm) ribbon.
Interfacings: Sew-in, woven or non-woven; same care as garment.
Linings: Usually; same care as garment.
Underlinings: Optional, depending on design and desired warmth.

Machine Setup
Stitch Length: 2.5-3mm (8-10spi); zigzag or fur seam (W,4-L,1)
Tension: Lightly balanced; light pressure.
Feet: Roller, even feed, wide straight stitch, zigzag.

Sewing Basics
Test Garment: Recommended.
Fabric Prep: Machine wash/dry, steam, or dry-clean, depending on manufacturer's recommendation.
Layout: Nap – single layer, wrong-side up; duplicate pattern pieces.
Seams: Zigzag, fur, sheared fur, taped.
Seam/Hem Finishes: Bound, serged; if lined, none.
Hems: Hand (blindstitch, blind catchstitch, catchstitch, double-stitched), interfaced, faced hem.
Edge Finishes: Facings (self-, contrast, or lining fabric, faux suede or leather), bands, bindings, ribbings.
Closures: Large hooks/eyes, covered snaps, buttons/loops, leather tabs, toggles, large zippers (machine, exposed), buttonholes (faced, inseam).
Pressing: Low to medium heat; thick towel, Velvaboard®.
Garment Care: Dry-clean or machine wash, depending on manufacturer's recommendation.

Faux Leather

Faux leather is a synthetic leather. Pleather and UltraLeather® are two of the most popular and best quality. These fabrics have no grain and do not fray. They have more stretch on the cross grain, tear easily under stress, and are easily damaged by hot irons, pins, tracing wheels, and machine stitching.

Faux Leather Types/Similar Fabrics: Pleather, UltraLeather®, leatherette, rubberized coatings, synthetic leather, vinyl coated fabrics, blackboard cloth, clear film, oilcloth, plastic laminates, PVC, resin coated fabrics, rubberized coatings, Tyvek®, vinyl.

Uses: Tailored sportswear, casual wear, outerwear, patio furnishings, tote bags, chair covers, hats.

Design Elements: Simple designs, minimal seaming, topstitching, extended shoulders, shirt and raglan sleeves. Avoid eased seams, gathers, pleats, and tucks.

Sewing Checklist

Essential Supplies
Needles: Sharp (HM, HJ), topstitching (HN), universal (H); sizes 80/12-100/116.
Thread: All purpose or topstitching (polyester).
Cutting: Shears, rotary cutter/mat.
Marking: Chalk, clips, water erasable pens.
Miscellaneous: Shim, quilting clothes pins, large paper clips, grommets, talcum or flour, tape, temporary pattern adhesive, silicone spray, water soluble stabilizer.
Interfacings/Linings/Underlinings: Low temp fusibles or sew-ins.

Machine Setup
Stitch Length: 2.5-3mm (8-10spi); topstitching – 3-4mm (6-8spi).
Tension: Lightly balanced; light pressure.
Feet: Teflon, roller, even feed, zigzag.

Sewing Basics
Test Garment: Depends on garment design and quality.
Fabric Prep: Not required.
Layout: Without nap, double layer.
Seams: Plain (pressed open or closed), topstitched, strap, non-woven flat fell.
Seam/Hem Finishes: None.
Edge Finishes: Facings (self, contrast, faux suede, ribbon), bindings, ribbings, bands.
Closures: Buttonholes (machine, bound, inseam), toggles, snaps, hook/loop tape, zippers (machine, decorative, invisible).
Hems: Topstitch (single fold), fuse.
Pressing: Low heat or press with scissor handles. Use a press cloth when in doubt.
Garment Care: Machine wash/dry or dry-clean, depending on the garment design and quality.

Workroom Secrets
Pattern Prep: To simulate the look of real leather, select a pattern with small garment sections or add seams on larger sections.

Layout/Cutting/Marking: Spread the fabric with the wrong sides together. To avoid pin damage, use weights, temporary pattern adhesive, or tape to hold the pattern in place or place pins only in the seam allowances. For a more economical layout on vinyl, clear films, and Tyvek, pattern pieces can be tilted slightly. Cut sleeves and pants 1" to 2" longer to allow for shortening when the garment is worn.

Stitching: To prevent the faux leather from sticking to the bottom of the foot, use a roller foot or foot with a non-stick coating (Teflon) on the bottom, dust the fabric with talcum or flour, or spray the presser foot with silicone spray. Begin with a new needle in the smallest size that will not skip stitches and change the needle frequently. If skipped stitches are a problem, insert a new needle; if they persist, use a larger needle. When making rainwear, use nylon or polyester thread which will not deteriorate from the excess moisture. Do not backstitch.

Seams/Darts: Use paper clips or quilting clothes pins to baste; or pin only in the seam allowances. Topstitch seams and darts so they will lie flat. Trim close to the stitching. At dart ends, stitch the point with three short stitches along the fold to prevent puckering.

Buttonholes: Lengthen the stitch for machine buttonholes. Cover the fabric with water soluble stabilizer so the foot will not stick to the fabric.

Ventilation: Use grommets under the arm to provide ventilation.

Garment Care: Dry-clean to maintain the garment's pristine appearance. Machine wash and dry casual and everyday garments. To remove wrinkles, machine dry for a short period; smooth the fabric and hang to cool.

This lightweight faux leather is the perfect choice for a rainy day. (Burda pattern – 8816, courtesy of Burda.)

Faux Suede

Faux suede and suede look-alikes are synthetic fabrics. Ultrasuede® is perhaps the best known, but there are many others. These fabrics have no obvious grain, do not fray, tear easily under stress, and are easily damaged by abrasion, hot irons, pins, and machine stitching.

Some, like the original Ultrasuede®, are very crisp while others, like Ultrasuede® Light, are much lighter and softer.

Workroom Secrets

Pattern Prep: To simulate the look of real suede, select a pattern with small garment sections or add seams on larger sections.

Fabric Prep: Check the manufacturer's recommendations. You can machine wash/dry most faux suedes. Remove from the dryer while damp, shake well, and hang to dry. Do not over-dry.

Layout/Cutting/Marking: Mark the nap direction on the wrong side of the fabric with chalk arrows. For a more economical layout, spread the fabric in a single layer, right-side up; and use duplicate pattern pieces. Pattern pieces can be tilted very slightly. Use super fine pins to avoid damaging the fabric. Cut sleeves and pants 1" to 2" (2.5-5cm) longer to allow for shortening when the garment is worn.

Stitching: Begin with a new needle in the smallest size that will not skip stitches. Change the needle frequently. If skipped stitches are a problem, insert a new needle; if they persist, use a larger needle and a needle lubricant.

Seams: Generally plain seams are better for dressy designs while non-woven flat fell and lapped seams are attractive on sportswear. To stitch plain seams, use quilting clothes pins, spring hair clips, or a glue stick to baste; or use super fine pins only in the seam allowances. To flatten seams, press the seam open. Brush the open seam with a 50/50 vinegar/water solution; press again and cover with a clapper. Hold the clapper in place about 20 seconds. (Always test for colorfastness before using vinegar on a garment.) Topstitch seams and darts so they will remain flat. Trim close to the stitching. Topstitch sporty designs with a longer stitch ¼" (6mm) from the seamline. Stabilize all seams which will be stressed.

Hems: Topstitch or fuse hems in place.

Sleeves: Reduce sleeve cap ease so it can be set smoothly.

Buttonholes: Lengthen the stitch for machine buttonholes. To prevent machine stitches embedding in the fabric, stitch with water soluble stabilizer on top of the fabric. For more defined buttonholes, cord them.

Interfacings: Interface edges to preserve the shape.

Linings: Line garments to preserve the shape, reduce clinging, and prevent the color from crocking.

Pressing: Test press on scraps. Faux suedes are very sensitive to hot irons. When pressing the right side, use a press cloth or press with a steamer.

Garment Care: You can machine wash/dry most faux suedes if the design and other elements are washable; but to maintain the garment's pristine appearance, dry-clean.

Faux suedes are most attractive in simple designs like this suit. (Photo courtesy of KWIK-SEW®.)

Faux Suede Types/Similar Fabrics: Buttersuede, Facile®, Ultrasuede® Elite, Ultrasuede® Light, Ultrasuede® Soft, Sensuede, sherpa, sueded reversible sherpa.

Uses: Tailored designs, casual wear, sportswear, jackets, skirts, outerwear, tote bags.

Design Elements: Simple designs, minimal seaming, extended shoulders, shirt and raglan sleeves. For crisp fabrics – topstitching, structured silhouettes; for softer fabrics – shirring, pleats, draped designs.

Sewing Checklist

Essential Supplies

Needle type: Stretch (HS), sharp (HM, HJ), universal (H); sizes 70/10-90/14.

Thread: All purpose (cotton, polyester, cotton covered polyester). Topstitching – all purpose, machine embroidery/topstitching threads.

Cutting: Sharp shears, rotary cutter/mat, duplicate pattern pieces.

Marking: Chalk, clips, erasable pens.

Miscellaneous: Shim, quilting clothes pins or spring hair clips, washable glue stick, temporary spray adhesive, super fine pins, needle lubricant, water soluble stabilizer, fusible web, vinegar, steamer.

Interfacings: Low temp fusibles or sew-ins.

Linings: Outerwear, quality garments; same care requirement.

Machine Setup

Stitch Length: 2.5-3mm (8-10spi); topstitching – 3-4mm (6-8spi).

Tension: Lightly balanced; light pressure.

Feet: Teflon, roller, even feed, zigzag.

Sewing Basics

Fabric Prep: Machine wash and dry for easier stitching.

Layout: Nap – single layer, right-side up.

Seams: Plain (pressed open or closed), topstitched, non-woven flat fell, non-woven lapped.

Seam/Hem Finishes: None.

Edge Finishes: Facings (self, contrast, faux leather), bindings, ribbings, bands.

Closures: Buttonholes (machine, bound, inseam), zippers (machine, invisible).

Pressing: Low heat; press cloth, steamer.

Garment Care: Dry-clean or machine wash/dry.

Felt

Felt is made of fibers which are pounded, compressed, shrunk, and felted to give it a unique no-fray quality with no visible grain. Made of wool, fur, mohair, cotton, rayon, or polyester fibers, it is reversible and frequently tears when stressed. It is susceptible to abrasion and stretches out of shape easily.

Similar Fabrics: Boiled wool, duffel, friezé, loden, faux suede, wadmal.
Uses: Casual jackets, coats, capes, ponchos, vests, sportswear, skirts, hats, bags, children's wear, costumes, banners.
Design Elements: Structured designs, minimal seaming, color blocking, topstitching.

Sewing Checklist

Essential Supplies
Needles: Universal (H); sizes 70/10-80/12.
Thread: All purpose (cotton, polyester, cotton covered polyester). Topstitching – all purpose, machine embroidery/topstitching (cotton, polyester, acrylic, cotton covered polyester, silk).
Cutting: Sharp shears, rotary cutter/mat.
Marking: Chalk, clips, pins, erasable pens.
Miscellaneous: Pinking or scalloping shears, safety pins, fusible web, glue stick.
Interfacings/Linings/Underlinings: Rarely used.

Machine Setup
Stitch Length: 2-2.5mm (10-12spi).
Tension: Lightly balanced.
Feet: All-purpose.

Sewing Basics
Test Garment: Rarely needed.
Fabric Prep: Steam.
Layout: Without nap – double layer.
Seams: Plain (pressed open or closed), non-woven lapped, stand-up pinked, dinosaur, strap, abutted.
Hems: Topstitched, fused, wrong-side-out.
Seam/Hem Finishes: Rarely required, serged, pinked.
Edge Finishes: Facings (self-fabric, lining), foldover braid, bindings, raw edge, pinked.
Closures: Buttonholes (slashed, machine), buttons/loops, toggles, frogs, ties, decorative clasps, zippers (machine, decorative).
Pressing: Medium heat, little or no moisture.
Garment Care: Dry-clean, discard.

Workroom Secrets
Fabric Prep: Preshrink only if garment will be cleaned. Steam carefully to avoid shrinking wool felt unevenly.
Layout/Cutting/Marking: Tilt pieces slightly for fabric economy. Mark right side of each piece with safety pins.
Seams/Darts: Seams can be plain or fancy, depending on the garment design, seam location, and your whimsy. For inconspicuous seams, press open and topstitch close to the seamline; trim close to the stitching. For darts, stitch, slash open, topstitch, and trim.
Seams: The no-fray quality permits a variety of interesting and unusual seams such as non-woven lapped, stand-up pinked, and dinosaur seams. To make stand-up pinked, stitch on the seamline with wrong sides together; then pink the raw edges. To make dinosaur seams, cut seam allowances 1" to 1¼" (2.5cm-3.1cm) wide. Wrong sides together, stitch on the seamline; trim to make oversized "pinking."
Edge Finishes: To add body to unfinished straight or pinked edges, fuse a felt facing to the edge; then trim or pink.
Buttonholes: The slashed buttonhole is the easiest fastener. For machine stitched buttonholes, lengthen the stitch to avoid chewing the fabric.
Pressing: Test press.

A popular choice for banners and fun fashions, felt is easy to sew. (Photo courtesy of Simplicity Patterns.)

Fleece

Fleece is a double-napped knit. Comfortable to wear, durable, hypo-allergenic, and odor resistant, it does not fray, has good stretch, retains its insulating properties when wet, and dries quickly. Many are reversible or printed. Poor quality fleeces have poor shape retention when stretched and pill badly. Fleece is easily damaged by hot irons.

Workroom Secrets

Fabric Selection: To determine if the fabric has good shape retention, measure, stretch, and remeasure. To check for pilling, rub two layers of fabric together.

Layout/Cutting/Marking: Mark right side of fabric with safety pins. On most fabrics, the selvage edge will curl to the right side when stretched.

Basting: Use washable basting tape or spray adhesive to baste zippers, pockets, decorative trims, and appliqués.

Stitching: Clean machine frequently to remove lint. Staystitch curves and openings just inside the seamline.

Seams: For more elastic seams, use polyester thread and a narrow zigzag (W,.5-L,3). When sewing border prints, the vertical seams are on the crossgrain; stabilize seams at shoulders, neck, and waist to prevent stretching. Nonwoven lapped or abutted seams are flat and attractive for color blocked designs. Serge or zigzag seams together for a neat, flat finish. To avoid stretching serged seams, set differential feed 1.8 to 2.

Topstitching: Lengthen the stitch length.

Edge Finishes: Understitch or topstitch to prevent facings from rolling to the outside. For a ready-to-wear look, use medium-weight Lycra-blend knits to bind edges or finish edges with ribbing.

Closures: Stabilize buttonhole area and zipper opening with fusible interfacing. Stitch machine buttonholes on lengthwise grain when possible.

Hems: To prevent rippling, fuse a strip of lightweight knit interfacing to the hem allowance. Turn under and machine stitch using an even-feed foot. Fold the hem to the right side for a decorative effect.

Embroidery: Fleece is an easy fabric to embroider. Use water soluble stabilizer on top of the fabric with cut-away stabilizer on the wrong side.

The border trim on this easy-to-wear jacket is just one of many unusual trims you can create with fleece fabrics. (Photo reprinted from Polar Magic: New Adventures with Fleece *by Nancy Cornwell, published by Krause Publications.)*

Fleece Types/Similar Fabrics: AirCore Berber, Arctic Fleece, berber, bunting, Chinella®, GlenPile, HiLo Fleece, Nordic Fleece, Plush Fleece, Polarfleece®, PolarPlus®, Polarlite®, Polartec® 100, 200, sherpa, Windbloc®, Yukon Fleece.

Uses: Casual garments, coats, jackets, pants, sweatshirts, tops, vests, activewear, linings, insulations, underwear, children's wear, hats, scarves.

Design Details: Topstitching, color blocking, loose fitting, ribbings, bindings, embroidery, wrong-side out facings and hems, zipper trims.

Sewing Checklist

Essential Supplies

Needles: Universal (H), stretch (HS), ballpoint (H-SUK); sizes 80/12-90/14.

Thread: All purpose (polyester). Topstitching/decorative serging – topstitching/machine embroidery (polyester), all purpose.

Cutting: Sharp shears, large rotary cutter/mat.

Marking: Chalk, clips, erasable pens, safety pins.

Miscellaneous: Flower pins, safety pins, washable basting tape, temporary spray adhesive, water soluble and cut-away stabilizers.

Interfacings: Optional, knit fusible.

Linings/Underlinings: Optional, washable.

Machine Setup

Stitch Length: 3-4mm (6-8spi) or narrow zigzag (W,.5-L,3).

Tension: Lightly balanced; light pressure.

Machine Feet: Wide straight stitch, roller, even-feed, zigzag.

Sewing Basics

Fabric Prep: Not required for many fabrics. Polartec® Power Stretch® shrinks about 5 percent.

Layout: Nap – double layer; if thick, single layer.

Seams: Plain (open or closed), topstitched, abutted, zigzagged, safety-stitch serged, non-woven lapped, non-woven flat fell, strap, taped.

Hems: Narrow, topstitched (single fold), hand (blindstitch), fused, wrong-side out.

Seam/Hem Finishes: Serged, zigzag, pinked, unfinished.

Edge Finishes: Facings (self, lining, woven fabrics, wrong-side out), bindings (stretch fleece or knits, foldover braid, ribbon), self-fabric fringe, ribbings, lycra cuffs and waistbands.

Closures: Buttonholes (machine), ties, toggles, zippers (machine, separating, exposed).

Pressing: Steam and finger press; low heat or press cloth.

Garment Care: Wrong side out, machine wash/dry low heat. Do not dry-clean, bleach, or use fabric softeners.

Real fur is an animal skin with the hair still attached. All furs have two parts: the skin and the fur. Tanned and processed to make it soft and supple, fur can be sheared, bleached, dyed, tipped, stenciled, let out, or curled to make it more interesting and more fashionable. The most common sources for furs are garage sales and thrift shops. Generally they are inexpensive, but the quality and condition will vary.

Fur is warmer than faux fur fabrics. It has a nap, is bulky and easily damaged by ripping; but it is not difficult to sew, and most mistakes can be corrected.

Similar Fabrics: Faux fur.

Uses: Jackets, skirts, pants, vests, coats, capes, ponchos, linings, collars, cuffs, hats, muffs, pillows, bedspreads, dog beds.

Design Elements: Simple uncluttered designs, leather or suede trims, inseam pockets, hook and eye fasteners. Avoid patch pockets, intricate details, pleats, gathers, and double-breasted styles.

Sewing Checklist

Essential Supplies
Needles: Leather (HLL, NTW), sharp (HJ); sizes 80/12-100/16.
Thread: All purpose (polyester).
Cutting: Mat knife, sharp shears.
Marking: Chalk, erasable pens, clips, pencil.
Miscellaneous: Flower pins, quilting clothes pins, fabric surgical tape, wire dog comb, masking tape, pencil, mat knife, polyester fleece, sponge, vinegar, twill tape.
Linings: Quality satin lining.
Underlinings: Muslin, hair canvas, polyester fleece.

Machine Setup
Stitch Length: Narrow zigzag seams (W,4-L,1); plain seams – 2.5-3mm (8-10spi).
Tension: Lightly balanced; light pressure.
Feet: Zigzag.

Sewing Basics
Test Garment: Recommended.
Layout: Nap – single layer, wrong-side up; duplicate pattern pieces.
Seams: Fur, taped, plain.
Seam/Hem Finishes: None.
Hems: Hand (catchstitch), interfaced, faced.
Edge Finishes: Facings (self cut-on facing, suede, leather), edge to edge lining, bands, bindings, ribbings.
Closures: Large hooks/eyes, covered snaps, buttons/loops, leather tabs, toggles, large zippers (machine), buttonholes (faced, inseam).
Pressing: Low to medium heat; thick towel, press cloth.
Garment Care: Fur clean.

Workroom Secrets
Pattern Prep: To reduce bulk, eliminate non-fitting seams at center back and straight seamlines at the front edges. (See Any Fabric page 14.) If you are using fur seams, trim seam allowances to ⅛" (3mm). On the collar pattern, add a seam at center back. The hair can run away from the center, toward it, or down to the floor.
Fur Prep: To clean a used fur, wipe with a sponge and a 50/50 vinegar/water solution; air dry. Test for colorfastness first.
Layout/Cutting/Marking: Mark the fur direction and any pelt markings with chalk on the wrong side. Lay out in single layer, wrong-side out. Use duplicate pattern pieces, and weights or tape the pattern in place. Trace around the pattern with a pencil or erasable marking pen. Before cutting, double check to be sure there is a pair of each section. Use scissor points or a mat knife to cut just the backing. Do not clip-mark when using fur seams.
Stitching: Avoid cotton thread; the tannin in the fur will rot it.
Seams: Baste, using quilting clothes pins or flower pins. For fur seams, trim seam allowances to ⅛" (3mm). For stronger seams, tape edges with fabric surgical tape. Before stitching, brush or tape pile away from the edge. Right sides together, stitch (W,4-L,1) so the needle will swing off the fabric edge. Wrong side up, press stitching line with the scissor handles. Use a dog comb to brush the seam on the right side. To stitch plain fur to fabric seams, stitch with the fabric uppermost.
Edge Finishes: Sew ½" (1.2cm) twill tape to all unfaced edges. To reduce wear at edges, interface with polyester fleece. To reduce bulk, face hem with lining fabric.
Pockets: Generally inseam pockets are best. Cut the pocket sacks from velveteen or cotton flannel.
Collars/Cuffs: Cut the collar facing from fur or fabric. Cut with ¼" (6mm) seam allowances. Underline the fur with muslin or polyester fleece.
Garment Care: Hang fur on well padded hanger in a cool closet. To protect from moths, store in a cedar chest or sealed cedar closet. Avoid shoulder strap bags.

Embellish your favorite gown or coat with a touch of mink. (Photo courtesy of PtakCouture.com.)

Gabardine

Gabardine is a firm, hard-finished fabric with a prominent twill-weave. Made of wool, silk, cotton, or manufactured fibers, it spans the seasons, wears well, and does not wrinkle badly; but it is difficult to ease and press.

Workroom Secrets

Layout/Cutting/Marking: Use a nap layout, even though there is no obvious nap.

Seams/Darts: For flatter seams, cut seams 1" (2.5cm) wide. Slash and press darts open.

Seam/Hem Finishes: To avoid pressing imprints, serge or zigzag with lightweight serger thread or textured thread. Avoid bound finishes, which are bulky.

Underlining: Yves Saint Laurent underlines tailored jackets with bias-cut lightweight hair canvas.

Sleeves: Shrink and shape sleeve caps before setting into the garment. Reduce the ease as needed to ease the fullness smoothly. (See Any Fabric page 14.)

Topstitching: To flatten seams and edges, topstitch. For dressy designs, topstitch close to the edge or seam. For sportswear, topstitch ¼" (6mm) away.

Pressing: Test press to determine the appropriate amount of heat, moisture, and pressure for the fiber. Be patient when pressing. Gabardine is easily damaged by too much heat and overpressing. Use a wool press cloth when pressing the right side. To avoid pressing imprints, use a seam roll, seam stick, or ham, or place strips of brown paper under cut edges. Rub both sides of the stitched line with a bar of Ivory soap. Steam generously without touching the fabric; spank with a clapper. Repeat until the seam is flat. For sharp edges, press seams open over a point presser; then fold facing into position, and baste about ¼" (6mm) from the edge with soft cotton thread. Cover edge with a press cloth, press firmly.

Garment Care: Dry-clean.

Similar Fabrics: Bedford cord, blazer flannel, cassimere, cheviot, covert, elastique, pinstripes, serge, sharkskin, tartans, tricotine, tropical worsted, whipcord, wool poplin, worsted flannel.

Uses: Tailored garments, jackets, coats, dresses, pants, skirts, shirts.

Design Elements: Topstitching, pleats, dropped shoulders, raglan or dolman sleeves, pockets (all types). Avoid bias skirts.

Sewing Checklist

Essential Supplies

Needles: Sharp (HJ), universal (H); sizes 70/10-90/14.

Thread: All purpose (cotton, polyester, cotton covered polyester). Topstitching – all purpose, machine embroidery/topstitching threads (silk, cotton, polyester, silk). Serger – lightweight serger threads, textured thread.

Cutting: Sharp shears, rotary cutter/mat.

Marking: Chalk, clips, pins, tailor's tacks, thread.

Miscellaneous: Soft cotton thread (hand embroidery floss), seam roll, clapper, Ivory soap.

Interfacings: Generally, sew-ins, hair canvas.

Linings: Frequently.

Underlinings: Optional.

Machine Setup

Stitch Length: 2-2.5mm (10-12spi).

Tension: Lightly balanced.

Machine Feet: Wide straight stitch, zigzag.

Sewing Basics

Test Garment: Recommended, depending on garment design and quality.

Fabric Prep: Steam or dry-clean.

Layout: Nap – double layer.

Seams: Plain (pressed open or closed), topstitched.

Hems: Hand (blindstitch, blind catchstitch, double-stitched), topstitched, interfaced.

Seam/Hem Finishes: Serged, zigzag, hand overcast.

Edge Finishes: Facings (self-fabric), bindings, bands.

Closures: Buttonholes (machine, bound, inseam), buttons/loops, zippers (hand, machine, invisible).

Pressing: Medium heat, steam, wool press cloth.

Garment Care: Dry-clean; wash manufactured fibers

Smart and comfortable, this gabardine ensemble will look good from morning to night. (Photo courtesy of KWIK·SEW®.)

Georgette

Georgette is a sheer crepe fabric. Usually made of silk, rayon, or polyester, it is soft and drapeable. It wrinkles, has little elasticity, frays badly, and is easily damaged by ripping and improper pressing. It is more durable and easier to sew than chiffon, but not as easy to sew or crisp as organza.

Similar Fabrics: Double georgette, marquisette, mousseline, soft organza.

Uses: Special occasion designs, dresses, coats, blouses, skirts, jackets, linings, underlinings, interfacings.

Design Elements: Gathers, pleats, tucks, lace trims, drapes, lace insertions. Avoid bound buttonholes unless the section is underlined.

 Sewing Checklist

Essential Supplies

Needles: Sharp (HM, HJ), universal (H); sizes 60/8-70/10.

Thread: Lightweight (cotton, cotton covered polyester, silk), all purpose. Topstitching – lightweight or all purpose. Serger – lightweight serger thread, textured thread.

Cutting: Serrated shears, rotary cutter/mat, tissue.

Marking: Chalk, clips, erasable pens, tailor's tacks, thread.

Miscellaneous: Serrated shears, super fine pins, hand sewing needles (sizes 9-12), weights, flesh-colored chiffon, water soluble stabilizer, tissue.

Interfacings: Lightweight sew-ins, self-fabric, organza, lightweight silks, soft organza.

Linings/Underlinings: Optional for modesty, color, or design.

Machine Setup

Stitch Length: 2-2.5mm (10-12spi).

Tension: Lightly balanced.

Feet: Wide straight stitch, roller foot; small hole throat plate.

Sewing Basics

Test Garment: Depends on design and quality.

Fabric Prep: Silk georgette – preshrink with steam or dry-clean; polyester – wash/dry; rayon – according to manufacturer's direction.

Layout: Without nap – double layer.

Seams: Plain (pressed open or closed), topstitched, French, faux French, bound, safety-stitch.

Hems: Narrow (machine-rolled, merrow, pin, satin stitch, shirttail), hand (blindstitch, catchstitch); wide double hems.

Seam/Hem Finishes: Serged, zigzag, bound (chiffon, China silk), hand overcast.

Edge Finishes: Facings (bias, tulle, decorative), bound, edge-to-edge linings.

Closures: Buttonholes (machine, inseam, bound), buttons/loops, zippers (hand, invisible), snaps, hooks/eyes.

Pressing: Medium heat; steam, press cloth.

Garment Care: Dry-clean; casual designs wash/dry if fabric was preshrunk.

Workroom Secrets

Layout/Cutting/Marking: Spread fabric in double layer; pin selvages together. Lay out pattern; and pin only in the seam allowances. Cut, using sharp serrated shears or a rotary cutter/mat. Mark the right side of each section with a cross-stitch.

Basting: Hand baste to ensure stitching accuracy and prevent ripping. To pin baste, use super fine pins or fine needles (sizes 9-12).

Stitching: Begin with a new, sharp needle (HM). Use a wide straight stitch or roller foot to reduce stitching problems. If using a zigzag foot, decenter needle and move it to the right-hand position. Sandwich stitch seams. Sandwich and pin the seam between strips of water soluble stabilizer. Stitch; then steam press to remove the stabilizer. Shorten the stitch length when stitching curves. Do not backstitch; knot the thread ends.

Seams: Bind seams with flesh-colored chiffon to make them inconspicuous. When both sides of the garment will show, use French or faux French seams.

Darts: Trim dart take-up to ¼" (6mm) and overcast by hand or zigzag (W,2-L,2) the edges.

Edge Finishes: Replace facings with bindings, edge to edge linings, or underlinings to avoid unattractive shadows.

Buttonholes: To stitch machine buttonholes, sandwich the georgette between two layers of water soluble stabilizer. Stitch with a fine, sharp needle (HM) and lightweight embroidery thread.

Pressing: Test press; georgette is easily damaged by improper pressing and too much heat.

A good choice for rayon georgette, this lush duster is sheer enough to show the dress underneath. (Photo courtesy of KWIK·SEW®.)

Hair Fibers

Hair fibers are from the goat and camel families or from fur-bearing animals. The most common hair fibers are mohair, cashmere, camel's hair, alpaca, llama, and vicuña. A few hair fibers such as angora are from fur-bearing animals. Soft and comfortable to wear, they can be woven or knitted. Most are blended with wool (which is the wool from sheep) and other fibers for special effects, beauty, softness, drapeability, color, luster, durability, and economy. They can be used for woven or knitted fabrics and are sewn and handled like wool fabrics.

Common Hair Fibers: Alpaca, angora rabbit, camel's hair, cashmere, llama, mohair, pashmina.

Uses: Coats, jackets, capes, dresses, skirts, pants, tops, sweaters, wraps, dressing gowns.

Design Elements: Simple designs, minimal seaming, topstitching. Avoid intricate details.

Similar Fabrics: Any hair fiber from the camel and goat families, alpaca, angora, camel's hair, cashmere, llama, mohair, pashmina.

Designed by Ila Erickson, this luxurious mohair cape will complement any outfit—casual or dressy. (Photo courtesy of Clark Marten, Columbus, MT.)

Sewing Checklist

Essential Supplies
Needles: Universal (H); sizes 70/10-90/14.
Thread: All purpose (cotton, polyester, cotton covered polyester). Topstitching – machine embroidery/topstitching threads (cotton, polyester, silk) all purpose threads. Serger – lightweight serger, textured thread.
Cutting: Sharp shears, rotary cutter/mat.
Marking: Chalk, clips, safety pins, tailor's tacks, thread.
Miscellaneous: Flower pins, shim, safety pins, water soluble stabilizer, duplicate pattern pieces.
Interfacings: Fusible, sew-in, hair canvas, weft-insertion.
Linings: Generally.
Underlinings: Use silk organza or firm sew-in interfacing to prevent bagging on skirts, pants, dresses, lightweight silk; to add structure on coats, jackets, and capes.

Machine Setup
Stitch Length: 2.5-3mm (8-10spi).
Tension: Lightly balanced.
Feet: Wide straight stitch, roller, zigzag.

Sewing Basics
Test Garment: Recommended, fabrics are easily damaged by ripping.
Fabric Prep: Dry-clean.
Layout: Nap – if thick, single layer, duplicate pattern pieces.
Seams: Plain (pressed open or closed), topstitched, taped.
Hems: Hand (blindstitch, blind catchstitch, catchstitch), double-stitched, topstitched, interfaced.
Seam/Hem Finishes: Serged, pinked, bound; if lined, none.
Edge Finishes: Facings (self-fabric, lining), bindings, linings.
Closures: Buttonholes (machine, corded, bound, inseam), buttons/loops; zippers (hand, machine, invisible).
Pressing: Cool to medium heat; steam, wool press cloth.
Garment Care: Dry-clean.

Mohair

The best known and most commonly used hair fiber, mohair is from angora goats. Recognized by its fluffy, lustrous appearance, it feels soft and silky. It resists abrasion and does not shrink, felt, or soil as readily as wool, but it is more difficult to press. It is generally used for suitings and novelty fabrics. To sew, see Mohair (page 63).

Cashmere

From domesticated Kashmir goats in the Himalayas, Tibet, Iran, Afghanistan, India, and China, cashmere is more like wool than any other fiber. Obtained by brushing the goats during the spring, the fibers are extremely fine and soft. Fabrics drape beautifully and usually have a nap. Select cashmere for its beauty, not its durability. It is easily abraded by shoulder straps.

Cashmere is about 50 percent warmer than wool and available in a variety of fabrications from soft jerseys to woven coatings. Sew it like similar wool fabrics such as wool jersey, wool flannel, or melton.

Camel's Hair

Similar to wool, camel's hair is known for its warmth without weight, natural tan color, luster and softness. Obtained from the Bactrian (two-humped) camel, only the soft, downy hair near the camel's skin is used for fine fabrics. The coarser outer hair is used for rugs and blankets. Camel's hair is warmer than wool but does not wear as well. It has a nap and is frequently blended with wool for durability and economy.

Generally used for tailored designs, it is sewn and pressed like similar wool fabrics such as wool flannel and melton.

Alpaca

A member of the camel family, the alpaca is raised in the mountains of Peru for its soft, fine hair. Strong and lustrous, the long hair is 8" to 12" (20-30cm) when sheared every two years. It is used for suitings and dress-weight fabrics and sometimes blended with silk or cotton.

Llama

Another member of the camel family, the llama is closely related to the alpaca. Its fleece is coarser and weaker than the alpaca; and the colors are usually brown or black.

Angora

Angora is from the angora rabbit. Generally used for yarns and felt, it is sometimes used in fabrics.

Designed by Molly Murphy, the 2003 Junior Winner of the Make It Yourself With Wool Contest, the coat was fabricated in a blend of lambs' wool and cashmere and worn with a wool top and trousers. (Photo courtesy of Make It Yourself With Wool.)

Workroom Secrets

Layout/Cutting/Marking: Refold fabric to cut around original crease. Mark the right side of the fabric with safety pins. Use flower pins to hold pattern pieces in place.

Stitching: Use polyester thread for more elastic seams. Generally when stitching, it is better to stitch with the nap than with the grain. Understitch by hand for a soft, inconspicuous finish.

Buttonholes: Stabilize machine and hand buttonholes. For machine buttonholes, use water soluble stabilizer on top of the fabric to prevent the stitches from embedding in the fabric.

Zippers: Stabilize the opening with stay tape to prevent stretching. On heavy fabrics such a camel's hair or cashmere, machine stitch around the zipper opening; then sew the zipper in by hand.

Underlinings: To preserve the shape and prevent bagging, underline skirts, pants, and dresses with lightweight silk. For a softer, more tactile garment, cut the underlining on the bias. To add structure for coats, jackets, and capes, use a lightweight fusible interfacing or hair canvas.

Pressing: Before pressing, cover the ironing board with a piece of wool. Use a wool press cloth when pressing the right side. Test press. Hair fiber fabrics are easily damaged by steam and improper pressing. Generally a dry iron and low heat is best. When steaming, watch for shrinkage on a fabric scrap before steaming a large piece.

Garment Care: Dry-clean. To protect skirts and pants from clip hangers, sew in ribbon hanger loops at the waist. Hair fiber fabrics are easily damaged by abrasion such as handbags with shoulder straps.

Handkerchief Linen

Handkerchief linen is a lightweight, crisp fabric. It wrinkles, ravels, does not ease well, has little elasticity, and varies in transparency. It is easily damaged by wax, colored chalk, and erasable pens.

Workroom Secrets

Fabric Preparation: Dry-clean or steam dark colors which fade badly and become white at edges. Wash and dry light colors if you plan to wash the garment.

Layout/Cutting/Marking: Mark the right side of the fabric with small safety pins. Avoid erasable pens; they may stain permanently.

Stitching: Begin with a new, sharp (HM) needle in the smallest recommended size. Use a wide straight stitch or roller foot to reduce stitching problems; or use a zigzag foot, and move the needle to the right-hand position. When stitching curves, shorten the stitch length.

Seams: Use topstitched seams and hems for unlined and washable designs. For dressy designs, topstitch close to the seam. For sportswear, topstitch ¼" (6mm) away or use a wide twin needle to simulate flat fell seams. When both sides of the garment show, use French, faux French, or strap seams.

Hems: The most attractive are very narrow or wide double hems.

Edge Finishes: To avoid unattractive facing shadows, replace facings with bindings, bands, or ribbings. When facings cannot be avoided, cut them straight or make them a design element.

Interfacing: Self-fabric and lightweight sew-ins are good choices.

Buttonholes: Machine stitch with a sharp needle and lightweight embroidery thread (60/2). To add crispness before stitching, spray the buttonhole area with spray starch.

Pressing: Use a cooler iron than for regular linen. To avoid slicking dark fabrics, press from the wrong side or use a press cloth.

Embroidery: Handkerchief linen is an easy fabric to embroider. Use water soluble stabilizer on top of the fabric with tearaway or cut-away stabilizer underneath.

Sophisticated enough to wear alone or layered, this linen easy shirt is cool and smart for warm weather dressing. (Butterick Pattern-3473, Linda Allard Ellen Tracy; photo courtesy of The McCall Pattern Co.)

Similar Fabrics: Cotton organdy, dimity, cotton dobby, dotted swiss, eyelet, eyelash voile, gazar, lawn, leno, marquisette, organzine, satin faced organza, shirtings, voile.

Uses: Reversible or unlined garments, casual jackets, blouses, skirts, lingerie, interfacings, men's shirts, and children's garments.

Design Elements: Topstitching, crisp silhouettes, ruffles, gathers, tucks, dropped shoulders, lace trims, lace insertions, decorative embroidery.

Sewing Checklist

Essential Supplies

Needles: Sharp (HM, HJ), universal (H); sizes 70/10-90/14; twin needles.

Thread: Lightweight or all purpose (cotton, polyester, cotton covered polyester, silk). Topstitching – lightweight machine embroidery/topstitching or all purpose.

Cutting: Sharp shears, rotary cutter/mat.

Marking: Chalk, clips, pins.

Miscellaneous: Safety pins, spray starch, super fine pins, stabilizers – water soluble, burn-away, tearaway, cut away.

Interfacings: Optional; self-fabric, lightweight sew-ins or fusibles.

Linings/Underlinings: Rarely.

Machine Setup

Stitch Length: 2.5-3mm (8-10spi).

Tension: Lightly balanced.

Feet: Wide straight stitch, roller, zigzag; small hole throat plate.

Sewing Basics

Test Garment: Optional, depending on design.

Fabric Prep: For washable garments, hand or machine wash/dry; otherwise dry-clean. Fabric will soften some when washed.

Layout: Without nap – double layer.

Seams: Plain (pressed open or closed), topstitched, bound, strap, French, faux French.

Seam/Hem Finishes: Serged, pinked, zigzag, bound.

Hems: Hand (blindstitch, catchstitch), topstitched, twin needle, wrong-side out, shirttail, pin.

Edge Finishes: Facings, bindings, ribbing, bands.

Closures: Buttonholes (machine, corded, bound, inseam); buttons/loops, ties, zippers (hand, machine, invisible).

Pressing: Medium to high heat, damp cloth or steam.

Garment Care: Machine wash/dry casual designs if fabric was pretreated; dry-clean quality garments.

Handwoven Fabric

Handwoven fabrics range from firmly woven Harris tweeds to novelty, loosely woven materials. Some have long floats, slubs, and metallic yarns, which make them pick, pull, and ravel badly while others have stripes with no regular repeat. This chapter focuses on loosely woven handwovens.

Similar Fabrics: Bouclé, hopsacking, loosely woven fabrics, monk's cloth, wool lace.
Uses: Tailored or unstructured designs, coats, jackets, skirts, pants, dresses, jumpers, wraps.
Design Elements: Simple designs to showcase the fabric, minimal seaming, soft pleats, extended shoulders, pockets (welt, inseam), collars (all types). Avoid intricate details.

Sewing Checklist

Essential Supplies
Needles: Sharp (HM, HJ), universal (H); sizes 70/10-90/14.
Thread: All purpose (cotton, polyester, cotton covered polyester). Topstitching – all purpose.
Cutting: Sharp shears, duplicate pattern pieces.
Marking: Chalk, erasable pens, flower pins, safety pins, tailor's tacks, thread.
Miscellaneous: Flower pins, safety pins, seam sealant, white glue, spray starch, thick towel, water soluble stabilizer.
Interfacings: Fusible, weft-insertion, knit; sew-in such as Armo Press® Firm or hair canvas.
Linings: Optional, depends on garment type/design.
Underlinings: Sew-in or fusible, silk organza, soft organza, polyester chiffon.

Machine Setup
Stitch Length: 2-3mm (8-12spi) or narrow zigzag (W,.5-L,2).
Tension: Lightly balanced.
Feet: Roller, wide straight stitch.

Sewing Basics:
Test Garment: Recommended.
Fabric Prep: Steam or dry-clean.
Layout: Nap – single layer right-side up.
Seams: Plain (pressed open), topstitched, piped, strap, taped.
Hems: Hand (blindstitch, catchstitch, double-stitched), interfaced, topstitched.
Seam/Hem Finishes: Serged, zigzag, bound, Hong Kong finish.
Edge Finishes: Facings (self-fabric, leather, faux suede, lining), bindings (smooth fabrics, faux suede/leather), bands, ribbings, fringing, edge-to-edge linings.
Closures: Buttonholes (machine, corded, bound, inseam), buttons/loops, zippers (machine, hand, invisible).
Pressing: Cool to medium heat; steam, self-fabric or wool press cloth.
Garment Care: Dry-clean.

Workroom Secrets
Layout/Cutting/Marking: Think twice before cutting the garment on the crossgrain. The hem edge may not be straight or attractive. If the fabric has stripes without a regular repeat, use piped seams; cut sleeves on the bias; or match one dominant color bar on the jacket to the same bar on the sleeve and ignore the color bars above and below it. To ensure accuracy when cutting a single layer, use duplicate pattern pieces. For fabrics which fray badly, cut 1" (2.5cm) seams. Before moving the sections from the table, spray the edges lightly with seam sealant, a thin solution of white glue and water, or spray starch. Use small safety pins to mark the right side of the fabric and construction symbols.
Stitching: To avoid vertical seamlines that "hike" at the hemline, use a narrow zigzag (W,.5-L,2).
Stays: Stabilize necklines, shoulder seams, buttonholes, zipper openings, and front edges with lightweight stays.
Buttonholes: To prevent machine stitches from embedding in the fabric, stitch with water soluble stabilizer on top of fabric. For more defined buttonholes, stitch over cording and/or stitch with machine embroidery thread (30/2,40/2). For bound buttonholes, fuse a narrow strip of interfacing to the wrong side of the fabric.
Underlinings: To add structure as well as control fraying, underline each garment section with a lightweight fusible interfacing. Cut the interfacing precisely; then assemble the garment, using the cut edges of the interfacing as a guide. Do not be concerned if the fabric has grown larger. For a softer, more supple underlining, use silk organza, polyester chiffon, or soft organza; quilt the fabric to the underlining if necessary to prevent stretching.
Pressing: To avoid flattening, cover pressing surface with thick towel. Use a press cloth to prevent iron from snagging fabric.

Designed by Gloria Young, the simple styling of this jacket showcases a unique handwoven fabric. (Photo courtesy of photographer Francine Walls.)

Hemp

Hemp is a bask fiber, similar to linen, but more absorbent. Frequently combined with other fibers, it is cool and comfortable to wear. It does not ease well, may fray badly, and wrinkles. It is easy to embroider.

Workroom Secrets

Fabric Prep: Dry-clean or steam dark colors which may fade badly and become white at edges. Machine wash/dry light colors if you plan to wash the garment. Purchase an additional ¼ to ½ yard for washable garments.

Layout/Cutting/Marking: Mark the right side of the fabric with small safety pins. Avoid wax or colored chalks and erasable pens, which may stain hemp permanently.

Stitching: To machine stitch through multiple thicknesses easily, rub seams with a bar of Ivory soap to lubricate the needle or pound with a cloth-covered hammer to soften fibers. When crossing bulky seams, use a shim to level the foot and prevent skipped stitches.

Seams: Use sturdy topstitched seams and hems for washable designs. To flatten seams, topstitch. For dressier designs, topstitch close to the seam. For sportswear, topstitch ¼" (6mm) away or use a wide twin needle to simulate flat fell seams.

Topstitching: Lengthen the stitch (3-4mm). Use a topstitching needle which has a deeper groove. Use a twin needle (HJ) to double stitch. Use a zipper foot when topstitching edges so the foot will remain level.

Sleeves: Shrink and shape sleeve caps before setting into the garment. Reduce the ease as needed to ease fullness smoothly. (See Any Fabric page 14.)

Buttonholes: Machine stitch with a sharp needle and all-purpose or embroidery thread. Lengthen the stitch length.

Embroidery: Hemp is an easy fabric to embroider. Use water soluble stabilizer on top of the fabric with tear-away or cut-away stabilizer on the wrong side.

Sophisticated and versatile, this hemp shirt jacket features classic tailored details and an easy fit. (Burda pattern - 8816, courtesy of Burda.)

Similar Fabrics: Butcher linen, crash, linen-like, linen-look, raw silk, silk linen, silk noil.

Uses: Unlined or reversible garments, tailored designs, casual jackets, coats, skirts, pants, vests.

Design Elements: Minimal seaming, extended shoulders, kimono or raglan sleeves, topstitching, decorative embroidery.

Sewing Checklist

Essential Supplies

Needles: Sharp (HM, HJ), universal (H); sizes 70/10-90/14; twin needle (ZWI HJ 40/100).

Thread: All purpose (cotton, polyester, cotton covered polyester). Topstitching – all purpose or machine embroidery/topstitching (cotton, polyester).

Cutting: Sharp shears, rotary cutter/mat.

Marking: Chalk, clips, pins.

Miscellaneous: Shim, safety pins, hammer, Ivory soap, stabilizers – spray starch, water soluble stabilizer, tearaway, cut away.

Interfacings: Optional, fusible, sew-in, self-fabric, linen.

Linings/Underlinings: Optional, same care as garment.

Machine Setup

Stitch Length: 2.5-3mm (8-10spi).

Tension: Lightly balanced.

Feet: Wide straight stitch, roller, zigzag, zipper.

Sewing Basics

Test Garment: Generally not required.

Fabric Prep: Preshrink. Steam, dry-clean, or machine wash/dry, depending on color and design.

Layout: Without nap – double layer.

Seams: Plain (press open or closed), topstitched, bound, strap.

Seam/Hem Finishes: Serged, zigzag, bound; if lined, none.

Hems: Hand (blindstitch, catchstitch, double-stitched), topstitched, twin needle, wrong-side out.

Edge Finishes: Facings, bindings, linings.

Closures: Buttonholes (machine, corded, bound, inseam); buttons/loops, ties, zippers (hand, machine, invisible).

Pressing: High heat, damp cloth or steam.

Garment Care: Machine wash/dry. Dry-clean to maintain the garment's pristine appearance.

Interfacing and Stabilizer

For every fabric, you have a choice of several interfacings. Your selection will be determined by availability; the fabric care; amount and direction of stretch; quality, weight, hand, and color; the fiber content; garment quality, type, design, use, and desired finished appearance; your sewing skills, time available, and personal preference. It is not uncommon to use several different interfacings in a single garment.

The most common interfacings are listed in the Interfacing Checklist (Appendix G). The chart is divided into two sections: fusible and sew-in; then the interfacings are listed by weight. Similar products are grouped together so you can make substitutions when necessary.

For most fabrics, you can use several different interfacings; and even though the results may be different, there is rarely a wrong choice. Recently I made two jackets—same pattern, same fabric. On one, I used only fusibles; on the other, traditional hair canvas. Both look great. The fused jacket has a crisper, slick look while the hair canvas design is a little softer with a more supple, tactile quality.

Application

Sew-in interfacings are sewn into the garment by hand or machine. Available in most fibers, they can be woven, nonwoven, or knit.

Fusible interfacings have a resin on one side and are bonded to the fabric when heat, moisture, and pressure are applied. They can be woven, nonwoven, tricot, warp-insertion or weft-insertion knits. All fusibles will make fabrics crisper after fusing and less tactile. Fusibles cannot be used on some fabrics because fusing will damage them or they will not adhere well.

Fabric Structure

Woven interfacings have stability in the lengthwise grain and slight give in the crossgrain. Sew-in or fusible, they are suitable for all woven fabrics. They can be machine washed and dried or dry-cleaned.

Hair canvas is a woven interfacing for tailoring. Woven with wool, goat's hair, and other fibers, the quality improves with the amount of wool and hair. It requires dry-cleaning.

Nonwoven interfacings are felt-like materials which do not ravel. Well-suited for washable garments and knits, nonwovens can be machine washed and dried or dry-cleaned.

Stable nonwoven interfacings have no grain and no give. They are firm and can be cut in any direction.

Stretch nonwoven interfacings have crosswise stretch. They are suitable for knits, bias-cut fabrics, and stretch wovens.

All-bias nonwoven interfacings have some give in all directions. They are suitable for supple, unstructured shapes.

Tricot interfacings have crosswise stretch and can be used to interface or underline knit and woven fabrics.

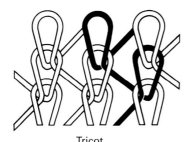

Tricot

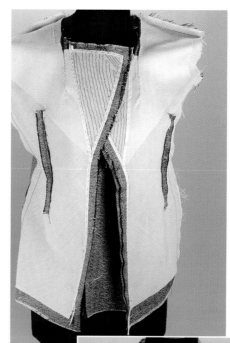

This sample jacket utilizes a combination of sew-ins and fusibles on the front and the back. (Photo by Robert Best.)

Stabilized tricot is a sew-in knit which is stable in the length and width, with stretch on the bias. It does not fray or run when edges are left raw.

Stabilized tricot

Warp-insertion interfacings are fusible knit interfacings with yarns inserted lengthwise. This structure produces stability in the length and stretch in the width.

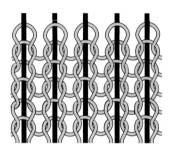

Warp insertion

Weft-insertion interfacings are fusible knit interfacings with yarns inserted horizontally. This structure produces stability in the crossgrain and stretch and recovery in the length. Well suited for tailoring, weft-insertions are more supple than woven fusibles and more stable than knits.

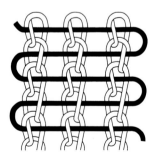

Weft insertion

Fusible woven interfacings describe themselves. The limited selection in the interfacing department can be expanded by applying a fusible web to a sew-in interfacing with a fusible web on release paper or a Teflon release sheet.

Fusible web is a mesh of polyamides which melt. With heat, moisture, and pressure, fusible webs can join two fabric layers permanently for hemming, appliqués, or interfacing. They can be applied to a single layer of fabric with a Teflon release sheet. Some fusible webs are packaged on paper release sheets.

Release sheets are Teflon-type sheets which allow you to bond a fusible web to a fabric without gumming up the iron.

Fusing Interfacings

Heat and moisture melt the resin, and pressure pushes it into the fibers.

1. Read the instructions with the interfacing.

2. Cover the pressing surface with paper towels. Place the fabric, wrong-side up, on the paper towels.

3. Place the interfacing, resin side down, on the fabric.
Hint: *When fusing to a portion of a section, trim the edge with pinking shears to avoid a demarcation line.*

4. Cover with a press cloth, dry or wet depending on the instructions.

5. Baste press lightly in several areas if the section is large.
Note: *When working with loosely woven fabrics, the garment section is frequently larger than the interfacing, even though they were cut by the same pattern. Do not force the edges to match; the fashion fabric has stretched out of shape. If you have cut accurately, use the interfacing as a guide.*

6. Set the iron on "wool."

7. Beginning in the center of the section, fuse toward the edges. Press hard with steam, unless the instructions indicate otherwise, for 10 to 15 seconds. Overlap the fused areas carefully to avoid a bare section. Do not slide the iron.

8. Turn the section over; cover with a press cloth; and fuse the other side.

9. Allow the section to cool before moving it.

10. Test to be sure all corners are securely fused.

Stabilizers

Stabilizers support the fabric during construction for tissue stitching, appliqué, seaming, buttonholes, embroidery. They tear away or dissolve with water, steam, or heat after stitching. (See Appendix E – Stabilizers.)

Claire's Hints

1. Interfacings should have the same care requirements as the garment.
2. Preshrink all interfacings before using. Place in a sink with very hot water; leave about 30 minutes; then hang to dry. Do not shrink fusibles in a washer or dry in dryer.
3. Always test fuse when using fusibles. This is particularly important when fusing to a portion of a section because the fusible may change the hand or drape or make a demarcation line at the edge.
4. Keep a record of the products you use with notes about the results.

Jersey

Jersey is a single knit with lengthwise ribs on one side and horizontal rows on the back. Generally the ribs are on the right side. Available in wool, silk, cotton, nylon, and polyester, jersey is soft and drapeable with moderate stretch. It runs from both ends, will not hold a crease, and tends to bag and sag.

Jersey Types/Similar Fabrics: Interlock knits, jacquard jersey, lisle, milanese, pointelle, simplex, single knits, tricot, wool jersey.
Uses: Tee shirts, blouses, dresses, skirts, pants, lingerie, evening wear, casual jackets, coats.
Design Elements: Soft, fluid or draped designs, unpressed pleats, gathers, casings, ribbings, bindings.

Sewing Checklist

Essential Supplies
Needles: Universal (H), stretch (HS), ballpoint (H-SUK), twin needle; sizes 60/8-80/12.
Thread: All purpose (cotton, polyester, cotton covered polyester, silk). Topstitching – all purpose or fine machine embroidery thread (60/2).
Cutting: Sharp shears, weights, tissue.
Marking: Chalk, clips, erasable pens, thread, tailor's tacks.
Miscellaneous: Super fine pins, lightweight zippers, nylon stocking scrap, stabilizers – water soluble, cut-away.
Interfacings: Detail areas; lightweight fusibles or sew-ins, bias-cut organza or China silk.
Linings/Underlinings: Optional, same care as garment. Cut on bias to retain stretch.

Machine Setup
Stitch length: 2-2.5mm (10-12spi), narrow zigzag (W,.5-L,1.5)
Tension: Lightly balanced.
Feet: Wide straight stitch, roller, zigzag.

Sewing Basics
Fabric Prep: Preshrink cottons and synthetics, machine wash/dry; non-washables, steam or dry-clean.
Layout: Nap – double layer.
Seams: Plain (pressed open or closed), zigzagged (W,.5-L,1.5), topstitched, twin needle, safety-stitch serged, tissue-stitched, taped.
Seam/Hem Finishes: Serged, zigzag, none.
Hems: Hand (blindstitch, catchstitch), pinked, topstitched, twin needle, lettucing, fused, interfaced.
Edge Finishes: Facings (self-fabric, bias), bindings, ribbings.
Closures: Buttonholes (machine, corded, bound, inseam); buttons/loops, ties, zippers (hand, machine, invisible).
Pressing: Medium to high heat, depending on the fiber; damp cloth or steam.
Garment Care: Dry-clean, machine wash/dry, depending on fiber.

Workroom Secrets
Fabric Prep: To preshrink cotton and cotton-blend fabrics, machine wash/dry three times. Steam or dry-clean silk and wool.
Layout/Cutting/Marking: Let fabric relax overnight before cutting. To find right side, stretch crosswise; edge will curl to the right side. To cut silk jersey, pin to tissue. Lay out pattern; cut through fabric and tissue.
Seams: Check needle for burrs before stitching by stitching through a nylon stocking scrap. To prevent snagging on the feed dogs, tissue stitch seams. For more elastic seams, use polyester or textured thread and zigzag (W,.5-L,1.5), or use a twin needle seam. Narrow serged seams are a good choice for casual garments. Tape seams at shoulders, neck, and waist to prevent stretching.
Hems: Let hems hang at least 24 hours before hemming. To avoid runs, zigzag (W,.5-L,1) close to the raw edge. Use loose blindstitches, blind catchstitches, or catchstitches to hem quality designs. Topstitch everyday garments with a straight or twin needle. To prevent rippling, fuse a strip of lightweight knit interfacing to the hem allowance. For a soft, feminine look, use a lettuce edge.
Facings: Understitch or topstitch to prevent facings from rolling to the outside.
Buttonholes: Stabilize buttonhole area with a strip of interfacing. Use water soluble stabilizer on top of fabric to prevent the stitches from embedding in the fabric. Stitch with fine embroidery thread (60/2). Consider buttons/loops for wool or silk jerseys.
Zippers: Stabilize the opening to prevent stretching. Hand stitch zippers on quality designs.
Embroidery: Use water soluble stabilizer on top of the fabric and cutaway stabilizer on wrong side.

This go-anywhere ensemble in jersey will be a welcome addition to any wardrobe. (Petite Plus Patterns® – 102, 601; Photo courtesy of Petite Plus Patterns®.)

Knits

Differences and Similarities of Knits and Wovens

Knits are just as diverse as woven fabrics. To sew them successfully, it's important to recognize the similarities and differences between knits and woven fabrics.

- *Generally, knits have more give than woven fabrics, but woven fabrics with stretch yarns may stretch more than stable knits.*
- *Knits mold and fit the body better than woven fabrics.*
- *The amount of stretch in a knitted fabric ranges from almost none to 100 percent, depending on the kind of knit, the fiber, yarn, and fabric finish.*
- *Knits have lengthwise stitches called ribs and crosswise rows called courses instead of a lengthwise grain and a crossgrain.*
- *Woven fabrics and most knits have more give in the crossgrain than in the lengthwise grain.*
- *Unlike wovens, some knits have more stretch in the crossgrain than on the bias. And a few knits have more stretch in the length than in the width.*
- *Garments made from stretch knits do not need as much ease as those made of stable knits and woven fabrics.*
- *Pattern selection for both knits and wovens is based on fabric weight, bulk, crispness, drapeability, texture, opaqueness, fabric pattern, and care.*
- *Generally, knit fabrics are thicker than woven fabrics, but they are not as wind-resistant.*
- *Knits do not hold a crease as well as woven fabrics.*
- *Knits are more resistant to wrinkles.*
- *Knitted and woven fabrics with permanent-press finishes cannot be straightened if they are off-grain.*
- *On knits, the course or crossgrain cannot be determined by pulling a thread; instead, square the ends of knit fabrics with the edge of a rectangular table.*

- *Knits shrink more frequently and in larger amounts than woven fabrics.*
- *All knits have a one-way pattern or nap which is caused by the way the fabric is structured. Shading differences that go undetected in uncut fabric may be noticeable in the finished garment.*
- *Stretch fabrics need stretch seams and hems; when no stretch is desired, seams and edges need to be stabilized with a non-stretch tape.*
- *Knits do not ravel like woven fabrics; but some knits run and many curl at cut edges.*
- *Since knits do not ravel as woven fabrics, seam and hem finishes are frequently optional.*
- *When sewing knits, choose threads with stretch such as long-staple polyester or textured threads.*
- *Generally, knit fabrics are stitched with ballpoint needles which will slide between the yarns instead of penetrating them. Woven fabrics are stitched with sharp point needles. Needles with sharp or damaged points will make holes and cause runs.*
- *Generally, knits are stitched with shorter stitches and looser tension than woven fabrics, so that seams will elongate with the fabric. Both usually require a balanced tension.*
- *Knits are less likely to require interfacings, linings, and underlinings than woven fabrics. When selecting interfacings, consider both the purpose—for shape and support—and the relationship of the interfacing to the general characteristics of the fiber.*
- *For knits and wovens, the fiber content as well as the fabric structure determines the garment's durability, pressing temperature, and general care.*

Appropriate for every age, knits are easy to sew and comfortable to wear. (Photo courtesy of KWIK·SEW®.)

Knit Stretch Guide

Knits stretch more than wovens. Most stretch more in the width than in the length, but they can stretch in either or both directions.

Stable knits stretch little, if any, while super stretch knits can stretch as much as 100 percent. The amount of stretch is determined by the type of knit, the size of the knitted loops, and the number and type of yarns.

When working with stretch knits, choose patterns designed with an appropriate amount of stretch.

To determine the amount of stretch, fold the knit about 3" (7.5cm) from a crosswise edge. Measure and mark a 4" (10cm) length on the folded edge. Stretch gently and measure the folded edge.

- Stable knits such as double knits stretch 10 percent or less. 4" (10cm) stretches ½" (1.2cm) or less.
- Moderate stretch knits such as jerseys and interlocks stretch 20 to 25 percent. 4" (10cm) stretches 1" to 1¼" (2.5-3.1cm).
- Stretch knits such as stretch terry and stretch velour stretch about 50 percent. 4" (10cm) stretches about 2" (5cm).
- Super stretch knits such as ribbing, swimwear, and slinky stretch 50 to 100 percent. 4" (10cm) stretches up to 8" (20cm).

Lace

Laces are decorative fabrics which run the gamut from very fine, sheer materials to heavy, coarse fabrics. Available in a variety of fibers—nylon, polyester, linen, wool, cotton, and rayon, most have no selvage and do not ravel. They do not have a grainline, but have more stretch in the width than in the length. Many have a one way design with motifs which must be matched. Some have scallops on one edge; others have them at both edges.

Lace Types: Alençon, all-over lace, Breton lace, chantilly, cluny, guipure, metallic, re-embroidered, Schiffli.

Uses: Formal gowns, dressy or casual dresses, jackets, blouses, skirts, pants.

Design Elements: Minimal seaming to showcase the fabric, bindings, lace edgings, buttons and loops, pockets (inseam).

Sewing Checklist

Essential Supplies

Needles: Sharp (HM, HJ), universal (H); sizes 70/10-80/12.

Thread: Delicate laces – fine machine embroidery, extra-fine cotton covered polyester). Coarse laces – all purpose (cotton, polyester, cotton covered polyester).

Cutting: Sharp shears, duplicate pattern pieces.

Marking: Safety pins, thread tracing, erasable pens, flower pins.

Miscellaneous: Flower pins, safety pins, stabilizers – water soluble, tearaway, cut away.

Interfacings: Organza, tulle.

Linings/Underlinings: Optional, depends on lace and design.

Machine Setup

Stitch Length: 1.75-2mm (12-15spi).

Tension: Lightly balanced; light pressure.

Feet: Wide straight stitch, roller, embroidery, zigzag.

Sewing Basics

Test Garment: Recommended for expensive laces.

Fabric Prep: Preshrink with steam.

Layout: Nap – double layer; single layer right-side up to match motifs or to cut coarse lace.

Seams: Plain (pressed closed), lace appliqué, serged.

Seam/Hem Finishes: Serged, zigzag, unfinished.

Hems: Hand (blindstitch, catchstitch), horsehair braid, lace edging.

Edge Finishes: Facings (bias, tulle, ribbon, lining), bindings (satin, light-weight silk), bands, edge - to edge linings.

Closures: Buttonholes (hand, machine, corded, bound, inseam); buttons/loops, zippers (hand, invisible), covered snaps, hooks/eyes.

Pressing: Medium, damp cloth or steam.

Garment Care: Dry-clean, machine wash/dry, or hand wash, depending on lace and design.

Workroom Secrets

Layout/Cutting/Marking: Spread the lace in a single layer right-side up. Examine the lace to determine if it has motifs to be matched and whether you want to lay out the pattern on the lengthwise grain and/or crossgrain. Use duplicate pattern pieces; and position pattern pieces on the lace so the long scalloped edge is at the hem or front edge. When this is not possible, trim away the scalloped edge and reapply it later, using a zigzag stitch (W,1-L,1) or hand overcasting.

Stitching: To avoid snagging the lace, stitch with water soluble stabilizer between the lace and feed dogs. Stitch slowly to reduce puckered seams.

Seams: Use narrow seams on casual designs and less expensive laces. Use lace appliqué seams on better garments. (See Sewing Techniques page 108.)

Hems: If lace motifs cause an uneven foldline at the hem, consider other edge finishes such as bindings, applied lace trim, facing, or horsehair braid.

Closures: When possible, replace zippers and buttonholes with covered snaps or buttons and loops.

To machine stitch buttonholes, use water soluble stabilizer on top of the fabric to prevent the stitches from embedding in the lace. Use lightweight zippers and stabilize the opening with light-weight selvage to prevent stretching.

Pressing: Test press. Lace is easily damaged by hot irons and careless handling. Cover the pressing surface with a thick terry towel to avoid flattening the lace design.

Garment Care: To protect skirts and pants from clip hangers, sew in ribbon hanger loops at the waist.

This simply styled gown is stunning in an allover lace fabric. (Photo courtesy of KWIK-SEW®.)

Lamé

Lamé is a woven or knit fabric with metallic yarns in the length and/or width. Today's lamés include metal, metal-coated plastic, plastic-coated metal or a metal-wrapped core yarn.

Lightweight and drapeable, lamé frays and snags, dulls shears and machine needles, and is easily damaged by needles, pins, and improper pressing.

Workroom Secrets

Layout/Cutting/Marking: Before cutting, check to be sure the foldline is not permanent. Use weights, temporary pattern adhesive, or position pins within the seam allowances. To control fraying, do not cut until you are ready to sew. Handle the sections as little as possible after cutting. Cut seams 1" (2.5cm) wide, and use a seam sealant on the cut edges applied carefully to avoid spotting the fabric. Do not mark with clips.

Stitching: Start all new projects with a new needle in the smallest recommended size. Change needles frequently; metallic lamé dulls needles faster than natural fibers. To test the needle, stitch through an old nylon stocking. Baste seams as needed to avoid ripping.

Seam/Hem Finishes: To reduce fraying, turn under and stitch raw edges. For seams, use a safety-stitch seam; or stitch the seam allowances together with a narrow zigzag; then trim to 3/8" (1cm).

Seams: Self-finished seams such as French and faux French are often too bulky. To reduce seam slippage, stitch seams again 1/8" (3mm) away.

Interfacings: Many designs do not require interfacing. If you want to add crispness, experiment with fusibles to determine if the lamé will be damaged by heat and/or steam.

Linings: To avoid skin irritations, line the garment, bind seams with tricot or chiffon, or wear a slip.

Embroidery: Use water soluble stabilizer on top and bottom of fabric.

Pressing: Test press. Some lamé fabrics are easily damaged by hot irons and steam; others are not.

Garment Care: To protect skirts and pants from clip hanger marks, sew in ribbon hanger loops at the waist.

This stunning gown, designed by Tammy O'Connell, is panné velvet with hologram and accent piping with metallic drapes and revers. (Photo courtesy of Tammy O'Connell of Jitney Patterns and Patrick Manning.)

Similar Fabrics: Cloth of silver, cloth of gold, hologram, Lurex®, Metlon®, sheer metallics, stretch lamé, tissue lamé, tricot-backed lamé.

Uses: Dresses, blouses, bustiers, skirts, pants, eveningwear.

Design Elements: Minimal seaming, bindings, pockets (inseam), casings. Avoid close fitting designs if you are not underlining.

Sewing Checklist

Essential Supplies

Needles: Sharp (HM, HJ), stretch (HS) universal (H); sizes 60/8-70/10.

Thread: Lightweight (machine embroidery cotton, cotton covered polyester), all-purpose (cotton, polyester, cotton covered polyester).

Cutting: Stainless steel shears, weights, rotary cutter/mat.

Marking: Chalk, erasable pens, super fine pins, safety pins, tailor's tacks.

Miscellaneous: Super fine pins, seam sealant, weights, nylon stocking scrap, temporary pattern adhesive, water soluble stabilizer.

Interfacings: Optional, sew-in or low temp fusibles.

Linings/Underlinings: Generally for formal designs, and scratchy fabrics.

Machine Setup

Stitch Length: 2-2.5mm (10-12spi).

Tension: Lightly balanced; light pressure.

Machine Feet: Wide straight stitch, roller, zigzag.

Sewing Basics

Test Garment: Recommended.

Fabric Prep: Hand wash or dry-clean, depending on manufacturer's recommendation.

Layout: Nap – double layer.

Seams: Plain (pressed open or closed), tissue stitched.

Seam/Hem Finishes: Serged, turn under and stitch, zigzag.

Hems: Hand (blindstitch), topstitched, shirttail, pin, twin needle.

Edge Finishes: Facings (self-fabric, lining, bias), bands, bindings, edge to edge linings.

Closures: Buttons/loops, buttonholes (machine, bound, inseam), ties, covered snaps, zippers (hand, machine, invisible).

Pressing: Medium heat, dry iron.

Garment Care: Dry-clean or hand wash, depending on manufacturer's recommendation.

Leather and Suede

Technically not a fabric, leather is the outside of an animal skin; suede is the underside. When the wool is left on, it is called sherpa. Sold by the skin instead of by the yard, leather is easily marred by pins and needles. It frequently crocks, and may be expensive to clean.

Leather Types/Similar Materials: Cabretta, chamois, cowhide, faux suedes, pigskin, lambskin, faux leather, fur, pleather, Sensuede®, snakeskin, shearling, sherpa, stretch suede, suede-like fabrics, Ultrasuede®.

Uses: Tailored or casual garments, jackets, coats, dresses, skirts, pants, tunics, vests, handbags, belts, pillows.

Design Elements: Minimal seaming, topstitching, bindings, non-woven lapped and flat fell seams.

Sewing Checklist

Essential Supplies
Needles: Leather (HLL, NTW), sharp (HM, HJ), universal (H); sizes 70/10-100/16. Hand sewing, glover's needles.
Thread: All purpose (polyester). Topstitching – all purpose or heavy (polyester). Hand sewing – waxed polyester or quilting thread.
Cutting: Sharp shears, duplicate pattern pieces.
Marking: Chalk, clips, erasable pens, pencil.
Miscellaneous: Weights, shim, quilting clothes pins, hair clips, rubber mallet, rubber or Barge cement, washable glue stick, cardboard tube, single-edge razor blade or mat knife, glover's needles, beeswax.
Interfacings: Low temp fusibles or sew-ins.
Linings: Outerwear, all quality designs.

Machine Setup
Stitch Length: 2.5-4mm (6-10spi).
Tension: Lightly balanced.
Feet: Teflon, roller, leather, zigzag; small hole throat plate.

Sewing Basics
Fabric Prep: None.
Layout: Nap – single layer, right-side up.
Seams: Plain (pressed open or closed), topstitched, nonwoven lapped, nonwoven flat fell.
Seam/Hem Finishes: None.
Edge Finishes: Facings (leather, suede, ribbon, fabric), bindings, bands.
Closures: Buttonholes (machine, bound, inseam), buttons/loops, snaps, ties, lacings, zippers (machine, invisible, decorative).
Pressing: Dry, medium heat, press cloth, brown paper.
Garment Care: Leather clean or dry-clean.

Workroom Secrets

Selection: Choose skins which are similar in color, texture, and thickness. Check the care requirements before purchasing. To determine the amount needed, multiply the yardage requirement by 12—the number of square feet in a yard of 45" (112mm) fabric. Add 15 percent for flaws and waste.

Layout/Cutting/Marking: Lay skins flat, right-side up. Examine for imperfections, holes, scratches, and thin spots. The center of full skins is most attractive and strongest. Cut duplicate pattern pieces; arrange them on the right side with the tops toward the neck area. Leather does not have grain, but it has less stretch in the length. Anchor the pieces with weights or drafting tape; pins leave holes. Remove the tape as soon as possible. Cut sleeves and pants 1" to 2" (2.5cm-5cm) longer to allow for shortening when the garment is worn.

Stitching: Use polyester thread: the tannin in leather causes cotton to rot. When sewing lightweight leathers, use a sharp needle. When sewing medium and heavy-weight leathers, use a leather needle. Do not backstitch. Tie knots at the end.

Seams: Use quilting clothes pins for basting. Stabilize seams which will be stressed. Before stitching corners, reshape sharp points so they are rounded. Draw the stitching lines on the leather to be sure they are identical when stitched. To flatten seams, pound with a mallet or cloth-covered hammer. Glue or topstitch seams so they will remain flat. Apply rubber or Barge cement to the wrong side and finger press seams flat. (Always test before using to be sure it won't show through on the outside.) When topstitching, stitch sporty designs with a longer stitch ¼" (6mm) from the seamline. When sewing medium and heavy-weight leathers, use non-woven flat fell or non-woven lapped seams.

Darts: Stitch, then slash and glue darts open. If appropriate, topstitch.

Hems: Topstitch or glue hems in place.

Sleeves: Reduce ease in the sleeve cap. (See Any Fabric page 14.)

Buttonholes: To avoid damaging the leather when machine stitching buttonholes, lengthen the stitch.

Interfacings: Interface edges to preserve the shape.

Linings: Line garments to preserve the shape, reduce clinging, and prevent color crocking.

Pressing: Test press on scraps. Do not use steam which may cause shrinkage. Wrong side up, press with a press cloth or plain brown paper. Do not slide the iron.

Garment Care: Add ribbon hanger loops at the waist for skirts and pants. Store jackets on sturdy wood hangers.

This handsome leather top contrasts attractively with the duchesse silk satin skirt. (Photo courtesy of PtakCouture.com.)

Linen

Linen is a bask fiber. It wrinkles, does not ease well, and is easily damaged by wax or colored chalk and erasable pens. To sew lightweight linens, see Handkerchief Linen page 46.

Workroom Secrets

Fabric Preparation: Dry-clean or steam dark colors which fade badly and become white at edges. Wash and dry light colors if you plan to wash the garment.

Layout/Cutting/Marking: Mark the right side of the fabric with small safety pins.

Stitching: Begin with a new sharp needle in the smallest recommended size. When crossing bulky seams, use a shim to level the foot and prevent skipped stitches.

Seams: Use sturdy topstitched seams and hems for unlined and washable designs. To flatten seams, topstitch. For dressy designs, topstitch close to the seam. For sportswear, topstitch ¼" (6mm) away or use a wide twin needle to simulate flat fell seams.

Topstitching: Lengthen the stitch (3-4mm). Use a topstitching needle (HE) which has a deeper groove for heavier threads. Use a twin needle (HJ) to double stitch.

Interfacing: Consider bias-cut self-fabric when interfacing. For jackets, interface the entire front.

Edge Finishes: Use a zipper foot to topstitch edges so the foot will be level.

Sleeves: Shrink and shape sleeve caps before setting into the garment. Reduce the ease as needed to ease fullness smoothly.

Buttonholes: Machine stitch with a sharp needle. For more definition, lengthen the stitch, and use machine embroidery thread (40, 30). If the fabric is soft, spray the buttonhole area with spray starch.

Pressing: To avoid slicking the fabric, use a press cloth when pressing the right side.

Embroidery: Linen is an easy fabric to embroider. Use water soluble stabilizer on top of the fabric with tearaway or cut-away stabilizer underneath.

Designed to flatter, this linen ensemble is cool and smart. (McCall's Pattern – 3939, Sewing with Nancy; courtesy of The McCall Pattern Co.)

Linen Types/Similar Fabrics: Butcher linen, cotton jacquard, crash, damask, flax tweed, hemp, linen-like, linen jacquard, linen-look, moira, pembroke, raw silk, silk linen, silk noil.

Uses: Reversible or unlined garments, tailored designs, casual jackets, coats, skirts, pants, vests.

Design Elements: Minimal seaming, topstitching, crisp silhouettes, decorative embroidery.

Sewing Checklist

Essential Supplies

Needles: Sharp (HM, HJ), universal (H); sizes 70/10-90/14; twin needle (ZWI HJ); embroidery (HE).

Thread: All purpose (cotton, polyester, cotton covered polyester, silk). Topstitching – all purpose, machine embroidery/topstitching.

Cutting: Sharp shears, rotary cutter/mat.

Marking: Chalk, clips, pins.

Miscellaneous: Shim, safety pins, spray starch, water soluble stabilizer, burn-away, tearaway, cut away.

Interfacings: Optional, fusible, sew-in, self-fabric.

Linings/Underlinings: Generally on better garments; care, same as garment.

Machine Setup

Stitch Length: 2.5-3mm (8-10spi).

Tension: Lightly balanced.

Feet: Wide straight stitch, roller, zigzag.

Sewing Basics

Test Garment: Optional, depending on design.

Fabric Prep: Preshrink. Steam, dry-clean, or hand wash, depending on design. Purchase additional ¼ to ½ yard for washable garments.

Layout: Without nap – double layer.

Seams: Plain (pressed open or closed), topstitched, bound, strap, piped.

Seam/Hem Finishes: Serged, pinked, zigzag, bound; if lined, none.

Hems: Hand (blindstitch, catchstitch, double-stitched), topstitched, twin needle, wrong-side out.

Edge Finishes: Facings, bindings, linings.

Closures: Buttonholes (machine, corded, bound, inseam); buttons/loops, ties, zippers (hand, machine, invisible).

Pressing: High heat, damp cloth or steam.

Garment Care: Machine wash/dry, dry-clean.

Lining/Underlining

Linings and underlinings are optional for many fabrics and designs. Traditional tailored garments are always lined, but a contemporary or casual design in the same fabric might be unlined.

Linings and underlinings improve the durability, comfort, and quality of a garment. Simply explained, linings cover the seams and construction details to finish the inside of garments while underlinings do not.

Assembled separately, linings are sewn to the garment at the neckline, armholes, garment opening, waistline, and sometimes at the hem. In addition to adding comfort and quality, linings protect the seams from abrasion, reduce wrinkling, prolong the garment's life, add warmth, preserve the shape of the garment, allow the garment to slip easily over other garments, reduce clinging, and protect the body from irritating fabrics. Although linings are usually inconspicuous, they can be an important design feature.

Underlinings are attached to the individual garment sections before the garment is assembled. Generally used to add support and body, underlinings can change the characteristics of the fabric. They conceal construction details from the outside of the garment, add opaqueness, change the color, reduce wrinkling, and support the garment shape. Within one garment, you may use different underlinings for different effects.

Flat linings are a combination lining/underline. The individual garment sections are lined so there are no raw edges at the seams; then the garment is assembled.

Lining/Underlining Fabrics

Most fabrics can be used both for linings and underlinings; and almost all interfacing fabrics can be used as underlinings. The fabrics listed here are readily available from local, mail order, or Internet retailers.

Acetate/nylon lining combines acetate for breathability and nylon for strength and wrinkle-resistance.

Ambiance is a plain weave Bemberg lining.

Batiste is a lightweight cotton or cotton/blend which shrinks and ravels. It is heavier than silk, rayon, and polyester fabrics.

Bemberg is a quality rayon lining. Available in plain and twill weaves, it is more comfortable to wear than polyester and more durable than silk.

Coat lining is a satin-weave with a flannel backed lining.

Cling Free is 100 percent polyester. It is inexpensive, wrinkles, and shrinks when steam pressed.

Coup de Ville is a quality 100 percent polyester.

Faux fur, fur, and wool jersey are bulky linings which add warmth and design.

Mesh linings are used for waterproof and water-repellent garments. They are lightweight, stretch slightly, and breathe.

Microfibers are lightweight and slide on and off easily. They breathe better than traditional synthetic fabrics but not as well as rayon or silk.

Polartec® fleeces are good for insulating, but do not slip on easily.

Polyesters range from inexpensive materials which shrink and do not breathe to quality linings which are more absorbent and more comfortable to wear. They are washable and may ravel badly.

Posh is a 100 percent polyester lining.

Stretch linings are well-suited for stretch wovens and knits.

Lightweight silks such as China silk, chiffon, crêpe de Chine, and charmeuse are comfortable to wear, expensive, and not very durable.

Wicking linings are used for waterproof and water-repellent garments. They breathe well and are heavier than taffeta.

Sewing Checklist

Lining/Underlining Selection

1. Linings/Underlinings should have the same care requirements as the fashion fabric. Always preshrink.

2. They should be colorfast, static free, wrinkle-resistant, and comfortable to wear. The color should match or complement the fabric. To reduce soiling, spray whites and light colored linings with a fabric protector.

3. Linings should add strength and protection without adding bulk. Generally, the best choice is lighter in weight and slightly softer than the fabric. Twill weaves wear better and are more durable than plain- or satin-weaves. If the threads separate when you scrape your thumbnail across the fabric, the fabric will slip at seams.

4. Underlinings can be crisper and thicker than the fabric; but they should not be heavier.

Above: *Made of silk, the edge-to-edge lining completely covers the construction elements on this tailored dress. (Photo courtesy of Claire Shaeffer.)*

Left: *Underlined with silk organza, the seams are exposed on the wrong side. (Photo courtesy of Claire Shaeffer.)*

Loosely Woven Fabric

Loosely woven fabrics are novelty fabrics with a loose weave. Many are bulky with slubs and long floats. They pick, pull, and ravel badly.

Workroom Secrets

Layout/Cutting/Marking: Many loosely woven fabrics stretch badly; do not allow them to hang off table. For fabrics which fray badly, cut with 1" (2.5cm) seams. Then, before moving the sections from the table, spray lightly with seam sealant or thin solution of white glue and water. Use small safety pins to mark the right side and construction symbols. Avoid clips if the fabric frays badly. Understitch facings to prevent them from popping out.

Stitching: Use a roller foot or wrap toes with tape to avoid snagging long floats. Stitch with a narrow zigzag (W,.5-L,2) to prevent puckered seams. Hold the fabric firmly in front and behind the presser foot; use a roller or even-feed foot, or tissue stitch seams.

Seams: Stabilize necklines, shoulder seams, buttonholes, and zipper openings. (See Any Fabric page 13.)

Seam/Hem Finishes: If the fabric frays badly, serge or bind seams before assembling. Work carefully to avoid changing or varying the seam allowance widths.

Buttonholes: For more definition, use water soluble stabilizer on top of fabric and/or cord the buttonholes.

Underlinings: Use sew-ins for stability, fusibles for added structure.

Pressing: To avoid flattening the fabric, cover pressing surface with thick towel. Use a press cloth to prevent iron from snagging fabric.

Designed by Susan Fears, this jacket features a loosely woven silk suiting which has been embellished with machine embroidery. (Photo courtesy of Susan Fears and Bernina of America.)

Similar Fabrics: Handwovens, alpaca, bouclé, hopsacking, matka, mohair, monk's cloth, wool lace.

Uses: Tailored or unstructured garments, coats, jackets, skirts, pants, dresses, jumpers, wraps.

Design Elements: Simple designs, minimal seaming, gathers, soft pleats, pockets and collars (all types). Avoid close fitting garments and fussy details.

Sewing Checklist

Essential Supplies

Needles: Sharp (HM, HJ), universal (H); sizes 70/10-90/14, depending on fabric weight.

Thread: All purpose (cotton, polyester, cotton covered polyester, silk). Topstitching – all purpose, machine embroidery/topstitching.

Cutting: Sharp shears, rotary cutter/mat, duplicate pattern pieces.

Marking: Chalk, clips, flower pins, safety pins, tailor's tacks, thread tracing.

Miscellaneous: Flower pins, safety pins, weights, tape, seam sealant, white glue, spray bottle, terry towel, water soluble stabilizers – burn away, tearaway.

Interfacings: Fusible, weft-insertion, knit; sew-in, hair canvas.

Linings: Optional, depends on garment type/design.

Underlinings: Organza, sew-in and fusible interfacings.

Machine Setup

Stitch Length: 2-3mm (8-12spi); or narrow zigzag (W,.5-L,2).

Tension: Lightly balanced.

Feet: Roller, wide straight stitch, even-feed, zigzag.

Sewing Basics

Test Garment: Recommended, easily damaged by ripping.

Fabric Prep: Preshrink with steam or dry-clean.

Layout: Nap – double layer; single layer, right-side up for bulky fabrics and to match fabric patterns.

Seams: Plain (pressed open), topstitched, strap, lapped, piped, taped.

Hems: Hand (blindstitch, blind catchstitch, catchstitch), double-stitched, interfaced, topstitched.

Seam/Hem Finishes: Serged, zigzag, bound.

Edge Finishes: Facings (self-fabric, lining), bindings (contrast, leather or faux suede), bands, ribbings, fringing, edge-to-edge linings.

Closures: Buttonholes (machine, corded, bound, in-seam), buttons/loops, zippers (machine, hand, invisible).

Pressing: Cool to medium heat; steam, self-fabric press cloth.

Garment Care: Dry-clean.

Matelassé

Matelassé is a blistered or quilted-effect fabric with a fine, plain-weave on the back. Made in all fiber types, it may be bulky, difficult to ease, and ravel badly. Its uneven surface helps to hide stitching irregularities.

Similar Fabrics: Blister, brocade, brocatelle, broché, cloqué, cotton suiting, crinkle, embossed, imperial brocade, plissé, soufflé, tapestry, upholstery, upholstery satin, venetian.

Uses: Special occasion and formal wear, suits, coats, dresses, skirts, pants, handbags.

Design Elements: Simple designs to showcase the fabric. Avoid intricate seams, fussy details, and close fitting designs.

Sewing Checklist

Essential Supplies
Needles: Sharp (HM), universal (H); sizes 70/10-80/12.
Thread: All purpose (cotton, polyester, cotton covered polyester, silk). Serger – lightweight serger thread, textured thread.
Cutting: Sharp shears, rotary cutter/mat.
Marking: Chalk, clips, pins, tailor's tacks, thread.
Miscellaneous: Super fine pins, weights, covered snaps.
Interfacings: Sew-in.
Lining: Generally on jackets, but not necessarily on soft skirts and pants.
Underlinings: Frequently; organza, China silk, soft organza, voile, batiste.

Machine Setup
Stitch length: 2-3mm (8-12spi).
Tension: Lightly balanced.
Feet: Wide straight stitch, zigzag, roller.

Sewing Basics
Test Garment: Recommended.
Fabric Prep: Preshrink with steam or dry-clean.
Layout: Nap – double or single layer.
Seams: Plain (pressed open), piped, lapped.
Hems: Hand (blindstitch, catchstitch), interfaced, double-stitched.
Seam/Hem finishes: Serged, zigzag; if lined, none.
Edge Finishes: Facings (lining, self-fabric, bias), bindings, edge to edge linings.
Closures: Buttonholes (machine, bound, in-seam) buttons/loops, zippers (hand, invisible), covered snaps.
Pressing: Low to medium heat, steam.
Garment Care: Dry-clean.

Workroom Secrets
Stitching: Stitch carefully; most matelassé fabrics are easily marred by ripping.
Underlinings: When making a suit, underline the skirt with silk organza, soft organza, or voile to maintain the suppleness and reduce seam slippage on seams which will be stressed.

Underline the jacket with a crisp woven interfacing in cotton or cotton/blend to add body and maintain the design's shape.
Buttonholes: To prevent stitches from embedding in the fabric, stitch with water soluble stabilizer on top of fabric. To stitch inconspicuous buttonholes, use fine embroidery thread (60/2).
Zippers: To prevent the opening stretching, stabilize opening with a lightweight interfacing.
Pressing: Test press to determine the appropriate heat, moisture, and pressure for the fiber content. When steaming, watch for shrinking. Always use a press cloth when pressing the right side. To avoid flattening the fabric, cover pressing surface with a thick towel. To prevent seam and hem impressions, use a seam roll and brown paper strips under the edges.
Garment Care: Store special-occasion garments on well-padded hangers.

Designed by Geoffrey Beene, this timeless design showcases a luxurious matelassé fabric. (Vogue Pattern, Geoffrey Beene-2232, courtesy of The McCall Pattern Co.)

Melton

Melton is a bulky wool coating with a thick nap. Warm, water and wind resistant, it frays little, is difficult to ease and press, and wears badly at edges.

Workroom Secrets

Layout/Cutting/Marking: Spread the melton in a single layer with wrong-side up. Use duplicate pattern pieces. Cut the seams 1" (2.5mm) wide so they will lie flatter when pressed.

Stitching: To position bulky fabrics under the presser foot, cover the fabric with a small piece of water-soluble stabilizer so you can slide it under the foot easily.

Seams: Press seams open; then topstitch each side to hold the seams flat. For unlined garments, serge seam edges, then topstitch; or zigzag edges flat against garment.

Facings: For a separate facing, stitch the facing and garment together. Press the seam flat; then press it open. Trim the seam evenly to a scant ¼" (6mm). Fold the facing to the wrong side, and topstitch a generous ¼" (6mm) from the edge. To avoid bulk at the front edges, cut the facing in one piece with the front. Stabilize the folded edge with a strip of lightweight selvage so the edges will hang perpendicular to the floor even when the garment is unfastened.

Topstitching: Topstitching is especially attractive on simple, uncluttered designs; and it helps control bulk and hold seams flat. When topstitching over bulky seams, use a shim to balance the foot and prevent skipped stitches.

Pockets: Stabilize pocket openings to prevent stretching. To reduce bulk, line patch pockets and flaps with lining.

Pressing: Cover the pressing surface with wool. When pressing the right side, use a wool press cloth to avoid damaging the nap.

This handsome casual jacket is easy-fitting and comfortable to wear. (Photo courtesy of KWIK·SEW®.)

Similar Fabrics: Astrakan, baize, blazer cloth, bolivia, blanket cloth, buffalo cloth, camel's hair, cashmere, cavalry, chinchilla, coatings, duffel, fleece, friezé, homespun coating, jumbo corduroy, kersey, loden cloth, lumberjack, mackinac, molleton, ottoman, polo cloth, ratiné, wool fleece, wool velour, zibeline.

Uses: Tailored garments, loose fitting coats and jackets, capes, ponchos.

Design Elements: Simple structured designs, topstitching, fur or stand collars. Avoid fussy details, gathers, pleats.

Sewing Checklist

Essential Supplies

Needles: Universal (H); sizes 80/12-100/16.

Thread: All-purpose (cotton, polyester, cotton covered polyester). Topstitching – machine embroidery/topstitching (cotton, polyester, silk, rayon).

Cutting: Large, sharp shears; duplicate pattern pieces.

Marking: Chalk, clips, tailor's tacks, thread.

Miscellaneous: Flower pins, shim, water soluble stabilizer.

Interfacings: Sew-ins, hair canvas; fusibles, knit.

Lining: Generally (Bemberg or silk); underlining, rarely.

Machine Setup

Stitch Length: 2.5-3mm (8-10spi).

Tension: Lightly balanced; light pressure.

Feet: Wide straight stitch, zipper, zigzag.

Sewing Basics

Fabric Prep: Steam or dry clean.

Layout: Nap – single layer, right-side up.

Seams: Plain (pressed open or closed), topstitched, abutted.

Hems: Hand (blindstitch, blind catchstitch, catchstitch), double- or triple-stitched, interfaced, topstitched.

Seam/Hem Finishes: Serged, zigzag, tricot bound, Hong Kong binding, seam tape; if lined, none.

Edge Finishes: Facings (self-fabric, lining), bindings.

Closures: Buttonholes (machine, bound, inseam), buttons/loops, zippers (machine, decorative), toggles, frogs.

Pressing: Medium heat, steam; wool press cloth, clapper, point presser, needleboard.

Garment Care: Dry-clean.

Metallic

Metallic fabrics contain metal, plastic-coated metal, metal-coated fibers, or metal-wrapped core. Generally woven with the weaker metallic threads in the filling, they are available in a variety of structures with the metallic yarns throughout the fabric or concentrated in small areas.

Metallic Types: Brocade, embroideries, handwovens, knit, lace, lamé, matelassé, metallic denim, metallic organza mesh, saris, stretch lamé, tulle.
Uses: Evening/formal wear, jackets, coats, dresses, blouses, bustiers, skirts, pants.
Design Elements: Minimal seaming, bindings, pockets (welt, inseam). Avoid fussy details.

Sewing Checklist

Essential Supplies
Needles: Sharp (HM, HJ), stretch (HS), universal (H); sizes 60/8-90/14.
Thread: All-purpose (cotton, polyester, cotton covered polyester, silk). Topstitching – all-purpose, machine embroidery/topstitching.
Cutting: Old or stainless steel shears, rotary cutter/mat, duplicate pattern pieces.
Marking: Chalk, clips, tailor's tacks, erasable pens, safety pins.
Miscellaneous: Super fine pins, seam sealant, weights, ¼" (6mm) ribbon, stabilizers – water soluble, tearaway, cut away.
Interfacings: Optional, sew-in or low temp fusibles for details.
Linings/Underlinings: Generally for outerwear, formal designs, scratchy fabrics, and quality garments.

Machine Setup
Stitch Length: 2-3mm (8-12spi).
Tension: Lightly balanced; light pressure.
Machine Feet: Wide straight stitch, roller, zigzag.

Sewing Basics
Test Garment: Recommended.
Fabric Prep: To preshrink, hand wash or dry-clean, depending on manufacturer's recommendation.
Layout: Nap – double layer; single layer – right-side up to match patterns.
Seams: Plain (pressed open), tissue stitched.
Seam/Hem Finishes: Serged, zigzag, tricot binding, Hong Kong finish; if lined, none.
Hems: Hand (blindstitch, blind catchstitch, catchstitch), topstitched, twin needle.
Edge Finishes: Facings (self-fabric, lining, bias), bands, bindings, edge-to-edge linings.
Closures: Buttons/loops, buttonholes (machine, bound, inseam, corded), ties, snaps, zippers (hand, machine, invisible).
Pressing: Medium heat, dry iron.
Garment Care: Dry-clean or hand wash, depending on manufacturer's recommendation.

Workroom Secrets
Fabric Prep: Follow the manufacturer's recommendation or use the non-metallic fibers as a guide to select an appropriate method.
Layout/Cutting/Marking: When matching fabric patterns, spread in a single layer, right-side up. Use duplicate pattern pieces. To reduce fraying, do not cut until you are ready to sew and handle as little as possible after cutting. Use clips sparingly.
Stitching: Metallics dull needles quickly; replace as needed with new needles. Hand baste to avoid ripping.
Seams: Wide seams are easier to press flat than narrow ones.
Seam/Hem Finishes: For an elegant finish in unlined garments, use tricot binding, or Hong Kong finish with lightweight silk.
Underlinings: To prevent seam slippage, underline close fitting designs. To add body to lightweight or soft metallic fabrics, use sew-ins or fusibles. Experiment with fusibles to determine if the metallic yarns will be damaged by heat and/or steam.
Linings: To avoid skin irritations, line the garment or bind seams with tricot or chiffon.
Buttonholes: Use water soluble stabilizer on top of the fabric to prevent the stitches from embedding in the fabric.
Zippers: Stabilize the opening with lightweight selvage or tape to prevent stretching.
Pressing: Test press. Some metallics are damaged by steam and high heat.
Garment Care: To protect skirts and pants from clip hanger marks, sew in ribbon hanger loops at the waist.

This simply shaped coat is a stunning metallic knit. (Photo courtesy of Simplicity Patterns.)

Microfiber

Microfibers are finer than silk filaments. Made of manufactured fibers such as polyester, nylon, acrylic, and rayon, they can be woven, knit, or non-woven and used for a variety of fabric types and textures from sheer chiffon to velvet to synthetic suede and insulating material.

They are lightweight and combine the aesthetics and comfort of natural fibers with the easy care, durability, and versatility of manufactured fibers. Some fray badly; others, very little. All are difficult to ease.

Workroom Secrets

Fabric Prep: Preshrink to relax and soften fabric.

Layout/Cutting/Marking: Set pins parallel to selvage. Cut with serrated shears or rotary cutter/mat. Keep extra rotary cutting blades on hand; microfibers dull them quickly. Erasable pens are very convenient for marking, but they may stain permanently.

Stitching: Begin with a new needle with a sharp point (HM, HJ). Replace needles frequently.

Seams: When basting, use super fine pins. To reduce puckered seams, avoid seams on the straight grain. (See Any Fabric page 13.) Hold the fabric firmly in front of and behind the foot when stitching or stitch with a narrow zigzag (W,.5-L1.5). To flatten seams, topstitch.

Seam/Hem Finishes: To reduce thread imprints when serging, use textured thread in the loopers.

Buttonholes: Machine stitch with fine machine embroidery or very fine serger thread and a new needle in a small size.

Sleeves: To sew sleeves smoothly, reduce the ease in the cap. (See Any Fabric page 14.)

Pressing: Test press. Microfibers are easily damaged by heat and difficult to press. Always use a press cloth. To press seams, place on a seam roll or seam stick. Brush with 50/50 solution of white vinegar/water; press and cover with a clapper until cool.

Garment Care: To avoid permanent stains, remove any grease spots before laundering. I use talcum powder or fuller's earth—diatomaceous earth used by auto shops to absorb grease and in pools as a filter—which will absorb most stains.

Softly draped, this microfiber design is comfortable to wear and resistant to wrinkles. (Photo courtesy of New Look Patterns.)

Microfiber Fabrics: MicroFinesse, MicroMattique®, Micro-Supplex®, MicroSupreme®, rayon twill, sandwashed rayon, sandwashed Tencel®, Trevira Finess®, Satin Gab, Silky Touch®, Supplex®.

Uses: Casual sportswear, jackets, coats, pants, shorts, tops, raincoats, sleepwear, linings.

Design Elements: Minimal seaming; kimono, raglan, dolman, cap, and shirt sleeves; gathers, drapes, cowl necklines, and topstitching. Avoid sharp creases, tucks, pressed pleats, and designs which require hand sewing.

Sewing Checklist

Essential Supplies

Needles: Sharp (HM, HJ), universal (H); sizes 60/8-70/12.

Thread: Lightweight threads (polyester, cotton covered polyester, silk), textured thread. Topstitching – lightweight, all purpose.

Cutting: Sharp serrated shears, rotary cutter/mat.

Marking: Chalk, clips, erasable pens.

Miscellaneous: Super fine pins, brush, vinegar, water soluble stabilizer, talcum powder or fuller's earth.

Interfacings: Very lightweight sew-in or low-temp fusible, polyester organdy, Sewin' Sheer™; same care as fabric.

Linings/Underlinings: Optional, same care as fabric.

Machine Setup

Stitch length: 1-2mm (12-24spi), narrow zigzag (W,1-L,1)

Tension: Lightly balanced; light pressure.

Feet: Wide straight stitch, roller, zigzag.

Sewing Basics

Fabric Prep: Machine wash/dry.

Layout: Without nap – double layer.

Seams: Plain (pressed open or closed), topstitched.

Hems: Topstitched, fused, hand (blindstitch); avoid very narrow machine-rolled.

Seam/Hem Finishes: Serged, pinked.

Edge Finishes: Facings, bindings, ribbings, bands, casings.

Closures: Buttonholes (machine), buttons/loops, ties, toggles, zippers (machine, invisible, separating, decorative).

Pressing: Low to medium heat; steam, press cloth, seam roll, seam stick, clapper.

Garment Care: Machine wash/dry; better garments, dry-clean.

Mohair

Mohair is a hair fiber from the angora goat. Soft and comfortable to wear, it can be woven or knitted. Sewn and handled like wool, its textured surface helps to hide stitching irregularities. Mohair is easily damaged with improper pressing.

Similar Fabrics: Alpaca, angora, camel's hair, cashmere, llama, pashmina.

Uses: Skirts, pants, dresses, jackets, coats, capes, sweaters, baby blankets, lap robes.

Design Elements: Soft designs with minimal seaming, gathers, unpressed pleats, gored skirts, elastic waists. Avoid fussy details.

Sewing Checklist

Essential Supplies

Needles: Universal (H); sizes 60/8-70/12.

Thread: All-purpose (cotton, polyester, cotton covered polyester, silk). Topstitching – all-purpose, machine embroidery/topstitching.

Cutting: Sharp shears, rotary cutter/mat.

Marking: Clips, tailor's tacks, safety pins.

Miscellaneous: Flower pins, fusible web, burn away or water soluble stabilizer, wool press cloth.

Interfacings: Fusible, sew-in, hair canvas, weft-insertion, silk organza, polyester chiffon, China silk.

Linings: Depends on design.

Underlinings: Soft lightweight silks, very lightweight fusibles.

Machine Setup

Stitch Length: Woven fabrics, 2-3mm (8-12spi); knits, (W,.5-L,1.5).

Tension: Lightly balanced.

Feet: Wide straight stitch, zigzag, roller, even-feed.

Sewing Basics

Test Garment: Recommended; it is easily damaged by ripping.

Fabric Prep: Dry-clean.

Layout: Nap – single/double layer, depending on thickness.

Seams: Plain (pressed open), topstitched, taped.

Hems: Hand (blindstitch, catchstitch), twin needle.

Seam/Hem Finishes: Serged, zigzag, tricot binding, Hong Kong finish; if lined, none.

Edge Finishes: Facings (extended, lining, self-fabric), bindings, foldover braid, edge to edge lining.

Closures: Buttonholes (machine, corded, hand, bound, inseam), buttons/loops, zippers (hand, machine, invisible).

Pressing: Cool to medium heat, wool or self-fabric press cloth.

Garment Care: Dry-clean.

Workroom Secrets

Layout/Cutting/Marking: If the fabric looks the same on both sides, mark the right side with safety pins. Refold the fabric to avoid the original crease. Use flower pins to hold pattern pieces in place.

Stitching: Use polyester thread for more elastic seams. To avoid stretching the seams when stitching, stitch with the seam sandwiched between two layers of stabilizer. Generally, when stitching it is better to stitch with the nap than with the grain. Understitch by hand for a soft, inconspicuous finish.

Seams: Stabilize shoulder seams, necklines, and front edges.

Buttonholes: Stabilize machine and hand buttonholes with a small rectangle of lightweight fusible interfacing. Or use a small piece of fusible web, tucked between the layers. For machine buttonholes, use water soluble stabilizer on top of the fabric to prevent the stitches from embedding in the fabric.

Zippers: Use lightweight zippers, and stabilize the opening to prevent stretching.

Underlinings: To preserve the shape and prevent bagging, underline skirts, pants, and dresses with lightweight silk. For a softer, more tactile garment, cut the underlining on the bias. To add structure for coats, jackets, and capes, use lightweight hair canvas, knit or weft fusible interfacing, or hair canvas. When underlining with silk, quilt the layers together to prevent the mohair from sagging.

Pressing: Test press. Mohair is easily damaged by steaming and improper pressing. When steaming, watch for shrinking. Before pressing, cover the ironing board with a piece of wool. Use a wool or self-fabric press cloth when pressing the right side.

A couture jacket from Phillipe Venet, the classic princess line showcases this luxurious wool/mohair plaid. (Photo courtesy of Claire Shaeffer.)

Net and Tulle

Net and tulle are open-mesh fabrics. Available in cotton, silk, nylon, and polyester, they are easy to sew, transparent, do not fray, and have no grain or right side. They have more stretch in the width, tear easily, and are easily damaged with the point of the iron. When sewing stretch tulle, review Stretch Knit page 83.

Workroom Secrets

Layout/Cutting/Marking: When cutting multiple layers, use safety pins or flower pins to hold the layers together. To economize, pattern pieces can be tilted slightly; but you should avoid cutting some pieces on the straight grain and some on the crossgrain.

Stitching: To avoid snagging the net, use a roller or wide straight stitch foot or wrap the toes of the zigzag foot with transparent tape. To avoid tearing the net on the feed dogs, place a stabilizer under the net. When stitching nets with large holes, shorten the stitch length. To prevent puckered seams, stitch slowly .

Seam Finishes: To avoid scratchy seams, bind seams with tricot or flesh-colored chiffon. When both sides of the garment show, use French or faux French seams.

Edge Finishes: To avoid snagging your nylon hose, bind edges of net skirts or petticoats with ribbon, tricot, or fabric. To finish necklines and armholes inconspicuously, use narrow tulle or flesh-colored silk facings. To give hems more definition, use horsehair braid or zigzag over monofilament thread. To create decorative hems, use a merrow stitch, narrow zigzag, bias binding, or ribbon facing on the right side.

Underlinings: Net is an excellent support material, but it may have too much stretch in the width to stabilize the fashion fabric. If so, cut the net on the crossgrain. When making sleeve boosters to support gathered sleeve caps, cut a football shape about 10" (25cm) long from the net. Fold it in half lengthwise and gather the raw edges. Sew it into the armhole at the top of the cap. Use a skirt booster to support heavy, full skirts. Cut a net strip 60"-72" (150-180cm) wide and 18" (45cm) long. Fold the net in half; stitch ¾" (2cm) from the fold. Insert narrow braided elastic; pull up the elastic until it fits the waist comfortably. Stitch through all layers at each end; trim, and sew on a hook and eye at the waist.

Pressing: Avoid hot irons. Use a press cloth or tissue to press. To restore crispness, use spray starch.

Designed by Joi Mahon, this stunning gown features 100 yards of hand-dyed tulle skirt trimmed with satin-band hems and a beaded bodice. (Photo courtesy of Joi Mahon, Dress Forms Design Studio, LLC.)

Similar Fabrics: Athletic mesh, bobbinet, embroidered net, English net, illusion, maline, metallic net, point d'esprit, stretch tulle.

Uses: Special occasion and evening designs, wedding veils, petticoats, costumes, underlining, interfacing, sleeve boosters.

Design Elements: Minimal seaming, full skirts, bands, bindings, ribbon facings.

Sewing Checklist

Essential Supplies

Needles: Universal (H); sizes 70/10-80/12.

Thread: All-purpose (polyester, cotton, cotton covered polyester).

Cutting: Shears, rotary cutter/mat.

Marking: Clips, safety pins.

Miscellaneous: Flower pins, safety pins, transparent tape, spray starch, tricot binding, stabilizer.

Interfacings: Self-fabric.

Linings/Underlinings: Use for modesty or design.

Machine Setup

Stitch Length: 1.75-2.5mm (10-15spi).

Tension: Lightly balanced.

Feet: Wide straight stitch, roller, zigzag.

Sewing Basics

Test Garment: Rarely required.

Fabric Prep: Press to remove wrinkles.

Layout: Without nap – double layer.

Seams: Plain (open or closed), narrow, double-stitched, French, faux French, safety-stitch serged.

Seam/Hem Finishes: None, serged, bindings (tricot, tulle, chiffon).

Hems: None, narrow, merrow, horsehair braid, lace, wired.

Edge Finishes: Unfinished, bindings and bands (lightweight silk, satin, ribbon, tricot), facings (tulle, lightweight silk, ribbon).

Closures: Buttons/loops, buttonholes (machine, bound) covered snaps.

Pressing: Warm, dry heat; press cloth.

Garment Care: Machine wash/dry or dry-clean, depending on fiber and garment design.

Nylon

The first true synthetic, nylon is a polyamide made from hard, white chips which are melted and extruded through a spinnerette to form monofilaments. Known for its strength, durability, and resistance to abrasion, it is frequently blended with natural and other manufactured fibers to make fabrics in all weights and a variety of fabrications. It is available in bottom and top weights and can be woven, knitted, or nonwoven and used for all type fabrics from waterproof Cordura® to very sheer tulle.

Nylon dulls needles and scissors quickly; woven fabrics fray badly. It does not ease well, pills, retains static electricity, and soils easily. Skipped stitches and puckered seams are frequently a problem. It is easily damaged by hot irons and dull or damaged needles or pins.

Nylon Trademarks/Fabrics: Antron®, Antron III®, Cordura®, ninon, Qiana®, Helanca, Micro Supplex®, Silky Touch®, Supplex®, Ultron®, Wear-Dated®, waterproof fabrics, water-repellent fabrics.

Uses: Casual sportswear, blouses, dresses, lingerie, foundations, activewear, evening wear, rainwear, ski and swimwear, leotards, windbreakers.

Burn Test: Nylon shrinks from the flame, melts, and fuses. It has a white smoke, is self-extinguishing, smells like celery, and leaves a hard gray or tan bead.

Sewing Checklist

Essential Supplies

Needles: Woven fabrics – sharp (HM), universal (H). **Knit fabrics** – stretch (HS), universal (H), ballpoint (H-SUK). Sizes – lightweight nylons, 60/8-70/10; medium-weight, 70/10-80/12; heavy-weight, 80/12-90/14; very heavy-weight, 90/14-110/18.
Thread: Lightweight fabrics – lightweight (cotton, polyester, cotton covered polyester, silk), all purpose thread. **Medium-weight fabrics** – all purpose thread. **Heavy-weight fabrics** – machine embroidery/topstitching or all purpose threads. **Very heavy-weight fabrics** – machine embroidery/topstitching threads.
Cutting: Sharp shears; rotary cutter/mat.
Marking: Chalk, clips, erasable pens.
Miscellaneous: Super fine pins, flower pins, water soluble stabilizer, nylon stocking scrap.
Interfacings/Linings/Underlinings: Depends on the fabric weight, garment type, quality, and structure; same care properties.

Machine Setup

Stitch Length: Lightweight wovens – 1.5-1.75mm (15-18spi). **Medium-weight fabrics** – 2-2.5mm (10-12spi). **Heavy-weight fabrics** – 2.5-3mm (8-10spi). **Very heavy-weight fabrics** – 3-4mm (6-8spi). **Knits** – zigzag (W,.5-L,2).
Tension: Depends on the fabric.
Feet: Straight stitch, zigzag, roller, even-feed.

Sewing Basics

Test Garment: Rarely required.
Fabric Prep: Nylon fabrics do not shrink. Machine wash/dry to relax the fabric.
Layout: Knits – with nap; wovens – generally without nap.
Seams/Hems: Depends on the fabric weight, structure, and transparency; and garment quality, design, use, and care.
Seam/Hem Finishes: All types.
Closures: Buttonholes (machine, inseam), buttons/loops, ties, zippers (hand, machine, invisible).
Pressing: Medium heat, press cloth and steam.
Garment Care: Machine wash/dry or dry-clean, depending on garment structure and quality.

Workroom Secrets

Stitching: Start all new projects with a new needle in the smallest recommended size. Change needles frequently; nylon dulls needles faster than natural fiber fabrics. To check the needle for burrs, stitch through an old nylon stocking. Use polyester or textured thread for more elastic seams. Wind the bobbin slowly. When wound on high, the thread heats up and stretches; then, when sewn into the seam, it relaxes and the seam puckers. Puckered seams cannot be pressed out. To reduce stitching problems, use a wide straight stitch foot and a small-hole throat plate. Hold fabric firmly in front and back of foot when stitching.

Pressing: Test press. Use warm heat; nylon is easily damaged by hot irons.

Garment Care: Sort garments according to color and soil. Nylon will pick up both during the washing process. Use warm water to machine wash with fabric softener in final rinse. Dry on low temperature. To reduce static electricity, do not overdry. Quality sportswear will maintain its pristine appearance longer when dry-cleaned.

Fabricated in a quick drying nylon/spandex, this two piece swimsuit is ideal for a custom fit. (Photo courtesy of KWIK-SEW®.)

Organza

Organza is a crisp, lightweight, transparent fabric. Usually silk or polyester, it is durable, comfortable to wear, and easy to press. It wrinkles, has little elasticity, varies in transparency, and may fray badly.

Workroom Secrets

Layout/Cutting/Marking: Mark the right side of each section with a cross-stitch. Spread fabric in a double layer; pin selvages together. Lay out pattern and pin only in the seam allowances. Cut, using sharp, serrated shears or a rotary cutter/mat.

Basting: Hand baste to ensure stitching accuracy and prevent ripping. Pin baste with super fine pins or fine needles (sizes 9-12).

Stitching: Begin with a new, sharp (HM) needle. Use a wide straight stitch or roller foot to reduce stitching problems; or use a zigzag foot, and move the needle to the right-hand position.

Sandwich stitch seams. Sandwich and pin the organza seam between strips of water soluble stabilizer. Stitch; then steam press to remove the stabilizer. When stitching curves, shorten the stitch length. Do not backstitch; knot the thread ends.

Seams/Darts: To make seams inconspicuous, bind seams with flesh-colored chiffon or trim very evenly. When both sides of the garment show, use French or faux French seams. Trim dart to $1/4$" (6mm) and overcast edges by hand or zigzag (W,2-L,2).

Hems: Very narrow and wide double hems are most attractive.

Edge Finishes: To avoid unattractive facing shadows, replace facings with bindings, edge-to-edge linings, or underlinings. When facings cannot be avoided, cut them straight or make them part of the overall design element.

Buttonholes: To machine stitch, sandwich the organza between two layers of water soluble stabilizer. Stitch with a fine, sharp (HM) needle and lightweight embroidery thread.

Pressing: Test press; organza is easily damaged by improper pressing and too much heat.

Cool and crisp, this organza jacket is the perfect topper for chilly summer evenings. (Burda Pattern – 8789, courtesy of Burda.)

Similar Fabrics: Cotton organdy, dotted swiss, gazar, leno, marquisette, mikado organza, ninon, organzine, satin faced organza, voile.

Uses: Special occasion designs, dresses, coats, blouses, skirts, jackets, underlinings, interfacings, sleeve heads and boosters.

Design Elements: Gathers, pleats, tucks, lace trims and insertions. Avoid bound buttonholes unless the section is underlined.

Sewing Checklist

Essential Supplies

Needles: Sharp (HM, HJ), universal (H); sizes 60/8-70/10.

Thread: Lightweight (cotton, polyester, cotton covered polyester, silk), lightweight serger thread, all purpose. Topstitching – lightweight or all purpose. Serger – lightweight serger thread.

Cutting: Sharp, serrated shears, rotary cutter/mat, tissue.

Marking: Chalk, clips, erasable pens, tailor's tacks, thread.

Miscellaneous: Super fine pins/needles, weights, flesh-colored chiffon, water-soluble stabilizer, tissue.

Interfacings: Lightweight sew-ins, self-fabric, lightweight silks, polyester chiffon, georgette.

Linings/Underlinings: Optional for modesty, color, or design.

Machine Setup

Stitch Length: 2-2.5mm (10-12spi).

Tension: Lightly balanced.

Feet: Wide straight stitch, roller; small hole throat plate.

Sewing Basics

Test Garment: Depends on design.

Fabric Prep: Preshrink with steam, wash/dry, or dry-clean. Most organzas soften only a little when washed.

Layout: Without nap – double layer.

Seams: Plain (pressed open or closed), topstitched, French, faux French, bound.

Hems: Narrow hems – machine-rolled, merrow, satin stitched, lettuce, shirttail; wide double hems – topstitch or hand (blindstitch, catchstitch).

Seam/Hem Finishes: Serged, zigzag, bindings (tricot, tulle, chiffon), hand overcast.

Edge Finishes: Facings (bias, tulle, ribbon, decorative), bindings, edge-to-edge linings.

Closures: Buttonholes (machine, bound, inseam), buttons/loops, zippers (hand, machine), snaps, hooks/eyes.

Pressing: Medium heat; steam, press cloth.

Garment Care: Dry-clean to maintain the garment's pristine appearance. Wash/dry casual designs if fabric was pretreated.

Plaid

Plaid fabrics have bars and spaces on both the lengthwise grains and crossgrains. Available in all fibers and weights, they can be woven, knitted, or printed.

Avoid plaids which are printed, woven, or knitted off-grain.

All plaids require additional fabric for matching. For small plaids, purchase an extra ¼ to ½ yard; for large ones, ½ to 1 yard.

Plaid Fabrics: Gingham, Glen plaid, madras, tartans, houndstooth, tattersall, windowpane check.

Uses: All type garments.

Design Elements: Simple designs, minimal seaming, piped seams, bias details, bindings, bands. Avoid patterns which are "not suitable for plaids."

Sewing Checklist

Essential Supplies

Needles: Woven fabrics – sharp (HM), universal (H). **Knit fabrics** – stretch (HS), universal (H), ballpoint (H-SUK). Sizes – lightweight, 60/8-70/10; medium-weight, 70/10-80/12; heavy-weight, 80/12-90/14; very heavy-weight, 90/14-120/20.

Thread: Size/fiber depends on fabric weight and elasticity and the garment design and use.

Cutting: Sharp shears, rotary cutter/mat, duplicate pattern pieces.

Marking: Chalk, clips, pins, safety pins, erasable pens.

Miscellaneous: Small safety pins, washable glue stick, double-stick washable tape, temporary adhesive spray.

Interfacings/Linings/Underlinings: All types depending on the fabric and garment design.

Machine Setup

Stitch Length: Lightweight fabrics – 1.5-1.75mm (15-18spi). **Medium-weight fabrics** – 2-2.5mm (10-12spi). **Heavy-weight fabrics** – 2.5-3mm (8-10spi). **Very heavy-weight fabrics** – 3-4mm (6-8spi). **All weights** – zigzag (W,.5-L,2).

Tension: Depends on the fabric.

Feet: Even-feed, roller, zigzag.

Sewing Basics

Test Garment: Recommended for quality fabrics and intricate designs.

Fabric Prep: Depends on fabric, garment design, quality, and use.

Layout: Nap or without nap, depending on plaid pattern; single layer, duplicate pattern pieces.

Seams: Plain (pressed open or closed), piped, lapped.

Hems/Edge Finishes: All types, depending on fabric and design.

Seam/Hem Finishes: All types.

Closures: Buttonholes (machine, bound, inseam), buttons/loops, ties, zippers (hand, machine, invisible).

Pressing: Depends on the fiber and fabric.

Garment Care: Depends on fiber content, fabric structure, and garment quality.

Workroom Secrets

Test Garment: Recommended when sewing quality fabrics and intricate designs.

Fabric Prep: Depends on manufacturer's recommendation, fiber content, fabric structure, garment design, quality, and use.

Layout/Cutting/Marking: A nap layout is often preferred. Spread the fabric in a single layer, right-side up, and use duplicate pattern pieces. When possible, lay out pieces so adjoining seams are next to each other. Lay out the pattern pieces, matching the plaid pattern at center front, center back, and side seams. Match the sleeve and front about 4" below the shoulder seam; the sleeve may not match at the back. Front and back shoulder seams do not have to match. Always match the seamlines, not the cutting lines. This is frequently easier if you trim away or fold back the seam allowances on the tissue pattern. Lay out the pieces so the stitching lines match. Using chalk, measure and mark the cutting lines on the fabric. To create a different look, cut small sections and/or sleeves on the bias. Do not cut major pieces on the bias; the bias will stretch vertically, making it too small in the width.

Designer Tip: To match pockets, flaps, and welts, begin by marking the location on the garment sections. Lay the smaller pattern piece on the garment section. Place a fabric scrap on the tissue pattern, matching the plaid pattern. Tape it in place. Remove the small pattern. Lay it on the fabric to be cut, matching the plaid design, and cut. (This also works for sleeves.)

Designed by Susan Fears, this smashing ensemble is a wool/mohair blend. (Photo courtesy of Susan Fears and photographer

Stitching: Use the fabric weight and structure as a guide when choosing needle types and sizes. Then make a test seam. Using an even-feed or roller foot, stitch directionally with the grain, generally from the bottom to the top. When pin basting, set the pins on the seamlines with the heads toward the raw edges. Insert every other pin from the underside. Stitch, removing the pins as you go to avoid stitching over them. If you must stitch over them, stitch slowly and walk the machine over each pin. When stitching knits, use a narrow zigzag (W,.5-L,2) for a more elastic seam.

Seams: The most popular seams include plain, piped, and lapped. When the plaids do not match, insert piping between the sections. To stitch lapped seams accurately, press under the seam allowance on the overlap. Right sides up, align the seamlines and baste the sections together with a glue stick, double-stick washable tape, temporary adhesive spray, or pins. Edgestitch close to the folded edge.

Buttonholes: All types of buttonholes—machine, hand, bound, inseam—are suitable. For bound buttonholes, cut the strips on the bias and cord them so they will not stretch out of shape.

This simply-styled skirt is smart and easy to sew. (Photo courtesy of KWIK·SEW®.)

Plaid Types

Repeat: One complete plaid pattern. Some hand-woven fabrics do not have a regular repeat.

Even Plaid: A perfect square. The color bars and spaces are balanced: same size, color, and sequence horizontally and vertically; and when folded diagonally through the center of the repeat, the fold is on the true bias and the bars and spaces match.

Uneven Plaid: A rectangular repeat which is not a perfect square. An uneven plaid can be balanced crosswise with a symmetrical arrangement of vertical bars, lengthwise with a symmetrical arrangement of horizontal bars, or in both directions. When balanced in both directions, it looks like an even plaid, but it forms a rectangle instead of a square.

Balanced Plaid: A symmetrical arrangement of color bars and spaces. When folded through the center of the repeat, the two halves are identical. Plaids can be balanced crosswise, lengthwise, or both. They can be even or uneven.

Unbalanced Plaid: An uneven plaid which, when folded into quarters has four different quarters. They have no center of design, but usually have a repeat.

Pleated Fabric

Pleated fabrics can be purchased or custom made of manufactured or natural fibers and heat set to hold their pleats permanently. They are generally pleated on the crossgrain. Many fabrics do not drape well and are easily damaged by careless handling.

Pleated Types and Similar Fabrics: Accordian, crystal, marii, and sunburst pleating; crinkle fabrics, plissé.

Uses: Dresses, pull-on skirts and pants, tops.

Design Details: Minimal seaming, elastic casings, bound edges, lettuce hems, surplice necklines.

Sewing Checklist

Essential Supplies

Needles: Sharp (HM, HJ), universal (H); sizes 60/8-80/12.

Thread: All-purpose (cotton, polyester, cotton covered polyester, silk), nylon, monofilament.

Cutting: Shears, rotary cutter/mat, duplicate pattern pieces.

Marking: Chalk, clips, pins, erasable pens.

Miscellaneous: Monofilament thread, 20-lb. fishing line, stay tape, vinegar, spray bottle, ¼" (6mm) ribbon, safety pins, small trimming scissors.

Interfacings: Avoid fusibles.

Linings/Underlinings: Outerwear, quality garments.

Machine Setup

Stitch Length: 2-2.5mm (10-12spi).

Tension: Lightly balanced; light pressure.

Feet: Zigzag, wide straight stitch.

Sewing Basics

Test Garment: Rarely required.

Fabric Prep: Rarely needed.

Layout: Without nap – single layer, right-side up.

Seams: Plain (pressed closed), safety-stitch serged, taped.

Seam/Hem Finishes: Serged, zigzag.

Hems: Hand (blindstitch, catchstitch), machine rolled, pin, lettuce, merrow, satinstitch, selvage.

Edge Finishes: Facings (smooth fabric, tulle, tricot, organza), bands, bindings, casings.

Closures: Buttonholes (machine), buttons/loops, zippers (invisible, hand, machine).

Pressing: Warm, dry setting.

Garment Care: Dry-clean.

Workroom Secrets

Layout/Cutting/Marking: Spread fabric in a single layer, right-side up. Smooth it until it lies flat without stretching. Most pleated fabrics do not have a nap. Lay out pattern pieces so the grainline is parallel to pleats. Use duplicate pattern pieces to avoid cutting two left sleeves. Place pins in the seam allowances.

Stitching: To avoid distorting seams and edges, use the pattern pieces as a guide to stabilize the neckline, armholes, and all seams on the bias or crossgrain with lightweight selvage or tape. (See Any Fabric page 13.)

Hems: For a quick and easy finish, place the selvage edge at the hemline. For fluted edges, turn under the selvage and stretch; zigzag (W,2-L,1). For more fluting, zigzag over monofilament nylon or 20-lb. fishing line. If there is no selvage at the hem edge, use small scissors to trim close to the stitching. For a softer hem, turn under ¼" (6mm) and blindstitch by hand. If desired, use small glass beads to give the hem weight.

Edge Finishes: Bias bindings made from unpleated self- or contrast fabrics are particularly attractive. When using pleated self-fabric, stretch and pin the fabric flat. Spray with white vinegar and cover with a damp cloth. Use a hot iron and press quickly until dry. Repeat as needed until flat.

Underlinings: To stabilize garment sections and control stretch, underline with organza or other lightweight silks.

Closures: Zippers and buttonholes are less conspicuous when placed parallel to the pleats. When the pleats are perpendicular to a zipper opening, bind the edges of the opening with self-fabric before setting the zipper.

Pressing: Avoid overpressing. Use plenty of steam and finger press.

Garment Care: To protect skirts and pants from clip hanger marks, sew in ribbon hanger loops at the waist.

"Go for Baroque" designed by Marinda Stewart for the Fairfield "Heart and Soul" Fashion Show 1999-2000, the simple pleated skirt is the perfect companion for the richly embellished jacket. (Design 163; photo courtesy of Frank Biemer and Fairfield Processing Corporation, Inc.)

Polyester

The most popular synthetic, polyester is produced from petroleum by-products. Known for its durability and easy care properties, it is frequently blended with natural and other manufactured fibers to make fabrics in top and bottom weights and a variety of fabrications. Polyester fabrics can be woven, knitted, or nonwoven and used for all type fabrics from luxury lingerie to heavy outerwear.

Workroom Secrets

Layout/Cutting/Marking: Nap layout, depending on the fabric. If foldline does not press out, refold and cut around it, or position the fold inconspicuously. Before cutting, redraw seams on the straight grain so they are on a slight bias to prevent puckering. Do not tilt sections off-grain. (See Any Fabric page 14.) Use erasable pens with care; they may stain some fabrics permanently. Polyester dulls rotary cutter blades quickly; change blades frequently.

Stitching: Begin with a new needle in the smallest recommended size. Change needles frequently; synthetic fibers dull needles faster than natural fibers. Use a wide straight stitch foot. Use polyester thread for more elastic seams. Wind the bobbin slowly. When wound on high, the thread heats up and stretches; then, when sewn into the seam, it relaxes and the seam puckers. Puckered seams cannot be pressed out. Hold fabric firmly in front and back of foot when stitching. Understitch or topstitch to keep facings from rolling to the outside.

Pressing: Test press; polyesters are difficult to press and are easily damaged by hot irons. To press seams, place on a seam stick wrong-side up. Brush with a 50/50 solution of white vinegar. Press and cover with a clapper until cool. Repeat if necessary.

Garment Care: Treat any stains immediately. Use dress shields to protect garments. Many polyesters retain body odors. Machine wash casual wear in warm water. To reduce static electricity, add fabric softener to the final rinse. Dry on low temperature, and remove garment immediately to avoid unwanted wrinkles and static electricity. Dry-clean to maintain the garment's pristine appearance.

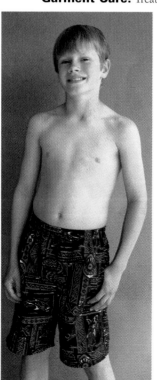

Versatile as well as practical, polyester is easy care and looks great in many fabrications. (Photo courtesy of Claire Shaeffer.)

Polyester Trademarks: Comfort Fiber®, Dacron®, Ecofil, ESP®, Fortel®, MicroFinesse, MicroMattique®, Trevira®, Trevira Finesse®.

Uses: All type garments, tailored and dressy ensembles, crisp and draped designs, casual sportswear, activewear, lingerie, foundations, rainwear, windbreakers.

Burn Test: Polyester shrinks from the flame, melts, and fuses. It has a black smoke, is self-extinguishing, has a sweet smell, and leaves a hard black or brown bead.

Sewing Checklist

Essential Supplies

Needles: Woven fabrics – sharp (HM), universal (H). **Knit fabrics** – stretch (HS), universal (H), ballpoint (H-SUK). Sizes – lightweight, 60/8-70/10; medium-weight, 70/10-80/12; heavy-weight, 80/12-90/14.

Thread: Lightweight fabrics – lightweight (polyester, cotton covered polyester), all purpose thread. **Medium-weight fabrics** – all purpose thread. **Heavy-weight fabrics** – all purpose, machine embroidery/topstitching threads. **Very heavy-weight fabrics** – machine embroidery/topstitching threads.

Cutting: Stainless steel shears; rotary cutter/mat.

Marking: Chalk, clips, erasable pens, pins.

Miscellaneous: Super fine pins, water soluble stabilizer.

Interfacings/Linings/Underlinings: All types, depending on the fabric structure and weight, garment design and quality.

Machine Setup

Stitch Length: Lightweight fabrics – 1.5-1.75mm (15-18spi). **Medium-weight fabrics** – 2-2.5mm (10-12spi). **Heavy-weight fabrics** – 2.5-3mm (8-10spi). **Very heavy-weight fabrics** – 3-4mm (6-8spi). **All weights** – zigzag (W,.5-L,2).

Tension: Depends on the fabric.

Feet: Straight stitch, zigzag, roller; small hole throat plate.

Sewing Basics

Test Garment: Rarely required.

Fabric Prep: Most polyesters do not shrink, but preshrinking relaxes the fabric and removes excess finishes, making it easier to sew.

Layout: Depends on fabric.

Seams/Hems/Edge Finishes: Depends on the fabric weight, structure, and transparency; garment quality, design, and use.

Closures: Buttonholes (machine, bound, inseam), buttons/loops, ties, zippers (hand, machine, invisible).

Pressing: Medium heat; steam.

Garment Care: Dry-clean or launder.

Quilted Fabric

Quilted fabrics can be purchased or custom made. They have three layers: face fabric, filling, and backing. Single-faced fabrics have a lightweight cheesecloth, gauze, or tricot backing. Double-faced fabrics have two face fabrics.

Easy-to-sew and available in a variety of materials, quilted fabrics are bulky, crisp, and stand away from the body. Many have a quilted or printed one-way design.

Quilted Types/Similar Fabrics: Broadcloth, calico, corduroy, nylon, satin, and velvet quilteds; matelassé.

Uses: Casual or dressy designs, depending on the face fabric. Jackets, coats, capes, ponchos, skirts, vests, robes, loungewear, place mats.

Design Elements: Minimal seaming, bindings, kimono and raglan sleeves, collarless designs, turned back cuffs. Avoid pleats, tucks, gathers, and notched collars.

Sewing Checklist

Essential Supplies

Needles: Sharp (HM, HJ), quilting (HQ); universal (H); sizes 80/10-100/16.

Thread: All-purpose (cotton, polyester, cotton covered polyester). Topstitching – machine embroidery/topstitching, all-purpose.

Cutting: Sharp shears; rotary cutter/mat, duplicate pattern pieces.

Marking: Chalk, clips, erasable pens, pins.

Miscellaneous: Flower pins, shim, safety pins, permanent felt tip pens, transparent tape, temporary pattern adhesive, fusible fabric spray, fusible web, stabilizers – water soluble, tear-away.

Interfacings: Generally, not used for double-faced fabrics.

Linings/Underlinings: Usually to hide an unattractive backing on single-faced fabrics.

Machine Setup

Stitch Length: 2.5-3mm (8-10spi).

Tension: Lightly balanced.

Feet: Zigzag, roller, even-feed, wide straight stitch.

Sewing Basics

Test Garment: Rarely required.

Fabric Prep: Machine wash/dry or steam press.

Layout: Nap – single layer, right-side up, duplicate pattern pieces.

Seams: Plain (pressed open or closed), topstitched, decorative serged, bindings, strap.

Seam/Hem Finishes: Serged, zigzag, bound (tricot, lightweight fabric, seam tape).

Hems: Hand (blindstitch, catchstitch), single fold, topstitch, fuse, wrong-side out.

Edge Finishes: Bindings, piping, foldover braid, facings (traditional, decorative), edge-to-edge lining.

Closures: Buttonholes (machine, corded, inseam), buttons/loops, frogs, toggles, ties, zippers.

Workroom Secrets

Fabric/Pattern Prep: When shrinking by machine, serge ends or join them to prevent unraveling. To reduce bulk, eliminate straight seams by pinning pattern pieces together on seamlines and cutting them in one piece. (See Any Fabric page 14.)

Layout: If fabric is printed off grain, decide whether the quilted stitches, grain, or fabric pattern is most important when planning the layout. Spread the fabric in a single layer, right-side up. Lay out the pattern using duplicate pattern pieces.

Stitching: To avoid damaging quilted materials with a gauze backing, tissue stitch with stabilizer between the fabric and feed dogs. To reduce raveling and prevent stretching, staystitch edges just inside the seamline.

Seams: When selecting the seam type or finish, consider the garment type, the fabric, whether it has a lining, and your personal taste. On double-faced fabrics, clean finish seams on the inside by stitching seams with wrong sides together. Finish the edges with decorative serging or cover the seam with a strap or binding.

Buttonholes: To machine stitch, cover fabric with water soluble stabilizer to prevent the stitches from embedding in the fabric. Use a permanent felt tip pen to color the batting.

Lining: To convert a single-faced quilted to a double-faced fabric, apply a contrast fabric to the wrong side, using fusible web or fusible fabric spray. The latter will be more supple.

Always in style, this smart jacket has a relaxed fit. (Butterick Pattern – 3577; courtesy of The McCall Pattern Co.)

Raschel Knit

Raschel knits are versatile warp knits, and run the gamut from fine, lightweight machine-made laces to bulky, three-dimensional sweater knits with little or no stretch. This chapter focuses on raschel knits with little or no stretch, including bulky, sweater-like fabrics which have looped yarns, chenille or embroidered-type designs on the right side and parallel rows of chainstitching on the wrong side. Many shrink or pill and cannot be straightened if off-grain.

Workroom Secrets

Fabric Prep: Preshrink or let fabric relax overnight before cutting.

Layout/Cutting/Marking: Use flower pins to secure the pattern. Mark construction details with safety pins.

Stitching: Use a roller foot to avoid snagging the fabric; or wrap the toes of the zigzag foot with transparent tape. When stitching, stop occasionally with the needle down. Raise the foot so the fabric can relax. Lower the foot and continue. Use a shim when crossing bulky seams.

Seams: Tape seams at shoulders, neck, and waist to prevent stretching. (See Any Fabric page 13.)

Hems: To prevent rippling when topstitching, fuse a strip of lightweight knit interfacing to the hem allowance; then topstitch. If the topstitching looks crooked, experiment with a narrow zigzag stitch (W,.5-L,2).

Facings: Understitch or topstitch to prevent facings from rolling to the outside.

Buttonholes: When possible, replace machine buttonholes with a zipper; or face the buttonhole area with grosgrain ribbon or firmly woven fabric. If buttonholes cannot be avoided, cord the buttonholes and use water soluble stabilizer on top of fabric to prevent the stitches from embedding in the fabric.

Zippers: Stabilize the opening with a strip of fusible interfacing applied to the seam allowances. Hand stitch zippers on quality designs. On bulky fabrics, machine stitch the opening; then sew the zipper in by hand.

This simply styled sweater is ideal for a novelty raschel knit. (Burda Pattern – 8804; photo courtesy of Burda.)

Similar Fabrics: Crochet lace knit, mali, malimo, wool lace.

Uses: Casual wear, unlined jackets, coats, tops, dresses, skirts, sweaters, sweatshirts.

Design Elements: Minimal seaming, easy fitting shapes, elastic waistbands, collarless cardigans, bindings, ribbings, foldover braids, bands.

Sewing Checklist

Essential Supplies

Needles: Universal (H), twin needles; sizes 80/12-90/14.

Thread: All purpose (cotton, polyester, cotton covered polyester), textured thread. Topstitching – machine embroidery/topstitching threads, textured thread, all purpose.

Cutting: Sharp shears, rotary cutter/mat, duplicate pattern pieces.

Marking: Chalk, clips, erasable pens, safety pins.

Miscellaneous: Flower pins, shim, safety pins, transparent tape, grosgrain.

Interfacings: Rarely. Weft or knit fusibles.

Linings: Optional.

Machine Setup

Stitch Length: 2.5-3mm (8-10spi), narrow zigzag (W,.5-L,2).

Tension: Lightly balanced.

Feet: Roller, wide straight stitch, even-feed, zigzag.

Sewing Basics

Test Garment: Rarely needed.

Fabric Prep: Preshrink appropriately for fiber content and planned care. Purchase additional fabric to wash and dry.

Layout: Nap – double layer; bulky fabrics – single layer with duplicate pattern pieces.

Seams: Plain (pressed open or closed), taped, strap.

Seam/Hem Finishes: Serged, zigzag, tricot binding, Hong Kong finish.

Hems: Topstitch (single or twin needle), fused, hand (blindstitch, catchstitch), faced.

Edge Finishes: Facings (self-fabric, contrast fabric, lining, bias), bindings (jersey, faux leather/suede), foldover braid, bands, ribbing.

Closures: Buttonholes (machine, corded, inseam); buttons/loops, zippers (machine, invisible), ties.

Pressing: Medium heat, damp cloth or steam.

Garment Care: Machine wash/dry or dry-clean, depending on fiber content and garment design.

Rayon

The oldest manufactured fiber, rayon was introduced in 1884 and called "artificial silk." The name "rayon" was adopted in 1924. A cellulosic fiber, it is made from wood pulp and passed through spinnerettes to form filaments.

A very versatile fiber, rayon can be made to look like cotton, linen, wool, or silk. It is known for its softness, drapeability, sheen, and absorbency. Comfortable to wear, easy to dye, and economical, it is resistant to moths, static electricity, and pilling. It ravels badly, fades, deteriorates when exposed to light for long periods, burns rapidly, and shrinks.

Most rayons are made by the viscose process. It is called "rayon" in the United States, "viscose" and "modal" in the United Kingdom, and "fibranne" in France. All are similar in quality.

There are three types of viscose rayon: regular, high tenacity, and high-wet-modulus. High tenacity rayons are stronger and more resistant to abrasion and wrinkling. High-wet-modulus rayons are firmer than regular viscose, stronger when wet or dry, and absorb less moisture.

Cupramonium rayon is made by a different process. Used to make chiffon, satin, net, ninon, and other sheer fabrics, the filaments are finer and stronger than viscose. Bemberg is a high-quality silk-like lining.

Uses: Accessories, blouses, dresses, jackets, lingerie, linings, pants, sportswear, suits.

Design Details: Draped designs, soft pleats, gathers.

Burn Test: Rayon burns rapidly with an afterglow, leaving a small amount of light, fluffy ash. It smells like paper or rags.

Rayon Fabrics/Trademarks: Challis, chiffon, crepe, damask, Fibro®, Galaxy, interfacings, linings, net, rayon blends, sandwashed, satin, slinky, velour, velvet, Viscose by Lenzing.

Sewing Checklist

Essential Supplies

Needles: Woven fabrics – sharp (HM), universal (H). **Knit fabrics** – stretch (HS), universal (H), ballpoint (H-SUK). Sizes – lightweight, 60/8-70/10; medium-weight, 70/10-80/12; heavyweight, 80/12-90/14.

Thread: Lightweight fabrics – lightweight (cotton, polyester, cotton covered polyester, silk), all purpose thread. **Medium-weight fabrics** – all purpose thread. **Heavy-weight fabrics** – all purpose, machine embroidery/topstitching threads. **Very heavy-weight fabrics** – machine embroidery/topstitching threads.

Cutting: Lightweight fabrics – serrated shears; other fabrics – sharp shears; rotary cutter/mat.

Marking: Chalk, clips, erasable pens, pins.

Miscellaneous: Fine pins, water soluble stabilizer.

Interfacings/Linings/Underlinings: All types, depending on the fabric structure and garment design.

Machine Setup

Stitch Length: Lightweight fabrics – 1.5-1.75mm (15-18spi). **Medium-weight fabrics** – 2-2.5mm (10-12spi). **Heavy-weight fabrics** – 2.5-3mm (8-10spi). **Very heavy-weight fabrics** – 3-4mm (6-8spi). **All weights** – zigzag (W,.5-L,2).

Tension: Depends on the fabric.

Feet: Straight stitch, zigzag, roller foot.

Sewing Basics

Test Garment: Rarely required.

Fabric Prep: Machine wash/dry, steam, or dry-clean.

Layout: Double layer without nap.

Seams: All types.

Hems/Edge Finishes: All types, depending on fabric and design.

Seam/Hem Finishes: Serged, pinked, zigzag.

Closures: Buttonholes (machine), buttons/loops, ties, zippers (hand, machine, invisible).

Pressing: Medium heat; press cloth and steam.

Garment Care: Clean the garment using the method to preshrink.

Workroom Secrets

Fabric Prep: Check the bolt when purchasing. Washability depends on the rayon type, fabric weave, and garment design. Many rayons will shrink and waterspot if laundered. It has progressive shrinkage and may waterspot or streak when wet. Machine wash on gentle or hand wash in cold water with cold rinse; machine dry on low and remove while damp. Shake well and hang to dry on a plastic hanger. Using medium heat, press as needed from the wrong side before the garment dries. When pressing from the right side, use a press cloth. When hand washing, rinse thoroughly. Press excess water out; do not wring or twist.

Garment Care: If the fabric was preshrunk, launder it using the same method. Dry-clean it to maintain the garment's pristine appearance.

Soft and sheer, this rayon georgette skirt features a unique stripe design. (Burda Pattern – 8666; photo courtesy of Burda.)

Rayon Challis

One of the most popular rayon fabrics, rayon challis is a lightweight, plain weave fabric. It is soft, drapeable, and comfortable to wear. It dyes well and is frequently used for prints. It ravels badly, wrinkles easily, fades, shrinks, and is easily damaged by hot irons. When sewing cotton challis, see Batiste page 17; for wool challis, see Wools – Lightweight page 103.

Workroom Secrets

Fabric Prep: Preshrink. Check the care label when purchasing. Some challis can be hand or machine washed in cold water; many cannot. Most will shrink more when washed than when dry-cleaned. For dry-clean only fabrics, steam or dry-clean to preshrink. Before preshrinking washable rayons, serge the raw edges to prevent raveling. Wash at least three times to preshrink.

Stitching: To preserve the fabric's soft drape, use lightweight threads for seams. Begin with a new sharp (HM) needle. To reduce stitching problems, use a straight stitch foot. Hold fabric firmly in front of and behind the presser foot when stitching. Tissue stitch seams to reduce puckering.

Seams: To avoid fraying when laundered, finish seams with serging or zigzagging; or use topstitched or safety-stitch serged seams. To maintain the softness and drape at seamlines, press the seams open and serge or zigzag separately with lightweight serger or textured thread. Avoid bound finishes. Substitute topstitched seams for flat fell seams.

Topstitching: To flatten seams and edges, topstitch. For dressier designs, topstitch close to the edge or seam. For sportswear, lengthen the stitch and topstitch ¼" (6mm) away.

Buttonholes: Before stitching, spray area with starch to add body or place water-soluble stabilizer on top before stitching. Stitch using a new sharp needle and lightweight thread.

Zippers: Use a lightweight zipper. Stabilize opening to prevent stretching.

Interfacings: Lightweight sew-ins and low-temp fusibles work well. Many crisp interfacings will overwhelm the fabric.

Pressing: Rayon challis is easily damaged by hot irons. Test press to determine the appropriate heat, moisture, and pressure.

Soft and drapeable, the Keesamba and Kintamani ensembles feature hand-dyed and hand-stamped batik prints. (Photo courtesy of The Batik Butik.)

Similar Types/Fabrics: Lyocell, modal, rayon batik, lightweight rayon twill, Tencel® challis, sandwashed Tencel®, viscose.

Uses: Casual wear, blouses, skirts, pants, dresses, unstructured jackets and coats.

Design Elements: Gored skirts, topstitching, soft pleats, gathers, elastic waists, draped designs, cowl necklines. Avoid close fitting designs.

Sewing Checklist

Essential Supplies

Needle types: Sharp (HM, HJ), universal (H); sizes 70/10-80/12; twin needle.

Thread: All purpose (cotton, polyester, cotton covered polyester). Topstitching – all purpose, machine embroidery/topstitching threads.

Cutting: Sharp shears, rotary cutter/mat.

Marking: Chalk, clips, erasable pens, pins.

Miscellaneous: Lightweight zippers, spray starch, stabilizers – water soluble, tearaway.

Interfacings: Lightweight, low-temp fusibles, sew-ins, same care properties as fashion fabric.

Machine Setup

Stitch Length: 2mm-2.5mm (10-12spi).

Tension: Balanced.

Feet: Wide straight stitch, zigzag; small hole throat plate.

Sewing Basics

Test Garment: Not required.

Fabric Prep: Machine wash/dry, steam or dry-clean, depending on manufacturer's recommendation and garment quality.

Layout: Without nap – double layer, right sides together.

Seams: Plain (pressed open or closed), topstitched, safety-stitch serged, taped.

Hems: Hand (blindstitch, slipstitch), topstitched, twin needle, shirttail.

Seam/Hem Finishes: Serged, zigzag.

Edge Finishes: Facings, bindings, bands, ribbing.

Closures: Buttonholes (machine), buttons/loops, decorative snaps, zippers (machine, invisible).

Pressing: Medium heat, damp cloth or steam.

Garment Care: Dry-clean to maintain the garment's pristine appearance. Hand or machine wash/dry if fabric has been preshrunk.

Sandwashed Fabric

Sandwashed fabrics have a smooth lustrous surface. Generally woven in silk, rayon, or polyester, they are heavier than similar fabrics which are not sandwashed. Fabrics are easily marred by pins, jewelry, ripping, and improper pressing.

Sandwashed Types/Similar Fabrics: Microfibers, sandwashed rayon, sandwashed silk, sandwashed polyester, peachskin, petalskin.

Uses: Casual jackets, blouses, dresses, pants, skirts, sleepwear, trims.

Design Elements: Soft pleats, twists, cowls, gored skirts, shirt sleeves, elastic waists.

Sewing Checklist

Essential Supplies

Needles: Sharp (HM, HJ), universal (H); sizes 60/8-70/10; twin needle,

Thread: All purpose (cotton, polyester, cotton covered polyester, silk). Topstitching – all purpose. Serger – lightweight serger thread, textured thread.

Cutting: Serrated shears, rotary cutter/mat.

Marking: Chalk, clips, tailor's tacks, thread.

Miscellaneous: Super fine pins/needles, temporary pattern adhesive, brown paper strips, seam roll, water soluble stabilizer.

Interfacings: Detail areas; lightweight sew-ins and low-temp fusibles, silk organza, polyester chiffon, net. Apply only to facings.

Linings/Underlinings: Rarely.

Machine Setup

Stitch Length: 2-2.5mm (10-12spi).

Tension: Lightly balanced; light pressure.

Feet: Wide straight stitch, roller, zigzag; small-hole throat plate.

Sewing Basics

Test Garment: Rarely needed.

Fabric Prep: Steam silk; hand wash/dry rayon; machine wash/dry polyesters.

Layout: Nap – double layer, right sides together.

Seams: Plain (pressed open or closed), tissue stitched, topstitched, safety-stitch serged.

Hems: Hand (blindstitch, catchstitch), topstitched, twin needle.

Seam/Hem Finishes: Serged, zigzag, pinked; if lined, none.

Edge Finishes: Facings, bindings, lace trim.

Closures: Buttonholes (machine, bound, inseam); buttons/loops; zippers (invisible, machine, hand).

Pressing: Cool to medium heat; steam, press cloth.

Garment Care: Dry-clean or launder.

Workroom Secrets

Fabric Prep: Preshrink using the fiber content as a guide.

Layout/Cutting/Marking: Use weights or super fine pins placed in the seam allowances. Set pins parallel to selvage. Mark lightly. Avoid erasable pens and colored chalk which may stain permanently.

Basting: Pin baste with super fine pins or needles.

Stitching: Begin with a new, sharp needle (HM). Check to be sure there are no burrs on the needle. Use a wide straight stitch foot. Stitch first onto water soluble stabilizer, then onto the fabric. Press with steam to remove the stabilizer. To reduce puckered seams, hold the fabric firmly in front and back of foot when stitching.

Seams: Avoid seams on the straight grain. (See Any Fabric page 13.) Topstitch seams on unlined designs which will be laundered. Avoid French, faux French, and flat fell seams; they are too bulky for most sandwashed fabrics.

Hems: Hand-rolled and double fold hems such as the shirttail hem are bulky and not as attractive as single fold hems. Topstitched hems are attractive on casual designs. Serge the raw edge, fold to the wrong side, and topstitch with a single or twin needles with fine thread. When using a twin needle, use textured thread on the bobbin. On dressy garments, use a blindstitch to hand sew the hem.

Seam/Hem Finishes: To reduce thread imprints, use textured thread in the serger loopers.

Buttonholes: Machine stitch with a new, sharp needle (HM). Generally, all purpose thread is the best choice, but a fine machine embroidery thread is sometimes more attractive. Experiment before choosing.

Sleeves: Reduce the ease in the cap. (See Any Fabric page 14.)

Pressing: Test press. Press lightly with a warm, dry iron. Sandwashed fabrics are easily damaged by improper pressing and some waterspot. Unwanted creases may be impossible to remove. Use a press cloth when pressing the right side. To avoid seam impressions, use a seam roll and insert brown paper strips under the edges. For hard to press fabrics, press over a seam roll with steam. Cover immediately with a clapper; hold until cool—at least 20 seconds.

Garment Care: Dry-clean to maintain the garment's pristine appearance.

The soft styling of this dress is well-suited for the sandwashed fabric. (Photo courtesy of New Look Patterns.)

Satin

Satin has a smooth, lustrous surface. Generally woven in silk, rayon, acetate, or polyester, satins vary in weight from very light, single faced fabrics to heavy, double-faced materials. Satins with a tighter weave fray less, are more durable and resistant to seam slippage while those with a looser weave have longer floats, more luster, and drape better. Satin snags easily, frays badly, and is easily marred by pins, rough hands, jewelry, abrasion, ripping, and improper pressing.

Workroom Secrets

Fabric Prep: Steam or dry-clean.

Layout/Cutting/Marking: Before cutting, scrape your nail across the satin floats. If yarns separate, fabric will ravel badly and seams will pull out when stressed. Cut wider seam allowances. Use super fine pins placed only in the seam allowances. Set pins parallel to selvage. Mark lightly. Avoid erasable pens and colored chalk, which may stain permanently.

Basting: Pin baste with super fine pins or needles. Hand baste to ensure stitching accuracy and reduce ripping. Baste with soft cotton or fine silk thread to avoid pressing imprints.

Stitching: Begin with a new, sharp needle (HM). Check to be sure there are no burrs on the needle by stitching through an old nylon stocking. Use a wide straight stitch foot and a small hole throat plate. Stitch first onto water soluble stabilizer, then onto the fabric. Press with steam to remove the stabilizer.

Hems: Interface the hem for a softer edge with cotton flannel. On prom and wedding dresses, use narrow horsehair braid or lace so the hem will stand away.

Seam/Hem Finishes: To reduce thread imprints, use textured thread in the serger loopers.

Buttonholes: Machine stitch with a new, sharp needle (HM) and fine machine embroidery thread.

Sleeves: To set the sleeve smoothly, reduce the ease in the cap to 1" (2.5cm).

Underlinings: Use underlinings to give the design shape, support heavy skirts, cushion seams, hide hemming stitches, and prevent seam slippage at stress points on close fitting designs.

Pressing: Test press. Press lightly with a warm, dry iron. Satin is easily damaged by improper pressing and waterspots. Unwanted creases are often impossible to remove. When pressing from the right side, use a press cloth. To avoid seam and hem impressions, use a seam roll and brown paper strips under the edges of the seam.

Garment Care: Most satin garments require dry-cleaning, even when made of manufactured fibers. Use dress shields to avoid unwanted perspiration stains.

Designed by Pamela Ptak, this stunning gown is fabricated in polyester satin. (Photo courtesy of PtakCouture.com.)

Similar Fabrics: Antique satin, chintz, cotton satin, crepe backed satin, cretonne, devoré satin, double-faced satin, duchesse satin, hammered satin, flannel back satin, peau d'ange, peau de soie, polished cotton, sateen, satin doupioni, slipper satin.

Uses: Dressy garments, blouses, dresses, pants, lingerie, special occasion, evening wear, linings, underlinings.

Design Elements: Gathers, pleats, ruffles, flares, drapes, cowl necklines, bias cuts. Avoid seams on the straight grain.

Sewing Checklist

Essential Supplies

Needles: Sharp (HM, HJ), universal (H); sizes 60/8-70/10.

Thread: Lightweight (cotton, polyester, cotton covered polyester, silk), all purpose. Topstitching – lightweight thread (lightweight cotton embroidery thread, silk). Serger – lightweight serger, textured thread. Basting – cotton basting or hand embroidery floss.

Cutting: Serrated shears, rotary cutter/mat.

Marking: Chalk, clips, tailor's tacks, thread.

Miscellaneous: Super fine pins/needles, weights, nylon stocking scrap, dress shields, brown paper strips, seam roll or seam stick, water-soluble stabilizer.

Interfacings: Lightweight sew-ins and fusibles, silk or polyester organza, polyester chiffon, China silk, net.

Linings/Underlinings: Generally on quality designs.

Machine Setup

Stitch Length: 2-2.5mm (10-12spi).

Tension: Lightly balanced; light pressure.

Feet: Wide straight stitch, roller, zigzag; small hole throat plate.

Sewing Basics

Test Garment: Recommended.

Fabric Prep: Steam; hand wash/dry synthetic fibers only.

Layout: Nap – double layer.

Seams: Plain (pressed open or closed), tissue stitched, topstitched, safety-stitch serged.

Hems: Hand (blindstitch, catchstitch), interfaced, horsehair braid, faced, lace, trims.

Seam/Hem Finishes: Serged, pinked, hand overcast; if lined, none.

Edge Finishes: Facings, bindings (self-fabric or contrast), bands.

Closures: Buttonholes (machine, hand, bound, inseam); buttons/loops; covered snaps, zippers (hand, invisible, machine).

Pressing: Cool to medium heat; steam, press cloth.

Garment Care: Dry-clean.

Shantung and Doupioni

Shantung and doupioni are cross-rib fabrics woven with slubbed filling yarns. They can be dull or lustrous, soft or crisp, lightweight or heavy. Selected for beauty, not durability, these fabrics crease and fray badly, are difficult to ease, susceptible to seam slippage, and easily marred by pins, needles, ripping, and improper pressing.

Similar Fabrics: Bengaline, canton crepe, faille, grosgrain, gros de Londres, honan, marocain, ottoman, pongee, repp, Thai silk, upholstery fabrics, silk basketweave, silk linen, tussah, wild silk.
Uses: Special occasion, evening wear, dressy garments, blouses, dresses, pants, lingerie, linings, underlinings.
Design Elements: Minimal seaming, gathers, pleats, ruffles, gores, flares, drapes, A-line skirts, gathered sleeves. Avoid seams on the straight grain. (See Any Fabric page 13.)

Sewing Checklist

Essential Supplies
Needles: Sharp (HM, HJ), universal (H); sizes 60/8-80/12.
Thread: Lightweight (cotton, cotton covered polyester, silk), all purpose. Topstitching – all purpose, lightweight cotton embroidery thread, silk. Serger – lightweight serger thread, textured thread.
Cutting: Sharp shears, rotary cutter/mat.
Marking: Chalk, clips, tailor's tacks, thread.
Miscellaneous: Super fine pins/needles, weights, dress shields, cotton basting thread or embroidery floss, wigan, batting, polyester fleece, water soluble stabilizer.
Interfacings: Lightweight fusibles and sew-ins, silk organza, lightweight silks, net. Apply fusibles to facings.
Linings: Generally for outerwear and quality designs.
Underlinings: Sew-in interfacings, silk organza, polyester chiffon.

Machine Setup
Stitch Length: 2-3mm (8-12spi).
Tension: Lightly balanced.
Feet: Wide straight stitch, roller, even-feed, zigzag.

Sewing Basics
Fabric Prep: Dry-clean; steaming may waterspot. Fabric will shrink, soften, lose its body, and fray badly when washed.
Layout: Nap – double layer right sides together; heavy – single layer right-side up.
Seams: Plain (pressed open or closed), topstitched.
Seam/Hem Finishes: Serged, pinked, zigzag; if lined, none.
Hems: Hand (blindstitch, double-stitched), faced, interfaced.
Edge Finishes: Facings (self-fabric, lining, bias), bias bindings.
Closures: Buttonholes (machine, corded, bound, in-seam); buttons/loops, frogs, covered snaps, ties, zippers (hand, machine, invisible).
Pressing: Cool to medium heat; press cloth and steam. To avoid spitting and spewing, be sure the iron has warmed up and steams properly before pressing.
Garment Care: Dry-clean or launder if the fabric was preshrunk.

Workroom Secrets
Fabric Prep: Steam or dry-clean. Shantung can be washed but will shrink badly and lose some of its body.
Layout/Cutting/Marking: To reduce seam slippage, do not cut on the crossgrain so the ribs run vertically. Use weights, temporary pattern adhesive, or place pins in seam allowances. Extend both ends of the grainline and pin in the seam allowances. Mark lightly. Erasable pens and colored chalk may stain permanently.
Basting: Pin baste with super fine pins or needles. Hand baste to ensure stitching accuracy and reduce ripping. Baste with soft cotton or fine silk thread to avoid pressing imprints.
Stitching: Begin with a new, sharp needle (HM). To hide needle holes if you have to rip, scratch the fabric lightly with your thumbnail or a fine needle.
Hems: Make the hem at least 2" wide. Interface hems with muslin or wigan for a softer edge. Use cotton batting or polyester fleece to create a padded hem.
Seam/Hem Finishes: To reduce thread imprints, use textured thread in the serger loopers.
Buttonholes: Machine stitch with a new, sharp needle (HM). For more defined buttonholes, cord the buttonholes; or cover fabric with water soluble stabilizer, then stitch.
Sleeves: Reduce the ease in the sleeve cap or cut the sleeves on the bias.
Underlinings: Use underlinings to give the design shape, support heavy skirts, cushion seams, hide hemming stitches, reduce wrinkling, and prevent seam slippage at stress points. Use sew-in underlinings for quality garments. Fusibles will make shantung and doupioni look stiff.
Pressing: Press lightly with a warm, dry iron. Use a press cloth when pressing the right side. Use a seam roll and brown paper strips to avoid seam and hem impressions on the right side. Press carefully. Unwanted creases may be impossible to remove.
Garment Care: Dry-clean to maintain the garment's pristine appearance. Use dress shields to avoid unwanted perspiration stains.

Made from gold-colored shantung, these crisply tailored trousers are elegant to wear and easy to sew. (Photo courtesy of Simplicity Patterns.)

Silk

Sometimes called the queen of fibers, silk is the only natural filament fiber and the most luxurious. Silks are generally selected for their beauty, not their durability.

Comfortable to wear, silk is warm in winter and cool in summer. It is resilient and elastic, holds its shape, resists wrinkling, and absorbs moisture well. It is available in a variety of fabrications from soft and sheer to crisp and heavy. Many are easily damaged by needles, pins, ripping, improper pressing, and perspiration.

Workroom Secrets

Fabric Prep: Depends on manufacturer's recommendation, fabric structure, garment design, quality, and use. Silk does not shrink but many silk fabrics do.

Layout/Cutting/Marking: Generally a nap layout is best, even though the fabric does not have an obvious nap or one-way pattern. When marking on the body of the garment, mark lightly to avoid marring the fabric. Use only super fine pins or needles, tailor's tacks, or thread; avoid erasable pens, colored or wax chalk.

Seams/Hems: Depends on the fabric weight, structure, and transparency and garment quality, design, use, and care. Wider seams will press and drape better.

Interfacings/Linings/Underlinings: Depends on the fabric weight, garment type, quality, and structure; same care properties.

Pressing: Test press; silks are easily damaged by improper pressing, hot irons, and waterspots. When using steam, use a press cloth or be sure that the iron does not spit and sputter.

Garment Care: Silk can be either laundered or dry-cleaned, depending on the dyes, finishes, fabric structure, garment design, quality, and use. Dry-clean in order to preserve the original hand and maintain the fabric's pristine appearance.

Designed by Diane Tatara, using PatternMaster Boutique™, this elegant caftan showcases a dazzling silk chiffon border design. (Photo courtesy of Wild Ginger Software®.)

Silk Fabrics: Bengaline, brocade, charmeuse, chiffon, China silk, crepe de chine, doupioni, faille, fuji silk, gazar, georgette, grosgrain, habutai, honan, jacquard silk, jersey, marquisette, matelassé, matka, mikado silk, moiré, organza, ottoman, peau de soie, pongee, repp, satin, satin-faced crepe, shantung, silk noil, suiting, surah, taffeta, tussah, velvet, voile.

Uses: All type garments.

Burn test: Silk burns slowly, sputters, forming tiny bubbles along the burned edge. It is self-extinguishing, and leaves crushable black beads.

Sewing Checklist

Essential Supplies

Needles: Woven fabrics – sharp (HM), universal (H). **Knit fabrics** – stretch (HS), universal (H), ballpoint (H-SUK). Sizes – lightweight fabrics, 60/8-70/10; medium-weight fabrics, 70/10-80/12; heavy-weight fabrics, 80/12-90/14; very heavy-weight fabrics, 90/14-120/20.

Thread: Lightweight fabrics – lightweight (cotton, polyester, cotton covered polyester, silk), all purpose. **Medium-weight fabrics** – all purpose. **Heavy-weight fabrics** all purpose, machine embroidery/ topstitching threads. **Very heavy-weight fabrics** – embroidery/topstitching threads.

Cutting: Lightweight fabrics – serrated shears; other fabrics – very sharp shears; all fabrics – rotary cutter/mat, duplicate pattern pieces.

Marking: Chalk, clips, super fine pins, tailor's tacks, thread.

Miscellaneous: Super fine pins, water soluble stabilizer.

Interfacings/Linings/Underlinings: All types depending on the fabric structure and garment design.

Machine Setup

Stitch Length: Lightweight fabrics – 1.5-1.75mm (15-18spi). **Medium-weight fabrics** – 2-2.5mm (10-12spi). **Heavy-weight fabrics** – 2.5-3mm (8-10spi). **Very heavy-weight fabrics** – 3-4mm (6-8spi). **All weights** – zigzag (W,.5-L,2).

Tension: Depends on the fabric.

Feet: Straight stitch, even-feed, roller, zigzag.

Sewing Basics

Test Garment: Recommended for quality fabrics and intricate designs.

Fabric Prep: Depends on fabric, garment design, quality, and use.

Layout: Nap – Single layer when matching patterns.

Seams: Plain (pressed open or closed); lightweight and sheer fabrics, French, faux French.

Hems/Edge Finishes: All types, depending on fabric and design.

Seam/Hem Finishes: All types. Avoid bulky finishes on lightweight fabrics.

Closures: Buttonholes (machine, bound, inseam), buttons/loops, ties, zippers (hand, machine, invisible).

Pressing: Medium heat; press cloth and steam.

Garment Care: Dry-clean quality garments. Hand wash/line dry lingerie silks.

Silky

Sometimes called silk look-alikes, most silkies are actually lightweight polyesters. They are resistant to wrinkles, slippery, easily damaged by hot irons, retain static electricity, and do not ease or breathe well. Microfiber polyesters and polyester blouse fabrics are more comfortable to wear than polyester lining materials; but they are not as comfortable as silk.

Polyester Types/Similar Fabrics: Polyester georgette, organza, chiffon, satin, taffeta, linings, crepe, jacquard; microfibers, sandwashed rayon.

Uses: Blouses, tailored shirts, dresses, skirts, pants, jackets, lingerie, sleepwear.

Design Elements: Gathers, pleats, ruffles, flounces, drapes, bindings, elastic casings. Avoid seams on the straight grain.

Sewing Checklist

Essential Supplies

Needles: Sharp (HM, HJ), universal (H); sizes 60/8-70/12.

Thread: Fine or all purpose (polyester, cotton covered polyester), textured thread.

Cutting: Sharp serrated shears, rotary cutter/mat.

Marking: Chalk, clips, erasable pens, pins.

Miscellaneous: Super fine pins, paint brush, vinegar, flannel-backed cloth, water soluble stabilizer, seam stick, clapper.

Interfacings: Very lightweight sew-ins, self-fabric, polyester organdy, Sewin' Sheer™; low-temp fusibles .

Linings/Underlinings: Optional, washable.

Machine Setup

Stitch Length: 2-2.5mm (10-12spi).

Tension: Lightly balanced; light pressure.

Feet: Wide straight stitch, roller, zigzag; small hole throat plate.

Sewing Basics

Test Garment: Rarely required.

Fabric Prep: Machine wash/dry to soften.

Layout: Without nap – double layer.

Seams: Plain (pressed open or closed), safety-stitch serged, French, faux French, topstitched, tissue stitched.

Hems: Topstitched, shirttail, merrow, hand (blindstitch), narrow machine-rolled, pin.

Seam/Hem Finishes: Serged, zigzag, turn and stitch, pinked.

Edge Finishes: Facings, bindings, bands, casings, ribbings.

Closures: Buttonholes (machine, inseam), buttons/loops, ties, zippers (machine, invisible).

Pressing: Low to medium heat; steam, press cloth, seam stick, clapper.

Garment Care: Everyday designs – machine wash/dry; quality garments – dry-clean or hand wash.

Workroom Secrets

Fabric Prep: Most polyesters do not shrink; but preshrinking removes excess finishes, making them easier to sew.

Layout/Cutting/Marking: To control lightweight polyesters, cover the cutting table with a flannel-backed vinyl cloth, flannel side up. Before cutting, redraw the seams on the straight grain so they are on a slight bias. Do not tilt sections off-grain. (See Any Fabric page 14.) Use sharp serrated shears or rotary cutter/mat to cut. Mark lightly. Avoid erasable pens and colored chalk; they may stain permanently.

Stitching: Begin with a new needle. Needles dull quickly; replace them frequently. When using polyester thread, wind the bobbin slowly. When wound on high, the thread heats up and stretches; then, when sewn into the seam, it relaxes and the seam puckers. To prevent fabrics from being drawn into the needle hole, tissue stitch seams. Hold fabric firmly in front and back of foot when stitching. To flatten seams, topstitch.

Seams: For washable garments, choose sturdy seams such as French, faux French, topstitched, safety-stitched seams.

Seam/Hem Finishes: To reduce thread imprints, use very fine serger or textured thread in the serger.

Buttonholes: Machine stitch with fine thread and a new sharp needle (HM) in a small size. To reduce tunneling when stitching, cover the fabric with a piece of water-soluble stabilizer.

Sleeves: To set sleeves easily, cut the sleeves on the bias or reduce the ease in the sleeve cap. (See Any Fabric page 14.)

Pressing: Test press; polyesters are difficult to press and easily damaged by hot irons. To press seams, place on a seam stick. Brush with a 50/50 solution of white vinegar and water. Press and cover with a clapper until cool. Repeat as necessary. When pressing with higher temperatures, use a press cloth to avoid melting the fabric.

Soft and silky, this summer shell is practical and easy to sew. (Burda Pattern – 8804, photo courtesy of Burda.)

Silk Suiting

Silk suitings range from firmly woven shantungs to unique loosely woven tweeds. Many are bulky with slubs, thick ribs, and long floats which make them pick, pull, and ravel badly.

Workroom Secrets

Layout/Cutting/Marking: Many silk suitings stretch badly. Do not allow them to hang off the table when cutting. Use weights, temporary pattern adhesive, or flower pins. To match patterns, use single layer and duplicate pattern pieces. For fabrics which fray badly, cut 1" (2.5cm) seams. Before moving the sections, spray cut edges lightly with seam sealant, thin solution of white glue and water, or spray starch. Use small safety pins to mark the right side of the fabric and construction symbols.

Stitching: To prevent underlayer creep, use a roller or even-feed foot, hold the fabric firmly in front and behind the presser foot. Stitch several inches, then rest; raise and lower the foot; and stitch again. Tissue stitch seams as needed. Use polyester thread and a narrow zigzag (W,.5-L,2) for more elastic seams.

Seams: Stabilize necklines, shoulder seams, buttonholes, and zipper openings with stay tape. (See Any Fabric page 13.) When it is difficult to match fabric patterns, piped seams are a good choice.

Seam/Hem Finishes: If the fabric frays badly, serge or bind seams before assembling. Work carefully to avoid changing or varying the seam allowance widths. On unlined garments, finish quality garments with a Hong Kong finish using silk chiffon or China silk. Use tricot bindings on everyday designs. Avoid double-fold bias bindings; they are too bulky and may show through.

Buttonholes: For more definition on machine stitched buttonholes, use water soluble stabilizer on top of fabric and/or cord the buttonholes.

Underlinings: Use sew-ins for stability and lightweight fusibles for added structure. Sew-in underlinings are more tactile than fusibles.

Pressing: To avoid flattening the fabric, cover pressing surface with thick terry towel. Use a press cloth to prevent iron from snagging fabric.

This fabulous swing coat is from the Custom Couture Collection by Claire Shaeffer. (Vogue Pattern – 7539; courtesy of The McCall Pattern Co.)

Similar Fabrics: Doupioni, handwovens, Indian tussah, heavy spun hopsacking, matka, muggah, raw silk, raj Indian silk, monk's cloth, shantung, silk/linen blend, silk tweed.

Uses: Tailored or unstructured designs, coats, jackets, straight skirts, pants, dresses, and wraps.

Design Elements: Simple designs, minimal seaming, pleats, pockets (all types), collars (all types), piped seams.

Sewing Checklist

Essential Supplies

Needles: Sharp (HM, HJ), universal (H); sizes 70/10-90/14, depending on fabric weight.

Thread: All purpose (cotton, polyester, cotton covered polyester, silk). Topstitching – all purpose, machine embroidery/topstitching.

Cutting: Sharp shears, rotary cutter/mat, duplicate pattern pieces.

Marking: Chalk, clips, flower pins, safety pins, tailor's tacks, thread.

Miscellaneous: Flower pins, safety pins, weights, stay tape, temporary pattern adhesive, seam sealant, white glue, spray starch, spray bottle, covered snaps, stabilizers – water soluble, burn away, tearaway.

Interfacings: Fusible, weft-insertion, knit; sew-in, hair canvas.

Linings: Outerwear, quality garments.

Underlinings: Organza, polyester chiffon, sew-in interfacings, very lightweight fusibles.

Machine Setup

Stitch Length: 2-3mm (8-12spi); or zigzag (W,.5-L,2).

Tension: Lightly balanced.

Feet: Roller, wide straight stitch, even-feed, zigzag.

Sewing Basics

Test Garment: Recommended; fabric is easily damaged by ripping.

Fabric Prep: Steam or dry-clean.

Layout: Nap – double layer; bulky fabrics and matching patterns – single layer right-side up, duplicate pattern pieces.

Seams: Plain (pressed open), topstitched, strap, lapped, piped, taped.

Hems: Hand (blindstitch, blind catchstitch, catchstitch), double-stitched, interfaced, topstitched.

Seam/Hem Finishes: Serged, tricot binding, Hong Kong finish, zigzag; if lined, none.

Edge Finishes: Facings (self-fabric, lining), bindings (contrast, synthetic leather, or suede), ribbings, edge-to-edge linings.

Closures: Buttonholes (machine, corded, bound, in-seam), buttons/loops, zippers (machine, hand, invisible).

Pressing: Cool to medium heat; steam, self-fabric or wool press cloth.

Garment Care: Dry-clean.

Slinky

Slinky is an elastic acetate knit. Available in different qualities, weights, and stretch, it is sometimes combined with spandex to eliminate bagging. It is comfortable to wear, has a soft, supple hand, and drapes attractively. It is easily damaged by hot irons.

Similar Fabrics: Beaded slinky, bubble knit, crystal pleating, slinky crepe, stretch crepe, stretch ottoman.
Uses: Dresses, pants, skirts, blouses.
Design Elements: Minimal seaming, slip-on designs, loose-fitting sleeves, elastic casings, turtleneck collars, bindings, ribbings. Avoid close fitting garments.

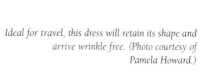 Sewing Checklist

Essential Supplies
Needles: Stretch (HS), universal (H), twin needle (HS); sizes 70/10-90/14.
Thread: All purpose (polyester, cotton covered polyester), textured thread. Serger: lightweight serger thread, textured nylon.
Cutting: Rotary cutter/mat, serrated shears.
Marking: Chalk, clips, erasable pens, pins, safety pins.
Miscellaneous: Flower pins, quilting clothes pins, lightweight invisible zippers, firm non-roll elastic, clear elastic, tissue, water soluble stabilizers.
Interfacings: Sewin' Sheer™; avoid fusibles.
Linings/Underlinings: None.

Machine Setup
Stitch Length: Zigzag W,.5-L,1; W,2-2.5;L,2.
Tension: Lightly balanced; light pressure.
Machine Feet: Embroidery, roller, zipper, zigzag.

Sewing Basics
Test Garment: Rarely needed.
Fabric Prep: Machine wash/dry.
Layout: Nap – double layer.
Seams: Narrow plain (zigzag closed), safety-stitch serged, taped.
Hems: Topstitch, twin needle, lettuce edging, hand (catchstitch).
Seam/Hem Finishes: Serged, zigzag.
Edge Finishes: Facings (self-fabric, lining), bindings, ribbings, elastic casings.
Closures: Buttonholes (machine), buttons or loops, zippers (invisible). Avoid hook and loop tape.
Pressing: Low heat; test press to avoid damage.
Garment Care: Machine wash/dry. Store flat; do not hang.

Workroom Secrets
Fabric Prep: Preshrink to relax fabric. Machine wash/dry.
Layout/Cutting/Marking: Before cutting, compare the amount of fabric stretch with the amount required for the design. Mark the right side of the fabric with small safety pins. Slinky stretches in the length more than most knits; do not allow it to hang off the table when cutting. Anchor with weights; cut using a rotary cutter and mat. If necessary, lay out on tissue paper, pin, and cut through all layers.
Stitching: To reduce creeping underlayer, use light pressure or serge using differential feed. To baste, use flower pins or quilting clothes pins. To begin, stitch onto a piece of stabilizer, then onto the fabric. Stitch with an embroidery foot to reduce stretching. If the fabric does not feed well, stop regularly; raise the foot and smooth the fabric; then continue.
Seams: Use polyester thread and zigzag for more elastic seams. Stitch long, straight seams with a long zigzag (W,.5-L,2-2.5); stitch short seams, which will be stressed, with a short zigzag (W,.5-L,1.5). To handle easily, cut and stitch seams with ⅝" (1.5cm) seam allowances; then serge and trim to ¼" (6mm). Stitch with the slinky on the bottom when joining to a stable fabric. Stabilize shoulder seams, necklines, and long side seams when needed with clear elastic.
Edge Finishes: Self-fabric bindings, stretch foldover braid, and ribbings are attractive edge finishes. Cut the ribbing and binding strips on the crossgrain 25 to 30 percent shorter than the edge. To apply slinky ribbing, join the ends of the strip; then fold it in half lengthwise with wrong sides together. Mark the ribbing and garment edge in quarters and stretch the ribbing to fit. Stitch to the right side; serge the edges. To apply a binding, join the ends. With right sides together, stitch one edge of the binding to the edge, stretching as needed. Wrap the ribbing around the edge, and ditch-stitch, using a zipper foot. For elasticized waists, choose a firm, non-roll elastic to support the weight of the fabric.
Closures: Most closures will interfere with the garment drape. When using a zipper, choose a lightweight invisible zipper. Machine stitch buttonholes parallel to the ribbing.
Hems: When marking hems, mark 10" above finished hemline. Lay flat; connect the marks; measure and mark at hemline. Fold hem to the wrong side and topstitch with a twin needle (HS) and textured thread in the bobbin. Loosen the needle and bobbin tensions. Trim away excess.

Ideal for travel, this dress will retain its shape and arrive wrinkle free. (Photo courtesy of Pamela Howard.)

Spandex

Known for its extraordinary elasticity, spandex has been used extensively for foundation garments and all types of active sportswear since its introduction in 1958. Spandex is frequently called by one of its trade names: Lycra. There are several other trade names: Cleerspan, Glospan, and Dorlastan.

Known as elastane or EL in some European countries, spandex can be stretched repeatedly and still snap back to its original shape and length. It can be stretched from four to seven times its length without breaking.

When compared to rubber, it is stronger, more durable with greater tear resistance. It is more resistant to abrasion, flexing, sunlight, weather, heat, detergent, body oil, and perspiration. It is lighter weight and can be made into finer yarns. It can be stitched through without damaging the fiber and reducing the recovery.

Spandex can be added to any fabric, knit or woven, and to a variety of fibers to add stretch in the length, width, or both directions.

Today, it is used in small amounts (2 to 5 percent) to add stretch and freedom of movement; improve the look, feel, fit, and comfort; maintain the shape; and eliminate bagging. It is used in large amounts (15 to 50 percent) for high stretch designs such as foundation garments, swimwear, skiwear, swimsuits, and skating costumes.

Workroom Secrets

Layout/Cutting/Marking: Let fabric relax overnight. Before cutting, compare the amount of fabric stretch with the amount required for the design. Generally the greatest stretch goes around the body.

Stitching: Start each new project with a new needle in the smallest recommended size. Change needles frequently; synthetic fibers dull needles faster than natural fibers. To check the needle for burrs, stitch through a nylon stocking scrap. Use polyester thread, which is more elastic than cotton. Wind the bobbin slowly. When wound on high, the thread heats up and stretches. Then, when sewn into the seam, it relaxes, and the seam shortens or puckers. For more elastic seams, stitch with a narrow zigzag (W,.5-L,1), and stretch slightly when stitching. Or stitch on a serger with a safety-stitch and textured thread on the loopers.

Seams: Use stretch seams where appropriate. Stabilize shoulder and waist seams and edges with stay tape or clear elastic. (See Any Fabric page 13.)

Frequently used for swim and active wear, spandex provides a close fit and permits freedom of movement. (Photo courtesy of Claire Shaeffer.)

Fabric Types: Stretch wovens, stretch knits, two-way and four-way stretch fabrics.

Uses: Traditional tailored and dressy designs, casual wear, activewear, lingerie, foundation garments, bindings, cuffs, ribbings.

Design Elements: Minimal seaming, topstitching, soft pleats.

Sewing Checklist

Essential Supplies

Needles: Woven fabrics – universal (H), sharp (HM). **Knit fabrics** – stretch (HS), ballpoint (H-SUK), twin needle; sizes 70/10-90/14.

Thread: All purpose (polyester), textured thread. Topstitching – machine embroidery/topstitching (polyester), all purpose. Serger: lightweight serger thread, textured thread.

Cutting: Sharp shears, rotary cutter/mat.

Marking: Chalk, clips, erasable pens, pins.

Miscellaneous: Super fine pins, clear elastic, stay tape, nylon stocking scrap.

Interfacings/Lining/Underlinings: Depends on garment type, design, and fabric. Examine carefully to be sure there is enough stretch for the fabric.

Machine Setup

Stitch Length: 1.5-2.5mm (10-18spi); zigzag (W,.5-L,1).

Tension: Lightly balanced.

Machine Feet: Roller, wide straight stitch, zigzag.

Sewing Basics

Test Garment: Depends on design and fabric.

Fabric Prep: Preshrink using the recommendations for the non-spandex fiber, garment design, use, and construction.

Layout: Depends on fabric design and construction; knits and wools – nap; wovens – depends on fabric design.

Seams: Depends on fabric and location.

Seam/Hem Finishes: Serged, zigzag, pinked.

Hems/Edges Finishes: All types, Depending on fabric stretch, garment type, and location.

Closures: All types.

Interfacings/Underlinings/Linings: Depends on design and fabric. Examine carefully to be sure there is enough stretch for the fabric.

Pressing: Test press to determine the appropriate amount of heat, moisture, and pressure. Spandex is more heat sensitive.

Garment Care: Depends on fabric, garment, and use.

Stretch Knit

Stretch knits can be weft or warp knits and stretch in one or both directions. The amount of stretch varies with the type knit and amount of spandex. Moderate stretch knits stretch 25 to 50 percent; super stretch knits stretch as much as 100 percent.

Good quality knits have good recovery and return to their original shapes after stretching. All are easily snagged by damaged pins, needles, and hook and loop tape.

Stretch Knits: Stretch tricot, stretch raschel, power knit, two-way and four-way stretch knits.
Uses: Activewear, tights, shorts, bindings, cuffs, ribbings.
Design Elements: Minimal seaming, close fitting garments with minimal ease. Thin fabrics and light colors often become transparent when wet.

Sewing Checklist

Essential Supplies
Needles: Stretch (HS), ballpoint (H-SUK), universal (H), twin needle; sizes 70/10-90/14.
Thread: All purpose (polyester), textured thread. Serger – lightweight serger thread, textured thread.
Cutting: Sharp shears, rotary cutter/mat, duplicate pattern pieces.
Marking: Chalk, clips, erasable pens, pins.
Miscellaneous: Super fine pins, temporary pattern adhesive, clear elastic, nylon stocking scrap.
Interfacings: Rarely, same stretch as fabric; lightweight tricot fusible, Sof-Knit™.
Linings: Lightweight stretch tricot, self-fabric, stretch banlon, lightweight power net, swimsuit lining.
Underlinings: Use to make light colors less transparent. Must have same stretch as fabric.

Machine Setup
Stitch Length: 1.5-2mm (12-18spi); zigzag (W,.5-L,1).
Tension: Loose, lightly balanced.
Feet: Roller, wide straight stitch, zigzag.

Sewing Basics
Test Garment: Rarely.
Fabric Prep: Washable fabrics – machine wash, line dry; non-washables – dry-clean or steam.
Layout: Nap – double layer; prints – single layer, right-side up, using duplicate pattern pieces.
Seams: Plain (pressed open or closed), topstitched, safety-stitch serged, 3-thread serged.
Hems: Topstitch, twin needle, lettuce edging.
Seam/Hem Finishes: Serged, zigzag, pinked.
Edge Finishes: Facings (self-fabric), bindings, elastic (casings, applied), ribbings, snap tape. Avoid hook and loop tape.
Closures: Buttonholes (machine), buttons or loops, zippers (machine, invisible, exposed), ties.
Pressing: Low heat,
Garment Care: Machine wash with no bleach, line dry.

Workroom Secrets
Layout/Cutting/Marking: Let fabric relax overnight. Before cutting, compare the amount of fabric stretch with the amount required for the design. Generally the greatest stretch goes around the body. Use weights, temporary pattern adhesive, or super fine pins in the seam allowances.
Stitching: Start each new project with a new needle in the smallest recommended size. Change needles frequently; synthetic fibers dull needles faster than natural fibers. To check the needle for burrs, stitch through a nylon stocking scrap. Use polyester thread which is more elastic. Wind bobbin slowly. Use a twin needle for topstitching with textured thread in the bobbin.
Seams: For elastic seams, stitch with a narrow zigzag (W,.5-L,1) or twin needle, and stretch very slightly when stitching. Or stitch on a serger with a safety-stitch and textured thread on the loopers. Reinforce seams which will be stressed with stay tape or clear elastic. Do not use textured threads on seams which will be stressed.
Edge Finishes: Self-fabric, two-way stretch, and cotton/spandex bindings are attractive substitutes for elastic.

Clear elastic can be applied directly or in a casing; it is resistant to perspiration, body oil, sun, salt water, and chlorine. Use braided elastic for casings, and knit, woven, or clear elastic for direct applications. When applying elastic, cut 10 to 25 percent shorter than edge.
Buttonholes: Reinforce or cord to prevent stretching.
Linings/Underlinings: Generally, not used except for comfort or modesty; must have the same stretch as the fabric.

Lena Stepanenko used a stretch knit to create this dazzling asymmetrical gown for a special evening. (Photo courtesy of Yelena Couture.)

Stretch Woven

Stretch-woven fabrics are made by blending cotton, silk, wool, hair fibers or manufactured fibers with a stretch fiber such as spandex or Lycra or by weaving the fabric from core-spun yarns. For most, the stretch fiber is less than 5 percent. They combine the appearance of traditional woven fabrics with the comfort and flexibility of knits. They have better shape retention and are less bulky than knits. They are more difficult to press than similar non-stretch fabrics; and most will not retain a sharp crease.

Workroom Secrets

Fabric Prep: Preshrink using the recommendations for the non-stretch fibers as a guide.

Stitching: Use polyester thread, which is more elastic. Wind bobbin slowly. Use a twin needle for topstitching with textured thread on the bobbin.

Seams: For more elastic seams, use textured or polyester thread and a narrow zigzag (W,.5-L,1), or stitch with a twin needle. Stabilize shoulder, crotch, and waist seams, necklines, and zipper openings with stay tape. Use clear elastic to stabilize seams with stretch.

Hems: Some fabrics are difficult to hem inconspicuously. Use a very fine hand needle (size 10), lightweight thread, and a blindstitch. Pick up just the back of the fabric yarns, leaving the thread loose between the stitches. Make a small backstitch on the hem allowance every third stitch.

Interfacings/Underlinings/Linings: Examine these fabrics carefully to be sure that they have enough stretch for the fashion fabric.

Pressing: Test press to determine the appropriate amount of heat, moisture, and pressure. Spandex is more heat sensitive than most fibers. Use a press cloth when pressing the right side. For sharper folds and seamlines, rub the crease on the wrong side with a bar of Ivory soap. Fold in place and press. For sharp, well-pressed seams and edges, use lots of steam or a damp press cloth. Press, then cover with clapper. Examine the results. If necessary, press again and spank with clapper. Do not move until the fabric is dry. To apply additional moisture when pressing, first cover garment with a dry cloth. Rub a wet, but not dripping, sponge over section to be pressed; then press. To hold the layers in position when pressing, baste about 1/4" (6mm) from the edge. Use soft cotton basting thread or hand embroidery floss to avoid a pressing imprint.

Career dressing at its best, this stretch woven ensemble will look fresh from early to late. (Photo courtesy of Monica McMurray, Stephens College.)

Stretch Woven Types: Brocade, corduroy, denim, gabardine, flannel, lace, linen, poplin, satin, seersucker, twill, velvet, velveteen.

Uses: Tailored and dressy garments, casual wear, jackets, coats, dresses, pants, shirts, skirts, riding habits.

Design Elements: Topstitching, soft pleats, gathers, flares, pockets (all types).

Sewing Checklist

Essential Supplies

Needles: Universal (H), sharp (HM, HJ); sizes 70/10-90/14.

Thread: All purpose (polyester, cotton covered polyester). Topstitching – machine embroidery/topstitching, all purpose. Serger – lightweight serger, textured thread.

Cutting: Sharp shears, rotary cutter/mat.

Marking: Chalk, clips, pins, tailor's tacks, thread.

Miscellaneous: Soft cotton basting thread, hand embroidery floss, sponge, Ivory soap, stabilizers – water soluble, cut away.

Interfacings: Generally; fusibles, fusible tricot, Sof-Knit™, sew-ins.

Linings/Underlinings: Quality garments; same care and stretch as garment.

Machine Setup

Stitch Length: 2-2.5mm (10-12spi); zigzag (W,.5-L,1).

Tension: Lightly balanced.

Feet: Wide straight stitch, zigzag.

Sewing Basics

Test Garment: Usually, depending on design.

Fabric Prep: Steam, dry-clean.

Layout: Nap – double layer.

Seams: Plain (pressed open or closed), topstitched.

Hems: Hand (blindstitch, blind catchstitch, catchstitch), fuse, topstitched, interfaced.

Seam/Hem Finishes: Serged, zigzag, pinked.

Edge Finishes: Facings (self-fabric), bindings, bands.

Closures: Buttonholes (machine, bound, inseam); buttons/loops, zippers (hand, machine, invisible).

Pressing: Medium heat, steam, press cloth, clapper, seam roll, point presser.

Garment Care: Dry-clean; machine wash/dry depending on design and fiber.

Stripe

Striped fabrics have colored bars and spaces on the lengthwise grain or the crossgrain, but not on both. Available in all fibers and weights, they can be woven, knitted, or printed. Stripes can have one, two, or many colors; be smooth or textured; have subtle solid color cross-ribs, vertical cords, or bold contrasting colors, be corded or flat. They are available in all sizes from tiny pinstripes to bold awning stripes.

Generally, vertical stripes are more attractive on more figures. They are not as difficult to match and are easier to sew than horizontal ones. Some stripes have a one-way pattern, requiring a nap layout and additional fabric for matching. Avoid stripes which are printed, woven, or knitted off-grain. They cannot be matched satisfactorily.

Sewing Checklist

Essential Supplies

Needles: Woven fabrics – sharp (HM), universal (H). **Knit fabrics** – stretch (HS), universal (H), ballpoint (H-SUK). Sizes – lightweight fabrics, 60/8-70/10; medium-weight, 70/10-80/12; heavyweight, 80/12-90/14; very heavy-weight, 90/14-120/20.

Thread: Size/fiber depends on fabric weight and elasticity and the garment design and use.

Cutting: Sharp shears, rotary cutter/mat, duplicate pattern pieces.

Marking: Chalk, clips, pins, safety pins, erasable pens.

Miscellaneous: Small safety pins, washable glue stick, double-stick washable tape, temporary spray adhesive.

Interfacings/Linings/Underlinings: All types depending on the fabric and garment design.

Machine Setup

Stitch Length: Lightweight fabrics – 1.5-1.75mm (15-18spi). **Medium-weight fabrics** – 2-2.5mm (10-12spi). **Heavy-weight fabrics** – 2.5-3mm (8-10spi). **Very heavy-weight fabrics** – 3-4mm (6-8spi). **All weights** – zigzag (W,.5-L,2).

Tension: Depends on the fabric.

Feet: Even feed, roller, straight stitch, zigzag, zipper.

Sewing Basics

Test Garment: Recommended for quality fabrics and intricate designs.

Fabric Prep: Depends on fabric, garment design, quality, and use.

Layout: Nap or without nap – depending on fabric and/or stripe design. Single layer – to match horizontal stripes, use duplicate pattern pieces.

Seams: Plain (pressed open or closed), piped, lapped.

Hems/Edge Finishes: All types, depending on fabric and design.

Seam/Hem Finishes: Serged, zigzag, bound, pinked.

Closures: Buttonholes (machine, hand), buttons/loops, ties, zippers (hand, machine, invisible).

Pressing: Depends on the fiber and fabric.

Garment Care: Depends on fiber content, fabric structure, and garment quality.

Workroom Secrets

Test Garment: Recommended when sewing quality fabrics and intricate designs.

Fabric Prep: Depends on manufacturer's recommendation, fiber content, fabric structure, garment design, quality, and use.

Layout/Cutting/Marking: For unbalanced stripes, use a nap layout so the stripe pattern will continue around the body. Use a without nap layout to mirror image the front and back. When sewing horizontal stripes, lay out the pattern pieces so the stripes match at center front, center back, and side seams. Match the sleeve and front about 4" (10cm) below the shoulder point; the sleeve may not match the back. Front and back shoulder seams do not have to match. A few horizontal stripes can be cut on the crossgrain; but most fabrics will not drape well. When possible, lay out pattern pieces so adjoining seams are next to each other. Always match the seamlines, not the cutting lines. This is frequently easier if you trim away or fold back the seam allowances on the tissue pattern, lay out the pieces so the stitching lines will match. Using chalk, measure and mark the cutting lines on the fabric.

Stitching: Use an even feed or roller foot to stitch directionally with the grain. Generally this is from the bottom to the top. When pin basting, set the pins on the seamlines with the heads toward the raw edges. Insert every other pin from the underside. Stitch, removing the pins as you go to avoid stitching over them. If you must stitch over them, walk the

Never sewn stripes? This attractive skirt belies the notion that stripes are always difficult. (Burda Pattern – 8687, photo courtesy of Burda.)

machine slowly. When stitching knits, use a narrow zigzag (W,.5-L,2) for a more elastic seam.

Seams: The most popular seams include the plain, piped, and lapped seams. Lapped seams are easier to stitch than plain seams. Press under the seam allowance on the overlap. With right sides up, align the seamlines and baste the sections together with a glue stick, spray adhesive, or double-stick washable tape, or pins. Use a zipper foot to edgestitch close to the folded edge. When stripes cannot be matched, consider piped seams.

Buttonholes: All types of buttonholes—machine, inseam, bound—are suitable. For bound buttonholes, cut the welt strips to match the color bars on the garment or on the bias. Always cord bias-cut welts so they will not stretch out of shape.

Matching Tip

Pockets/Flaps/Welts: To match pockets, flaps, and welts, begin by marking the location on the garment sections. Lay the smaller pattern piece on the garment section. Place a fabric scrap on the tissue pattern, matching the stripe design. Tape the scrap in place. Remove the small pattern; lay it out so the scrap matches the stripe design, and cut. (This also works for sleeves.)

Stripe Fabrics: Bedford cord, herringbone, ottoman, pique, shantung.
Uses: All type garments.
Design Elements: Simple designs, minimal seaming, bindings, bands, piped seams, bias designs trims.

Stripe Types

- **Repeat:** One complete stripe pattern.
- **Even Stripe:** A pattern with equal-width color bars and spaces.
- **Uneven Stripe:** A pattern with bars and spaces of unequal widths.
- **Balanced Stripe:** Sometimes called a mirror-image stripe, the stripes, when folded in the center of the most dominant bar, have the same sequence, color, and size on both sides.
- **Unbalanced Stripe:** A three or more color pattern with progressive or consecutive arrangement of bars and spaces.

This classic straight skirt is smart and flattering. (Burda Pattern – 8492, photo courtesy of Burda.)

Sweater Knit

Sweater knits run the gamut from weft knits, which look, stretch, and unravel like hand knits, to stable warp knits. This section focuses on the former. To sew stable sweater knits, see Raschel Knit page 72.

Sweater knits are available by the yard in a variety of fibers and pattern designs as well as in kits. They vary in stretch, add pounds to most figures, and are often bulky.

Sweater Knit Types/Similar Fabrics: Cable knits, french terry, fleece, intarsia designs, jacquard jersey, knitted terry, knitted velour, openwork designs, pointelle, ribbed patterns, simplex, single knits, tricot.

Uses: Sweaters, jackets, coats, dresses, skirts, pants, tee shirts, vests.

Design Elements: Easy-fitting shapes, minimal seaming, elastic bands, collarless cardigans, turtlenecks, ribbing trims, elastic casings.

Sewing Checklist

Essential Supplies
Needles: Universal (H), stretch (HS), ballpoint (H-SUK), twin needle; sizes 70/10-80/12.
Thread: All purpose (polyester, cotton covered polyester).
Cutting: Sharp shears, weights, rotary cutter/mat.
Marking: Chalk, clips, erasable pens, tailor's tacks, thread, safety pins.
Miscellaneous: Flower pins, stay tape, bias tape, clear elastic, safety pins, stabilizers – water soluble, lightweight tearaway, cut away.
Interfacings: Detail areas – lightweight knit or weft fusibles or sew-ins.
Linings/Underlinings: Optional, same care and stretch as fashion fabric.

Machine Setup
Stitch Length: 2-2.5mm (10-12spi); zigzag (W,.5-L,1.5)
Tension: Lightly balanced.
Feet: Wide straight stitch, roller, zigzag.

Sewing Basics
Fabric Prep: Preshrink washables – machine wash/dry; non-washables – steam or dry-clean.
Layout: Nap – double layer; bulky – single layer, duplicate pattern pieces.
Seams: Plain (pressed open or closed), twin needle, taped, safety-stitch serged.
Seam/Hem Finishes: Serged, zigzag.
Hems: Hand (blind catchstitch, catchstitch), top-stitched, coverstitch, twin needle, lettucing, fused.
Edge Finishes: Facings (self-fabric, grosgrain, lining, bias, tricot), bindings, ribbings, elastic casings, bands.
Closures: Buttonholes (machine, corded, inseam); buttons/loops, ties, zippers (hand, machine, invisible, decorative), snaps, snap tape; avoid hook/loop tape.
Pressing: Medium heat, damp cloth or steam.
Garment Care: Machine wash/dry or dry-clean, depending on fiber.

Workroom Secrets
Pattern Prep: Before cutting a "knits only" pattern, compare the fabric to the stretch gauge; then compare the pattern dimensions and body measurements. If the fabric has more stretch than recommended, consider a smaller size pattern. Change seam allowances to 1" (2.5cm) to avoid wavy seamlines.

Fabric Prep: Preshrink to reduce stitching problems, remove excess finishes, and relax the fabric; machine wash/dry washable fabrics. To preshrink cottons and cotton blends, wash/dry several times. For acrylics, remove fabrics from the dryer immediately to avoid heat-set wrinkles. For wool, steam or dry-clean.

Layout/Cutting/Marking: Let fabric relax overnight before cutting. To find right side, stretch crosswise; edge will curl to the right side. If both sides look the same, use safety pins to mark the right side. Steam press any creases. If permanent, refold so they will be inconspicuous. Identify and mark a lengthwise rib to use as the grainline. Use flower pins or weights to hold pattern in place.

Stitching: For more elastic seams, use polyester thread and a narrow zigzag (W,.5-L,1.5), a twin needle, or textured thread in the bobbin.

Seams: To prevent stretching, stabilize seams at the shoulder, waist, and garment edges with stay tape. At necklines and armholes, use bias-cut tape. To stabilize and allow stretch, use clear (polyurethane) elastic.

Hems: Machine stitch hems with a twin needle. Loosen the upper tension and use textured thread in the bobbin.

Edge Finishes: Use grosgrain ribbon to stabilize and face garment openings.

Garment Care: Dry-clean to maintain the garment's pristine appearance.

Look good and be comfortable wearing this smartly styled sweater knit. (Burda Pattern – 8593, photo courtesy of Burda.)

Sweatshirt Knit

Sweatshirt knits are medium to heavy-weight knits. Made of cotton, acrylic, polyester, and blends, they vary in stretch from very little to moderate (25 percent); and many have a napped surface on the face or back. Sweatshirt knits hold their shape well, do not run or unravel, and are comfortable to wear. They are easy to sew, even though the fabric is bulky.

Workroom Secrets

Fabric Prep: Choose fabrics which are finished with the ribs and courses at right angles. Check the label on the bolt and purchase additional fabric to allow for shrinkage. Sweatshirt knits shrink both in the length and width; and fabrics which contain cotton shrink most.

Layout/Cutting/Marking: Use a nap layout with right sides together. Use flower pins to pin the pattern pieces in place.

Stitching: For more elastic seams, use polyester thread and a narrow zigzag stitch. Use an even feed or roller foot to reduce underlayer creep.

Seams: Generally, inconspicuous serged plain or top-stitched seams are best. Stabilize seams at shoulders, neck, and waist with stay tape to prevent stretching. (See Any Fabric page 13.) When topstitching, use an even feed foot.

Hems: Generally, topstitched hems or ribbing trims are preferred. For very casual designs, a simple serged edge in matching or contrast thread is attractive. For topstitched hems, use a twin needle or multiple rows of stitching. To prevent rippling, fuse a strip of lightweight knit interfacing to the hem allowance before stitching.

Edge Finishes: Replace bulky facings with ribbing, bands, bindings, elastic, fold-over braids, or serging.

Buttonholes: Stabilize machine buttonholes with a small strip of fusible interfacing. Use water soluble stabilizer on top of the fabric to prevent the stitches from embedding in the fabric.

Zippers: Stabilize the opening to prevent stretching.

Embellishments: Use ruffled pintucks for a softer, feminine look. Fold the fabric on the crossgrain and stretch as much as possible. Zigzag, satin stitch, or serge the folded edge with matching or contrast thread. To showcase your embroidery skills, use a cutaway stabilizer under the fabric and a water soluble stabilizer on top.

Simply designed and easy to wear, this sweatsuit is a must-have for any wardrobe. (Photo courtesy of New Look Patterns.)

Similar Fabrics: French Terry, knitted terry, knitted velour, sweater knits.

Uses: Activewear, sweaters, skirts, sweatshirts, and sweat pants, casual dresses and jackets, bathrobes.

Design Elements: Minimal seaming, raglan and kimono sleeves, dropped shoulders, elastic waistbands, topstitched seams, soft pleats, ribbing and grosgrain trims, exposed zippers, lettuce edging, ruffled pintucks, embroidery.

Sewing Checklist

Essential Supplies

Needles: Stretch (HS), universal (H); sizes 70/10-90/14.

Thread: All purpose (polyester, cotton covered polyester). Topstitching – all purpose, machine embroidery/topstitching threads.

Cutting: Sharp shears, rotary cutter/mat, duplicate pattern pieces.

Marking: Chalk, clips, erasable pens, flower pins, safety pins.

Miscellaneous: Flower pins, weights, stay tape, fusible knit interfacing, stabilizers – water soluble, tearaway, cut away.

Interfacings/Linings: Rarely used.

Machine Setup

Stitch Length: 2.5-3mm (8-10spi).

Tension: Lightly balanced.

Machine Feet: Even feed, roller, wide straight stitch, zigzag.

Sewing Basics

Test Garment: Not required.

Fabric Prep: Machine wash/dry several times.

Layout: Nap – double layer right sides together; heavy fabrics – single layer, using duplicate pattern pieces.

Seams: Plain (pressed closed), taped, topstitched, safety-stitch.

Seam/Hem Finishes: Serged or zigzag together.

Hems: Topstitched, twin needle, serged edge.

Edge Finishes: Facings (self-fabric, lining), ribbing, bands, bindings, elastic, fold-over braid, serged edges.

Closures: Buttonholes (machine), toggles, zippers (machine, exposed, invisible).

Pressing: Medium to high heat, steam.

Garment Care: Machine wash/dry.

Taffeta

Taffeta is a crisp, fine-rib fabric with a distinctive rustle or scroop. Tightly woven in silk, rayon, acetate, polyester, or blends, it creases badly, is difficult to ease, and is easily marred by pins, needles, ripping, folding, and improper pressing.

Similar Fabrics: Antique taffeta, barathea, basket weave taffeta, bayadere, bengaline, ciré, faille, givrene, gros de Londres, iridescent taffeta, jacquard taffeta, mikado silk, moiré, paper taffeta, pongee, repp, tissue taffeta, tussah, watered silk.
Uses: Dressy garments, blouses, dresses, pants, lingerie, special occasion, evening wear, linings, underlinings.
Design Elements: Crisp silhouettes, gathers, pleats, ruffles, flares, drapes. Avoid seams on the straight grain. (See Any Fabric page 14.)

Sewing Checklist

Essential Supplies
Needles: Sharp (HM, HJ), universal (H); sizes 60/8-70/10.
Thread: Lightweight (cotton, polyester, cotton covered polyester, silk), all purpose. Topstitching – lightweight, all purpose threads. Serger – lightweight serger thread, textured thread.
Cutting: Serrated shears, rotary cutter/mat.
Marking: Chalk, clips, tailor's tacks, thread.
Miscellaneous: Temporary pattern adhesive, super fine pins/needles, weights, dress shields, horsehair braid, cotton flannel, water soluble stabilizer, cotton basting or hand embroidery floss.
Interfacings: Lightweight sew-ins and fusibles, silk organza, lightweight silks, polyester chiffon, net.
Linings/Underlinings: Generally on outerwear and quality designs.

Machine Setup
Stitch Length: 2-2.5mm (10-12spi).
Tension: Lightly balanced; light pressure.
Feet: Wide straight stitch, roller, zigzag; small-hole throat plate.

Sewing Basics
Test Garment: Recommended.
Fabric Prep: Rarely needed, steaming may spot.
Layout: Without nap – double layer, right sides together; moiré/iridescent – nap.
Seams: Plain (pressed open or closed), tissue-stitched, topstitched, bound, French, faux French, safety-stitch serged.
Hems: Hand (blindstitch, catchstitch), interfaced, double-stitched, horsehair braid, shirttail, machine rolled, faced, lace.
Seam/Hem Finishes: Pinked, serged, zigzag; if lined, none.
Edge Finishes: Facings (self-fabric, lining, bias, ribbon), bias bindings (self-fabric, contrast).
Closures: Buttonholes (machine, corded, bound, inseam); buttons/loops, covered snaps, ties, zippers (hand, invisible, machine).
Pressing: Cool to medium heat, press cloth.
Garment Care: Dry-clean.

Workroom Secrets
Layout/Cutting/Marking: Use weights or place super fine pins in the seam allowances. Extend both ends of the grainline and pin in the seam allowances or use temporary pattern adhesive. Mark lightly; erasable pens and colored chalk may stain permanently.
Stitching Tips: Start all new projects with a new needle in the smallest recommended size. Change needles frequently. To check for burrs on the needle, stitch through a nylon stocking scrap. Stitch onto water soluble stabilizer, then onto the taffeta. Press lightly with steam to remove the stabilizer. To reduce puckered seams, use a wide straight stitch foot, and hold the fabric firmly in front and back of the foot when stitching.
Seams: Pin baste with super fine pins or needles. Hand baste to ensure stitching accuracy and reduce ripping. Baste with soft cotton or fine silk thread to avoid pressing imprints. Wide seams (1"-2.5cm) are easier to press smoothly.
Hems: Interface the hem for a softer edge with bias-cut cotton flannel. On prom dresses, use lace or narrow horsehair braid so the hem will stand away from the legs.
Seam/Hem Finishes: To reduce thread imprints, use textured thread in the serger loopers.
Buttonholes: Machine stitch with a new, sharp needle (HM) and fine machine embroidery thread.
Sleeves: To set the sleeve smoothly, reduce the ease in the cap.
Underlinings: Use underlinings to give the design shape, support heavy skirts, cushion seams, hide hemming stitches, and prevent seam slippage on close fitting designs. Use a net booster at the waist under gathered skirts to support the weight. (See Satin page 76.)

Pressing: Test press. Press lightly with a warm iron. Taffeta is easily damaged by improper pressing and water spots. Unwanted creases may be impossible to remove. Use a press cloth on the right side and a seam roll and brown paper strips to avoid seam and hem impressions.
Garment Care: Most taffeta garments require dry-cleaning, even when made of synthetic fibers. Use dress shields to avoid unwanted perspiration stains.

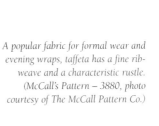

A popular fabric for formal wear and evening wraps, taffeta has a fine rib-weave and a characteristic rustle. (McCall's Pattern – 3880, photo courtesy of The McCall Pattern Co.)

Tencel®/Lyocell (knit and woven)

Tencel® is Courtauld's trade name for the fiber lyocell. An environmentally friendly fiber made of wood pulp, it has many of the properties of cotton. Fabrics can be knitted or woven and range from crepes and chambrays to poplins and twills. It can be used alone or blended with natural fibers or other manufactured fibers. It has a soft hand and is durable, comfortable to wear, resistant to wrinkles, and easy to clean. It has little elasticity.

Workroom Secrets

Fabric Prep: Tencel® will shrink. If 100 percent lyocell, machine wash and rinse in cool water; dry on low. Remove immediately from the dryer to avoid wrinkles. If the fabric is a blend, preshrink using the other fiber as a guide.

Stitching: Use sharp (HM, HJ) needles. Begin each new project with a new needle. Use a straight stitch foot and throat plate to reduce stitching problems. For more elastic seams on knits, use polyester thread and a narrow zigzag (W,.5-L,2). Hold fabric firmly in front of and behind presser foot when stitching.

Seams: To avoid fraying when laundered, finish seams with serging or zigzag; or use safety-stitch serged seams. To maintain the softness and drape at seamlines, press the seams open and serge or zigzag separately with lightweight serger thread or textured thread. Avoid bound finishes.

Topstitching: To flatten seams and edges, topstitch. For dressier designs, topstitch close to the edge or seam. For sportswear, lengthen the stitch and topstitch ¼" (6mm) away.

Sleeves: Reduce the ease as needed to ease the cap fullness smoothly.

Buttonholes: Before machine stitching, spray area with starch to add body or place water-soluble stabilizer on top. Stitch, using a new sharp needle (HM).

Zippers: Use a lightweight zipper. Stabilize opening to prevent stretching.

Interfacings: Lightweight sew-ins and fusibles work well. Many crisp interfacings will overwhelm the fabric.

Pressing: Test press to determine the appropriate heat, moisture, and pressure for the fiber content. Fabrics are damaged by too much heat.

Environmentally friendly, Tencel® resists wrinkles and is comfortable to wear. (Photo courtesy of KWIK-SEW®.)

Similar Types/Fabrics: Lenzing lyocell, Tencel® denim, Tencel®/wool, rayon challis, sandwashed Tencel®.

Uses: Tailored or dressy designs, casual wear, blouses, skirts, pants, dresses.

Design Elements: Gored skirts, topstitching, soft pleats, gathers, twists, shirt sleeves, decorative snaps. Avoid close fitting designs.

Sewing Checklist

Essential Supplies

Needle types: Sharp (HJ), universal (H); sizes 70/10-80/12.

Thread: All purpose (cotton, polyester, cotton covered polyester). Topstitching – all purpose, machine embroidery/topstitching threads.

Cutting: Sharp shears, rotary cutter/mat.

Marking: Chalk, clips, erasable pens, pins.

Miscellaneous: Super fine pins, stay tape, lightweight zippers, spray starch, stabilizers – water soluble, tearaway.

Interfacings: Fusible, sew-in, washable.

Linings: Outerwear, same care properties as fashion fabric.

Machine Setup

Stitch Length: 2-2.5mm (10-12spi).

Tension: Balanced.

Feet: Wide straight stitch, zigzag.

Sewing Basics

Test Garment: Not required.

Fabric Prep: Machine wash/dry, steam or dry-clean, depending on the garment structure and fiber content.

Layout: Generally without nap; double layer with right sides together.

Seams: Plain (pressed open or closed), topstitched, safety-stitch serged.

Hems: Hand (blindstitch, catchstitch), topstitched, shirttail.

Seam/Hem Finishes: Serged, zigzag, pinked.

Edge Finishes: Facings, bindings, bands, ribbing.

Closures: Buttonholes (machine), buttons/ loops, decorative snaps, zippers (machine, invisible).

Pressing: Medium heat; damp cloth or steam.

Garment Care: Machine wash/dry, dry-clean depending on garment type, design, and fibers.

Terry Cloth and Velour

Terry cloth and velour are warp pile fabrics. Terry cloth has uncut loops on one or both sides; and velour has cut loops which look like velveteen. Made of cotton, hemp, rayon, or blends, better fabrics have a closely woven back with closely packed loops or pile, but they are bulky and creep badly when stitched. Unlike fleece, velvet, and velveteen, terry and velour are much sturdier and easier to sew. This section focuses on woven fabrics and knits with little, or no, stretch. To sew stretch terry or velour, see Stretch Knit page 83.

Similar Fabrics: French terry, no-wale corduroy, plush knit, sculptured velour, terry knit, velour knit, velveteen plush.

Uses: Casual jackets, coats, tee tops, shorts, pants, bathrobes, children's wear, towels.

Design Elements: Minimal seaming, wrap fronts, elastic casings, ribbing, bias trims, extended shoulders, kimono, raglan, and shirt sleeves, decorative seams. When possible, eliminate fasteners.

Sewing Checklist

Essential Supplies

Needles: Sharp (HM, HJ), universal (H); sizes 70/10-90/14.

Thread: All-purpose (cotton, polyester, cotton covered polyester, silk).

Cutting: Large, sharp shears, rotary cutter/mat, duplicate pattern pieces.

Marking: Chalk, clips, erasable pens, safety pins.

Miscellaneous: Flower pins, washable glue stick, shim, water soluble stabilizers.

Interfacings: Sew-ins, fusibles.

Linings/Underlinings: Rarely used.

Machine Setup

Stitch Length: 2.5-3mm (8-10spi); topstitching: 3-3.5mm (7-8spi).

Tension: Lightly balanced; light pressure.

Feet: Even feed, roller, wide straight stitch, zipper, zigzag.

Sewing Basics

Test Garment: Rarely needed.

Fabric Prep: Machine wash/dry several times if cotton or rayon.

Layout: Nap – wrong sides together; heavy fabrics – single layer, wrong-side up.

Seams: Plain (pressed open, closed), piped, bound, strap, safety-stitched serged.

Hems: Topstitched, twin needle, hand (catchstitch, blindstitch), wrong-side out.

Seam/Hem Finishes: Serged, zigzag, bound (tricot, cotton bias tape); if lined, none.

Edge Finishes: Facings (self-, contrast trim), bindings, fold-over braid.

Closures: Buttonholes (machine, inseam), buttons/loops, ties, zippers (machine, invisible, exposed).

Pressing: Medium to high heat; steam, self-fabric press cloth on right side.

Garment Care: Machine wash/dry.

Workroom Secrets

Fabric Prep: To preshrink natural fiber fabrics, machine wash/dry several times.

Layout/Cutting/Marking: Mark the right side with safety pins. Use flower pins to hold pattern pieces in place. Mark notches with short ⅛" (3mm) clips. Spread velour with wrong sides together. If fabric is double-faced velour, spread in a single layer.

Stitching: To simulate quality ready-to-wear, reduce or eliminate hand sewing as much as possible. To stitch over uneven layers, use a zipper foot or shim. When joining to a smooth fabric, stitch with the smooth fabric uppermost. Topstitching is more attractive on terry cloth than velour. When topstitching, lengthen the stitch. Topstitch with the nap.

Seams: Use serged, topstitched, strap, and bound seams to finish unlined jackets attractively. For decorative bound seams, stitch wrong sides together. Trim seam to ¼" or ⅜" (6-10mm). Bind seam with contrast bias fabric or ribbon. Fold seams toward back or down when joining to another section.

Hems: Topstitch hems with a single or twin needle or coverstitch. For a decorative hem, use a wrong-side-out hem or contrast facing as a trim.

Edge Finishes: Replace self-fabric facings with contrast smooth fabric facings, lightweight bindings, bands, or ribbings.

Garment Care: Turn garment inside out to wash. Use a fabric softener to reduce lint.

Soft and absorbent, terry is ideal for bath or beach. (Photo courtesy of New Look Patterns.)

Tricot

Tricot is a warp knit with vertical ribs on the face and horizontal rows on the back. It is easy to sew, run resistant, and durable. A favorite for lingerie, it is available in a variety of fabrications and weights. Made of nylon, polyester, acetate, triacetate, or cotton, it is sometimes knitted with monofilament nylon for stability or spandex for stretch. Tricot attracts oil stains, snags easily, and may cling.

Workroom Secrets

Fabric Prep: Generally, tricot does not need to be preshrunk. To relax fabric, remove excess fabric finishes, reduce static electricity, and reduce skipped stitches, machine wash/dry. Add fabric softener to final rinse.

Layout/Cutting/Marking: To determine right side, stretch crosswise, the edge will roll to right side. Mark the right side with a chalked "X" or small safety pins. Cut seam allowances ¼" (6mm) wide for easier stitching; mark with short ⅛" (3mm) clips.

Stitching: To reduce stitching problems, use polyester thread and fill the bobbin slowly. Begin with a new needle and change needles frequently. Hold threads when you begin stitching, stitch at a medium speed, and hold the fabric firmly, stretching it slightly. For more elastic seams, stitch with a narrow zigzag (W,.5-L,1.5).

Seams: Stabilize seams at shoulders, neck, and waist to prevent stretching. Use clear elastic to stabilize and preserve the stretch.

Hems: For a plain finish, topstitch hems with a straight stitch, narrow zigzag, or twin needle. To prevent rippling, fuse a strip of lightweight knit interfacing to the hem allowance.

Edge Finishes: Applied lace is frequently used on lingerie, sleepwear, and loungewear. To avoid stretching the tricot or lace, lay the garment flat on a table to pin. Position the lace on the right side; use pins, temporary spray adhesive, or glue stick to baste. Stitch permanently at the top of the lace using a narrow zigzag (W,1-L,1); trim away the excess fabric under the lace. To apply straight lace, serge the garment edge. Glue-baste the lace on the right side to cover the serging. Zigzag (W,.5;L,1) to secure permanently. For a soft, tailored look, use a binding.

Buttonholes: When buttonholes cannot be avoided, interface the buttonhole area with a strip of interfacing.

Comfortable to wear and easy to sew, tricot is the perfect choice for lingerie and sleepwear. (Photo courtesy of KWIK·SEW®.)

Tricot Types/Similar Fabrics: Antron III®, brushed nylon, glissinate, interlock knits, knit interfacings, Lustra, plain knits, pointelle, quilt backing, satin tricot, sheer tricot, single knits, stretch tricot, tricot tulle.

Uses: Slips, panties, nightgowns, loungewear, evening wear, veiling, overlays.

Design Elements: Soft, fluid designs, casings, elastic, lace trim. Avoid hook and loop tape.

Sewing Checklist

Essential Supplies

Needles: Stretch (HS), universal (H), ballpoint (H-SUK), twin needle; sizes 60/8-80/12.

Thread: All purpose (polyester), fine serger thread.

Cutting: Serrated shears, rotary cutter/mat.

Marking: Chalk, clips, erasable pens, pins.

Miscellaneous: Super fine pins, temporary spray adhesive, glue stick, lightweight zippers, clear elastic, stay tape.

Interfacings: Detail areas; lightweight knit fusibles.

Linings/Underlinings: Rarely.

Machine Setup

Stitch Length: 2-2.5mm (8-10spi), narrow zigzag (W,.5-L,1.5).

Tension: Lightly balanced.

Feet: Wide straight stitch, roller, zigzag; small hole throat plate.

Sewing Basics

Fabric Prep: Machine wash/dry.

Layout: Nap – double layer.

Seams: Plain (pressed closed), zigzag, double-stitched, twin needle, safety-stitch serged.

Seam/Hem finishes: Serged, zigzag, none.

Hems: Lettuce edging, merrow, narrow zigzag, topstitched, twin needle.

Edge Finishes: Bindings, facings (bias tricot, sheer tricot, self-fabric), applied elastic, applied lace, elastic casings.

Closures: Buttons or loops, ties, machine buttonholes.

Pressing: Low heat.

Garment Care: Machine wash/dry.

Two-way and Four-way Stretch Knit

Sometimes called Action Knits, stretch knits such as two-way and four-way knits are warp knits with spandex. Available in all weights from sheer illusion to moleskin, they stretch in both the length and width. Generally, four-way stretch knits have more stretch, are heavier, cover better, and pill less than two-way stretch knits. All have a nap and are easily snagged by damaged pins, needles, and hook and loop tape.

Nylon/spandex blends are better than polyester blends for swimwear. They dry faster, have more stretch, and resist abrasion better. Polyester/cotton blends are cooler and more comfortable to wear when exercising.

Stretch Knits: Athletic mesh, automan, glissinate, Hi Tech Supplex®, jumbo spandex, milliskin, moleskin, power net, satin spandex, sheer illusion, slinky, spandura, stretch hologram, stretch tricot, stretch raschel, stretch vinyl, tricot chiffon.

Uses: Activewear, swimwear, jumpsuits, unitards, leotards, tights, shorts, skiwear, skating and dance costumes, bindings, cuffs, trims.

Design Elements: Minimal seaming, close fitting garments with little ease, no ease, or minus ease. Avoid thin fabrics and light colors for swimwear or use a lining.

Sewing Checklist

Essential Supplies

Needles: Stretch (HS), ballpoint (H-SUK), universal (H), twin needle; sizes 70/10-90/14.

Thread: All purpose (polyester); heavy fabrics – machine embroidery/topstitching. Serger – lightweight serger thread, textured thread.

Cutting: Sharp shears, rotary cutter/mat.

Marking: Chalk, clips, erasable pens, pins.

Miscellaneous: Super fine pins, temporary pattern adhesive, weights, swimwear or clear elastic, nylon stocking scrap.

Interfacings: Rarely.

Linings: Lightweight stretch tricot, self-fabric, lightweight power net, swimsuit lining.

Machine Setup

Stitch Length: 1.5-2mm (12-18spi); zigzag (W,.5-L,1).

Tension: Lightly balanced.

Feet: Roller, wide straight stitch, zigzag.

Sewing Basics

Test Garment: Rarely.

Fabric Prep: Machine wash, line dry.

Layout: Nap – double layer; crossgrain; prints – single layer, right-side up, using duplicate pattern pieces.

Seams: Plain (pressed open or closed), topstitched, twin needle, safety-stitch serged, strap.

Hems: Topstitch, twin needle.

Seam/Hem Finishes: Serged or zigzag together, pinked.

Edge Finishes: Facings (self-fabric), bindings, elastic (casings, applied), ribbings, snap tape.

Closures: Buttonholes (machine), buttons/loops, zippers (machine, invisible, exposed), ties. Avoid hook and loop tape.

Pressing: Low heat.

Garment Care: Machine wash, no bleach; line dry.

Workroom Secrets

Fabric Prep: Wash and line dry to relax the fabric and remove any excess finishes which might cause skipped stitches.

Layout/Cutting/Marking: Before cutting, check the fabric to determine whether there is more stretch in the length. Generally, garments are cut so the greatest stretch goes around the body. Compare the amount of fabric stretch with the amount required for the design. Use a nap layout. When cutting on the crossgrain, position the tops of the pattern in one direction. Use weights, temporary pattern adhesive, or super fine pins in the seam allowances to secure the pattern pieces. When fitting as you sew, cut 1" (2.5cm) seam allowances. Pin fit. Baste with a wide, long zigzag and loose tension. Fit, adjusting as needed. Then stitch, and trim.

Stitching: Start each new project with a new needle in the smallest recommended size. Change needles frequently; synthetic fibers dull needles faster than natural fibers. To check the needle for burrs, stitch through a nylon stocking scrap.

Seams: Use polyester thread for more elastic seams. For heavier fabrics, use machine embroidery/topstitching thread (size 40). Generally, textured thread is not strong enough for seams which will be stressed. Stitch with a narrow zigzag (W,.5-L,1), stretching moderately while stitching. If the seam ripples, you stretched it too much. Topstitch seams to flatten and add strength. Topstitch with a plain zigzag, multi-stitch zigzag, or twin needle to retain elasticity.

Edge Finishes: Self-fabric, other action knits, cotton/spandex bindings are attractive substitutes for elastic. Swimwear and clear elastics are resistant to perspiration, body oil, sun, salt water, and chlorine. They can be applied directly or in casings. Avoid rayon elastic. When applying elastic, cut 10 to 25 percent shorter than edge.

Linings/Underlinings: Use for comfort and modesty. Linings and underlinings should have the same stretch as fabric.

Ideal for activewear, this two-way stretch ensemble is attractive as well as practical. (Photo courtesy of KWIK-SEW®.)

Velvet

Velvet is a pile fabric woven with an extra set of warp yarns. Made of fibers such as cotton, rayon, acetate, polyester, microfibers, spandex, and various blends, velvets range in weight from chiffon to heavy upholstery fabrics. Velvets have a nap, creep badly when stitched, and are easily marred by pins, machine needles, improper pressing, folding, and ripping. When sewing stretch velvet, review Stretch Woven page 84 or Stretch Knit page 83.

Workroom Secrets

Fabric Prep: Depends on manufacturer's recommendation. To create washable crushed velvet, machine wash/dry inexpensive rayon velvet. To store, hang by the selvage. Do not fold.

Layout/Cutting/Marking: Use chalk to mark the direction of the nap on the wrong side. Spread the fabric in a single layer with wrong-side up or double layer with wrong sides together. Use super fine pins, and pin only in the seam allowances. Try to avoid marking on the nap itself. When necessary, make tailor's tacks with fine silk thread or soft cotton embroidery floss. Avoid wax chalk and erasable pens, which may stain permanently.

Stitching: To avoid stitching problems and ripping, baste seams with water soluble thread; then baste a second time to fill in the spaces. Stitch with a velvet "V" foot, even feed, or roller foot; then press the seam flat using steam to dissolve the thread. When joining velvet to a lining or a smooth fabric, stitch with the velvet on top. Stitch with the nap, even if you must stitch against the grain. Understitch by hand.

Seam/Hem Finishes: Use a stiff brush to brush away loose pile at cut edges. Finish with a serger, tricot binding, or Hong Kong finish.

Hems: Interface with bias-cut cotton flannel for a soft hemline. To press the hemline, steam generously. Cover with a velvet scrap, and pat with the bristles of a stiff brush.

Pressing: Cover the pressing surface with a thick towel if you do not have a needleboard or a VelvaBoard®. Rayon and silk velvets are easily damaged; do not handle them while damp.

Garment Care: To protect skirts and pants from clip hangers, sew in ribbon hanger loops at the waist. To freshen the pile, hang in a steam-filled bathroom for 30 minutes. Do not handle or wear until completely dry.

From the Custom Couture Collection by Claire Shaeffer, this stunning coat features a dropped waist and flared skirt with shirring. (Vogue Pattern – 7634; courtesy of The McCall Pattern Co.)

Velvet Types: Bagheera, brocade, burnt out, crushed, cut, devoré, faconné, Lyon, mirror, nacré, panné, sculptured, stretch, transparent, voided.

Uses: Dressy and tailored designs, dresses, jackets, coats, capes, skirts, pants, evening wear.

Design Details: Simple designs, minimal seaming, soft gathers, pleats, flares, elastic casings. Avoid topstitching, tucks, close fitting garments, seams and folds on the cross grain.

Sewing Checklist

Essential Supplies
Needles: Sharp (HM, HJ), universal (H); sizes 70/10-80/12.
Thread: All-purpose (cotton, polyester, cotton covered polyester core, silk). Serger – lightweight serger.
Cutting: Large, sharp shears, duplicate pattern pieces.
Marking: Chalk, clips, tailor's tacks, thread.
Miscellaneous: Super fine pins, hand embroidery floss, water soluble, or fine silk for basting, stiff bristled brush, ¼" (6mm) wide ribbon, cotton flannel, needleboard or VelvaBoard®, stabilizers – water soluble, burn away, cut away.
Interfacings: Sew-ins, hair canvas.
Linings: Generally on quality designs and outerwear.
Underlinings: Rarely.

Machine Setup
Stitch Length: 2.5-3mm (8-10spi).
Tension: Lightly balanced; light pressure.
Feet: Velvet "V" foot, even feed, roller, wide straight stitch, zigzag.

Sewing Basics
Test Garment: Recommended.
Fabric Prep: Preshrink natural fibers with steam or dry-clean. Machine wash/dry microfibers and synthetics for casual designs.
Layout: Nap – single layer, wrong-side up, using duplicate pattern pieces; double layer – wrong side together.
Seams: Plain (pressed open), piped.
Hems: Hand: (blindstitch, blind catchstitch, catchstitch) double-stitched, interfaced.
Seam/Hem Finishes: Serged, zigzag, Hong Kong finish, bound; if lined, none.
Edge Finishes: Facings (self-fabric, smooth fabric), bindings, fold-over braid.
Closures: Buttonholes (machine, bound, inseam), buttons/loops, frogs, zippers (hand, invisible).
Pressing: Medium heat; steam, velvet press cloth.
Garment Care: Generally dry-clean; machine wash/dry casual designs if fabric was preshrunk.

Velveteen

Velveteen is a pile fabric woven with an extra set of filling yarns. Made from several fibers such as cotton, polyester, and various blends, velveteens are made in a variety of weights and designs. Velveteens have a nap, and the pile separates on seams and folds on the lengthwise grain. It does not ease well, creeps badly when stitched, and is easily marred by pins, improper pressing, and ripping.

Similar Fabrics: No-wale corduroy, velveteen plush, velour.
Uses: Dresses, jackets, coats, capes, skirts, pants, evening wear, sportswear, pillows, children's designs, trims.
Design Details: Minimal seaming, soft gathers, pleats, flares, topstitching on casual designs. Combines well with wool, fleece, cotton, faux suede, faux leather, and satin. Avoid tucks, close fitting garments, seams and folds on straight grain. (See Any Fabric page 14.)

Sewing Checklist

Essential Supplies
Needles: Sharp (HM, HJ), universal (H); sizes 70/10-90/14.
Thread: All-purpose (cotton, polyester, cotton covered polyester, silk). Topstitching – machine embroidery/topstitching thread, 2 threads all purpose. Serger – lightweight serger, textured thread.
Cutting: Large, sharp shears; rotary cutter/mat.
Marking: Chalk, clips, tailor's tacks, thread.
Miscellaneous: Super fine pins, cotton embroidery floss or silk for basting, stiff bristled brush, needleboard, point turner, thick towel, wigan, muslin.
Interfacings: Sew-ins, hair canvas; fusibles, weft.
Linings: Generally on quality designs and outerwear.
Underlinings: Rarely.

Machine Setup
Stitch Length: 2.5-3mm (8-10spi); topstitching – 3-3.5mm (7-8 spi).
Tension: Lightly balanced; light pressure.
Feet: Even feed, roller, wide straight stitch, zipper, zigzag.

Sewing Basics
Test Garment: Recommended.
Fabric Prep: Preshrink natural fibers with steam or dry-clean. Machine wash/dry several times to preshrink cottons and blends for casual designs.
Layout: Nap – wrong sides together; heavy fabrics – single layer, wrong-side up; matching – single layer right-side up, using duplicate pattern pieces.
Seams: Plain (pressed open), topstitched, piped.
Hems: Hand (blindstitch, blind catchstitch, catchstitch), double-stitched, interfaced.
Seam/Hem Finishes: Serged, zigzag, tricot binding, Hong Kong finish; if lined, none.
Edge Finishes: Facings (self-, lining), bindings, foldover braid.
Closures: Buttonholes (machine, bound, inseam), buttons/loops, toggles, zippers (hand, machine, invisible).
Pressing: Medium to high heat; steam, velveteen press cloth.
Garment Care: Dry-clean to maintain the garment's pristine appearance. If fabric was preshrunk, launder casual designs. Turn garment wrong-side out.

Workroom Secrets
Fabric Selection: Twill weave velveteens have a denser pile, wear better, and shed less than plain weave fabrics. To store, hang by the selvage. Do not fold.
Pattern Prep: Redraw seams on straight grain so they are off-grain.
Layout/Cutting/Marking: Spread the fabric wrong sides together, except when working with heavy velveteens or prints which require matching. Spread heavy fabrics wrong-side up and prints right-side up. For a rich, deep color, lay out so nap runs up; for wear and lighter color, lay out so nap runs down. Place pins only in the seam allowances. Try to avoid marking on the right side.
Stitching: To avoid stitching problems and ripping, baste seams; baste again to fill in the spaces. Hold firmly in front and behind foot. Stitch with the nap. When joining to a smooth fabric, stitch with the velveteen on top. When topstitching, lengthen stitch; use a zipper foot to topstitch edges and a shim to stitch over uneven layers.
Seams: At edges, press seams open before trimming. Trim to a scant ¼" (6mm). At corners, do not trim too closely. Before turning, fold the seam toward the underside, and sew it flat at the corner. Turn the seam right-side out and straighten with a point turner.
Hems: For soft hems on quality garments, interface with bias-cut wigan or muslin. To press the hemline, steam generously. Cover with self-fabric scrap and pat with bristles of a stiff brush. Double stitch hems on heavier fabrics.
Buttonholes: Cut welts for bound buttonholes on the bias.
Pressing: Cover the pressing surface with a thick terry towel or piece of velveteen. Set heat higher for cottons. Avoid touching pile with iron.
Garment Care: To freshen the pile, tumble in dryer with several damp towels for 10 minutes. Remove and hang immediately.

A favorite for all ages, this velveteen party dress is trimmed with satin. (Photo courtesy of KWIK-SEW®.)

Waterproof Fabric

Waterproof fabrics are available in a variety of qualities. Fabrics with thicker coatings are more waterproof but do not breathe as well. Fabrics which do not breathe will keep you dry, but are uncomfortable to wear if they do not have ventilation features. Frequently bulky and difficult to stitch, most waterproof fabrics are damaged by pins, needles, ripping, hot irons, light bulbs, clothes dryers, campfires, and heaters.

This chapter focuses on breathable waterproof fabrics. If these fabrics are not available from your local retailer, they can be ordered from several mail order companies.

Breathable Types: Avalite, Extreme, Gore-Tex®, Supplex®, Ultrex®.

Non-Breathable Types: Cordura®, Imperial PVC, packcloth, coated nylon, coated Tasnyl, vinyl.

Uses: Breathable types – vests, jackets, pullovers, rainwear, parkas; non-breathables – pack sacks.

Design Elements: Minimal seaming, raglan sleeves, hoods, storm and zipper flaps, extended and reinforced shoulders, air vents. Avoid shoulder seams at the top of the shoulder, gathers, close fitting designs.

Workroom Secrets

Layout/Cutting/Marking: If a fabric looks the same on both sides, sprinkle water on it; mark the least absorbent side "right side." Place pins only in the seam allowances or use temporary pattern adhesive. Spread the fabric in a single layer to cut thick fabrics.

Stitching: Begin with a new needle in the smallest size; change frequently. Use nylon or polyester thread. Stitch using a teflon foot, even-feed, or roller foot; or place stabilizer on top of the fabric. To prevent puckered seams, place stabilizer under the fabric to stitch. Hold the fabric firmly in front of and behind the presser foot. Stretch when stitching stretch fabrics. Wipe the needle frequently with alcohol on a cotton ball to remove build-up on the needle and reduce skipped stitches. When using topstitching or upholstery thread, loosen the bobbin tension or use an extra bobbin case. To avoid ripping, baste; pin-baste only in the seam allowances, or use quilting clothes pins, glue stick, or washable basting tape.

Seams: Backstitch to secure thread ends. Shorten stitch length for curves and corners. When crossing thick seams, use a shim to balance the foot. Double stitch seams that will be stressed. Seal seams with liquid seam sealer or iron-on sealing tape.

Simply styled, this coat is comfortable to wear as well as waterproof. (Photo courtesy of www.rochelleharper.net.)

Sewing Checklist

Essential Supplies

Needles: Sharp (HM, HJ), topstitching (N), universal (H); sizes, light to medium-weight – 60/8-80/12, heavy-weight – 80/12-18/110.

Thread: All purpose or machine embroidery/topstitching (polyester), nylon upholstery.

Cutting: Sharp shears; lightweight fabrics – rotary cutter/mat.

Marking: Chalk, clips, erasable pens.

Miscellaneous: Shim, weights, quilting clothes pins, washable basting tape, temporary pattern adhesive, grommets, rubbing alcohol, cotton, liquid seam sealers, iron-on sealing tape, waterproof seam tape, invisible zippers, glue stick, DWR (durable water-repellent) treatments.

Interfacings: Lightweight sew-in for storm and zipper flaps.

Linings/Underlinings: Wicking fabrics – PowderDry®; Polartec® 100 wt; CoolMax®; insulating, Thinsulate®.

Machine Setup

Stitch Length: 1.75-2.5mm (10-15spi).

Tension: Lightly balanced; light pressure.

Feet: Teflon, roller, even feed, overlock, zigzag.

Sewing Basics

Test Garment: Depends on design, quality, and your skills.

Fabric Prep: Depends on fabric; do not preshrink coated fabrics.

Layout: Without nap – double layer; heavy fabrics – single layer, duplicate pattern pieces.

Seams: Plain (closed), twin needle, zigzag, French, topstitched, strap, abutted, lapped.

Seam/Hem Finishes: None, serged, sear, zigzag.

Hems: Topstitched (double, single fold), twin needle.

Edge Finishes: Facings (self- or contrast fabric), bands, ribbings, bindings (self-, contrast, fleece), casings.

Closures: Buttonholes (machine, inseam), zippers (decorative, two-way separating), snaps, grommets, toggles, hook/loop tape.

Linings: Wicking fabrics – taffeta, micro mesh, Polartec®, PowderDry®, tricot.

Interfacings: Lightweight sew-ins at openings; avoid fusibles.

Ventilation: Grommets, eyelets, nylon mesh, or under armpit zippers.

Pressing: Low heat or press with scissor handles.

Garment Care: Machine wash frequently. Machine dry on hot for short period. To restore DWR temporarily, machine dry. Nikwax and Tectron make special soaps and water-repellent treatments. Dry garments completely before storing.

Water-Repellent Fabric

Water-repellent fabrics are tightly woven, wind-resistant, and resistant to tearing and snagging. Some are water-repellent due to the weave and/or fiber; others are coated with a DWR (durable water-repellent) which must be renewed occasionally.

Available in a variety of weights, some are bulky, difficult to stitch, and fray badly. Some of the microfiber and lighter weight fabrics are particularly challenging. Most water-repellent fabrics are easily damaged by pins, needles, ripping, hot irons, light bulbs, clothes dryers, campfires, and heaters.

Water-Repellent/Similar Fabrics: Fabrics coated with DWR, ripstop, sueded microfiber, Savina®, Savina® DPR, Sunbrella®, Supplex®, Tactel®, Tuftex, Versatech®.
Uses: Vests, jackets, pullovers, rainwear, snowsuits.
Design Elements: Minimal seaming, raglan sleeves, hoods, storm and zipper flaps, extended and reinforced shoulders, air vents. Avoid close fitting garments.

Sewing Checklist

Essential Supplies
Needles: Sharp (HM, HJ), topstitching, universal (H); sizes 70/10-100/116.
Thread: All purpose or machine embroidery/topstitching (polyester), nylon upholstery thread.
Cutting: Shears, rotary cutter/mat.
Marking: Chalk, clips, erasable pens.
Miscellaneous: Shim, weights, temporary pattern adhesive, large paper clips, grommets, rubbing alcohol, cotton, liquid or iron-on seam sealers, quilting clothes pins, nylon mesh, invisible zippers, candle, water soluble stabilizers.
Interfacings: Rarely, except openings, storm and zipper flaps.
Linings/Underlinings: Windbreakers – fleece, cotton flannel, quilted linings. Rainwear – wicking fabrics, taffeta, micro mesh, Polartec®, PowderDry®, tricot.

Machine Setup
Stitch length: 1.75-2.5mm (10-15spi).
Tension: Lightly balanced; light pressure.
Feet: Teflon, roller, even feed, zigzag.

Sewing Basics
Test Garment: Rarely.
Fabric Prep: Generally not required; do not preshrink coated fabrics.
Layout: Without nap – double layer.
Seams: Plain (closed), topstitched, strap, French, double-stitched.
Seam/Hem Finishes: None, serged, sear.
Hems: Topstitched (double or single fold), twin needle.
Edge Finishes: Facings (self- or contrast fabric), bands, ribbings, bindings, casings.
Closures: Buttonholes (machine, inseam), zippers (machine, decorative, two-way separating), snaps, grommets, toggles, hook/loop tape.
Pressing: Low heat or press with scissor handles, no steam.
Garment Care: Machine wash/dry frequently.

Workroom Secrets
Layout/Cutting/Marking: When cutting fabrics which look the same on both sides, mark the right side with transparent tape. Use weights, temporary pattern adhesive, or place pins in the seam allowances.
Stitching: Begin with a new needle in the smallest size that will not skip stitches. Change the needle frequently. Use polyester or nylon thread and a teflon foot; or place stabilizer on top of the fabric. To prevent puckered seams, place stabilizer under the fabric to stitch. Hold the fabric firmly in front of and behind the presser foot. To remove build-up from the needle and reduce skipped stitches, wipe the needle frequently with alcohol on a cotton ball. When using topstitching or upholstery thread, loosen the bobbin tension or use an extra bobbin case.
Seams: Use quilting clothes pins, paper clips, or pin baste only in the seam allowances. When crossing thick seams, use a shim to balance the foot. Double stitch seams that will be stressed. Sear raw edges on synthetics to prevent fraying. To sear, move the edge quickly over a lighted candle. Do not inhale the fumes.
Ventilation: Use grommets, eyelets, nylon mesh, or invisible zippers under the arm to provide ventilation.
Garment Care: If water no longer beads on the right side, wash with non-detergent soap such as Blue Magic, Down Wash, Nikwax Tech Wash, or Pro Wash. To restore water-repellency, use Nikwax or Tectron products.

*An original design by Rochelle Harper, this reversible vest is fabricated in taslanized nylon and Polartec® fleece.
(Photo courtesy of www.rochelleharper.net.)*

Wool

Wool is the most versatile fiber. A natural, protein fiber, it is available in a wide range of weights, textures, weaves, and qualities. It absorbs moisture better than any other natural fiber. Wools are easily damaged by moths, chlorine bleach, and improper pressing.

There are two types of wool fabrics: woolens and worsteds. Woolens are woven from woolen yarns; worsteds, from worsted yarns.

Woolen yarns are made of short fibers, loosely spun with a low to medium twist. They are carded, but not combed, giving them a hairy surface which is easy to identify. Most woolen fabrics are soft with a rough or fuzzy texture that obscures the weave or knit. They are used to make bulkier, heavier, and warmer fabrics such as tweeds, coatings, washable wools, textured wools, and some flannels. Worsted yarns are carded and combed to make them smooth, strong, and more lustrous than woolen yarns. They have a medium-to-high-twist and the weave is quite prominent.

Worsted fabrics are lighter weight, clear-surfaced fabrics. They are tightly woven with a smooth, hard surface which wears well but shines easily, They tailor well, rarely sag or bag, crease and press well. They wear longer than woolens, but are more difficult to sew.

Woolens are easier to sew, less expensive, and better suited for casual designs. They are easier to ease and remove stains; but they are scratchier, sag, pill, mat, and soil more easily.

Woolen Types: Army blankets, blanket cloth, bouclé, cheviot, coating, Donegal, fleece, Glen plaid, Harris tweed, herringbone, houndstooth, homespun, kasha, loden, melton, Saxony, Scottish tweed, tartans, wool flannel, wool tweeds.

Worsted Fabrics: Bedford cord, blazer cloth, cassimere, cavalry twill, cheviot, covert, elastique, gabardine, jacquard, menswear suiting, ottoman, serge, sharkskin, tartans, tricotine, tropical wool, whipcord, wool challis, wool poplin, wool satin, worsted flannel, worsted suitings, zibeline.

Uses: All type garments.

Burn test: Wool burns slowly, and is self-extinguishing. It smells like hair and leaves small brittle black beads.

Designed by Ashley Marcu, the winner of the Exemplary Construction Award for Make It Yourself With Wool (2003), this classic ensemble is as modern as it is timeless. (Photo courtesy of Make It Yourself With Wool.)

Secrets for Pressing Wool

- Wools are easily damaged by improper pressing and hot irons.
- Test press to determine the appropriate amount of heat, moisture, and pressure.
- Before pressing, cover pressing surface with wool fabric.
- Use a wool press cloth when pressing the right side. Use a white wool cloth to press light colors.
- To generate a lot of steam, wrap the iron with a synthetic chamois cloth.
- Place bound buttonholes and welt pockets wrong-side up on a thick towel or needleboard.
- For sharper foldlines, rub the fold on the wrong side with a bar of Ivory soap. Fold in place; press, using a press cloth.
- For sharp, well-pressed seams, press the seam flat. Then rub each side of the stitching line with a bar of Ivory soap, and press it open over a seam roll or seam stick, using steam or a damp press cloth. Cover with clapper. Examine the results. If necessary, press again and spank with clapper. Do not move until fabric is dry.
- To apply additional moisture when pressing, first cover the garment with dry cloth. Rub a wet, but not dripping, sponge over the section to be pressed; then press.
- For a sharper press at edges, place the open seam over a point presser and press before trimming and turning right-side out.
- To hold layers in position when pressing an edge, baste about ¼" (6mm) from edge, using soft cotton basting thread or hand embroidery floss to avoid a pressing imprint.
- To remove pressing imprints, place the garment wrong-side up on a needleboard. Fill the garment with steam and press firmly. If possible, press underneath the seam allowance or pocket which has caused the imprint. Repeat until the imprint has been removed.

Sewing Checklist

Essential Supplies

Needles: Woven fabrics – sharp (HM, HJ), universal (H). **Knits** – stretch (HS), universal (H), ballpoint (H-SUK). Sizes – lightweight, 60/8-70/10; medium, 70/10-80/12; heavy, 80/12-90/14.

Thread: Lightweight fabrics – lightweight (cotton, polyester, cotton covered polyester, silk), all purpose thread. **Medium-weight fabrics** – all purpose thread. **Heavy-weight fabrics** – all purpose, machine embroidery/topstitching threads. **Very heavy-weight fabrics** – machine embroidery/topstitching threads.

Cutting: Lightweight fabrics – serrated shears; other fabrics – sharp shears; rotary cutter/mat.

Marking: Chalk, clips, pins, tailor's tacks, threads, wax chalk.

Miscellaneous: Fine pins, flower pins, water soluble stabilizer, thick towel, needleboard, sponge, large piece of wool fabric, press cloths – synthetic chamois, wool, cotton, silk organza.

Interfacings/Linings/Underlinings: Depends on the fabric weight, garment type, quality, and structure; same care properties.

Machine Setup

Stitch Length: Lightweight fabrics – 1.5-1.75mm (15-18spi). **Medium-weight fabrics** – 2-2.5mm (10-12spi). **Heavyweight fabrics** – 2.5-3mm (8-10spi). **Very heavy-weight fabrics** – 3-4mm (6-8spi). **All weights** – zigzag (W,.5-L,2).

Tension: Depends on the fabric.

Feet: Straight stitch, zigzag, roller, even feed.

Sewing Basics

Test Garment: Depends on design and fabric quality.

Fabric Prep: Steam or dry-clean, except when working with washable wool. Many wools can be washed, but it may change the character of the fabric.

Layout: Nap, even though the nap may be imperceptible.

Seams/Hems: Depends on the fabric weight and structure and the garment quality, design, use, and care.

Seam/Hem Finishes: All types. Avoid bulky finishes on lightweight fabrics.

Closures: Buttonholes (machine, bound, inseam), buttons/loops, ties, zippers (hand, machine, invisible).

Pressing: Test press.

Garment Care: Dry-clean to maintain the garment's pristine appearance. When out of season, store in an air-tight cedar closet.

Above: Detail – woolen. (Vogue Pattern - 7467; courtesy of The McCall Pattern Co.)

Right: Detail – wool crepe. (Vogue Pattern – 7540; courtesy of The McCall Pattern Co.)

Beautifully tailored, these go-anywhere pants ensembles are worn by Ashley Marcu and Molly Murphy, winners at the National Make It Yourself With Wool Contest – 2003. (Photo Courtesy of Make It Yourself With Wool.)

Wool Crepe

Wool crepe has a dull crinkled surface. Suitable for a variety of designs from dressy to tailored to casual, it is available in all weights from very light to heavy. It is not difficult to sew, but is easily damaged when ripped or pressed carelessly.

Workroom Secrets

Fabric Prep: Ask your dry-cleaner to preshrink it or preshrink by hanging over the shower rod in a steam-filled bathroom. When steamed with an iron, wool crepe may shrink unevenly.

Layout/Cutting/Marking: Mark the right side with small safety pins. Cut seams 1" (2.5cm) so they will lie flatter when pressed open. On quality garments, cut the hem allowance 2" (5cm).

Stitching: To reduce puckered seams, use a wide straight stitch foot; and hold fabric firmly in front and back of foot when stitching.

Hem/Seam Finishes: Hand overcast or serge with textured thread in the loopers for a flat, inconspicuous finish. Bound and Hong Kong finishes are generally too bulky for light and medium-weight crepes.

Sleeves: Shrink and shape sleeve caps before setting them into the garment. If the fullness cannot be eased smoothly, reduce the ease. (See Any Fabric page 14.)

Underlining: For dresses, use silk organza, silk chiffon, or Sewin' Sheer™. For jackets, use bias-cut hair canvas in a light to medium-weight for a supple silhouette; use a very lightweight fusible for more structure.

Zippers: Stabilize the opening with a strip of lightweight selvage.

Pressing: Before pressing, cover pressing surface with wool fabric. Test press to determine the appropriate amount of heat, moisture, and pressure. Use wool press cloth to press right side. When pressing light colors, use a white wool press cloth. For sharp, well-pressed seams and edges, press the seam flat, then press the seam open. For additional pressing hints, see Wool page 98.

Fabricated in wool crepe, this simple shift is from the Custom Couture Collection by Claire Shaeffer. (Vogue Pattern – 7540; courtesy of The McCall Pattern Co.)

Similar Fabrics: Bark crepe, stretch crepe, wool flannel.

Uses: Tailored designs, dressy garments, jackets, coats, dresses, pants, skirts.

Design Elements: Topstitching, gores, pleats, flares, drapes.

Sewing Checklist

Essential Supplies

Needles: Sharp (HJ), universal (H); sizes 70/10-90/14.

Thread: All purpose (cotton, polyester, cotton covered polyester). Topstitching – machine embroidery/topstitching (cotton, polyester, cotton covered polyester, silk), all purpose. Serger – lightweight serger, textured thread.

Cutting: Sharp shears, rotary cutter/mat.

Marking: Chalk, clips, pins, tailor's tacks.

Miscellaneous: Soft cotton thread, hand embroidery floss, Ivory soap, small safety pins, water soluble stabilizers.

Interfacings: Generally; sew-ins, fusibles, Sofknit™, Feather Weft™.

Linings: Generally on quality garments; care, same as garment.

Underlinings: Depends on garment design, weight of wool crepe.

Machine Setup

Stitch Length: 2-2.5mm (10-12spi).

Tension: Lightly balanced.

Machine Feet: Wide straight stitch, zigzag.

Sewing Basics

Test Garment: Usually, depending on design.

Fabric Prep: Dry-clean, steam.

Layout: Nap – double layer.

Seams: Plain (pressed open or closed), topstitched.

Hems: Hand (blindstitch, blind catchstitch), double-stitched, topstitched, interfaced.

Seam/Hem Finishes: Serged, zigzag, hand overcast, Hong Kong binding; if lined, none.

Edge Finishes: Facings (self-fabric), bindings, bands.

Closures: Buttonholes (machine, bound, inseam); buttons/loops, zippers (hand, machine, invisible).

Pressing: Medium heat, steam, wool press cloth, clapper, point presser, seam roll.

Garment Care: Dry-clean.

Woolen

Woolens are made of yarns with short fibers which have been loosely spun with a low to medium twist. They are carded, but not combed; this gives them a hairy surface which is easy to identify. Most woolen fabrics are soft with a rough or fuzzy texture that obscures the weave or knit. Woolen fabrics such as tweeds, coatings, washable wools, textured wools, and some flannels are bulkier, heavier, and warmer than similar worsteds.

Woolens are easier to sew than worsteds, less expensive, and better suited for casual designs. They are easier to ease but pill, mat, sag, and soil more easily.

Woolen Types: Army blankets, blanket cloth, bouclé, cheviot, coating, Donegal, fleece, Glen plaid, Harris tweed, herringbone, houndstooth, homespun, kasha, loden, melton, Saxony, Scottish tweed, tartans, wool flannel, wool tweeds.
Uses: Tailored and casual garments, jackets, coats, dresses, pants, skirts.
Design Elements: Topstitching, unpressed pleats, gathers, flares.

Sewing Checklist

Essential Supplies
Needles: Universal (H); sizes 70/10-90/14.
Thread: All purpose (cotton, polyester, cotton covered polyester, silk). Topstitching – machine embroidery/topstitching (cotton, polyester, cotton covered polyester, silk), all purpose. Serger – lightweight serger thread.
Cutting: Sharp shears, rotary cutter/mat, duplicate pattern pieces for single layer.
Marking: Chalk, clips, pins, tailor's tacks, thread.
Miscellaneous: Soft cotton basting thread, hand embroidery floss, sponge, Ivory soap, water soluble stabilizers.
Interfacings: Generally; fusibles or sew-ins.
Linings: Frequently; care, same as garment.
Underlinings: Optional; silk organza, polyester chiffon; hair canvas for structure.

Machine Setup
Stitch Length: 2-2.5mm (10-12spi).
Tension: Lightly balanced.
Feet: Wide straight stitch, zigzag.

Sewing Basics
Test Garment: Usually, depending on design.
Fabric Prep: Steam, dry-clean.
Layout: Nap – double layer; heavy fabrics – single layer, using duplicate pattern pieces.
Seams: Plain (pressed open or closed), topstitched, twin needle, taped.
Hems: Hand (blindstitch, blind catchstitch, catchstitch), fused, topstitched, interfaced, double-stitched.
Seam/Hem Finishes: Serged, zigzag; if lined, none.
Edge Finishes: Facings (self-fabric), bindings, bands.
Closures: Buttonholes (machine, bound, inseam); buttons/loops, zippers (hand, machine, invisible).
Pressing: Medium heat, steam, wool press cloth, clapper, point presser, seam roll.
Garment Care: Dry-clean.

Workroom Secrets

Layout/Cutting/Marking: Always use a nap layout for woolens even though the nap is imperceptible. Spread bulky and thick fabrics in a single layer, right-side up. Cut using duplicate pattern pieces. Mark the wrong side with a chalked arrow in the direction of the nap.
Stitching: Lengthen the stitch slightly for medium-weight woolens and more for heavy fabrics. Understitch by hand or machine so the facings will not roll to the outside.
Seams: Stabilize shoulders, waists, and edges to prevent stretching.
Darts: For a flatter finish, slash and press darts open.
Underlinings: Underline pants and skirts to preserve the shape.
Buttonholes: To prevent machine stitches from embedding in the fabric, stitch buttonholes with water soluble stabilizer on top of the fabric. For more defined buttonholes, cord the buttonholes.
Zippers: Stabilize the opening to prevent stretching and roller coaster zippers.
Pockets: Stabilize pocket openings to prevent stretching. To reduce bulk, line patch pockets and flaps with a lightweight lining.
Pressing: See Wool page 98 for Pressing Tips.

This handsome tailored jacket is from the Custom Couture Collection by Claire Shaeffer. (Vogue Pattern – 7467; courtesy of The McCall Pattern Co.)

Wool Flannel

Wool flannels are familiar napped fabrics. Available in a variety of weights and quality, they can be woven from woolen or worsted yarns and have a twill or plain weave. On some fabrics, the weave is almost obscured by the nap. Better fabrics have a tight weave.

Workroom Secrets

Layout/Cutting/Marking: Mark the wrong side with a chalked arrow in the direction of the nap.

Darts: For a flatter finish, slash and press darts open.

Sleeves: Shrink and shape sleeve caps before setting them into the garment. If the fullness cannot be eased smoothly on worsted flannels, reduce the ease. (See Any Fabric page 14.)

Pressing: Before pressing, cover the pressing surface with wool fabric. Test press to determine the appropriate amount of heat, moisture, and pressure. Use a wool press cloth when pressing right side. For sharper fold-lines, rub fold on wrong side with a bar of Ivory soap. Fold in place and press.

For sharp, well-pressed seams and edges, use lots of steam or a damp press cloth. Press, then cover with clapper. Examine the results. If necessary, press again and spank with clapper. Do not move until fabric is dry. For sharper edges, open seams at edges and press over point presser before trimming and turning right-side out. To hold layers in position for pressing, baste about ¼" (6mm) from edge using soft cotton basting thread or hand embroidery floss to avoid a pressing imprint. Press with the wrong-side up. To apply additional moisture when pressing, first cover garment with dry cloth. Wipe with a wet, but not dripping, sponge over the section to be pressed; then press.

A classic with a difference, this reversible jacket features a simple shape and contrast trim. (Courtesy of Tammy O'Connell of Jitney Patterns and photographer Patrick Manning.)

Wool Flannel Types: Blazer flannel, cassimere, cheviot, covert, elastique, French flannel, gabardine, herringbone, kasha, menswear, pin stripes, serge, sharkskin, shirting flannel, tricotine, viyella, washable wool, whipcord, wool poplin, worsted flannel, woolen flannel.

Other Flannel Types: Baby flannel, chamois, cotton or outing flannel, duvetyn, flannelette.

Uses: Tailored and dressy garments, jackets, coats, dresses, pants, shirts, skirts, riding habits.

Design Elements: Topstitching. For woolens, unpressed pleats, gathers, flares; for worsteds, sharp pleats and creases.

Sewing Checklist

Essential Supplies

Needles: Universal (H); sizes 70/10-90/14.

Thread: All purpose (cotton, polyester, cotton covered polyester). Topstitching – machine embroidery/topstitching thread, all purpose. Serger – lightweight serger, textured thread.

Cutting: Sharp shears, rotary cutter/mat.

Marking: Chalk, clips, pins, tailor's tacks, thread, wax chalk.

Miscellaneous: Soft cotton basting thread, hand embroidery floss, sponge, bar of Ivory soap, wool press cloth.

Interfacings: Generally; fusibles, sew-ins, hair canvas.

Linings: Generally on quality garments.

Underlinings: Optional.

Machine Setup

Stitch Length: 2-2.5mm (10-12spi).

Tension: Lightly balanced.

Machine Feet: Wide straight stitch, zigzag.

Sewing Basics

Test Garment: Usually, depending on design and quality.

Fabric Prep: Steam or dry-clean.

Layout: Nap – double layer.

Seams: Plain (pressed open or closed), topstitched, taped.

Hems: Hand (blindstitch, blind catchstitch, catchstitch), topstitched, interfaced, double-stitched, fused.

Seam/Hem Finishes: Serged, zigzag; if lined, none.

Edge Finishes: Facings (self-fabric), bindings, bands, linings.

Closures: Buttonholes (machine, bound, inseam); buttons/loops, zippers (hand, machine, invisible).

Pressing: Medium heat, steam; wool and cotton press cloths, clapper, point presser, seam roll.

Garment Care: Dry-clean.

Wool – Lightweight

Most lightweight wools are lightweight, soft and drapeable, with good body. Many are firmly woven and easy to sew while others are loosely woven and ravel if overhandled. Light colors are often transparent; and even though they rarely have an obvious nap, they should be cut with a nap layout.

Similar Fabrics: Albatross, Cool Wool®, lightweight wool crepe, naked wool, printed challis, tropical worsteds, viyella, wool batiste, wool challis, wool gauze, wool voile.

Uses: Soft jackets and pants, skirts, dresses, blouses.

Design Elements: Gathers, unpressed pleats, flares, drapes, cowl necklines, bindings. Tropical worsteds can be pressed sharply. Avoid close fitting designs.

Sewing Checklist

Essential Supplies

Needles Sharp (HM), universal (H); sizes 70/10-80/12.

Thread: Lightweight (cotton, polyester, cotton covered polyester, silk), all purpose. Topstitching – lightweight, all purpose threads. Basting – soft cotton, fine silk. Serger – lightweight serger thread, textured thread.

Cutting: Sharp shears, rotary cutter/mat.

Marking: Chalk, clips, tailor's tacks, thread, wax chalk.

Miscellaneous: Lightweight zippers, tissue, water soluble stabilizer.

Interfacings: Lightweight knit fusible, low-temp fusibles, sew-ins, Sewin' Sheer™, batiste, organza, polyester chiffon, China silk.

Linings: Depends on garment design, use, and quality.

Underlinings: Sometimes to provide support or opaqueness.

Machine Setup

Stitch Length: 1.75-2mm (12-15 spi).

Tension: Lightly balanced tension; light pressure.

Feet: Wide straight stitch, zigzag; small hole throat plate.

Sewing Basics

Fabric Prep: Steam or dry-clean.

Layout: Nap – right sides together.

Seams: Plain (pressed open or closed), topstitched, French, faux French, safety-stitch serged, tissue stitched, taped.

Hems: Hand (blindstitch, blind catchstitch, catchstitch), interfaced, topstitched.

Seam/Hem Finishes: Serged, zigzag; if lined, none.

Edge Finishes: Facings (self-fabric, lightweight linings, synthetic suede or leather), bindings, ribbing.

Closures: Buttonholes (machine, bound, inseam), buttons/button loops, zippers (hand, machine, invisible).

Pressing: Medium heat, steam, press cloth.

Garment Care: Dry-clean; hand wash only if fabric was pretreated.

Workroom Secrets

Layout/Cutting/Marking: Mark the wrong side with chalked arrows to identify the nap.

Stitching: To preserve the fabric's soft drape, stitch seams with lightweight thread. Begin with a new needle. Use a straight stitch foot and small hole throat plate to reduce stitching problems. When using a zigzag foot, move the needle to the right-hand position. Hold the fabric firmly in front of and behind the presser foot when stitching. To reduce puckering, tissue stitch. Use a shorter stitch length when stitching curves. To reduce fraying, avoid overhandling and ripping.

Seams: Plain seams pressed open and serged with textured or lightweight serger threads are best for soft, fluid seams. Narrow serged seams work well for unlined garments, light colors, and fabrics that fray badly.

Hems: On flared skirts, cut the hem ⅝" to 1¼" (1.5-3.1cm) wide; on straight skirts, cut it 2" (5cm). For softer, more attractive hems, interface with bias-cut silk organza, polyester chiffon, or very lightweight batiste. Narrow single fold hems allow skirts to float and billow more than wide hems and double fold hems such as shirttail and machine rolled hems.

Buttonholes: Stitch machine buttonholes with fine machine embroidery thread.

Zippers: Use lightweight zippers. To avoid stretching the opening, stabilize with a strip of lightweight selvage.

Pressing: Test press to determine the heat, moisture, and pressure. Generally, a lower temperature is better for lightweight wools. When pressing lightweight wool crepe with steam, press carefully to avoid shrinking the fabric unevenly.

Garment Care: Dry-clean to maintain the garment's pristine appearance.

From the Custom Couture Collection by Claire Shaeffer, these traditional trousers are fabricated in a lightweight wool crepe. (Vogue Pattern – 7468; courtesy of The McCall Pattern Co.)

Wool – Textured

Textured wools and wool tweeds are widely used for casual sportswear. A good choice for beginners, most are firmly woven and have a rough surface which hides stitching irregularities. They have a nap and some are bulky or loosely woven making them more difficult to handle.

Workroom Secrets

Fabric Prep: Preshrink with steam or dry-clean. Do not wash unless you want to change the character of the fabric.

Layout/Cutting/Marking: Use small safety pins to mark right side of the fabric and construction symbols. Use flower pins to hold pattern pieces in place.

Stitching: Use polyester threads for more elastic seams. When stitching fabrics with slubs, use needles with sharp points. To prevent underlayer creep, use a roller or even-feed foot, hold the fabric firmly in front of and behind the presser foot, or tissue stitch seams. Understitch facings by hand or machine to prevent them from rolling out.

Seams: For crisper corners on collars and lapels, redraw sharp points so they will be rounded and can be turned smoothly. After stitching, press seams open at edges, and trim to reduce bulk. At corners, press and trim the seam. Fold the seam toward the facing and sew it flat so it won't rumple when turned. Use a point turner to turn and straighten the corner.

Buttonholes: For more defined buttonholes, cord the buttonholes and/or stitch with machine embroidery thread (30/2, 40/2).

Zippers: Stabilize the opening with lightweight selvage or stay tape to prevent stretching.

Pockets: Stabilize pocket openings to prevent stretching. To reduce bulk, line patch pockets and flaps with a light-weight lining.

Interfacing: When working with lightweight wools, use a textured weft fusible to give the fabric loft.

Underlinings: Underline pants and skirts to preserve the shape.

Linings: To reduce bulk on flaps and collars, replace self-fabric facings with lightweight linings.

Pressing: Test press. Textured wools are easily damaged by improper pressing. When steaming, watch for shrinking. Before pressing, cover the ironing board with a piece of wool over a thick towel. When pressing the right side, use a wool press cloth. To press seams, cover a seam roll with wool; then arrange the seam on it. Press the seam open; spank with a clapper until the seam is flat. Do not move the garment until dry. For a sharp press, cover with a damp press cloth. Remove the iron and spank with a clapper to flatten. To raise or brighten the fibers, steam the surface, holding the iron about ½" (1.2cm) from the surface.

This simply shaped jacket is stunning in a textured wool tweed trimmed with leather. (Burda Pattern – 8761, photo courtesy of Burda.)

Similar Fabrics: Alpaca, astrakan, bouclé, chenille, éponge, frisé, Harris tweed, Donegal tweed, mohair, ratiné, sponge cloth, wool crepe.

Uses: Tailored and dressy garments, sportswear, jackets, coats, capes, ponchos, dresses, skirts, sweaters, pants, vests.

Design Elements: Minimal seaming, piping, braid trims, bindings, faux and real leather or suede. Avoid self-fabric tie belts and fussy details.

Sewing Checklist

Essential Supplies

Needles: Sharp (H, HJ), universal (H); sizes 70/10 to 100/16, depending on fabric weight.

Thread: All purpose (cotton, polyester, cotton covered polyester). Topstitching – machine embroidery/topstitching (cotton, polyester, cotton covered polyester, silk-D, rayon). Serger – serger, all purpose threads.

Cutting: Large, sharp shears, duplicate pattern pieces.

Marking: Chalk, clips, safety pins, tailor's tacks, thread, wax chalk.

Miscellaneous: Flower-head pins, shim, point turner, thick towel, stay tape, water soluble stabilizer.

Interfacings: Fusibles, sew-ins, hair canvas, textured weft insertion.

Linings: Generally on quality garments.

Underlinings: Optional.

Machine Setup

Stitch Length: 2.5-3mm (8-10spi).

Tension: Lightly balanced tension; light pressure.

Feet: Wide straight stitch, zigzag, even feed, roller.

Sewing Basics

Fabric Prep: Steam or dry-clean.

Layout: Nap; lightweight – double layer, right sides together; heavy-weight – single layer, right-side up, using duplicate pattern pieces.

Seams: Plain (pressed open); topstitched.

Hems: Hand (blindstitch, blind catchstitch, catchstitch), double-stitched, interfaced, topstitched.

Seam/Hem Finishes: Serged, zigzag; if lined, none.

Edge Finishes: Facings (self-fabric, linings, synthetic suede or leather), bindings, fold-over braid, ribbing.

Closures: Buttonholes (machine, bound, in-seam), buttons/loops, toggles, zippers (hand, machine, invisible).

Pressing: Medium setting, steam, press cloth.

Garment Care: Dry-clean.

Worsted

Worsted yarns are carded and combed to make them smooth, strong, and more lustrous than woolen yarns. They have a medium-to-high twist and the weave is quite prominent.

Worsted fabrics are lighter weight clear-surfaced fabrics. They are tightly woven with a smooth, hard surface which wears well but shines easily. They tailor well, rarely sag or bag, crease and press well. They will wear longer than woolens, but are more difficult to sew.

Worsted Fabrics: Bedford cord, blazer cloth, cassimere, cavalry twill, cheviot, covert, elastique, gabardine, jacquard, menswear suiting, ottoman, serge, sharkskin, tartans, tricotine, tropical wool, whipcord, wool challis, wool poplin, wool satin, worsted flannel, worsted suitings, zibeline.

Uses: Tailored garments, jackets, coats, dresses, pants, skirts, vests.

Sewing Checklist

Essential Supplies
Needles: Sharp (HJ), universal (H); sizes 70/10-80/12.
Thread: All purpose (cotton, polyester, cotton covered polyester). Topstitching – all purpose, machine embroidery/topstitching threads (silk, cotton, polyester, silk). Serger – lightweight serger, textured thread.
Cutting: Sharp shears, rotary cutter/mat.
Marking: Chalk, clips, pins, tailor's tacks, thread, wax chalk.
Miscellaneous: Soft cotton thread or hand embroidery floss, stabilizers – water soluble, tearaway, cut away.
Interfacings: Generally; sew-ins, hair canvas, fusibles.
Linings: Used for outerwear and quality garments.

Machine Setup
Stitch Length: 2-2.5mm (10-12spi).
Tension: Lightly balanced.
Machine Feet: Wide straight stitch, zigzag.

Sewing Basics
Test Garment: Recommended, depending on garment design and quality.
Fabric Prep: Steam, dry-clean.
Layout: Nap – double layer.
Seams: Plain (pressed open or closed), topstitched.
Hems: Hand (blindstitch, blind catchstitch, catchstitch), interfaced, topstitched.
Seam/Hem Finishes: Serged, zigzag; if lined, none.
Edge Finishes: Facings (self-fabric, lining), bindings, bands.
Closures: Buttonholes (machine, bound, inseam), buttons/loops, zippers (hand, machine, invisible).
Pressing: Medium heat, steam, wool press cloth.
Garment care: Dry-clean.

Workroom Secrets
Layout/Cutting/Marking: Use a nap layout, even though the nap is not obvious. If the fabric looks the same on both sides, mark the wrong side with chalked arrows in the direction of the nap. Cut seams 1" wide so they will be easier to press flat.
Stitching: Use polyester thread for more elastic seams.
Seams/Darts: For flatter seams, cut them 1" (2.5cm) wide. Slash and press darts open to avoid a ridge.
Seam/Hem Finishes: To avoid pressing imprints, serge or zigzag with lightweight serger or textured thread. Avoid bound and Hong Kong finishes on light and medium-weight worsteds.
Sleeves: Shrink and shape sleeve caps before setting into the garment. Reduce the ease as needed to ease the fullness smoothly. (See Any Fabric page 14.)
Topstitching: To flatten seams and edges, topstitch. For a dressier design, topstitch close to the edge or seam. For sportswear, topstitch ¼" (6mm) away.
Buttonholes: For more defined buttonholes and longer wear, cord the buttonholes.
Pockets: Stabilize pocket openings to prevent stretching. To reduce bulk, line patch pockets and flaps with a lightweight lining.
Pressing: See Wool page 98 for Pressing Tips.

Designed by Sarah Walker, the 2003 Senior Winner for Make It Yourself With Wool contest, this avant garde design is fabricated in a traditional menswear pinstripe. (Photo courtesy of Make It Yourself With Wool.)

Zebra

A zebra is a rare or unusual fabric. Zebras can be divided into a variety of groups: fabrics which reflect new technology, unique fabrics which are not readily available, unusual fabrics which have limited use, specialty fabrics which interest only a few home sewers, any fabric or material which you have never sewn.

Fabrics which incorporate new technology include new fibers, unusual fabric construction, or a different finish. For example, familiar fabrics such as Ultrasuede®, microfibers, Polarfleece®, Slinky, and Tencel® were zebras not so long ago. Today, they are readily available and you have probably sewn on them.

Some unique fabrics which are not readily available or which have limited appeal to the home sewing market include Luminex®, rhinestone mesh, Kevlar®, Sunbrella®, Cordura®, and Tyvek®.

Fabrics which you have never sewn can include traditional favorites such as dotted swiss and marquisette as well as new special occasion fabrics, new fabrications for microfibers and lyocell, and other interesting materials such as chalkboard fabric.

While writing this book, I went to the trade shows—semi-annual events for fabric store buyers to see and purchase new fabrics. At one show, there was an incredible selection of unusual embellished special occasion fabrics—which are not covered in this book—so I immediately began thinking about how to sew them successfully. Here are some hints for sewing them or any other zebra.

Analyzing a zebra

Begin by analyzing the fabric. Most zebras have some characteristics which are similar to fabrics which you have sewn before.

Describe the fabric. What are its characteristics?

Is it a woven, knit, or non-woven? What kind of weave or knit does it have? Is it densely or loosely woven or knitted?

Does it have a nap or one-way design?

Does it have a border design, pattern, or weave which requires a layout on the crossgrain?

Is it a natural fiber such as cotton, linen, hemp, silk, wool, cashmere, mohair? Or a manufactured fiber such as rayon, lyocell, acetate, acrylic, nylon, polyester, spandex?

Does it stretch in the width, length, or both?

Is it soft or crisp? Lightweight or heavy? Thin or bulky?

Does it ravel? Do the yarns separate when you scrape your nail across the fabric?

Does it wrinkle? Waterspot? Is it absorbent?

Will it require an underlining for stability or body, support or shaping, modesty, comfort, or color?

Can it be cleaned? What are the recommendations for cleaning?

Are designers in the apparel industry using it? How? What type garments?

Describe some ready-to-wear designs you have seen and the details on them?

Identify any similar fabrics. How are they similar?

Is it similar to a fabric described in *Sew Any Fabric*?

What happens when you burn it? See the Burn Test on page 143.

What are its disadvantages? How will they affect the design?

What are its advantages? How can you utilize them?

One of the fabrics I saw at the trade show was a fabulous embroidered chiffon with a beaded design along one edge. It had a border design and incorporated many of the characteristics of chiffon, embroidered, and beaded fabrics. When considered as a whole, this fabric would be challenging; but, when the project is divided into many small steps, it is easier to manage. Yes, it's just like eating an apple—one bite at a time.

Designer Carol Lambeth used pliers and a seam ripper to "cut" the mesh fabric; then she sewed it together by hand. (Photo courtesy of Carol Lambeth Couture.)

Sewing a zebra

If the zebra is similar to fabrics which you have sewn before, apply what you learned from those experiences. Make some samples on the new fabric using techniques which have proven successful in the past.

When making seam samples, make them about 20" (50cm) long. Hang them vertically and stand back at least 5 feet (1.5m).

If the fabric is unlike any you have sewn previously, look for similar fabrics in *Sew Any Fabric* and experiment with the recommended techniques. If there are no similar fabrics, keep it simple and plunge ahead.

Occasionally, when there are no similar fabrics, you must think creatively. For the rhinestone mesh bodice shown at right, Carol Lambeth used pliers and a seam ripper to "cut" the fabric; then she sewed the mesh together by hand.

Hints for Sewing a Zebra

1. Analyze the fabric.
2. Identify the fiber(s), construction, advantages, disadvantages.
3. Identify similar fabrics.
4. Make samples, using what you know about similar fabrics.
5. Test press.
6. Talk to the fabric and listen to what it's telling you.
7. Select a simple design to showcase the fabric.

Designed by Carol Lambeth, this stunning gown features a rhinestone mesh bodice and four-ply silk skirt. (Photo courtesy of Carol Lambeth Couture.)

In Conclusion

From the beginning, this book has focused on basic, quality techniques, how they are applied to today's most popular fabrics, and how you can apply what you already know to sew any fabric successfully.

There will always be zebras and new fabrics to inspire, excite, and delight us. Some fabrics will be more challenging than others; but, with the knowledge you have acquired in the past, you can meet these challenges and unravel their secrets to sew any fabric successfully.

Breathtakingly luxurious, the metallic lace bodice trimmed with lamé is paired with a silk satin skirt. (Photo courtesy of Ptakcouture.com.)

part 2

Sewing Techniques

This mini-guide is included to avoid any misunderstandings about the techniques and terminology used throughout this book.

Seams

Plain Seams

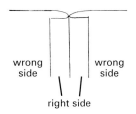

The plain seam is the simplest, most widely used, and easiest to alter. Many other seams such as taped, safety-stitch, and fur are variations of the plain seam.

1. Right sides together, stitch on the seamline.
2. Press flat; then press open.
3. Finish the edges separately. (See Seam and Hem Finishes page 112.)
4. For closed seams, finish edges together with serging or zigzag; press to one side.

Bound Seam

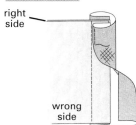

1. Right sides together, stitch a plain seam; press and trim to ¼" (6mm).
2. Bind edges with bias-cut strip 1½" (3.7cm). (Avoid purchased bias tape for better garments.)
3. To make a Decorative Bound Seam, begin wrong sides together. Topstitch flat against garment if desired.

Faux Flat Fell Seam

See Topstitched Seams.

Faux French Seam

1. Right sides together, stitch a plain seam; press.
2. Fold each seam allowance in half, and align folded edges.
3. Stitch the edges together by hand or machine.

Flat Fell Seams

Since these seams are bulky and more difficult to sew, I use topstitched seams which duplicate the look without the aggravation.

Fur Seam

1. Cut seam allowances ⅛" wide.
2. Brush pile away from edge using a damp sponge.
3. Right sides together, zigzag (W,4-L,1), allowing needle to swing off the edge.
4. Open seam flat; press with handles of your shears. Right-side up, brush pile with a wire dog brush.

Fur Seam (Sheared)

1. Right sides together, stitch a plain seam. Right-side up, brush pile with a wire dog brush.
2. Trim away pile on seam allowances.

Hairline Seam – Method One

1. Right sides together, stitch a plain seam using a short straight stitch.
2. Zigzag (W,1-L,1) close to the seamline; trim and press.

Hairline Seam – Method Two

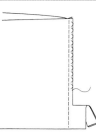

1. Right sides together, stitch a plain seam using a short straight stitch.
2. Trim to ⅛" (3mm).
3. Zigzag (W,2-L,1), allowing needle to swing off the edge; press.

Safety-Stitch (4-Thread) Serged

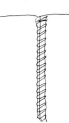

1. Use lightweight serger thread. For more elastic seams, use polyester textured thread.
2. Right sides together, stitch.

Sequin Appliqué Seams

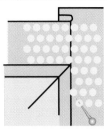

1. Mark the seamlines on the wrong side.

2. Remove the beads or sequins from the seam allowances plus ⅛" (3mm). Knot the threads to avoid additional unraveling.

3. Pin or tape the sequins out of the way; baste and stitch the seams, using a zipper foot. Press the seams open.

4. On the right side, restitch the sequins and beads by hand or machine; trim away the excess.

5. On sheer fabrics, trim the seam to ⅛" (3mm) and zigzag the edges together.

Strap Seam

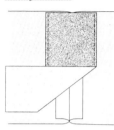

1. Wrong sides together, stitch a plain seam; press, trim as needed.

2. Cover with ribbon, decorative, lace, faux leather or suede, or contrast fabric; baste.

3. Edgestitch the strap in place.

Taped Seam

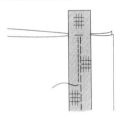

1. Using the paper pattern as a guide, measure and mark the seamline length on a stay tape.

2. Wrong side up, center tape over seamline; baste.

3. Right sides together, stitch seam; press.

Tissue-Stitched Seam

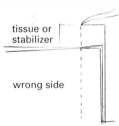

tissue or stabilizer

wrong side

right side

1. Cut strips of tissue or stabilizer.

2. Begin stitching on the "tissue." Place the seam on the tissue; continue stitching to the end.

Topstitched Seam

1. Right sides together, stitch a plain seam; press open.
2. Finish the seam edges.
3. Topstitch the desired distance on each side of the seamline. For a dressier look, topstitch close to the seamline; for sportswear, topstitch farther away.

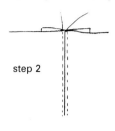

step 2　　step 3

Topstitched Seam (Faux Flat Fell)

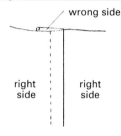

wrong side

right side　right side

1. Right sides together, stitch a plain seam; press to one side.

2. Finish the seam edges.

3. Topstitch ¼" (6mm) to ⅜" (1cm) away.

Twin Needle Seam

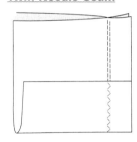

1. Fill bobbin with textured thread such as Woolly Nylon. Loosen upper tension.

2. Right sides together, stitch using a twin needle; press.

Wrong-Side-Out Seam

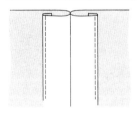

1. Wrong sides together, stitch seam; press.

2. Turn under raw edges; edgestitch flat.

Zigzag Seam

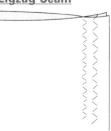

1. Right sides together, zigzag (W,.5-L,1.5) on the seam line; press.

2. For closed seams, stitch again ⅛" (6mm) away; trim.

Abutted Seam – Method One

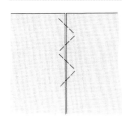

1. Cut away seam allowances.
2. Butt edges together and zigzag.

Abutted Seam – Method Two

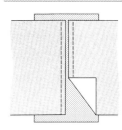

1. Use seam tape, lining, or muslin for underlay.
2. Cut away seam allowances
3. Stitch one edge to underlay.
4. Butt edges together, stitch remaining edge.

Appliqué Seams (Lace)

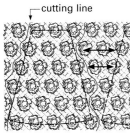

step 3

step 7   match seamline

1. Copy pattern pieces and make duplicates without seam allowances.
2. Right side up, pin pattern pieces to lace.
3. Mark seamlines with thread.
4. Add $\frac{3}{8}$" (1cm) seam allowances; mark cutting lines with flower pins.
5. Examine overlap sections, if cutting line goes through large motifs, re-mark allowing $\frac{3}{8}$" (1cm) around the edges of the motifs.
6. Cut out sections.
7. Right sides up, lap sections, matching seamlines; baste.
8. Baste around motif edges.
9. Zigzag (W,1.5-L,1) or hand sew sections permanently.
10. Trim away excess lace on both layers.

Claire's Hint: *When hand sewing, wax and press the thread. Pressing prevents knotting and keeps the wax from rubbing off on the fabric.*

French Seams

1. Wrong sides together, stitch $\frac{1}{4}$" (6mm) seam; press. Trim to $\frac{1}{8}$" (3mm).
2. Right sides together, stitch $\frac{1}{4}$" (6mm) seam, enclosing the first seam; press.

French Seam (Decorative)

1. Right sides together, stitch $\frac{1}{4}$" (6mm) seam; press.
2. Wrong sides together, stitch $\frac{3}{8}$" (1cm) seam, enclosing the first seam; press to one side.
3. Edgestitch seam to garment, if desired.

Lapped Seams

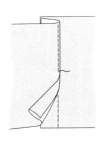

1. Right sides up, mark seamlines.
2. Turn under seam allowance on overlap.
3. Baste to underlap, matching seamlines.
4. Topstitch seam permanently.
5. For reversible designs, turn under seam.

Nonwoven Flat Fell

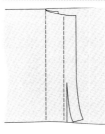

1. Wrong sides together, stitch seam; press to one side.
2. Trim inner layer to $\frac{1}{8}$" (3mm).
3. Fold untrimmed layer in place; stitch.

Nonwoven Lapped Seams

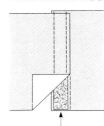

1. Cut overlap without seam allowance.
2. Mark seamline on underlap.
3. Fuse or glue sections together.
4. Stitch seam permanently.

Seam and Hem Finishes

Most finishes can be used on seams and hems; two—seam tape and folded edges—are rarely used on seams.

Bound

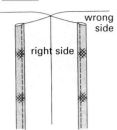

1. Use seam tape, lace, net, or tricot binding (Seams Great®); purchased bias binding is too bulky and the fabric is a poor quality.
2. With wrong sides together, press binding in half lengthwise.
3. Slip edge of seam allowance into binding.

4. Edgestitch or zigzag at edge of binding.

Folded Edge

Rarely used as a seam finish, the folded edge is a neat hem finish for lightweight fabrics, sheers, reversible and unlined garments.
1. Cut the hem 1/4" (6mm) wider than the desired finished width.
2. Turn under the raw edge 1/4" (6mm) and pin.
3. Finish the hem.

Hand Overcast

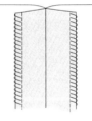

1. Hand overcasting is the flattest, least conspicuous seam finish.
2. Overcast each seam allowance separately or trim and overcast together.

Hong Kong Finish

This attractive finish will be noticeable on the right side of lightweight and many medium-weight fabrics.
1. Cut 1" (2.5cm) bias strips from chiffon, nylon tricot, georgette, lightweight lining, or polyester organza.
2. Right sides together, stitch binding to each edge with a scant 1/4" (6mm) seam. Trim to 1/8" (3mm).
3. Wrap binding around the edge; press.
4. Ditch-stitch to secure binding.

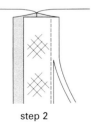 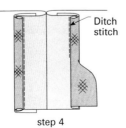

step 2   step 4

Pinked

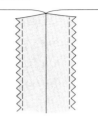

Pinking is a nice flat finish.
1. Pink edges, trimming away as little as possible.
2. Stitch close to the pinking for fabrics that ravel.

Seam Tape

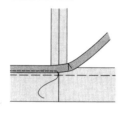

Rarely used as a seam finish, seam tape is suitable for hems on washable fabrics which fray.
1. Measure and mark the hem the desired depth.
2. Align the seam tape edge with marked line; edgestitch it in place.
3. Finish the hem.

Serged

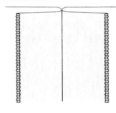

For most garments, this is the easiest to use and least conspicuous.
1. On the loopers, use 2-ply, lightweight serger thread or a textured thread such as Woolly Nylon to avoid an imprint.
2. Serge and trim seam allowances separately or together.

Turned-and-Stitched

This finish is bulky. Use it only on lightweight fabrics.
1. Cut 1" (2.5cm) seam allowances.
2. Stitch and press seam.
3. Turn under each raw edge about 1/4" (6mm); edgestitch.

Zigzag Finish

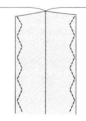

Suitable for a variety of fabrics which fray, this finish can be used instead of serging.
1. Stitch and press seam.
2. Zigzag seam allowances separately (W,2-L,2) or stitch with a multi-stitch zigzag. If the fabric rolls under the foot, use an overlock foot which has a small wire to hold the fabric flat or tissue stitch using water soluble stabilizer.
3. For a closed seam, stitch through both plies close to the seamline; trim close to the zigzag.

Plain Hems

Hand Hems

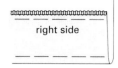
right side

Hand hems are used on quality garments.

The most common hand stitches include blindstitch, blind catchstitch, catchstitch, and slipstitch.

To hem invisibly, use a very fine needle. Keep the stitches loose, and take a backstitch in the hem allowance every 4" to 5" (10-12.5cm).

1. Mark the hemline.
2. Fold and baste ¼" (6cm) from the foldline; press.
3. Measure and mark the hem width.
4. Finish the edge of the hem allowance.
5. Baste hem in place; hem permanently by hand.
6. Wrong side up, press, allowing the iron to extend under the edge of the hem allowance.

Double Hem

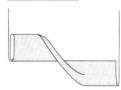

Use this hem to shadow-proof a hem on light colored and transparent fabrics. Hems can be very narrow or very wide.

1. Fold on hemline; press.
2. Fold so raw edge meets hemline; press.
3. Hem by hand or machine.

Double-stitched Hem

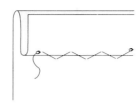

Use this hem on heavy or bulky fabrics.

1. Fold on hemline; baste midway between the hemline and top of hem allowance.
2. Hem at basting.
3. Hem again at top of hem allowance.

Interfaced Hem

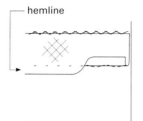
— hemline

Interface the hems on better garments to add body, prevent wrinkling, and avoid a sharp, creased edge. Interface with bias strips of wigan, organza, muslin, hair canvas, or interfacing materials.

1. On unlined garments, cut the interfacing the hem width; on lined garments, cut it wider.
2. Wrong side up, place the interfacing on the garment so the lower edge extends ½" (12mm) over the hemline.
3. At the hemline, sew the interfacing with a long loose blindstitch. On lined garments, use a catchstitch to sew the top of the interfacing to the wrong side.
4. Fold the hem in place; sew the hem to the interfacing on lined garments.

Other Hems

Faced Hem

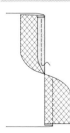

Use to finish shaped hemlines, reduce bulk, lengthen garments, or increase comfort. The facing can be lining, contrast, or self-fabric; purchased bias is a poor quality fabric.

1. Trim hem allowance to ¼" (6mm).
2. Cut facing 2" (5cm).
3. Right sides together, stitch a ¼" (6mm) seam.
4. Fold to wrong side, and press.
5. Hem by hand.

Horsehair Braid Hem

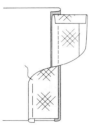

Use this hem to make the skirt stand away from the body.

1. Right side up, pin braid to garment edge.
2. Stitch a ¼" (6mm) seam.
3. Sew braid to the wrong side so the hem wraps around the braid; press.
4. Topstitch the edge or use a catchstitch.

Lettuce Hem

Use on fabrics with 50% stretch or bias-cut edges.

1. Fold under hem allowance; center folded edge under the foot. Zigzag (W,3-L,1), stretching edge as much as possible.
2. Trim away excess hem allowance; press.

Machine Rolled (Baby) Hem

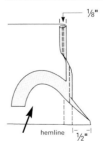
⅛"
hemline ½"

Use this narrow hem for lightweight fabrics.

1. Stitch ⅛" (3mm) below the hemline.
2. Right side up, fold under on stitching; edgestitch close to the fold.

Claire's Hint: *Use an edgestitch or zipper foot so you can stitch ¹⁄₁₆" (1.5mm) from the edge.*

continued

3. Trim as closely as possible to the stitching.

4. Wrong side up, fold again; stitch on top of the last stitched line.

Pin Hem

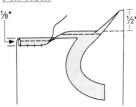

Use this narrow hand-sewn hem instead of a hand-rolled hem for fabrics. It is a little flatter, but easy to make.

1. Stitch ⅛" (3mm) below hemline.

2. Right side up, fold under on stitching; edgestitch close to the fold.

3. Trim close to the stitching.

4. With the wrong side up, fold again. Slipstitch the hem permanently.

Shirttail Hem

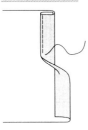

Suitable for lightweight fabrics.

1. Fold hem in place; fold raw edge under.

2. Wrong side up, topstitch close to top of hem.

3. Edgestitch near the hem edge, if desired.

Topstitched Hem

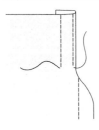

Suitable for many fabrics, top-stitched hems can be wide or narrow.

1. For a smoother finish on knits, fuse a strip of lightweight fusible knit interfacing to the hem allowance.

2. Finish the hem allowance edge.

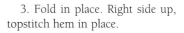

3. Fold in place. Right side up, topstitch hem in place.

4. Cut the hem wider and top-stitch several rows if desired.

Twin Needle Hem

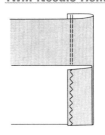

Soft and elastic, this hem is particularly well-suited for knits and stretch fabrics.

1. Fill bobbin with polyester or textured thread. Loosen the bobbin tension; set stitch length 2-3mm (8-12spi).

2. For a firmer, smoother hem, interface the hem allowance with a strip of lightweight fusible knit.

3. Finish the raw edge as needed.

4. Fold the hem allowance to the wrong side. Right side up, stitch; press.

Merrow Hem

Use this narrow hem for lightweight, firm fabrics, and napkins. Review the directions in your serger manual.

Overlocked Hem

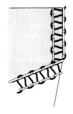

Use to finish edges under lace or embellish casual garments with decorative threads.

1. Mark the hemline.

2. Right side up, stitch on the hemline, trimming away the excess hem allowance.

Hemming Stitches

Blindstitch

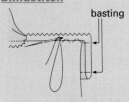

This stitch is most versatile and frequently used.

1. Work from right to left, fasten the thread on the hem allowance. Pick up a thread in the garment; then a stitch in the hem.

2. Repeat, alternating between the garment and hem to create a series of small "v's."

Blind Catchstitch

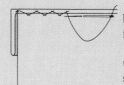

This hem is more elastic than the blindstitched hem; use on heavy fabrics and fabrics with stretch.

1. Work from left to right, pick up a thread in the garment; then a stitch in the hem.

2. Repeat, alternating between the garment and hem to create a series of small "x's."

Bindings

Frequently used to replace facings on transparent or double-faced fabrics, reversible and unlined garments, bindings are visible on both sides of the garment. Woven bindings are generally cut on the bias; stretch and knit fabrics can be cut on the crossgrain as well as on the bias. When making bindings, always make a sample before cutting the strips.

Single Bias Binding

1. Trim away the seam allowance at the edge.
2. For a finished $1/4"$ (6mm), cut a strip $1\frac{1}{2}"$ (3.7cm) wide.
3. Staystitch a scant $1/4"$ (6mm) from the edge.
4. Right sides together, stitch a $1/4"$ (6mm) seam.
5. Wrap the binding around the edge.

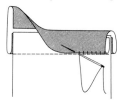

6. To finish by machine, turn under the raw edge so the binding is $1/8"$ (3mm) wider on the wrong side. Baste. Right side up, ditch-stitch close to the seamline, using a zipper foot.

7. To finish by hand, trim the binding so you will have only $1/4"$ (6mm) to turn under. Turn under the raw edge, aligning the fold with the stitched line. Hand sew the binding in place.

Claire's Hint: *If fabric is thick or bulky, do not fold in the edge.*

Double Bias Binding

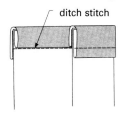

ditch stitch

1. For a double binding, cut a strip 2" (5cm) wide.
2. Fold the strip in half lengthwise, wrong sides together.
3. Proceed as above.

Ribbon or Braid Binding

These directions can also be used for leather and suede (real or faux) and purchased bias tape.

1. Trim away the seam allowance.
2. Fold the trim lengthwise, wrong sides together, so one edge is $1/16"$ (1.5mm) wider than the other; press and shape.
3. Right side up, slip garment edge into trim so that the edge touches the foldline; baste and stitch.

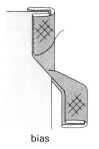

bias   ribbon

Bias strips

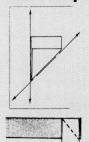

1. To establish the bias, fold a piece of paper, matching one short edge to a long edge. Align the long edge with the lengthwise grain. Chalk-mark the bias along the folded edge.

2. To join strips, square the ends. Right sides together, stack the strips as shown; stitch across the corner, using a short stitch – 1.5mm (18spi).

Catchstitch

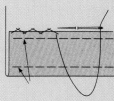

This stitch is frequently used to hem lined garments.

1. Work from left to right, pick up a thread in the garment; then a stitch in the hem.
2. Repeat, alternating between the garment and hem to create a series of small "x's."

Slipstitch

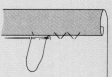

Use on lightweight fabrics to hem wide or narrow hems.

1. Finish hem edge with a turn-and-stitch finish or fold.
2. Work from right to left, pick up a thread in the garment; then a long stitch in the hem fold. Repeat, alternating between the garment and hem to create a series of small "v's."

Facings

Most patterns include shaped facings. Bias facings, lace, ribbon, and faux leather or suede are neat alternatives.

Bias

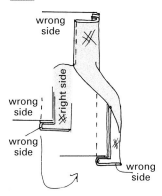

Bias facings are narrow and inconspicuous.

1. Trim garment seam allowance to ¼" (6mm).
2. Cut bias strips 1½" (3.7cm) wide.
3. Right sides together, baste bias to garment edge; stitch on seamline. Trim.
4. Fold bias to wrong side; press. Edgestitch or topstitch.

Facing as a Trim

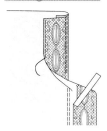

Use lace, ribbon, faux leather, or faux suede as a trim.

1. Finish any vertical seams with serging.
2. Trim garment seam allowance to ¼" (6mm). Staystitch a scant ¼" from the edge.

3. Wrong side up, place trim on edge so it barely covers stitched line; stitch.
4. Fold trim to right side. Stitch at top of trim.

Closures

Buttonholes

The most common buttonhole types include:

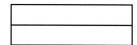

machine   hand   bound

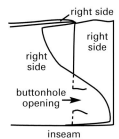

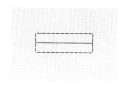

inseam   faced   slashed

Button Loops

Suitable for a variety of fabrics, button loops are particularly attractive on lightweight fabrics.

> **Claire's Hint:** *If it turns easily, the loop is too fat.*

5. Wet the tubing and squeeze it dry in a towel.
6. Pin one end to the ironing board, straighten the tube so the seam is not twisted. Stretch as much as possible; pin. Leave it to dry.

> **Claire's Hint:** *Even silks won't show water spots.*

Self-Filled Tubing

1. Cut bias strips 1" to 2" (2.5-5cm) wide.

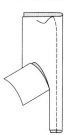

2. Right sides together, fold the strip lengthwise. Shorten the stitch; stitch parallel to the folded edge, stretching as much as possible as you stitch.
3. Trim the strip so the stitching is in the center.

> **Claire's Hint:** *Stitch the tube a little wider at each end.*

4. Using a tapestry needle, fasten a short length of topstitching thread at one end. Run the needle into the tubing. Turn the tube right-side out.

Flat Tubing

For decorative loops on casual garments, use flat tubing in self- or contrast fabric.

1. Cut strips 1½" (3.7cm) wide on the bias or straight grain.

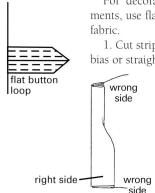

2. Wrong sides together, fold the strip lengthwise. Fold again so the raw edges touch the fold.
3. Edgestitch both sides of the strip.

Hints for Successful Machine Buttonholes

Machine stitched buttonholes are the most versatile and easiest to make.

1. Always make at least one sample buttonhole to be sure the size is correct and you like the way the buttonhole looks.
2. Interface the buttonhole with a small piece of lightweight interfacing so that the least amount of stretch is parallel to the buttonhole.
3. Mark the buttonhole length between the bars at each end.
4. Begin with a new needle. On woven fabrics, use a sharp (HM, HJ) needle; on knits, a universal (H) or stretch (HS) needle.
5. On lightweight fabrics, use lightweight machine embroidery thread, extra-fine cotton covered polyester, or polyester thread. On other fabrics, use all purpose thread.
6. Check to be sure there is enough thread on the spool and bobbin.
7. Loosen the upper tension; or insert the bobbin thread through the hole in the bobbin finger.
8. To prevent tunneling, place a piece of water soluble stabilizer under the fabric.
9. To prevent the stitches from sinking into the fabric, cover the fabric with water soluble stabilizer.
10. For more defined buttonholes, cord the buttonholes by stitching over two or four strands of thread.
11. Lengthen the stitch for bulky or heavy fabrics.
12. To cut, insert a very sharp seam ripper straight down into one end of the buttonhole. Slash toward the center. Repeat for the other end.
13. Use a permanent color marking pen to dye any interfacing that shows.

Zippers

The most common zippers include:

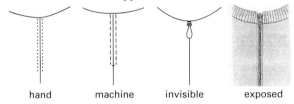

hand   machine   invisible   exposed

Claire's Super-Easy Zipper

This couture zipper is a very easy machine stitched zipper. These directions are for a slot zipper, but they can be adapted for a lapped or fly application.

1. Stabilize the zipper opening.
2. Press the seam allowances to the wrong side.
3. Right side up, stitch around the opening a scant ¼" (6mm) from the fold.
4. Wrong side up, baste the zipper in place, aligning the zipper teeth with the folded edge. When using a self-basting zipper, fuse.

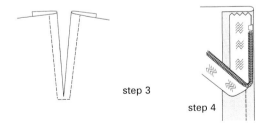

step 3

step 4

> **Claire's Hint:** *I place a strip of fusible web on the right side of the zipper tape to make a self-basting zipper.*

5. Using very short running stitches or backstitches, hand sew the zipper to the seam allowances permanently.

Hints for Successful Zippers

1. Use lightweight zippers for lightweight fabrics.
2. Key the top of the zipper by stitching across the top ⅜" (1cm) above the zipper. Key the garment on the seamline.
3. Shorten zippers at the bottom. Sew by hand or machine across the teeth. Trim ¾" (2cm) below the new stop.
   Hint: When zippers are on sale, I buy long ones which I can shorten later.
4. Make a self-basting zipper by fusing a narrow strip of fusible web to the right side of the zipper tapes.
5. To prevent roller coaster zippers, stabilize the opening with stay tape. Mark the length of the opening on the stay; make the opening fit the marked length. For general sewing, use a narrow strip of non-stretch fusible applied to the seam allowance. For fine garments, use a strip of organza; press out any stretch; center over the foldline and hand sew in place.
6. Press the seam allowances to the wrong side.
7. Baste the zipper into the opening.
   Note: I sew all zippers into an open placket without basting the opening closed.
8. To match plaids, baste one side. Close the zipper; mark several color bars on the tape on the remaining side of the zipper. Open the zipper; and baste, aligning the marks with the fabric pattern.
9. Try on the garment.
10. Sew permanently. For machine zippers, check the thread on the spool and bobbin; and begin with a new needle.
11. After sewing an invisible zipper, sew the ends of the zipper tape to the seam allowances.

part 3

Fabric/ Fiber Dictionary

Fabric/Fiber Dictionary

A

A.C.E.® Nylon fiber. See Nylon to sew.

Acetate Manufactured fiber made from cellulose acetate. Soft, pliable, colorfast to sunlight. It is weaker when wet and dissolves in acetone. See Acetate to sew.

Acetate by Avtex An acetate fiber. See Acetate to sew.

Activ-8® Stretch fiber. See Spandex to sew.

Acrilan® Acrylic fiber. See Acrylic to sew.

Acrylic Manufactured fiber made from coal, air, water, oil, and limestone. Soft, lightweight, warm, frequently used instead of wool; washable, quick drying, pills badly; resists moths, chemicals, oils, and sunlight. See Acrylic to sew.

Agilon® Stretch nylon fiber. Strong, durable, easy care. See Spandex and Nylon to sew.

Agrilan Stretch fiber. See Spandex to sew.

Alaskine Crisp, silk/wool blend. See Gabardine to sew.

Albert cloth Double cloth fabric. See Double Cloth to sew.

Alençon lace Small individual motifs are outlined with heavy thread; edge has chained beading instead of picot. Name frequently applied incorrectly to embroidered chantilly lace. See Lace to sew.

All-over embroidery Fabric with all-over embroidered pattern; ranges from inexpensive eyelet to expensive silks.

All-over lace Inexpensive lace with all-over, repetitive pattern. See Net to sew.

Alpaca Soft, lustrous, natural fiber from the alpaca—a kind of llama. Coarser than camel, frequently blended with wool. See Hair Fiber to sew.

Aluminized Mylar needlepunch Good insulator with reflective qualities for slim-line garments.

Angora (1) Long, white fleece from the angora goat. Soft and smooth; combined with other fibers. See Mohair to sew. (2) Light, fine hair from angora rabbits. Must be labeled angora rabbit. See Hair Fiber to sew.

Anidex Synthetic fiber with permanent stretch and recovery; less stretch than spandex but can withstand higher temperatures when laundered. See Spandex to sew.

Antelope Soft, fine-grained leather similar to deerskin. See Leather to sew.

Anti-crease finish Synthetic finish to reduce wrinkling of cotton, rayon, linen, and blends.

Antique satin Reversible satin-weave fabric with a lustrous face and a dull, slubbed back. See Satin to sew.

Antique taffeta Crisp, slubbed taffeta; some are iridescent. See Taffeta to sew.

Antron® Nylon fiber with unique luster, dry hand, and high opacity. See Nylon to sew.

Appliqué Design which is sewn, embroidered, glued, or fused to the face of another fabric.

Appliqué lace Lace fabric or trim with motifs which have been made separately from the background. Motifs can be clipped apart and appliquéd to another surface; same as clipped lace. See Lace to sew.

Aramid Synthetic fiber that is very strong and flame-resistant.

Argyle Knitting design motif featuring a diamond pattern.

Ariloft An acetate fiber. See Acetate to sew.

Armo Wool Interlining fabric, wool/polyester (90/10) blend. Incorrectly called lamb's wool.

Armure French term for pebbled surface or embossed effect; dress fabric made in a variety of fibers or blends. See Crêpe de Chine to sew.

Arnel® Triacetate fiber. Resists wrinkles and is washable with good pleat retention. See Acetate to sew.

Art linen Plain-weave fabric used for needlework.

Artificial silk Early name for rayon fabrics which imitated silk. See Rayon to sew.

Artillery tweed Twill-weave fabric using bulky yarns in the warp to create a sharply defined upright diagonal on the face. Same as whipcord. See Worsted to sew.

Astrakhan (1) Curly fur from the karakul sheep. See Fur to sew. (2) Woven fabric with a thick curly pile, imitating fur. Wool or synthetic; best quality has mohair warp to add luster and curl. See Melton to sew.

Athletic mesh Open work woven or knit pattern; same as dishrag. See Net to sew.

Avisco® XL High tenacity rayon fiber; strong and resistant to abrasion and wrinkling. See Rayon to sew.

Avlin Polyester fiber. See Polyester to sew.

Avril® High-wet-modulus (HWM) rayon fiber. See Rayon to sew.

Avron® High tenacity rayon fiber; strong and resistant to abrasion and wrinkling. See Rayon to sew.

Avsorb Rayon fiber. See Rayon to sew.

B

Backed cloth Extra filling and/or warp woven into a fabric to define pattern, add thickness, weight, strength, or warmth; piqué, matelassé, and satin-backed crepe. See Matelassé and Double-Faced Fabric to sew.

Bagheera Crease-resistant velvet with uncut, looped pile. See Velvet to sew.

Balanced fabric Cloth with same number of picks and ends per inch, which are identical in size and character.

Balanced twill Simplest twill weave, which alternates same number of picks and ends (e.g. 2/2 or 3/3). Sometimes called even twill.

Bandanna Colored, cotton square with a tie-dyed design in white. See Broadcloth to sew.

Ban-Lon® Process that adds bulk and stretch to synthetic yarns. See Spandex to sew.

Bannockburn tweed Made by alternating single ply and two-ply yarns. See Woolen to sew.

Barathea High-quality, fine wool twill-weave fabric. See Wool Flannel to sew.

Bark crepe Rough-textured crepe which resembles tree bark; made in wool, rayon, and polyester. See Wool Crepe to sew.

Baronet satin Weave fabric with cotton warp and rayon filling; drapes and wears well. See Satin to sew.

Bars Connecting threads in lace; same as brides and bridges.

Basket weave Variation of plain weave. Utilizes two or more threads in both the warp and filling; ex.: monk's cloth, hopsacking. See Loosely Woven to sew.

Bast fibers From the bark of flax, ramie, hemp, and jute. See Linen or Hemp to sew.

Batik Resist method of printing which utilizes wax. See Broadcloth to sew.

Batiste Soft, lightweight, plain weave fabric; durable, varies in sheerness. See Batiste to sew.

Battenberg lace Made by joining narrow tapes with brides.

Batting Originally, carded cotton or wool sold in sheets; today, usually polyester fleece which is sold by the yard.

Bayadere Silk with brightly colored cross rib. See Shantung to sew.

Beaded velvet Made with extra loops on the surface which are then cut to form the pile; same as cut velvet. See Velvet to sew.

Beading Lace or embroidered insertion with holes for inserting ribbon.

Beaver Warm, soft, hard-wearing fur; may be sheared or natural. Redness is undesirable.

Beau-Grip Rayon fiber. See Rayon to sew.

Beaver cloth Expensive topcoat fabric with heavy nap on face. See Melton to sew.

Bedford cord Firm, medium-heavy fabric with cords in the warp. See Melton and Worsted to sew.

Beetled finish Sheen produced by pounding the fabric to close spaces between warp and filling, which produces a sheen.

Bemberg Soft, silky fabric made of cuprammonium rayon; same as cupro. See Lining to sew.

Benares Lightweight fabric with a metallic thread pattern. See Metallic to sew.

Bengaline Lustrous, cross-rib fabric; heavier than grosgrain. Silk or wool; firm, but drapeable. See Shantung to sew.

Billard cloth High-quality twill- or plain-weave fabric in merino wool; even, smooth, and durable. See Felt to sew.

Bird's eye Fine worsted in a dobby weave with a small indentation in the center of the pattern resembling the eye of a bird; made of cotton or rayon. See Chambray to sew.

Bi-Loft® An acrylic fiber. See Acrylic to sew.

Blanket cloth Heavily napped and fulled fabric made of wool, cotton, or blend. See Melton to sew.

Blazer cloth Satin-weave fabric with slight nap on the face. See Flannel to sew.

Bleach Chemical used to remove color.

Bleeding dye Dyes, usually vegetable, which run or fade when wet; undesirable, except on madras and perhaps denim.

Blend (1) Combination of two or more fibers in one yarn. (2) Fabric made of blended yarns.

Blister Puckers, crimps, or bulges on the fabric surface.

Block printing Hand-printing method using carved wooden or linoleum blocks.

Blotch printing Direct printing method; reverse side will be almost white.

Blue "C" Nylon fiber. See Nylon to sew.

Bobbin Device that carries filling yarns in weaving.

Bobbinet Net fabric which simulates bobbin lace. See Net to sew.

Bobbin lace Lace originally made with bobbins. Motifs are worked separately, then joined by a net ground. Today both the motifs and ground are machine made. See Lace to sew.

Boiled wool Knitted wool which has been shrunk and fulled. See Boiled Wool to sew.

Bolivia Twill-weave wool coating with a diagonal pattern. See Melton to sew.

Bolt Quantity of fabric.

Bombazine Twill-weave silk and worsted fabric; often dyed black for mourning cloth. See Worsted to sew.

Bonded batting Polyester batting coated with light resin to keep fibers from migrating.

Bonded fabrics Two fabrics which have been fused or glued wrong sides together to make one fabric. See Double-Faced and Double Cloth to sew.

Bonded knit Fabric bonded to another fabric.

Border design Printed, woven, or knitted design along one or both edges.

Borgana® Pile coat fabric. See Melton to sew.

Botany Soft, firm twill-weave worsted. See Worsted to sew.

Bottom weight Fabrics used for suitings, pants, or skirts that weigh more than 8 oz./yd.

Bouclé (1) Yarns with loops or curls. (2) Knitted or woven fabric woven with bouclé yarns. See Bouclé to sew.

Braid (1) Method of making tape, trim, and elastic by plaiting. (2) Narrow plaited band made in all major fibers; narrows when stretched. (3) Fancy narrow band woven on a jacquard loom.

Breton lace Delicate transparent net with embroidered design. See Lace to sew.

Brides Connecting threads in lace; same as bridges and bars.

Bridges Connecting threads in lace; same as brides and bars.

Broadtail Flat, wavy fur taken from unborn lambs. See Fur to sew.

Broadcloth Cross-rib fabric with very fine ribs; made of cotton, rayon, and silk. See Broadcloth to sew cotton and rayon. See Shantung to sew silk.

Brocade Embossed or raised floral and scroll design woven on jacquard loom with floating threads on back. See Brocade to sew.

Brocade velvet Made by removing areas of pile (burn-out) to create the pattern; looks like cut velvet woven on jacquard loom. See Velvet to sew.

Brocalette Heavy brocade fabric used for upholstery. See Brocade to sew.

Brocatelle Tightly woven, high relief fabric similar to brocade, but heavier. See Brocade to sew.

Broderie anglaise Fine quality, white eyelet on white cotton or cotton blend. See Batiste to sew.

Broken check Woven or printed patterns with checks which are not perfect squares. See Plaid to sew.

Broken-twill weave Twill-weave fabrics in which the twill changes direction; not always a herringbone. See Stripe to sew.

Brushing Finishing process to raise the nap; used on acrylics, wool, cotton, denim, and nylon. Same as scrubbing.

Brussels lace Orginially handmade, features heavy outline around motifs. See Lace to sew.

Buckram Very stiff open-weave stiffening fabric.

Buckskin (1) The flesh or sueded side of deerskin; soft, lightweight. (2) Rugged, satin-weave fabric, simulating buckskin. See Suede to sew.

Buffalo cloth Very heavy wool coating with long nap. See Melton to sew.

Bunting fleece Generic name for knitted fabrics which have been shrunk and felted. Reversible, with good shape retention; warm, soft, and lightweight. See Fleece to sew.

Burlap Coarse plain-weave fabric made of jute, hemp, or cotton, with distinctive odor.

Burn-out fabrics (1) Plain-weave fabric made of two different fiber types which is treated with chemicals to burn out one of the fibers, creating a pattern design. Most are lightweight blends with sheer and opaque areas; others are sculptured velvets; same as etched-out. See Velvet to sew. (2) Lace embroidered with a shiffli machine on water-soluble material; same as guipure or chemical lace. See Lace to sew.

Butcher linen (1) Stiff, heavy, durable plain-weave linen, sheds dirt easily, wears well. (2) Linen-look fabrics made of rayon or cotton. See Linen to sew.

Byrd Cloth® Closely woven twill-weave cotton that is windproof. See Water-Repellent to sew.

C

Cabretta Popular lightweight goat skin with a fine grain and rich finish. See Leather to sew.

Cadon Nylon fiber. See Nylon to sew.

Calendering Lustrous or embossed finish applied to fabric by rollers; may not be permanent.

Calf Coarse, flat fur with a sheen; frequently dyed to imitate other animals. See Fur to sew.

Calfskin suede Underlayer of calfskin. See Suede to sew.

Calico (1) Inexpensive, printed, plain-weave cotton. Firmly woven, wears and launders well. (2) In UK, same as muslin. See Broadcloth to sew.

Cambric Lightweight, crisp, plain-weave linen or cotton. See Broadcloth to sew.

Camel hair Lustrous, soft underhair of the bactrian camel. See Hair Fiber to sew.

Candlewick Heavy, plain-weave cotton fabric with coarse string tufts; originally by hand. See Chenille to sew.

Canton crepe Silk crepe with slight cross-rib. See Crêpe de Chine to sew.

Canton satin Soft, heavy satin with crepe back, heavier than crêpe de Chine, drapes well. See Satin to sew.

Canvas (1) Stiff, durable plain-weave cloth; similar to duck and sailcloth, but lighter. See Denim to sew.

Caprolan Nylon fiber used for linings and outerwear. See Lining and Water-Repellent to sew.

Captiva Nylon fiber. See Nylon to sew.

Carded cotton Yarns made of short irregular fibers. Durable, but not as smooth or lustrous as combed cotton; used for calico and muslin. See Broadcloth to sew.

Carding Process of cleaning, untangling, and straightening wool, silk, and cotton fibers.

Caressa A faux suede. See Faux Suede to sew.

Cashmere Soft, strong, and silky hair fiber from kashmir goat; mixed with wool for economy and durability. See Hair Fiber to sew.

Cassimere Plain or twill-weave suiting with a clear finish. See Wool Flannel to sew.

Casuwool® A fabric made from wool and cotton. See Woolen to sew.

Cavalry twill Durable twill-weave wool with distinctive double-twill line. See Worsted to sew.

Celanese Nylon fiber. See Nylon to sew.

Cellophane Thin, transparent, smooth cellulose film.

Cellulose Fiber made from the cell walls of plants, used to make rayons and acetates.

Chalk stripe Suiting fabric with a fine, light, or white line; may be printed or woven. See Worsted to sew.

Challis Soft, but firm, plain weave fabric in wool, cotton, rayon, or blends; lightweight, drapes and gathers well. See Wool Challis or Rayon Challis to sew.

Chambray Plain-weave, smooth fabric with colored warp and white filling; looks like light weighted denim; wears and launders well. See Broadcloth to sew.

Chameleon Fabric with a changeable effect; warp of one color and double yarn filling of different colors. See Taffeta and Silk to sew.

Chamois Soft suede originally from the chamois goat; today, from other goats, sheep, or deer. See Suede to sew.

Changeable Fabric woven with different colors in warp and filling; changes color when the fabric is moved. Same as shot and iridescent. See Taffeta and Silk to sew.

Chantilly lace Open lace with a fine net ground and elaborate floral motifs; finished with picots on edge(s). Sometimes re-embroidered. See Lace to sew.

Charmeuse Soft, satin-weave fabric with a dull back and lustrous face. May be silk, polyester, cotton, rayon , or blends; creases, snags, and wears poorly. See Charmeuse to sew.

Charvet silk Soft, twill-weave fabric with dull finish. See Charmeuse to sew.

Check Woven or printed pattern of squares. See Plaid to sew.

Cheesecloth Soft, open-weave cotton used for straining. See Net to sew.

Chemical lace Firm, stiff lace, machine-made on a background fabric which is dissolved, leaving only the lace; same as burn-out, guipure, Venise, or Venice Lace. See Lace to sew.

Chenille (1) Fabric woven with chenille yarns. See Bouclé to sew. (2) Pile fabric name for the caterpillar. See Chenille to sew.

Cheviot Rough-surfaced, twill-weave wool with same color in warp and filling; wears well, but loses its shape. See Woolen to sew.

Chevron A horizontal design of joined V's.

Chiffon Lightweight, sheer, plain-weave fabric made with fine, highly twisted yarns; soft, drapeable, filmy, and strong. See Chiffon to sew.

Chiffon velvet Lightweight, pile fabric in rayon or silk; durable, drapes well, crushes easily. See Velvet to sew.

China grass See ramie. See Handkerchief Linen to sew.

China silk Inexpensive, soft, lightweight plain-weave silk; not very durable. Same as Jap silk. See China Silk to sew.

Chinchilla Expensive, soft, blush-white fur with dark tips. See Fur to sew.

Chinchilla cloth Thick, heavily napped wool coating with a short, curly pile on the face, simulating chinchilla fur; spongy, usually gray in color. See Faux Fur Fabric to sew.

Chinella® A fleece fabric. See Fleece to sew.

Chino Durable, medium-weight fabric with a slight sheen on the face and a dull back. See Denim to sew.

Chintz Closely woven, plain-weave cotton with a glazed finish; wears well. Some glazes wash out; some are permanent. See Broadcloth to sew.

Circular knit Fabric or garment knitted in a circle without a seam.

Ciré (1) Sometimes used on silk and rayon to produce a smooth, lustrous finish similar to patent leather. See Satin to sew. (2) High-luster finish applied to heat-sensitive nylon and rayon; sometimes lined or quilted for warmth. See Water-Repellent to sew.

Cisele velvet (1) Pile fabric with cut and uncut loops. (2) Satin fabric with velvet pattern. See Velvet to sew.

Clear finish on wool fabrics such as gabardine and serge to remove nap and fuzz, making the weave easy to see. Fabrics hold creases well, but shine with wear. See Gabardine to sew.

Cleerspan® Spandex fiber. See Spandex to sew.

Climaguard® Soft, silky, water-repellent microfiber used for outerwear. See Microfibers and Water-Repellent to sew.

Clipped lace See appliqué lace. See Lace to sew.

Cloque Lightweight, woven fabric with a blistered surface. Soft and drapeable; made in silk, rayon, and polyester. See Matelassé to sew.

Cloth Material made with yarns by weaving, knitting, or braiding or by felting fibers with heat, pressure, and moisture.

Cluny lace Coarse, open, cotton lace. See Lace to sew.

Coated fabric Any fabric coated with a film to make it water-repellent, waterproof, or longer wearing. See Water-Repellent or Waterproof to sew.

Coating Fabric suitable for making coats. See Melton to sew.

Colorfast Color which will not wash out, rub off, or fade in normal use.

Coloray Rayon fiber. See Rayon to sew.

Combed cotton Fine fabrics such as organdy, lawn, percale, or batiste, made with long cotton fibers which remain after combing. See Batiste to sew.

Combing Process to remove short fiber lengths from cotton and man-made yarns after carding.

Comfort Fiber Polyester fiber. See Polyester to sew.

Comfort stretch Fabrics with less than 30 percent stretch; suitable for everyday wear. See Stretch Woven to sew.

ComFortrel® Polyester fiber with a soft hand. See Polyester to sew.

Comiso A high tenacity rayon; stronger, more resistant to abrasion and wrinkling. See Rayon to sew.

Companion fabrics Manufacturer's collection of two or more fabrics designed to be used together.

Continuous filament Uncut filament of silk or man-made fiber.

Cool Wool® A washable wool. See Woolen to sew.

Corded fabric With a noticeable rib. Cross-rib fabrics include bengaline, grosgrain, faille, ottoman, poplin, and shantung. Warp cords include piqué and Bedford cord. See Shantung to sew.

Cordura® Nylon canvas fabric. Strong, very resistant to abrasion, dries quickly, not affected by rot or mildew. See Waterproof Fabric to sew.

Corduroy A filling pile fabric with plain or twill weave; usually forms wales or vertical ribs. Fabric weight, drape, and stiffness vary with size of wales. See Corduroy to sew.

Cotton Soft, absorbent fiber obtained from seed pod of the cotton plant.

Cotton batting A thin sheet of unwoven cotton held together with a glaze.

Cotton linters Short cotton fibers used to make rayon, acetate, and cotton wadding.

Cotton satin Fabric woven with long-staple, combed cottons in the warp. See Satin to sew.

Cotton shantung Cross-rib cotton fabric. See Shantung to sew.

Count of cloth In a woven fabric, the number of picks and ends in a square inch; in a knit, the number of wales and courses.

Courcel Rayon fiber. See Rayon to sew.

Course One row of stitches across knitted fabric; corresponds to crossgrain or filling in woven fabrics. Easy to see on the back of single knits.

Courtaulds HT Rayon Rayon fiber. See Rayon to sew.

Courtaulds Nylon Nylon fiber. See Nylon to sew.

Courtaulds Rayon Rayon fiber. See Rayon to sew.

Courtek M An acrylic fiber. See Acrylic to sew.

Covert Rugged, medium-weight, twill-weave wool; usually has speckled effect; naturally water-repellent. See Worsted to sew.

Cowhide Smooth-grained leather in all weights. See Leather to sew.

Cowhide splits Soft, sueded skins. See Suede to sew.

Crash Coarse, rough textured, plain or twill-weaved fabric. See Linen to sew.

Crepe Light to heavy-weight fabric with dull, crinkled surface. Made by using hard-twist yarns, a crepe weave, chemicals, or embossing. See Crêpe de Chine and Wool Crepe to sew.

Crepe-back satin Reversible fabric with a satin face and crepe back; same as satin-back crepe. See Satin and Double-Faced Fabric to sew.

Crepe charmeuse Smooth, light- to medium-weight crepe with a dull luster and slight stiffness; drapes and clings gracefully; may be silk or polyester. See Charmeuse to sew.

Crepe chiffon A very lightweight, sheer crepe. See Chiffon to sew.

Crêpe de Chine Fine, light- to medium-weight with crepe yarns used in the warp and filling. See Crêpe de Chine to sew.

Crepesoft Polyester fiber. See Polyester to sew.

Crepon Heavy crepe with lengthwise crinkles. See Crêpe de Chine to sew.

Creslan® An acrylic fiber. See Acrylic to sew.

Crimp Waviness in the fiber; adds bulk and warmth to the fabric and increases resiliency, absorbency, and resistance to abrasion. Natural in wool; sometimes added to man-made yarns.

Crinkle crepe Same as plissé. See Broadcloth to sew.

Crinoline Stiff, open-weave interfacing with heavy sizing. See Interfacing to sew.

Crochet knit Open-work knit made on a raschel knitting machine with little or no strength; usually acrylic. See Raschel Knit to sew.

Crocking Process of surface dye rubbing off onto the skin or other fabrics.

Crocodile Expensive leather similar to alligator. See Leather to sew.

Cross-dyeing Piece dyeing fabrics with different fiber types and affinities for the dyestuff, to create different shades and heathers.

Crush resistance Finish applied to pile fabrics to improve ability to spring back after crushing.

Crushed velvet Pile is pressed in different directions to create a pattern with various color shades. See Velvet to sew.

Crystal pleating Small accordian pleats. See Slinky and Pleated Fabric to sew.

Cumuloft Nylon fiber. See Nylon to sew.

Cuprammonium rayon Soft, silky rayon fiber; ex.: Bemberg. See Rayon and Lining to sew.

Cupro Same as cuprammonium rayon. See Rayon and Lining to sew.

Cut Sample piece of fabric in a particular pattern or color to make one or more sample garments.

Cut-pile Fabrics like corduroy and velvet made by forming extra loops on the surface, which are then cut to form the pile.

Cut velvet Made with extra loops on satin surface which are then cut to form the pile. Same as beaded velvet. See Velvet and Satin to sew.

D

Dacron® Polyester fiber; resists stretching, abrasion, and wrinkles; launders well, dries quickly. See Polyester to sew.

Damask Reversible fabric with elaborate design woven on jacquard loom; flatter than brocade, made in cotton, linen, wool, worsted, silk, rayon, or man-made yarns. See Damask and Double-Faced Fabric to sew.

Dan-Press A durable press finish.

Dantwill® A fine, twill weave fabric in 50/50 blend of cotton/polyester. See Broadcloth to sew.

Darleen® Synthetic rubber. See Spandex to sew.

Darlexx® A waterproof fabric with stretch. See Waterproof and Spandex to sew.

Darlexx Superskin Laminated stretch fabric with plastic film. See Faux Leather and Spandex to sew.

Darned lace Design on netting. See Lace to sew.

Deep pile Faux fur fabrics woven or knitted to simulate real furs; often modacrylic, which is flame resistant. See Faux Fur Fabric to sew.

Deerskin Grain or skin edge of deer leather. See Leather to sew.

Deerskin splits Sueded on both sides, these splits are soft, lightweight, and washable; similar to chamois, but stronger. See Suede to sew.

Degummed silk Very lightweight silk which has been boiled to remove the gum (sericin). See China Silk to sew.

Denim (1) Densely woven twill fabric with colored warp and white filling. Medium- to heavy-weight, strong, hard wearing, stiff when new; softens with wear; shrinks, crocks, and fades. (2) Knitted or woven fabrics in a variety of fibers which look like denim. See Denim to sew.

Design Weave design on graph paper. The marker or black squares show the warp yarns.

Diagonal weave Twill weave running from left or right on the face of the material. Most run from the upper right-hand corner to the lower left at a 45 degree angle; steep twills may be 63, 70, or 75 degrees.

Dimity Lightweight sheer fabric woven with multi-ply yarns to create stripes or checks on plain-weave fabric; semi-crisp to crisp. See Batiste to sew.

Dishrag Open-work woven or knit pattern; same as athletic mesh or fishnet. See Net to sew.

Dobby Fabric woven on a dobby loom with small dots, or a geometric or floral pattern. Made in cotton, rayon, silk, or man-made fibers. See Broadcloth to sew.

Doeskin (1) Skin of white sheep; originally skin of deer. See Suede to sew. (2) Soft, slightly napped wool broadcloth. See Wool Flannel to sew.

Domette British name for lamb's wool interlining fabric; sometimes called llama wool or French wool. Uses: shoulder pads, sleeve heads, and underlinings. See Interfacing to sew.

Donegal tweed Rough herringbone tweed with slubs. See Woolen to sew.

Dorelastan A European spandex fiber. See Spandex to sew.

Dotted swiss Sheer, crisp cotton with woven dots, wears and launders well. Imitation dotted swiss has flocked or printed dots. See Organza to sew.

Double cloth Reversible fabric which can be separated and used on either side. The two faces may differ in weave, color, yarns, and/or pattern. See Double Cloth to sew.

Double-faced fabric (1) Reversible fabric woven with two sets of fillings and two sets of warps. Face and reverse can have two different patterns, same colors. Cannot be separated into two distinct layers by clipping the binding yarns. Varies in weight and firmness. (2) Two fabric layers fused together to make a double-faced fabric. (3) Single-ply fabrics which have no wrong side. See Double-Faced Fabric to sew.

Double-faced satin Reversible fabric with satin on face and back. See Satin to sew.

Double knit Medium to heavy fabric, knitted on a machine with two sets of needles so both sides look the same when there is no pattern; fabric has little or no stretch, holds its shape well. See Double Knit to sew.

Double sheer Lightweight fabric tightly woven with twisted yarns. Crisp or soft and almost opaque, looks like moiré. See Chiffon and Organza to sew.

Doupioni A cross-rib silk woven with an uneven, irregular slubbed yarn from two cocoons nested together; ravels badly. See Shantung to sew.

Down Natural insulator; breathes, allows body moisture to evaporate quickly. Difficult to handle, does not insulate when wet, shifts, mats.

Down proof Closely woven, fabric that does not allow down to escape. See Denim to sew.

Drape The way a fabric hangs when arranged in different positions.

Drill Durable, tightly woven, twill-weave cotton. See Denim to sew.

Drizzle cloth A medium-weight, water-repellent fabric with a DWR finish. See Water-Repellent Fabric to sew.

Duchesse satin Very heavy, stiff satin with plain back; made of silk or rayon. See Satin to sew.

Duck Closely woven plain-weave material similar to canvas but heavier and more durable. See Denim to sew.

Duffel A dense, twill-weave woolen with a heavy nap. See Melton to sew.

Dungaree Similar to denim. See Denim to sew.

Durable press cotton Fabric with a finish to retard wrinkling when laundered. See Broadcloth to sew.

Durene® Quality cotton yarns.

Duvetyne Soft, medium-weight fabric with a velvety nap and satin weave; drapes and wears well; spots easily. Cotton duvetyne is sometimes called cotton suede. See Velveteen to sew.

Durvil Rayon fiber. See Rayon to sew.

DWR A durable, water-repellent coating which will wash out in six to eight launderings. See Water-Repellent Fabric to sew.

Dynel® A modacrylic fiber which is strong, warm, quick-drying, and non-combustible. See Acrylic to sew.

E

Ecospun® Polyester fiber made from recycled plastic bottles. See Polyester to sew.

Egyptian cotton High-quality, plain-weave cotton, known for its long staple. Soft, but strong and hard wearing; dyes well. See Batiste to sew.

Elastic Cord or fabric with stretch and recovery; made of latex, spandex, or cut rubber.

Elastique Worsted suiting. See Worsted to sew.

Eloquent Luster Nylon fiber. See Nylon to sew.

Eloquent Touch Nylon fiber. See Nylon to sew.

Embossed fabric With relief pattern which has been pressed into it by passing it between heated rollers; usually permanent. See Matelassé to sew.

Embroidered fabric Any fabric embellished with hand or machine-made embroidery in an all-over or border design. See Embroidered Fabric to sew.

Encron® Polyester fiber. See Polyester to sew.

End (1) Warp yarn running lengthwise in cloth. Set of yarns put onto the loom to run the length of the cloth and parallel to the selvage. Same as ends and woof. (2) Fabric remnant.

End and end Shirting fabric with alternating colors in the warp. See Broadcloth to sew.

Enkacrepe Nylon fiber. See Nylon to sew.

Enkaire Rayon fiber. See Rayon to sew.

Enkalure Nylon fiber. See Nylon to sew.

Enkasheer Nylon fiber. See Nylon to sew.

Enka Viscose Rayon yarn. See Rayon to sew.

Enkrome Rayon fiber. See Rayon to sew.

Entrant® Non-stretch fabric with a polyurethane coating. More waterproof than water-repellent, it is flexible and tough with a good hand and drape; wash or dry-clean. See Waterproof Fabric to sew.

Éponge Soft, spongy wool. See Bouclé to sew.

Espa® A Japanese spandex fiber. See Spandex to sew.

Estron An acetate fiber. See Acetate to sew.

Eyelash (1) Reversible fabric with clipped yarns on the fabric surface to look like eyelashes. See Batiste to sew. (2) Fabric with long yarns on the face side of the fabric.

Eyelash voile Sheer, semi-crisp, plain-weave fabric with clipped yarns on the fabric surface to look like eyelashes. See Batiste to sew.

Eyelet (1) Fabric with embroidered, open-work pattern. Soft to crisp with an all-over or border design. See Batiste to sew.

F

Fabric Any woven, knitted, braided, felted, or nonwoven material; same as cloth or material.

Facile Soft synthetic suede. See Faux Suede to sew.

Faconné (1) Any fancy weave fabric, like a jacquard. (2) Fabric, such as sculptured velvet, made of two fiber types with different characteristics and printed with a chemical which dissolves one, leaving the other. See Velvet to sew.

Faconné velvet Velvet with burnt out design. See Velvet to sew.

Faille Cross-rib fabric with thicker yarns in the filling. See Shantung to sew.

Faille crepe Cross-rib fabric with a satin back; smoother, duller, and heavier fabric than crêpe de Chine. May be silk or synthetic. See Shantung to sew.

Faille taffeta Fabric with pronounced cross-ribs; softer with larger, flatter ribs than grosgrain. See Shantung to sew.

Fairtex® A metallic yarn. See Metallics to sew.

Fashion fabric Term used to describe the most visible fabric used in apparel.

Faux fur fabric Deep pile fabrics woven or knitted to simulate real furs. Often modacrylic, which is flame resistant. See Faux Fur Fabric to sew.

Felt fabric Sheeting produced by pounding and felting wet fibers together. See Felt to sew.

Felted fabric Woven or knitted fabric which has been shrunk 20% to 50% and fulled to obscure the weave and produce a felted finish. See Boiled Wool to sew.

Fiber The smallest unit in all fabrics; an individual strand with a definite length before it is made into yarn such as cotton.

Fiberfill Fluffy batting material, usually polyester, for quilting, padding, and shoulder pads.

Fibermet® A metallic fiber. See Metallics to sew.

Fibranne Same as viscose rayon. See Rayon to sew.

Fibro Rayon fiber. See Rayon to sew.

Filament Individual fiber of an indefinite length, before it is made into yarn; silk, the only natural filament, can be 300 to 1,800 yards long, while a synthetic filament can run several miles.

Filament fabric Smooth fabric made of filament yarns. May be transparent or opaque, light- or medium-weight; ex.: chiffon, taffeta, satin, ninon, and silk organza.

Fi-lana® An acrylic fiber. See Acrylic to sew.

Filling Crossgrain yarns which interlace with the warp (lengthwise yarns); may be decorative; usually weaker than the warp, with less twist. Same as pick, shoot, shute, weft, or woof.

Filling-face satin Satin-weave fabric with a predominance of filling yarns on the fabric face. See Satin to sew.

Filling-face twill Twill-weave fabric with a predominance of filling yarns on the fabric face. See Gabardine to sew.

Filling pile Fabric with pile created by extra set of filling yarns; ex.: corduroy. See Corduroy or Velveteen to sew.

Filling stretch See horizontal stretch.

Film Flexible, waterproof sheet; may be clear or colored, plain, printed, or embossed. Does not breathe. See Faux Leather to sew.

Findings Supplementary materials used in garment making: buttons, snaps, zippers, and belts. Same as notions or haberdashery.

Finish Treatments to make fabrics more attractive, such as embossing, felting, crinkling, flocking, and laminating, or processes which enable fabrics to perform better by wrinkling and shrinking less, resisting flames, or repelling water.

Fireproof Fabric which will not burn. See Zebra to sew.

Fire-resistant Fabric treated to resist burning and retard spreading flames. Same as fire-retardant. See Zebra to sew.

Flannel (1) Dull-surfaced woolens and worsteds with a light nap; plain or twill weave. See Wool Flannel to sew. (2) Lightweight, napped cotton or man-made fibers; may be napped on one or both sides. See Broadcloth to sew.

Flannelette Soft cotton with nap; same as outing. See Broadcloth to sew.

Flat crepe Smooth crepe with a flat warp or twisted filling. See Crêpe de Chine to sew.

Flat knit Fabric knitted on a flat machine instead of a circular one.

Flax A bast fiber from the flax plant, used to produce linen.

Fleece (1) Wool from live sheep. (2) Heavy wool with deep, soft nap on fabric face; knitted or woven. (3) Knitted synthetic with a deep nap. See Fleece to sew.

Fleece-lined Double-knit fabric with fleece on one or both sides. See Sweatshirt Knit to sew.

Fleeced Napped surface, usually on the back side of knitted fabrics. See Sweatshirt Knit to sew.

Float Portion of the filling or warp yarns which crosses two or more of the opposite yarns to form the pattern.

Flock Small bits of fibers bonded to the fabric surface in dots or patterns; usually permanent.

Fluflon Stretch fiber. See Spandex to sew.

Fortisan® Strong, high-tenacity rayon fiber. See Rayon to sew.

Fortrel® Various polyester fibers. See Polyester and Microfibers to sew.

Foulard Lightweight, printed silk or man-made fabric woven in a plain or twill weave. See Silk to sew.

Four-ply silk Silk crepe with four-ply yarns in the warp and filling. See Crêpe de Chine to sew.

Four-way stretch knits Knits with stretch in length and width; good stretch and recovery, usually heavier than two-way stretch knits. See Two-way and Four-way Stretch Knit to sew.

FOXFIBRE® Naturally colored cotton. See Broadcloth to sew.

French back Worsted fabric with twill-weave back, usually in cotton to add weight, warmth, and stability. See Worsted to sew.

French terry Densely knit, lightweight, pile fabric with tiny loops on wrong side; cotton, rayon, and blends. See Terry Cloth to sew.

Friezé A heavy, twill-weave coating with a rough nap. See Melton and Boiled Wool to sew.

Fuji silk A lightweight, cream-colored silk woven with spun yarns. See China Silk to sew.

Fulling Finishing process used on wools and wool blends to felt and shrink the yarns and make the fibers swell and thicken; used to make boiled wool.

Fur Animal pelt tanned with the hair on. See Fur to sew.

Fur fabrics Incorrect term, according to a Federal Trade Commission ruling, for fake-fur fabrics.

Fusible fabric Fabric with a fusible backing which can be bonded to another fabric. Any fabric can be made a fusible fabric by bonding a fusing agent to its back; ex.: some interfacings.

Fusible web® Web of polyamide resins which melt when heated; ex.: Wonder Under®, Jiffy Fuse, Stitch Witchery®, Fine Fuse Fusible Web, Sav-a-Stitch®, and TransFuseII.

G

Gabardine Firm, hard-finished, durable, twill-weave fabric. See Gabardine to sew.

Galatea Rugged twill-weave cotton fabric. See Denim to sew.

Galloon Lace finished with scallops or finished edge on both sides. See Lace to sew.

Gauze Sheer, open-weave fabric in a plain or leno weave. See Batiste to sew.

Gauze weave Leno-weave variation in which the warp yarns twist around each other, forming a figure eight.

Gazar Lightweight silk fabric woven with highly twisted yarns in a tight weave; almost opaque, it has a linen-like coarseness. See Organza or Handkerchief Linen to sew.

Georgette Soft, double sheer crepe fabric made by alternating tightly twisted S- and Z-twist yarns in both the warp and filling; usually silk or polyester. See Chiffon to sew.

Gingham Plain-weave fabric using dyed yarns to form a striped or checked pattern. See Plaid to sew.

Glazing (1) Finish for cotton fabrics like chintz to give them a shiny finish. Glue, paraffin, and sizing may not be permanent; synthetic resins are. (2) Damage caused by too hot iron to acetate, synthetics, and thermoplastic fibers.

Glen plaid Small plaid woven over a large plaid; sometimes called a Glen check. See Plaid to sew.

Glissade Cotton-lining fabric with a satin weave. See Broadcloth to sew.

Glore-Valcana Synthetic suede fabric. See Faux Suede to sew.

Glospan Spandex fiber. See Spandex to sew.

Golden Glow Polyester fiber. See Polyester to sew.

Golden Touch Polyester fiber. See Polyester to sew.

Gore-Tex® Trade name for film-like material sandwiched between breathable fabrics to provide warmth and dryness without bulk or weight. See Waterproof Fabric to sew.

Grain Yarn directions on woven fabric.

Granada Fine worsted with cotton warp and mohair or alpaca filling. See Worsted and Hair Fiber to sew.

Granite cloth Fabric made with a pebbly surface on both sides. See Crêpe de Chine to sew.

Gray goods Fabrics which have been knitted or woven but not finished, napped, pressed, printed, dyed, tentered, embossed, bleached, waterproofed, or mercerized.

Grisaille French term meaning gray. Gray-looking fabric made with black-and-white yarns in the warp and filling. See Silk Suiting to sew.

Gros de Londres Cross-rib fabric with alternating thick and thin ribs. See Shantung to sew.

Grosgrain Hard-finished, closely woven, cross-rib fabric. See Shantung to sew.

Ground The background of the fabric design; the basic part of the fabric.

Guipure Firm, stiff lace, machine-made on a background fabric which is dissolved, leaving only the lace. Same as chemical, burn-out, Venise, or Venice Lace. See Lace to sew.

Gun-club check Checked fabric woven with three colors of yarn. See Plaid to sew.

H

H2O A washable wool. See Woolen to sew.

Habutai Soft, lightweight, ecru-colored silk woven in Japan, heavier than China silk. See China Silk to sew.

Hair canvas Interfacing fabric made of wool, cotton, or rayon with mohair or horsehair woven into the filling. See Interfacing to sew.

Hair fibers Fiber from animals other than sheep; ex.: mohair, camel, cashmere, alpaca, and angora rabbit. See Hair Fiber and Mohair to sew.

Hand The tactile quality of fabric. The feel of the fabric: crispness, firmness, drapeability, softness, elasticity, and resilience.

Handkerchief linen Sheer, lightweight, crisp plain-weave linen. See Handkerchief Linen to sew.

Handkerchief Tencel® Sheer, lightweight, crisp, plain-weave tencil. See Handkerchief Linen to sew.

Handwoven Fabric woven on a loom by hand, often loosely woven with novelty filling yarns. See Handwoven to sew.

Hard finish Cotton, woolen, or worsted fabrics with no nap.

Harris tweed Trade name for rough, heavy wool, is spun, dyed, and handwoven on Harris and other Outer Hebrides Islands. See Woolen and Handwoven to sew.

Heathers Soft, muted colors made by blending different colored fibers into the yarns; examples: tweeds and other sport fabrics. See Woolen to sew.

Helanca® Nylon/polyester stretch fiber. Stretches 500% and is used for two way stretch fibers. See Spandex to sew.

Hemp A bast fiber, similar to linen, but more absorbent. See Hemp to sew.

Herringbone Broken twill-weave pattern which produces a chevron, striped effect. See Woolen, Worsted, Silk Suiting, and Stripe to sew.

High pile Fabric with pile longer than 1/8". See Faux Fur Fabric and Melton to sew.

Himalaya Cross-rib cotton fabric. Same as cotton shantung. See Shantung to sew.

Hollofil Polyester fiber used in fiberfill.

Homespun Rough, plain-weave cotton cloth which appears undyed. See Loosely Woven Fabric to sew.

Honan silk Crisp, pongee-type fabric made from silkworms. See China Silk to sew.

Honeycomb Reversible, woven or knit fabric with geometric, raised weave resembling a honeycomb. See Broadcloth and Knit to sew.

Hopsacking Loosely woven basket-weave wool or cotton. See Loosely Woven Fabric to sew.

Hopsack linen Basket-weave linen. See Linen and Loosely Woven Fabric to sew.

Horizontal stretch Fabric with stretch only in the crossgrain.

Horsehair Hair from the mane and tail of a horse; used in hair canvas.

Houndstooth check Broken-check wool fabric with a regular pattern. See Plaid to sew.

Hydrophilic fiber Fibers which absorb water; ex.: rayon, acetate, cotton, and wool.

Hydrophobic fiber Fibers with low absorbency which repel water; ex.: nylon, acrylic, polyester.

Hymo Interfacing fabric made of mohair and linen.

I

Illusion Any soft silk or nylon net or tulle; very lightweight. See Net to sew.

Imperial brocade Jacquard-weave fabric with gold or silver yarns. See Brocade to sew.

Imperial PVC A waterproof, vinyl-coated polyester; does not breathe. See Waterproof Fabric to sew.

Interfacing Woven, nonwoven, or knit fabric made of cotton, wool, hair, man-made fibers, or blends; used to reinforce, add body or support, or stiffen the garment.

Interlining Lightweight fabric layer placed between the outer fabric and lining for warmth. May be napped, wool, cotton, or polyester fiberfill.

Interlock knit Lightweight, drapeable knit with lengthwise ribs on both sides. Made of cotton and man-made fibers; has little stretch and runs from only one end. See Jersey to sew.

Iridescent Fabric woven with different colors in warp and filling; changes color when the fabric is moved. Same as shot and changeable. See Taffeta and Silk to sew.

Iridescent taffeta Fabric woven with different colors in warp and filling which changes color when the fabric is moved; same as shot and changeable. See Taffeta to sew.

Irish linen Fine, lightweight linen made from Irish flax and woven in Ireland. See Linen to sew.

Irish tweed Twill-weave tweeds from Ireland with a white warp and dark filling. See Woolen to sew.

J

Jacquard Fabric with tapestry or floral design woven on jacquard loom; often reversible. See Crêpe de Chine to sew.

Jacquard loom Loom which utilizes plain, twill, and/or satin weaves to create intricate designs; used to make brocade, damask, tapestry, matelassé, and jacquard fabrics.

Jacquard velvet Patterned velvet with a high-and-low pile created during the weaving process. See Velvet to sew.

Jap silk Inexpensive, soft, lightweight, plain-weave silk; not very durable. See China Silk to sew.

Jean (1) Sturdy fabric similar to denim. See Denim to sew. (2) Used to describe pants made from denim.

Jersey Cool, lightweight, plain-knit fabric with ribs on one side and purl wales on reverse; good elasticity, drapes well, comfortable to wear, snags and runs from both ends. See Wool Jersey to sew.

Jetspun Rayon fiber. See Rayon to sew.

Jumbo corduroy Corduroy with 3 to 10 wales per inch. See Corduroy to sew.

K

Karakul Woven fabric with a thick, curly pile, imitating fur. Wool or synthetic; best quality has mohair warp to add luster and curl. See Melton to sew.

Kasha Soft fabric with a slight nap made from Tibetan goat hair. See Hair Fiber to sew.

Kashmir Soft, strong, and silky hair fiber from the kashmir goat. Mixed with wool to reduce cost and improve durability. See Hair Fiber to sew.

Kersey A face-finished cloth with a short, lustrous nap. See Melton to sew.

Kevlar An aramid fiber. See Denim to sew.

K-Kote finish A waterproof polyurethane coating applied in a single layer. Super K-Kote is applied in a double layer. It is heavier, will withstand more water pressure, and wear longer than the regular K-Kote. See Waterproof Fabric to sew.

Kodel® Polyester fiber that resists pilling. See Polyester to sew.

L

Lace Knitted or woven, open-work, decorative fabric usually made with a netting background. See Lace to sew.

Lactron Synthetic rubber. See Spandex to sew.

Lamaire Synthetic leather. See Spandex to sew.

Lambskin suede A lightweight, easy-to-sew suede; sometimes called garment suede. See Suede to sew.

Lamb's wool (1) Very soft wool taken from the first clipping, before lambs reach seven months. See Wool – Lightweight to sew. (2) An interlining fabric for interlinings, sleeve heads, and batting.

Lamé Any woven or knitted fabric with metallic yarns in the warp, filling, or both; lightweight and drapeable. See Lamé to sew.

Laminated fabric Made by fusing two layers of fabric, film to fabric, simulated leathers to fabric, simulated fabric to foam, or fabric to foam. See Water-Repellent or Faux Leather to sew.

Lamous Nonwoven synthetic suede. See Faux Suede to sew.

Lappet weave Utilizes extra set of warp yarns to create a pattern at fixed intervals. Resembles embroidery; ex.: dotted swiss effects.

Lastex Synthetic rubber. See Spandex to sew.

Latex Liquid rubber, natural or synthetic. See Spandex to sew.

Lawn Fine, crisp, plain-weave cotton with luster and high thread count; more closely woven and stiffer than batiste; not as crisp as organdy. See Batiste to sew.

Leno Loosely woven, but firm, open-weave fabric. See Broadcloth to sew.

Leno weave The warp yarns are paired; and while one warp is positioned like the warp on a plain weave, the other passes to its opposite side. At the same time, the second warp alternates over and under the filling. The term "leno" is used interchangeably with gauze, but they are not exactly the same.

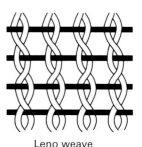
Leno weave

Lethasuede Polyester fiber. See Faux Leather to sew.

Leather Animal hide without fur. See Leather to sew.

Liberty Hand-blocked prints produced by Liberty Ltd., London, on lawn, silk, wool, challis, or wool/cotton blend. See Batiste and Wool Challis to sew.

Lifa® Polypropylene and worsted knit for undergarments; wicks and insulates. See Jersey to sew.

Light Spirit Blend® Polyester fiber that is more breathable than cotton; it wicks well and dries quickly. See Polyester and Broadcloth to sew.

Linen Fabric made from flax pant. Strong, lustrous, and very absorbent. See Linen to sew.

Linen-look Any fabric made to look like linen. Usually firmly woven and slightly coarse in a plain weave. See Linen to sew.

Lining fabric Firmly woven or knit fabric in a plain, twill, or satin weave. Usually slippery; yarns may be cotton, silk, man-made, or blends. Available in various weights to protect and hide seams, reduce wrinkling, prolong the garment's life, and improve its appearance. See Lining to sew.

Linton Tweed Very soft, nice hand, tweeds made by Linton Tweeds, Ltd. See Loosely Woven Fabric and Silk Suiting to sew.

Llama A hair fiber from the camel family. See Hair Fiber to sew.

Loden Thick, fleecy, coarse wool with water repellency. See Melton and Boiled Wool to sew.

London-shrunk Cold-water method of shrinking wool fabrics. Fabrics labeled London-shrunk do not need preshrinking.

Lorette® An Orlon/wool blend. See Wool and Acrylic to sew.

Lurelon Nylon fiber. See Nylon to sew.

Lurex® A metallic fiber; breaks easily, does not tarnish. See Metallic and Lamé to sew.

Lycra® Spandex two-way stretch fiber with good strength; resists heat and perspiration. See Spandex to sew.

Lyocell A environmentally friendly manufactured fiber made from wood pulp. See Tencel to sew.

Lyons velvet Heavier, crisp, short-pile velvet that does not drape well. See Velvet to sew.

M

Macintosh Rubber-coated fabric. See Waterproof Fabric to sew.

Mackinac or mackinaw cloth Heavy, warm fabric with a natural water repellency. See Melton and Water-Repellent Fabric to sew.

Madras Soft, cotton fabric with plaid, check, or stripe pattern. True madras is dyed with vegetable dyes, which bleeds when washed. See Broadcloth to sew.

Maline A fine, open net with diamond shape. See Net to sew.

Manufactured fiber Any fiber not provided by nature. Cellulosic fibers: lyocell, rayon, acetate, triacetate. Synthetics: polyester, nylon, acrylic, modacrylic, spandex, anidex, metallic, vinyon.

Marii pleats Very small vertical accordian pleats. See Pleated and Slinky to sew.

Marimekko® Hand-screened print. See Broadcloth to sew.

Marocain A heavy, cross-rib crepe with wavy, thick, twisted ribs. See Shantung to sew.

Marquisette Crisp, lightweight, open-weave fabric, made with a leno weave. See Organza to sew.

Matelassé Blistered or quilted-effect fabric, made on a dobby or jacquard loom with two extra sets of crepe yarns; made in cotton, silk, wool, rayon, acetate, polyester, and blends. See Matelassé to sew.

Matka A loosely woven silk suiting. See Silk Suiting and Loosely Woven Fabric to sew.

Matte jersey Dull tricot knitted with crepe yarns; usually rayon. See Rayon Jersey to sew.

Matte Touch® Polyester fiber. See Rayon Jersey to sew.

Melton A wool coating. See Melton to sew.

Merino Finest, softest wool available; from merino sheep. See Wool – Lightweight to sew.

Mesh Open-work, woven, or fabric. See Net to sew.

Messaline Very lightweight, loosely woven, lustrous, satin-weave silk. See Satin to sew.

Metalastic® Metal-coated elastic yarn. See Spandex and Metallics to sew.

Metallic Any metal, plastic-coated metal, metal-coated fiber, or metal-wrapped core. See Metallic to sew.

Metallic lace Lace featuring metallic yarns. See Metallic and Lace to sew.

Metlon® Non-tarnishing metallic yarn. See Metallic and Lamé to sew.

Micrell® Polyester microdenier yarn. See Microfibers to sew.

Microft® Wind and water resistent polyester microfiber used in activewear. See Microfiber and Water-Repellent Fabric to sew.

Micromattique MX® Polyester microfiber with body and resilience. See Microfibers to sew.

Microsoft® Soft, suede-like nylon microfiber; wind- and water resistant. See Microfiber and Water-Repellent Fabric to sew.

Microsupplex® Nylon microfiber. See Microfiber and Two-way Stretch Fabric to sew.

MicroSuprene® Acrylic microfiber. See Microfiber to sew.

Midwale corduroy Corduroy with 11 to 15 wales per inch. See Corduroy to sew.

Mikado silk A fine silk or silk-blend in a twill or plain weave. See Shantung or Satin to sew.

Milanese knit Fine, lightweight knit which does not run. See Tricot to sew.

Milium® An aluminum finish applied to the back of lining fabrics for additional warmth. See Lining to sew.

Miniwale corduroy Corduroy with more than 21 wales per inch. See Corduroy to sew.

Mirror velvet Fabric with an uncut pile which is pressed flat in different directions; softer and lighter than crushed velvet. See Velvet to sew.

Mitin® Permanent moth-proofing process for wool. See Wool to sew.

Modacrylic Modified acrylic, synthetic fiber. Soft, resilent, quick drying, very flame retardant, and resistant to acids and alkalies. See Faux Fur Fabric to sew.

Modal A high wet modulus rayon fiber. See Rayon to sew.

Mohair (1) Long, lustrous fibers from the Angora goat. (2) Spongy, plain-weave fabric made in a mixture of mohair and wool. See Mohair to sew.

Moiré Rippled, watermark pattern applied to fabrics like silk and acetate by calendering or printing. Usually permanent on acetate; may not be permanent on other fabrics.

Moiré faille Faille with moiré pattern; may be rayon, acetate, or silk. Pattern may not be permanent. See Shantung to sew.

Moiré taffeta Taffeta with moiré pattern. May be rayon, acetate, or silk. Moiré pattern may not be permanent. See Shantung or Taffeta to sew.

Molleton Wool coating fabric. See Melton to sew.

Momie weave Tight, irregular weave producing a rough, pebblelike surface. Same as crepe or granite weave. See Crêpe de Chine and Wool Crepe to sew.

Mommie A measuring unit for silk; 2-8, lightweight; 10-14 medium-weight; more than 14 heavyweight.

Monk's cloth Coarse, basket-weave fabric in cotton or linen; ravels badly. See Loosely Woven Fabric to sew.

Monofilament Single filament of man-made fiber.

Moreen Plain-woven worsted with a moiré finish. See Worsted to sew.

Moss crepe Rayon or polyester crepe with a mosslike surface. See Rayon Crepe to sew.

Motif Pattern or design.

Mountain Cloth Nylon/cotton poplin with a durable water-repellent finish. See Water-Repellent Fabric to sew.

Mousseline or mousseline de soie (Silk muslin) Sheer, lightweight, quality fabric with a soft hand; made in silk, polyester. See Chiffon and Organza to sew.

Moygashel A quality Irish linen. See Linen and Handkerchief Linen to sew.

Muga silk Fine, wild silk from India. See Silk Suiting to sew.

Multifilament Man-made yarn with several filaments twisted together.

Multisheer Nylon fiber. See Nylon to sew.

Muslin Inexpensive, plain-weave cotton or cotton-blends. See Broadcloth to sew.

N

Nacre velvet Iridescent velvet with one color in the background and another color in the pile. See Velvet to sew.

Nainsook Soft, fine, lightweight cotton in a plain weave; slightly coarser than batiste; wears and launders well. See Batiste to sew.

Naked wool Very light, sheer woolen. See Wool – Lightweight to sew.

Nankeen Same as shantung. See Shantung to sew.

Nap (1) Fuzzy fibers on the surface of a fabric, produced by brushing. (2) Pile and hair on fabrics which have a definite "up" and "down." (3) One-way design, with a definite top and bottom, printed on a fabric.

Napped fabric Any fabric which must be cut with the pattern pieces in the same direction, including hair fibers, knits, piles, and printed fabrics with a one-way design.

Natural Luster Nylon fiber. See Nylon to sew.

NatureTex™ Soft, drapeable duck that is water-repellent, durable, and breatheable; made from recycled plastic. See Water-Repellent Fabric to sew.

Naugahyde® Vinyl resin-coated fabric. See Faux Leather to sew.

Needlepunch Method of making fabrics by using needles to punch and entangle a web of fibers.

Net An open-weave, knotted fabric. See Net to sew.

Ninon Sheer, crisp, plain-weave voile in rayon, acetate, nylon, or polyester with a smooth finish. See Organza to sew.

Nomelle An acrylic fiber. See Acrylic to sew.

Non-woven fabric Fabric made from a web of fibers without knitting, weaving, or felting; ex.: Vinyl, felt. See Faux Leather or Felt to sew.

Norae® A water-repellent finish. See Water-Repellent Fabric to sew.

No Shock Nylon fiber. See Nylon to sew.

No-wale corduroy Corduroy without wales. See Corduroy to sew.

Nun's veiling Lightweight sheer, semi-crisp wool; silk and worsted. See Wool – Lightweight to sew.

Nupron® A high-wet-modulus rayon. See Rayon to sew.

Nylon First synthetic fiber. Very strong, supple, lustrous, wrinkle-resistant, easy to wash and dye; resists abrasion, oils, and many chemicals. See Nylon to sew.

Nylon Antron® taffeta Plain-weave fabric made with Antron® nylon; water and wind-repellent, quick drying, and easy-care. See Water-Repellent Fabric to sew.

Nylon oxford Smooth and shiny, it is heavier than nylon ripstop and taffeta. See Water-Repellent Fabric to sew.

Nylon Pack cloth A lightweight, water-repellant fabric with finer yarns in the warp than the filling. See Water Repellant Fabric to sew.

Nylon ripstop Plain weave nylon fabric designed to prevent rips and tears.

Nylon taffeta A tightly woven, smooth, plain-weave fabric. See Water Repellant Fabric to sew.

O

Oilcloth Waterproof fabric treated with linseed oil or varnish. See Faux Leather to sew.

Olefin Synthetic fiber made from polyethylene or polypropylene. See Fleece to sew.

Open-work raschel knits Open knits with little or no stretch. See Raschel Knit to sew.

Organdy Transparent, lightweight, plain-weave cotton fabric with a stiff finish. See Organza to sew.

Organza Sheer, lightweight, plain-weave fabric in silk, rayon, or polyester; not as crisp as cotton organdy. See Organza to sew.

Orlon® An acrylic fiber. See Acrylic to sew.

Osnaberg Coarse cotton cloth. See Denim to sew.

Ottoman Heavy, cross-rib fabric with round, prominent ribs; ribs can be small, medium, or large. See Shantung to sew.

Ottoman cord Cross-rib fabric with ribs in several sizes. See Shantung to sew.

Outing Soft, lightweight, cotton fabric with nap on the face and back; plain or twill weave. Same as outing flannel. See Broadcloth to sew.

Outing Flannel Same as outing. See Broadcloth to sew.

Oxford cloth Soft, basket-weave fabric, usually colored warp and white filling. See Broadcloth to sew.

P

Pailletes Large sequins with a single hole in the center. Usually plastic or metal. See Beaded to sew.

Paisley Printed or woven elaborate scroll design. See Wool – Lightweight to sew.

Palm Beach® Lightweight, summer suiting in cotton and mohair. See Wool – Lightweight to sew.

Panama Lightweight, plain-weave suiting with cotton warp and worsted filling; cool, wrinkle-resistant. See Wool – Lightweight to sew.

Panné satin Tightly woven, rather stiff, medium- to heavy-weight, satin-weave fabric; same as slipper satin. See Satin to sew.

Panné velvet Knit or woven fabric with soft, short, high-luster pile, flattened in one direction; comfortable to wear. See Velvet to sew.

Paper fabric Nonwoven fabric. See Felt to sew.

Paper taffeta Lightweight, very crisp, plain-weave taffeta with fine cross ribs. See Taffeta to sew.

Pa-Qel An acrylic fiber. See Acrylic to sew.

Patent leather Made by applying a solution to leather, which then becomes hard and shiny. See Leather to sew.

Pattern (1) Design or motif which is woven, knitted, or printed on the fabric. (2) Printed paper guide for cutting out a garment.

Patterned velvet Velvet with high-and-low pile; created by crushing the pile after weaving. See Velvet to sew.

Peasant lace Coarse Cluny lace. See Lace to sew.

Peau d'ange (1) Medium to heavy-weight satin-weave fabric with a dull finish; usually silk, heavier than peau de soie. See Satin to sew. (2) A kind of Chantilly lace. See Lace to sew.

Peau de soie Reversible, medium-weight, satin-weave fabric with a dull finish. May be made of silk, polyester, or other man-made fibers. See Satin to sew.

Pebble Grainy, rough-surfaced fabric formed by two different methods: (1) highly twisted yarns that shrink when wet or (2) a special weave. See Rayon Crepe to sew.

Pekin Stripes in the fabric length. Usually equal in width.

Pellon® Trade name for non-woven interfacings. See Interfacing to sew.

Pelt Another term for hide or skin.

Percale Closely woven, plain-weave cotton with smooth finish; wears and launders well. See Broadcloth to sew.

Permanent press cotton Cotton with permanent press finish. See Broadcloth to sew.

Petersham Narrow ribbed belting, similar to grosgrain.

Picks Filling yarns which run crosswise in woven fabrics.

Pigmented taffeta Dull-surfaced taffeta made with delustered yarns, which are called pigmented. See Taffeta to sew.

Pigskin Leather characterizd by a cluster of three marks where the bristles were removed. See Suede to sew.

Pile fabric Knit or woven fabric with cut or uncut loops on one or both sides. See Velvet, Velveteen, Terry Cloth, or Corduroy to sew.

Pile weave Weave utilizing an additional set of warp or filling yarns to create a pile. See Corduroy, Velveteen, Velvet, Terry, or Stretch Knit to sew.

Pillow ticking Tightly woven, down-proof fabric. See Denim to sew.

Pil-Trol™ Low pill acrylic fiber. See Acrylic to sew.

Pima cotton Fine, extra-long-staple cotton grown in America. See Broadcloth to sew.

Pin check Very small, checked pattern; may be woven or printed. See Plaid to sew.

Pin Stripe Fabric with a very small stripe; may be woven or printed. Popular worsted pattern. See Stripe or Worsted to sew.

Pinwale Very small wale or rib; usually found on corduroy or piqué. See Corduroy to sew.

Pinwale corduroy Corduroy with 16 to 21 wales per inch. See Corduroy to sew.

Pinwale piqué Fabric with vertical raised cords or wales of various widths and thickness. See Shantung to sew.

Piqué Light- to heavy-weight cotton with woven, raised design. Usually a lengthwise rib, but it may be another geometric pattern. See Broadcloth to sew.

Plaid Woven or printed pattern of stripes crossing at right angles. See Plaid to sew.

Plain knit Simple, flat-surfaced knit with vertical rows of plain ribs on the face, and horizontal rows of purl wales on the back. Looks like the hand-knit stockinette stitch. See Jersey to sew.

plain knit

Plain weave Simplest, most frequently used weave, in which each filling yarn passes alternately over and under one warp yarn; same as tabby weave; ex.: crepes, shantung, organdy, taffeta, and flannel.

plain weave

Plissé Lightweight fabric printed with caustic soda to create blistered stripes or pattern. See Broadcloth to sew.

Plush Compact, thick warp-pile fabric. See Terry Cloth to sew.

Ply Number of individual threads twisted together to make yarn.

Plyloc Polyester fiber. See Polyester to sew.

Point d'esprit Fabric with dots positioned at regular intervals. Generally net, but can be chiffon. See Net or Chiffon to sew.

Pointelle Single knit fabrics with skipped and/or slipped stitches to create an interesting pattern. See Knit to sew.

Polarfleece® Double-napped knit fabric made by Malden Mills. See Fleece to sew.

Polartec® Insulating fabrics. See Fleece to sew.

Polished cotton Plain-weave cotton with a permanently glazed finish; usually has less sheen than chintz. See Broadcloth to sew.

Polka dots Woven, knit, or printed circular design repeated at regular intervals. Dots range in size from pin dots to very large.

Polo cloth Wool coating. See Melton to sew.

Polyester Synthetic fiber; very strong, resistant to wrinkles, shrinkage, moths, mildew, and abrasion. Pills and attracts lint. See Polyester to sew.

Polynosic rayon A high-wet-modulus rayon; strong when wet or dry; less likely to shrink or stretch when wet. See Rayon to sew.

Polypropylene An olefin fiber. Strong, non-absorbent, but wicks. See Fleece to sew.

Polyurethane Synthetic fiber sometimes laminated to other fabrics. A component of Ultrasuede and Spandex. See Spandex to sew.

Pongee Light to medium-weight, plain-weave fabric with cross ribs and small slubs. Made of wild silk, polyester, or rayon. See Shantung to sew.

Poplin Lightweight, firm cross-rib fabric; ribs are formed by grouping yarns. See Broadcloth or Denim to sew, depending on weight.

Power Net Knit fabric with elastic fiber, superior holding power, good stretch and recovery. See Spandex and Two-way Knit to sew.

Power stretch Fabrics with 30 percent to 50 percent stretch in one or both directions. See Stretch Knit to sew.

Prima A high-wet-modulus rayon. See Rayon to sew.

Progressive shrinkage Shrinkage that continues to occur with repeated washing or cleaning.

Puckered nylon Lightweight fabrics similar to plissé or seersucker. See Nylon to sew.

Purl knit Fabric with horizontal ridges on both sides of the fabric. See Knit to sew.

PVC Polyvinyl chloride; waterproofing agent. Usually plain fabric with PVC applied. See Faux Leather to sew.

Q

Qiana® Nylon fiber; a variety of fabric types. See Microfiber to sew.

Qiviut® or qiviet Underwool from the domesticated musk ox; warm and soft like cashmere. See Hair Fiber to sew.

Quallofil® High loft polyester for insulating.

Quilted fabric Fabric with three layers: face, batting, backing of thin nylon jersey, gauze, or attractive contrast fabric; machine or heat quilted. See Quilted Fabric to sew.

Qwick Liner® Polyester fabric with brushed surface that wicks. See Polyester to sew.

R

Rabbit Popular, inexpensive fur; sheds and is not very durable. See Fur to sew.

Raccoon Long-haired, warm fur used primarily for trims, linings, jackets and coats. See Fur to sew.

Rajah May be silk or synthetic. See Shantung to sew.

Ramie Lustrous, absorbent bast fiber similar to flax, but more brittle; same as China grass. See Linen to sew.

Raschel knit Versatile, warp knit, variety of designs, lace, netting, and open-work. Stretch varies from minimal to maximal. See Raschel Knit to sew.

Ratiné Bulky coating with rough, fuzzy surface. Sometimes called éponge, frisé, or sponge cloth. See Bouclé to sew.

Raw silk (1) Silk fiber before processing. (2) Often used to describe wild silk, a dull silk with a rough texture. See Shantung to sew.

Rayon Manufactured fiber, made from regenerated cellulose, soft, comfortable to wear, weaker when wet. Leaves soft, gray ash when burned. See Rayon to sew.

Re-embroidered chantilly lace Chantilly lace embroidered with cording, ribbons, sequins, and/or beads; frequently incorrectly called Alençon lace. See Lace and Embroidered Fabric to sew.

Re-embroidered lace Any lace embroidered with cording, ribbon, sequins, and/or beads. See Lace and Embroidered Fabric to sew.

Remember An acrylic fiber. See Acrylic to sew.

Rep or Repp Medium- to heavy-weight, cross-rib fabric with prominent round ribs; similar to faille. See Shantung to sew.

Repeat A complete pattern which is repeated at regular intervals on the fabric. May be printed, woven or knit. Size varies from a fraction of an inch to several feet. See Plaid or Stripe to sew.

Revere® Synthetic rubber. See Spandex to sew.

Reverse knit Back side of a plain knit used as the right side.

Reversible fabric .One which can be used with either side as the face; ex.: damask, knit ribbing, antique satin, crepe-backed satin. See Double-Faced Fabric to sew.

Rexe® Spandex elastomeric fiber. See Spandex to sew.

Rib (1) Heavy yarn in the weave; (2) wale on knit fabric.

Ribbing Very elastic reversible fabric with alternating rows of ribs and wales. See Knit to sew.

Ribbon-embroidered lace Lace with narrow ribbon applied to the face in an elaborate pattern. See Lace to sew.

Rib cloth Fabric with rib in either warp or filling; ex.: corduroy, poplin, ottoman, rep, Bedford cord, and grosgrain. See Shantung to sew.

Rib-It® Stretch nylon ribbinng. See Knit to sew.

Rib knit Very elastic reversible fabric with alternating vertical rows of ribs and wales. See Knit to sew.

Rib weave Variation of plain weave with larger

yarns in the warp or filling. See Shantung to sew.

Richelieu Open-work embroidery. See Lace to sew.

Ripple cloth Coarse woolen fabric finished to form ripples. See Woolen to sew.

Ripstop Durable plain-weave fabric designed to prevent rips and tears from spreading. See Water-Repellent Fabric to sew.

Robia A cotton voile fabric. See Batiste to sew.

Roica Spandex fiber. See Spandex to sew.

Romaine Lightweight, plain-weave silk or rayon fabric with a predominance of filling yarns on the fabric face. See China Silk and Crêpe de Chine to sew.

Roman stripe Narrow, vertically striped fabric. May be reversible. See Stripe to sew.

Rubber Fiber made of natural or synthetic rubber; i.e., Lastex, Lactron, Revere, Darleen. See Spandex to sew.

Rustle Crunching noise made by taffeta. Same as scroop.

S

Sailcloth Very strong, firmly woven canvas made of cotton, linen, or nylon. See Denim to sew.

Salisbury English white wool flannel. See Wool Flannel to sew.

Salt and pepper Tweed fabric with black and white yarns. See Woolen to sew.

Sari Rectangular piece of fabric 45" (112 cm) wide and six yards long. See Silk or Batiste to sew.

Sarille Rayon fiber. See Rayon to sew.

Sateen Firmly woven, dull luster, cotton satin with filling, instead of warp, floats. See Satin to sew.

Satin Firmly woven fabric with satin weave. See Satin to sew.

Satin back Reversible fabric with satin-weave back and dull-finished face. See Satin or Double-Faced Fabric to sew.

Satin crepe Soft, lustrous, satin-weave fabric. See Satin to sew.

Satin-faced silk Reversible fabric with very lustrous satin face and dull, cross-rib back. See Satin to sew.

Satin-stripe sheers Sheer fabrics with satin-weave stripes. See Satin to sew.

Satin weave A basic weave with long warp floats to produce smooth, lustrous surface. For making sateen, the filling yarns have long floats. See Satin to sew.

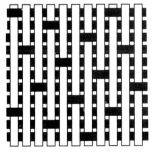

satin weave

Savina® DPR Soft, lustrous, drapeable polyester/nylon blend, usually heavier than two-way stretch knits. Wind- and water-repellent, breatheable. See Water-Repellent Fabric to sew.

Saxony Heavy, fine-quality woolen with a plain weave. See Melton to sew.

Schiffli embroidery Machine-made embroidery which duplicates a wide variety of hand-embroidered stitches. See Embroidered Fabric to sew.

Schiffli lace Delicate transparent net with embroidered design. See Lace to sew.

Scotchgard® Colorless finish used for soil and water repellency.

Scroop Crunching noise made by taffeta. Same as rustle.

Sculptured velvet Patterned velvet with high and low pile; created by crushing the pile after weaving. See Velvet to sew.

Sea Island cotton Lustrous, high-quality cotton. See Broadcloth to sew.

Seam slippage Fabric pulling away at the seams.

Seersucker Durable, firmly woven fabric with permanent puckered stripes or checks alternating with flat ones. See Broadcloth and Stripe to sew.

Selfedge or Self-edge Long, woven edge on each side of the fabric which does not ravel. Same as selvage.

Selvage Preferred term for long, woven edge on each side of the fabric which does not ravel. Same as selfedge or self-edge.

Serge Smooth, durable, twill-weave fabric. Made of wool in worsted, or blends; tailors, drapes well, holds creases, but shines with wear. See Wool Flannel to sew.

Sesua® Spandex/nylon warp knit used for swimwear. See Spandex and Two-way Stretch to sew.

Shadow stripes Subtle stripes created by weaving the stripes with the same-color yarn with a different twist, weave, or with blended yarns slightly lighter or darker. See Stripe to sew.

Shanton Polyester fiber. See Polyester to sew.

Shantung Dull or lustrous. Plain-weave fabric with irregular yarns and slubs in the filling. See Shantung to sew.

Shareen Nylon fiber. See Nylon to sew.

Sharkskin (1) Fine quality worsted in fancy weaves, resembles skin of shark, wears well. See Wool Flannel to sew. (2) Medium- to heavy-weight fabric with a sheen. See Melton to sew.

Shearing (1) Method of removing the wool from the animal. (2) Trimming the fabric pile as needed to the desired height.

Shearling Sheep or goat skin with wool left on; reversible and bulky. Same as sherpa and sheepskin. See Double-Faced Fabric and Leather to sew.

Sheepskin Sheepskin with wool left on; reversible and bulky. Same as shearling and sherpa. See Leather and Suede to sew.

Sheer (1) Lightweight fabric. (2) Transparent fabric. Weaves can be very tight or quite open. See Organza or Chiffon to sew.

Sheer tricot Transparent tricot knit. See Tricot to sew.

Sheeting Very wide, plain-weave fabric in plain colors and prints. See Broadcloth to sew.

Shepherd's check Twill-weave, plaid, black and white fabric with 1/4"-1" (6mm-2.5cm) checks. See Plaid to sew.

Sherpa Sheep or goat skin with wool left on; reversible and bulky. Same as shearling and sheepskin. See Leather to sew.

Shetland wool Originally very soft, expensive woolens made only from yarn pulled from the undercoat of sheep raised on the Shetland Islands, Scotland. Now it includes soft woolens which look as if they were made from Shetland wool. See Woolen to sew.

Shimmereen Nylon fiber. See Nylon to sew.

Shirred fabrics Fabrics with elastic fullness.

Shirting Lightweight, closely woven cottons and cotton-blends used for shirts and blouses; same as top-weight; ex.: oxford cloth, voile, batiste, end and end, handkerchief linen, Pima and Sea Island cottons, silk broadcloth. See Batiste and Broadcloth to sew.

Shot Fabric woven with different colors in warp and filling; changes color when the fabric is moved. Same as iridescent and changeable.

Shot Taffeta Iridescent taffeta. See Taffeta to sew.

Silesia Lightweight, loosely woven cotton twill used for linings and pocket sacks. See Broadcloth to sew.

Silicone finish Finish to repel water while allowing fabric to breathe. See Water-Repellent Fabric to sew.

Silk (1) Protein fiber made by silkworms; only natural filament fiber. (2) Luxury fabric made in a variety of weights, weaves, and qualities. See Silk to sew.

Silk noil Cross-rib silk with bits of cocoon left in the slub. See Broadcloth to sew.

Silk suede A lightweight suede that feels like silk. See Sandwashed Fabric to sew.

Silk twill Soft, twill-weave silk. See Crêpe de Chine to sew.

Silky Touch Polyester fiber. See Polyester to sew.

Single knit Knit with vertical rows of plain ribs on face, and horizontal rows of purl wales on back. Looks like a hand-knit stockinette stitch. Same as plain knit. See Jersey to sew.

Skinner satin Heavy, durable lining satin. See Satin to sew.

Slipper satin Tightly woven, rather stiff, medium- to heavy-weight, satin weave fabric. See Satin to sew.

Slub Small, thick section of yarn which gives the fabric a rough texture. Slubs in silk are natural imperfections, while slubs in man-made fibers are manufactured. Sometimes called nub.

Sofrina® Synthetic leather. See Faux Leather to sew.

Soft Quality of fabric hand.

Softalon® Nylon fiber. See Nylon to sew.

Soft Skin Synthetic leather. See Faux Leather to sew.

So-Lara® An acrylic fiber. See Acrylic to sew.

SolarKnit® Knit, sun protective fabrics. See Denim to sew.

Solarweave® Woven, sun protective fabrics. See Microfiber to sew.

Sorbit® Acrylic fiber that transports moisture; used for activewear. See Acrylic and Two-way Stretch to sew.

Spandaven Spandex yarn.

Spandex Manufactured elastic fiber with good stretch (500%) and recovery. See Spandex to sew.

Sponging Process for shrinking wool fabrics.

Spun rayon Fabrics made from yarns spun from rayon staple or cut rayon waste. See Rayon to sew.

Spun yarn Yarn made from man-made or silk filaments which have been cut into short lengths to imitate natural fibers. See Silk or Silky to sew.

Square cloth Any fabric having the same number of warp and filling yarns per inch.

Square fabric Fabric one yard long and one yard wide.

Square yard Same as square fabric.

Stable knit Knit with little or no stretch; ex.: boiled wool, raschel and double knits. See Boiled Wool, Double Knit, or Raschel Knit to sew.

Stretch fabrics (1) Fabrics woven with stretch fibers in either the warp or filling. (2) Fabrics woven or knit so they will stretch. See Stretch Woven and Stretch Knit to sew.

Stretch fibers Elastic, strongly crimped fiber; ex.: stretch nylon, stretch polyester, rubber, spandex, and anidex. See Spandex to sew.

Stretch nylon Tightly coiled yarn, heat-set into long-lasting springs. See Spandex to sew.

Stretch polyester Tightly coiled yarn, heat-set into long-lasting springs.

Stretch terry Knit with dense pile, loops on face and ribs on back; moderate to good stretch. See Stretch Knit to sew.

Stretch velour Knit with plush pile on face and ribs on back; moderate to good stretch. See Stretch Knit to sew.

Strialine Polyester fiber. See Polyester to sew.

Structural design Design woven, not printed, into a fabric, including plaids, stripes, brocade, tapestry, and jacquard. See Brocade, Matelassé, Shantung, Stripe, and Plaid to sew.

Stunner® Lightweight nylon fabric with cotton feel; used for activewear. See Two-way Stretch to sew.

S-twist Left-hand twist of yarns so they look like the middle of the letter "S."

Suede Leather skin which has been treated to the flesh side is used as the face. See Suede to sew.

Suede cloth (1) Soft, woven fabrics with nap, looks like suede. (2) Nonwoven fabrics with a nap. See Corduroy or Faux Suede to sew.

Suiting Medium- to heavy-weight fabric used for suits. Many weaves, textures, and all fibers and blends; ex.: flannel, tweed, piqué, faille, linen, and worsted. See Linen, Shantung, Silk Suiting, Woolen, or Worsted to sew.

Sunburst pleating Pleating that radiates out from small pleats at top to larger ones at hem. See Pleated Fabric to sew.

Superloft® Stretch fiber. See Spandex to sew.

Superwash® Process to make washable wool which will not shrink. See Woolen to sew.

Supima Trade name of fine, extra-long-staple cotton; grown in U.S. See Broadcloth to sew.

Supplex® Flat (2-Ply) Nylon with a soft, cotton-like hand; water and wind repellent. See Water-Repellent Fabric to sew.

Supplex® (3-Ply) More durable and heavier than 2-ply Supplex. See Water-Repellent Fabric to sew.

Surah Soft, printed, twill-weave fabric, does not wear well. See Crêpe de Chine to sew.

Sweater knits Medium-weight knit with look of hand-knit fabric. See Sweater Knit to sew.

Sweatshirt fabric Medium-weight, knit fabric with smooth face and fleece back. See Sweatshirt Knit to sew.

Swiss batiste High-luster, plain-weave cotton batiste. See Batiste to sew.

Synthetic suede Nonwoven fabric developed to simulate suede; ex: Ultrasuede®, Lamous, Sensuede®, and Facile. See Faux Suede to sew.

T

Tabby Same as plain weave.

Tackle Twill® Densely woven rayon-blend satin; used for rainwear, sportswear. See Satin and Water-Repellent to sew.

Tactel® Texturized nylon with acetate coating and matte finish; wind-, water-repellent, breathes well. See Water-Repellent to sew.

Tactel Micro® Microfiber nylon. See Water-Repellent to sew.

Taffeta Smooth, crisp, plain-weave fabric with very fine ribs; rustles, holds shape when draped, does not wear well. See Taffeta to sew.

Tana lawn Semisoft cotton lawn fabric from Liberty of London. See Batiste to sew.

Tanera® Faux leather. See Faux Leather to sew.

Tape lace Lace made with narrow tape and short bridges to create the design.

Tapestry Decorative fabric with woven design which may be floral or tell a story; stiffer and heavier than brocade. See Brocade to sew.

Tarlatan Open, plain-weave with a crisp finish. See Net to sew.

Tartan Twill-weave, checked designs belonging to individual Scottish clans. See Plaid to sew.

Taslan® Textured nylon with rough texture, matte finish; looks like cotton, made with a stretch fiber. Stronger, quick drying, wind-and water-repellant. See Water-Repellent to sew.

Tattersall check Two-colored overcheck pattern. See Plaid to sew.

T.E.N. Nylon fiber. See Nylon to sew.

Tencel® Lyocell fiber. See Tencel to sew.

Tentering Process for stretching and straightening fabric.

Terry cloth Absorbent, warp-pile fabric with uncut loops on one or both sides. See Terry Cloth to sew.

Terry knit Knit fabric that looks like woven terry; good absorbency, stretch and recovery. See Terry Cloth to sew.

Terylene Polyester fiber similar to Dacron. See Polyester to sew.

Texture Look and feel of fabric—smooth, rough, soft, crisp.

Thai silk Heavyweight, textured silk made in Thailand. See Shantung to sew.

Thermal Honeycomb-weave fabrics which trap the air for added warmth. See Knit to sew.

Thermoplastic Heat-sensitive fibers like synthetics, which can be changed when heat is applied. See Nylon and Polyester to sew.

Thick and thin Fabric with yarns of uneven sizes. See Shantung to sew.

Thinsulate® Polyester/polyolefin microfiber insulation.

Ticking Same as pillow ticking. See Denin to sew.

Tie silk Silk used to make ties. See Silk and Crêpe de Chine to sew.

Tissue Lightweight fabric in any fiber with some body. See Taffeta, Shantung, and Crépe de Chine to sew.

Tissue taffeta Very lightweight, transparent taffeta. See Taffeta to sew.

Toile (1) French word meaning cloth. (2) Sample garment. (3) Printed design.

Toray Japanese polyester microfiber. See Microfiber to sew.

Toraylon Acrylic fiber. See Acrylic to sew.

Tovis Japanese rayon fiber. See Rayon to sew.

Toweling Any fabric used for drying. See Terry Cloth to sew.

Tracing cloth Transparent, nonwoven fabric, printed with a dotted grid.

Traditional fabrics Fabrics which have been manufactured and used with little or no change for many years.

Transparent velvet Lightweight velvet which is translucent when held up to the light, drapes well, tends to crush. See Velvet to sew.

Trevira® Polyester fiber. See Polyester to sew.

Triacetate Modified acetate fiber which is stronger when wet, with greater resistance to heat, shrinkage, wrinkling, and fading. See Acetate to sew.

Triblends Blends of nylon, polyester, and cotton; fast drying, lightweight and durable. See Water-Repellent Fabric to sew.

Tricot Lightweight knit with ribs on face and moderate stretch. See Tricot to sew.

Tricotine Twill-weave worsted; double rib on the face. See Worsted and Wool – Lightweight to sew.

Triple sheer Tightly woven, sheer fabric that gives impression of being opague. See Organza to sew.

Tropical suiting Lightweight, crisp suiting, pleats and creases well, cool to wear. See Wool – Lightweight to sew.

Tubular knits Fabrics knit in a tube on a knitting machine. See Knit to sew.

Tulle Very fine, hexagonal net. See Net to sew.

Turkish toweling Thick, very absorbent terry. See Terry Cloth to sew.

Turtle Fur® Acrylic fleece. See Fleece to sew.

Tussah Cross-rib fabric with irregular filaments from uncultivated silkworms; ex.: wild silk, shantung, or rajah. See Shantung to sew.

Tweed Rough-textured fabric with slubs or knots on surface; usually yarn dyed, with fibers of different colors added before spinning. See Woolen or Silk Suiting to sew.

Twill fabric Fabric with a diagonal weave. See Denim and Worsted to sew.

Twill weave One of the three basic weaves; has a diagonal rib. Can be right- or left-handed.

Twill weave

Twist Term to describe the direction the yarn is rotated as it is manufactured. "S" twist yarns are turned to the left; "Z" twist yarns, to the right.

Two-faced fabric Fabric with two right sides. See Double-Faced Fabric to sew.

Two-way stretch Fabric with stretch in length and width. See Stretch Knit and Stretch Woven to sew.

Type 420 Nylon frequently blended with rayon or cotton to prolong garment's life.

Tyvek® Olefin fabric; used in FedEx bags. See Faux Leather to sew.

U

Ultraglow Polyester fiber. See Polyester to sew.

Ultraleather® Synthetic leather. See Faux Leather to sew.

Ultrasuede® Synthetic suede. See Faux Suede to sew.

Ultra Touch Polyester fiber. See Polyester to sew.

Ultrex® Supplex® nylon coated with urethane film; waterproof, breathable. See Waterproof Fabric to sew.

Ultron Nylon fiber. See Nylon to sew.

Unbalanced stripe Stripe pattern which, when folded in half, is not the same on both sides of the center. Sometimes called uneven stripe. See Stripe to sew.

Unbalanced plaid Plaid pattern which, when folded in half, is different on both sides of center. Same as uneven plaid. See Plaid to sew.

Uncut velvet Velvet fabric with uncut loops; same as terry velvet. See Velvet to sew.

Uniform cloth Serviceable fabric. See Denim to sew.

Upholstery fabrics Heavy fabric with ribbed design; ex: brocade, brocatelle, tapestry. See Shantung or Brocade to sew.

V

Val lace Common name for Valenciennes. See Lace to sew.

Valenciennes Narrow, flat lace with delicate floral design; used for edgings and insertions.

Veiling Net made from silk, rayon, or nylon. See Net to sew.

Velcro® A hook and loop fasteners.

Velour Knit or woven fabric with thick, short, warp pile; less absorbent than terry cloth. See Terry Cloth to sew.

Velvet Luxurious fabric with short pile on a knit or woven background; ranges from lightweight transparent velvet to heavy upholstery. See Velvet to sew.

Velveteen Cut pile on a woven background. See Velveteen to sew.

Velveteen plush Cotton velveteen with longer pile. See Velveteen to sew.

Velvet satin Satin weave silk with cut-velvet design. See Satin and Velvet to sew.

Venetian Satin-weave worsted used for suits and coats. See Worsted to sew.

Venetian lace A kind of guipure lace. See Lace to sew.

Venice or Venise lace Firm, stiff lace, machine-made on a background fabric which is dissolved, leaving only the lace; same as chemical, burn-out, guipure, or Venise. See Lace to sew.

Verel Modacrylic fiber.

Versatech® Densely woven polyester fabric; wind-, water resistant. See Water-Repellent Fabric to sew.

Vicuna Luxurious hair fiber from smallest member of camel family. See Hair Fiber to sew.

Vinal-vinyon Fiber similar to acrylic. Soft, flame-retardant. See Acrylic to sew.

Vincel® A high-wet-modulus (HWM) rayon. See Rayon to sew.

Vinyl (1) Fabric with vinyl base; (2) fabric covered with vinyl-based coating; (3) polyvinyl chloride. See Faux Leather to sew.

Virgin wool Wool made from new fibers; same as 100% wool or all wool. See Wool to sew.

Viscose Describes all rayons made by viscose process in United Kingdom. See Rayon to sew.

Viscose rayon Same as viscose. See Rayon to sew.

Viyella Trade name for soft, twill-weave fabric made of 55 percent lamb's wool and 45 percent cotton. See Wool – Lightweight to sew.

Voile Sheer, semi-crisp, plain-weave fabric. See Batiste to sew.

W

Wadding Lightweight batting made of cotton.

Wadmal Coarse, twill-weave fabric. See Melton and Boiled Wool to sew.

Waffle cloth Cotton or cotton blend that resembles breakfast waffles. See Broadcloth to sew.

Waffle weave Reversible, woven or knit fabric with geometric, raised weave resembling a honeycomb; same as honeycomb. See Broadcloth to sew.

Wale (1) Vertical rows of loops on knit fabrics; (2) pile ribs on corduroy. Corduroy wales vary in size from 5 to 21 per inch.

Warp Set of yarns put onto the loom to run the length of the cloth and parallel to the selvage. Same as ends and woof.

Warp knit Flat, dense fabrics knitted with multiple yarns; less elastic than weft knits; ex.: tricot, milanese, raschel knits. See Tricot and Raschel Knit to sew.

Warp-print taffeta Taffeta with warp yarns printed before weaving. See Taffeta to sew.

Warp stretch Lengthwise stretch in knits. See Two-way Stretch to sew.

Wash and wear Same as durable press and permanent press; blend of natural and synthetic fibers. See Broadcloth to sew.

Waste silk Waste or short filaments spun into thick and thin yarn.

Waterproof Fabric impervious to water; warm and clammy to wear; ex.: plastic, rubber, vinyl, coatings of lacquer, synthetic resin, or rubber. See Waterproof Fabric to sew.

Water-repellent Usually wax or silicone resin; resists water, retards soiling. See Water-Repellent Fabric to sew.

Water-resistant Resists water, retards soiling. See Water-Repellent Fabric to sew.

Weave Method of making fabric by interlacing yarns at right angles. The three primary weaves are plain, twill, and satin.

Weft Crossgrain yarns which interlace with the warp (lengthwise yarns).

Weft knit Fabrics knitted with a single yarn; ex.: jersey, ribbing, interlocks, double knits, sweater and sweatshirt knits. See Jersey, Double Knit, Sweater Knit, and Sweatshirt Knit to sew.

Wet look Shiny fabrics such as vinyl and ciré that look wet. See Faux Leather and Waterproof Fabric to sew.

Whipcord Twill-weave fabric using bulky yarns in the warp to create a sharply defined upright diagonal on the face. See Worsted to sew.

White-on-white White design woven or embroidered on white fabric.

Wick Ability of fabric to transfer moisture away from the body without absorbing it.

Wide wale Corduroy with large wales (5/inch) See Corduroy to sew.

Wigan Interfacing or backing, a plain-weave cotton fabric used in tailoring. See Broadcloth to sew.

Wild silk Rough, uneven textured silk with dull finish from uncultured silkworms. See Silk Suiting and Shantung to sew.

Woof Set of yarns put onto the loom to run the length of the cloth and parallel to the selvage. Same as warp and ends.

Wool Natural fiber from sheep with natural felting ability; comfortable to wear, easy to sew and press. See Wool to sew.

Woolblend mark Fabric composed or more than 60% wool, which has been quality tested. See Wool to sew.

Woolen Fabric made from loosely twisted woolen yarns which have short, fluffy fibers; ex.: tweeds, flannel, fleece. See Woolen, Wool Flannel, and Melton to sew.

Wool Velour Wool fabric with thick, dense pile. See Melton to sew.

Worsted Fabric made from high-twist, worsted yarns which have long, smooth fibers; ex.: gabardine, crepe, serge. See Worsted, Gabardine, and Wool Crepe to sew.

Woven stretch Fabric woven with stretch yarns. See Woven Stretch Fabric to sew.

X

Xena® A high-wet-modulus rayon. See Rayon to sew.

Y

Yarn Continuous thread used to weave or knit fabrics.

Z

Zankara A high tenacity rayon. See Rayon to sew.

Zantrel® A high-wet-modulus rayon. See Rayon to sew.

Zefran Blend of acrylic, nylon, and polyester fibers.

Zeftron Colored nylon fiber. See Nylon to sew.

Zepel Water-repellent finish. See Water-Repellent Fabric to sew.

Zephyr Very lightweight gingham. See Plaid to sew.

Zibeline (1) Heavily napped coating fabric. See Melton to sew. (2) Mikado silk twill. See Shantung or Satin to sew.

Zirpro® Treatment for wool to improve flame-resistance.

Zitkrome An acrylic fiber. See Acrylic to sew.

Z-twist Right-hand twist of yarns so they look like the middle of the letter "Z."

part 4
Appendices

APPENDIX A – SEWING MACHINE NEEDLES

The needles below are listed alphabetically by type. The letter designation for Schmetz needles is in parentheses. I have used the following brands with success: Abca, Groz-Beckert, Lammertz, Organ, Schmetz, Singer, and Sullivans.

Ballpoint (H-SUK)
Sizes: 70/10-100/16
Description: Medium ballpoint (Point spreads yarns to slip between them)
Use: Knits, especially bulky knits, elastics, and spandex

Denim (HJ)
Sizes: 70/10-110/18
Description: Sharp point, stiff shank to resist deflection
Use: Densely woven fabrics, denim, canvas, lace, shantung, embroideries

Embroidery (HE)
Sizes: 75/11;90/14
Description: Very light ballpoint, special scarf, deep groove, large eye
Use: Decorative stitching with metallic and machine embroidery threads; does not shred the thread

Hemstitch needle
Sizes: 100-110
Description: Very wide blade, sharp point
Use: Decorative stitching

Leather (HLL, NTW)
Sizes: 70/10-110/18
Description: Cutting point
Use: Leather, vinyl, heavy non-woven synthetics

Microtex (HM)
Sizes: 60/8-90/14
Description: Very sharp point
Use: Lightweight woven fabrics, chiffon, satin, lace, embroideries, shantung

Quilting (HQ)
Sizes: 75/11-90/14
Description: Slightly tapered sharp point
Use: Multiple layers, bulky seams, densely woven fabrics

Red Band (Singer)
Sizes: 65/9-110/18
Description: Sharp point
Use: Woven fabrics

Self-threading needle (same as calyx-eyed, quick threading, or slotted needle)
Sizes: 80/12-90/14
Description: Slotted eye to make threading easier
Use: General purpose needle

Serger or Overlock needle
Description: Varies with serger brand
Use: General purpose needle for sergers

Sharp or Standard point (HM,HJ)
Sizes: 60/8-90/14
Description: Very sharp point, slender shaft
Use: Woven fabrics, topstitching

Stretch needle (HS)
Sizes: 75/11;90/14
Description: Fine ballpoint with shaved shank and small hump above eye to prevent skipped stitches
Use: Lingerie, difficult-to-stitch fabrics, faux suede, elastic, stretch knits and wovens

Topstitching (N)
Sizes: 80/12-100/16
Description: Sharp point, extra large eye, and deep groove
Use: Topstitching with heavy threads

Twin needle (Universal)
Sizes: 1.6/80; 2.0/80; 2.5/80;4.0/80; 3.0/90; 4.0/90; 4.0/100; 6.0/100; 8.0/100
Description: Two needles on one shank spaced 1.6mm to 6.0mm apart
Use: Decorative stitching, stretch seams and hems

Universal (H)
Sizes: 60/8- 120/19
Description: Slight ballpoint
Use: Most knits and wovens

Yellow Band (Singer)
Sizes: 65/9-100/16
Description: Slight ballpoint, elongated scarf and shaved shaft
Use: General purpose for knits and many wovens

SPECIALTY NEEDLES

Metafil
Sizes: 70/10-90/14
Description: Large eye, square groove to accommodate rayon and metallic threads
Use: Embroidery, topstitching

Metafil Quilting
Sizes: 80/12
Description: Large eye, square groove
Use: Quilting, topstitching

Metafil twin
Sizes: 2.0/80; 3.0/80; 4.0/80
Description: Large eye, square groove
Use: Decorative stitching, topstitching, hems

Spring needle
Sizes: Universal:70/10-90/14; Embroidery: 75/11; 90/14; Quilting:75/11;90/14
Description: Needle set inside spring
Use: Freehand embroidery, monograms, quilting

Triple needle
Sizes: Triple 2.5,triple 3.0
Description: Three needles on one shank
Use: Decorative stitching

Twin Embroidery
Sizes: 2.0/75; 4.0/75
Description: Two embroidery needles on one shank
Use: Topstitch, pin tucks, decorative stitching

Twin Hemstitch
Description: One regular/one hemstitch needle on one shank
Use: Decorative openwork stitch

Twin Stretch
Sizes: 2.5/75; 4.0/75
Description: Two stretch needles on one shank
Use: Seams, hems, and decorative stitching on knits

APPENDIX B – THREAD

These threads are designed for assembling garments. There are also numerous threads for decorative stitching. The trade names will help you identify specific thread types.

All Purpose Threads - Medium-Weight

Cotton
C&C CottonMako-50/*, DMC Machine Embroidery-50/2; Gutermann Natural Cotton 50/3; Madeira Cotona-50; Mettler Silk Finish-50/3, Star Quilting 50/3, YLI Select
Description: Medium-weight, long staple, mercerized cotton thread. Mercerization gives luster and prevents shrinkage, little or no lint; least elastic.
Uses: All purpose sewing, particularly medium weight fabrics; do not use on leather, suede, fur, or waterproof fabrics.

Cotton covered polyester
Dual Duty
Description: Medium-weight. More durable, stronger than cotton; less static, easier to sew than polyester.
Uses: All purpose sewing; do not use on leather, suede, fur, or waterproof fabrics.

Polyester
Drima, Gutermann Sew-All, J.P.Coats Finesse, Metrosene Plus-100/3
Description: Medium-weight long staple polyester; very elastic, strong, durable, resistant to abrasion and chemicals, sensitive to heat, difficult to sew. Puckered seams and skipped stitches often problems.
Uses: All purpose sewing; all fabrics.

Silk
Clover/Tire-50; YLI-50; Gutermann Pure-Silk-A
Description: Soft, strong, long staple silk fiber.
Uses: Seaming, buttonholes, topstitching silks and wools, hand sewing.

Fine, Lightweight Threads

Cotton
Madeira Cotona-80/2; Mettler Fine Embroidery-60/2; YLI Heirloom 70/2, 100/2.
Description: Soft, lightweight thread; drapes well.
Uses: Seaming, buttonholes, topstitching lightweight fabrics; machine embroidery.

Poly/cotton
DMC Quilting-75/2
Description: 75%polyester/25% cotton.
Uses: Sewing lightweight fabrics; hand/machine quilting.

Cotton covered polyester
Extra Fine, Dual Duty
Description: Stronger than all cotton; drapes well.
Uses: Lightweight fabrics, microfibers; may cause seam slippage at stress points on lightweight silks.

Polyester
YLI-60/2; Metrolene--120/2
Description: Very lightweight, but strong; drapes well.
Uses: Sewing lightweight fabrics.

Silk
Very fine--YLI-200, Fine--YLI 100, Fine--Tire--90/2, 100/2
Description: Very lightweight, but strong; drapes well.
Uses: Sewing lightweight silks, may cause seam slippage at stress points on lightweight silks.

Heavy Threads for Seaming Heavy Fabrics (size 40 without glaze)

Heavy cotton
C&C Mako-40, Mettler Machine Quilting-40/3, Signature Cotton 40, Signature Machine Quilting-40/3, YLI Machine Quilting-40/3; YLI Select-40/2.
Description: Heavy, unglazed cotton thread, excellent sewability; least elastic.
Uses: Sewing heavy fabrics, machine quilting, topstitching, machine buttonholes. Do not use on leather, suede, fur, or waterproof fabrics.

Cotton covered polyester
Dual Duty Machine Quilting - 37/2; Signature Cotton Covered Polyester Machine Quilting Thread-40
Description: Provides strength with softness.
Uses: Sewing heavy fabrics, machine quilting, topstitching, machine buttonholes. Do not use on leather, suede, fur, or waterproof fabrics.

Polyester
Isacord-40/3; Mettler Poly Sheen-40/2; YLI
Description: Strong, elastic
Uses: Sewing all heavy fabrics, machine quilting, topstitching, machine buttonholes.

Overlock/Serging Threads

Overlock threads
Core-Lock, Mettler Overlock, Maxi-Lock, YLI Elite
Description: 100% polyester, strong, durable, lintfree, shrink-free.
Uses: Serging most fabrics.

Extra fine overlock threads
Metrolene 120/2; silk (100, 200)
Description: 100% polyester, very lightweight. Seaming, basting, and serging lightweight fabrics and fabrics easily marred by thread imprints.

Textured threads
Metroflock, YLI Woolly-Nylon, Bulky Lock (polyester)
Description: 100% textured nylon or polyester; crimped, stretchy, durable, soft. Stretch thread made of textured nylon or polyester.
Uses: Seaming and serging elastic fabrics, serging lightweight fabrics to avoid pressing imprints.

Topstitching/Machine Embroidery (See Heavy Threads above also.)

Cotton Topstitching/Machine Embroidery
Madeira Cotona-30/2; Mettler Machine Embroidery-30/2; Mettler Cordonnet-30/3,Perfect Quilter-30/3, YLI Colours (30/3)
Description: Mercerized cotton, 30 weight, soft luster.
Uses: Hand/machine embroidery, topstitching.

Polyester
Mettler Cordonnet 30/3, Superior Rainbows-35
Description: Buttonhole twist, topstitching thread.
Uses: Sewing buttons, topstitching, hand buttonholes.

Silk Topstitching

Guterman, Tire

Description: Heavy lustrous, topstitching thread.

Uses: Topstitching, hand buttonholes, gathers, sewing buttons.

Other Specialty Threads

Basting Thread (cotton)

Brooks, YLI

Description: Soft finished cotton thread on cardboard spool; breaks easily; crocks.

Uses: Basting seams, thread marking, tailor's tacks.

Basting (water soluble)

Wash-A-Way, Water soluble thread

Description: Thread which dissolves when steamed or wet.

Uses: Basting.

Bobbin threads

OESD, Gutermann, YLI Polyfil-60/2; YLI Soft Touch cotton-60/2

Description: Lightweight bobbin thread.

Uses: Bobbin thread for machine embroidery; seaming lightweight fabrics; basting.

Fusible threads

Gutermann, Thread Fuse, Stitch 'n Fuse

Description: Thread with adhesive coating that melts when pressed.

Uses: Basting, substitute for narrow strip of fusible web.

Embroidery threads-machine

Rayon, perle cotton, metallic, variegated Marlitt 40, Robison-Anton-40, Sulky-40, Signature-20

Description: Variety of threads with rayon, silk, and/or metallic content.

Uses: Decorative stitching, not suitable for seaming and general sewing.

Embroidery floss- hand

Description: All-cotton, loose twist, soft finish.

Uses: Tailor's tacks, hand basting.

Glacé or glazed threads

Dual Duty Cotton Quilting-35/3; Dual Duty Hand Quilting-29/2; Gutermann Hand Quilting-39/3, Mettler Hand Quilting-40, Signature Hand Quilting; YLI Cotton Quilting 40/3; Dual Duty Hand Quilting

Description: Strong, glazed thread to resist abrasion and prevent knots and tangles. Crisper than unglazed threads; may affect drape when used for seaming.

Uses: Machine gathering, hand/machine quilting, topstitching, very strong seams.

Heavy Duty: Button & Carpet

Dual Duty, Signature

Description: Cotton wrapped polyester; strong, durable glazed thread.

Uses: Sewing buttons, very strong seams.

Heavy Duty: Home Dec/Upholstery

Dual Duty, Gutermann, Signature

Description: Nylon for extra strength, home dec, upholstery.

Uses: Very strong seams.

Lingerie

IBC, YLI

Description: Extra fine nylon thread, some stretch; black and white.

Uses: Stretch seams.

Lingerie & Bobbin Thread

YLI-Sew Bob,

Description: Soft, supple thread; stretches as you stitch, loosening the bobbin tension.

Uses: Twin needle stitching, stretch seams.

Nylon monofilament

Nymo B, Sulky, YLI

Description: Fine single filament of nylon (.004); transparent, very wiry and stiff; ends scratchy.

Uses: Fluted hems, transparent vinyls, "invisibly" stitched hems.

Transparent/Invisible nylon

EZ Stitch-Thru, Gutermann, Invisible Nylon, Signature, Singer, Sulky, Transparent Nylon, Wonder Monofilament, Wonder Thread, Monofil

Description: Clear, lightweight, soft monofilament nylon thread. Appears invisible when used on the right side; smoke, clear.

Uses: Soft rolled hems, joining lace strips, soft seam finishes, serging, setting pockets.

Let the fabric do the talking with this fleece border design. (Photo courtesy of MacPhee Workshop.)

APPENDIX C – NEEDLE / THREAD GUIDE FOR MACHINE STITCHING

Use this handy needle and thread guide when machine stitching different fabrics.

Fabric Type: Featherweight and Very Lightweight Woven Fabrics

Batiste, chiffon, fine lace, marquisette, net, voile, organza, georgette, transparent fabrics, microfibers
Needle Type: Sharp points—microtex (HM), denim (HJ), Red Band. Universal (H)
Needle Sizes: 60/8 to 70/10
Threads: Very fine threads—extra-fine cotton covered polyester, serger thread (60/3, 100/2), silk machine thread, lingerie thread, fine cotton (70/2, 80/2), fine machine embroidery thread (60/2). All purpose threads—mercerized cotton (50/2), polyester 100/2.

Fabric Type: Lightweight Woven Fabrics

Challis, chambray, charmeuse, crepe, dimity, dotted swiss, handkerchief linen, cloque, satin, eyelet, lace, pleated fabrics, taffeta, lightweight silks and polyesters, lightweight wools
Needle Type: Sharp points—microtex (HM), denim (HJ), Red Band. Universal (H)
Needle Sizes: 60/8 to 70/10
Threads: Fine threads—extra-fine cotton covered polyester core, serger thread (100/2), silk machine thread, machine embroidery thread(60/2). All purpose threads—mercerized cotton (50/2 & 50/3), polyester (100/3).

Fabric Type: Lightweight Knits

Double knit, interlocks, jersey, mesh, panné velvet, metallics, rib knits
Needle Type: Universal (H), stretch (HS)
Needle Sizes: 60/8 to 70/10
Threads: Fine threads—extra-fine cotton covered polyester core, serger thread (100/2), silk machine thread, machine embroidery thread(60/2). All purpose threads—mercerized cotton (50/2 & 50/3), polyester (100/3).

Fabric Type: Light- to Medium-Weight Woven Fabrics

Metallics, chambray, gingham, percale, loosely woven fabrics, seersucker, sequinned, elasticized, and embroidered fabrics
Needle Type: Sharp points—microtex (HM), denim (HJ), Red Band, Universal (H)
Needle Sizes: 60/8 to 80/12
Threads: All purpose threads—polyester (100/3), cotton covered polyester, mercerized cotton (50/2, 50/3, 3 cord).

Fabric Type: Light- to Medium-Weight Knits

Rachel, sweater, sweatshirt, two-way stretch knits, power net, velours, fleece
Needle Type: Universal (H), stretch (HS), Yellow Band, ballpoint (H-SUK)
Needle Sizes: 60/8 to 80/12
Threads: All purpose threads—polyester (100/3), cotton covered polyester, mercerized cotton (50/2, 50/3, 3 cord).

Fabric Type: Medium-Weight Woven Fabrics

Broadcloth, brocade, linen, matelassé, piqué, shantung, silk suitings, chintz, faille, ottoman, velveteen tufted fabrics, felt, felted fabric, single/ply reversible fabrics, polyester blends, acrylics, woolens, worsteds, washable wools, fleece, gabardine, outerwear fabrics
Needle Type: Sharp points—microtex (HM), denim (HJ), Red Band Universal (H)
Needle Sizes: 70/10 to 90/14
Threads: All purpose threads—polyester (100/3), cotton covered polyester. For silks, mercerized cotton; for synthetics and outerwear, polyester.

Fabric Type: Medium-to Heavy-Weight Woven Fabrics

Denim, drapery fabrics, guipure lace, twill-weave fabrics, ticking, corduroy, terry, velour, fake fur, double-faced fabrics, quilted fabrics, outerwear
Needle Type: Sharp points—microtex (HM), denim (HJ), quilting (HQ), Red Band , Universal (H)
Needle Sizes: 70/10 to 100/16
Threads: All purpose threads—cotton (50/3), polyester (100/3), cotton covered polyester. Heavy threads—quilting, glacé, jeans, topstitching, machine embroidery (40/3, 40/2).

Fabric Type: Medium- to Heavy-Weight Knits

Fake fur, double knits, fleece
Needle Type: Universal (H), stretch (H), ballpoint (H-SUK), Yellow Band
Needle Sizes: 70/10 to 100/16
Threads: All purpose threads—polyester (100/3), cotton covered polyester. Heavy threads—glacé, quilting, jeans, topstitching, machine embroidery (40/3, 40/2).

Fabric Type: Heavy Woven Fabrics

Canvas, coatings, duck, awning fabrics, waterproof fabrics
Needle Type: Sharp points—jeans (HJ), quilting (HQ), Red Band, Universal (H)
Needle Sizes: 80/12 to 100/16
Threads: All purpose threads—polyester (100/3). Heavy threads—glacé, quilting, jeans, topstitching, machine embroidery (40/3, 40/2).

Fabric Type: Faux Suede

Ultrasuede®, Ultrasuede® Light, Sensuede
Needle Type: Stretch (HS), Universal (H), Yellow Band
Needle Sizes: 65/9 to 90/14
Threads: All purpose threads—polyester (100/3), cotton covered polyester.

Fabric Type: Faux Leather and Vinyl

UltraLeather®, plastics, plastic coatings, vinyl, other synthetic leathers
Needle Type: Sharp points—microtex (HM), jeans (HJ), Red Band, Universal (H)
Needle Sizes: 70/10 to 90/14
Threads: All purpose threads—polyester (100/3), cotton covered polyester. For clear vinyl, transparent, monofilament.

Fabric Type: Leather, Sherpa, Fur

Leathers, sherpa, fur
Needle Type: Leather (NTW,HLL), Sharp points—microtex (HM), jeans (HJ), Red Band
Needle Sizes: 70/10 to 100/16
Threads: All purpose threads—polyester (100/3).

Natural fibers- Vegetable

Fiber: Cotton
Burns: Rapidly, yellow flame; continues burning, afterglow
Odor: Paper
Residue: Brown-tinged end; light-colored, feathery ash

Fiber: Linen, ramie, hemp
Burns: Slower than cotton; continues burning, afterglow
Odor: Rope
Residue: Ash maintains shape of swatch

Natural fibers – Protein

Fiber: Silk
Burns: Slowly, sputters; usually self-extinguishing
Odor: Feathers
Residue: Crushable black bead

Fiber: Wool
Burns: Slowly; self-extinguishing
Odor: Hair
Residue: Lumpy ash; brittle, black bead

Manufactured fibers – Cellulosic

Fiber: Rayon
Burns: Rapidly; leaves creeping ember
Odor: Wood
Residue: Very little; light fluffy ash

Fiber: Lyocell
Burns: Rapidly; afterglow
Odor: Wood
Residue: Very little; light fluffy ash

Fiber: Acetate
Burns: Slowly with melting
Odor: Hot vinegar
Residue: Irregular shape; hard brittle charcoal

Fiber: Triacetate
Burns: Slowly with melting
Odor: Paper
Residue: Irregular shape; hard brittle charcoal

Manufactured fibers- Synthetic

Fiber: Nylon
Burns: Shrinks from flame; melts, fuses; self-extinguishing
Odor: Celery, boiling string beans
Residue: Hard gray round bead

Fiber: Polyester
Burns: Shrinks from flame; melts, fuses; black smoke, self-extinguishing
Odor: Sweet smell
Residue: Hard black or brown round bead

Fiber: Acrylic
Burns: Burns rapidly with melting; hot flame, sputters, smokes; not self-extinguishing
Odor: Hot vinegar
Residue: Hard, crisp, black mass

Fiber: Modacrylic
Burns: Burns slowly with melting; self-extinguishing
Odor: Acrid
Residue: Irregular, hard black bead

Fiber: Olefin
Burns: Shrinks from flame; melts, fuses; black smoke; not self-extinguishing
Odor: Acrid
Residue: Hard tan round bead

Fiber: Spandex
Burns: Burns and melts; not self-extinguishing
Odor: Acrid
Residue: Soft sticky gum

Designed by Pamela Isaacs-Erny, this casual hemp shirt will delight any man. (Photo courtesy of Pamela Isaacs-Erny/Off the Cuff.)

APPENDIX E – STABILIZER CHART

The Stabilizer Chart was developed with embroidery designer, Cheri Collins.

CUT AWAY STABILIZERS

■ Polymesh type
WEIGHTS AVAILABLE: Light, Medium
DESCRIPTION: Very soft and pliable
APPLICATIONS: Very good for knits, lightweight fabrics, and sheers.
COMMENTS: Will not show through to front when trimmed after embroidery. When using two or more layers, place the grains at right angles for more stability.

■ Non-woven Interfacing Type
WEIGHTS AVAILABLE: Light, Medium, Heavy
DESCRIPTION: Soft to the touch and pliable. Provides major stabilization.
APPLICATIONS: Use for knits and/or very dense embroidery designs. Use behind anything that needs extra strength, but make sure the project can take the thicker weight.**
COMMENTS: Be sure to hoop fabric smooth—don't stretch or distort. If using more than one layer, cut away at different distances (like grading a seam allowance), to avoid a ridge on the front of the work.

TEAR AWAY STABILIZERS

■ Light, Medium, Heavy
WEIGHTS AVAILABLE: Non woven material. Usually stiff and paperlike.
APPLICATIONS: Use for most applications, except lacy work where removal is important. Use more than one layer if needed, and tear away one layer at a time to avoid distorting the design.
COMMENTS: Probably most widely used stabilizer. Especially good for woven fabrics where stretch is not a big factor. Very dense designs will perforate the tear away and defeat its purpose. Not recommended for denim.

■ Adhesive Tear Away
WEIGHTS AVAILABLE: One weight
DESCRIPTION: 2 sheets bonded together: one paper, one adhesive. Peels apart like self-adhesive labels.
APPLICATIONS: Use for knits, and materials which should not be hooped. Not recommended for terrycloth, as the loops may pull out when removed.
COMMENTS: Hoop stabilizer, paper side up; score paper and tear away to reveal adhesive. Adhere fabric, embroider and tear away stabilizer.

■ Iron-On Tear Away
WEIGHTS AVAILABLE: One weight
DESCRIPTION: Paper with wax type coating on one side (resembles freezer wrap).
APPLICATIONS: Use primarily for knits. Iron wax coated side to wrong side of project. Hoop together for embroidery. **COMMENTS:** May cause problems with terry cloth loops and sweatshirt fleece when removing.

■ Easy Stitch™
WEIGHTS AVAILABLE: One weight
DESCRIPTION: Looks like perforated plastic type material.
APPLICATIONS: Use like lightweight tear away. Tears away very easily, leaves no whiskers.
COMMENTS: Use caution around the iron. This material WILL melt if heated, and makes a mess on the iron!

WATER SOLUBLE STABILIZERS

■ Gelatin Type
WEIGHTS AVAILABLE: Light, Medium, Heavy
DESCRIPTION: Made from gelatin—looks like cloudy plastic wrap.
APPLICATIONS: Stand-alone laces and any delicate fabrics or designs. Use as topping on napped fabrics to keep stitches from sinking into the nap.
COMMENTS: Can also hoop stabilizer, and use spray adhesive to adhere project when hooping the project is not feasible. Can use several layers fused together for heavier weight.*

■ Non- Woven Interfacing Type
WEIGHTS AVAILABLE: Light
DESCRIPTION: Looks like very lightweight non-woven interfacing.
APPLICATIONS: Use like gelatin type.
COMMENTS: Same as above, except layers are not fused, but simply laid cross grain to each other.

LIQUID STABILIZERS

■ Starch
DESCRIPTION: Open or lacy designs on washable fabrics. Starches well and hoops without other stabilizers for some designs. Brush on, let dry, press and stitch.
APPLICATIONS: For solid/dense designs, starch well, and use lightweight tear away under the hoop.

■ Perfect Sew ™
APPLICATIONS: Use like starch.
COMMENTS: Use like starch.

■ Dissolved Water Solubles
APPLICATIONS: Use like starch.
COMMENTS: Dissolve scraps of water-soluble stabilizer in water to obtain desired consistency. Use like starch.

HEAT SENSITIVE STABILIZERS

■ Fabric Type
DESCRIPTION: Looks like coarse muslin. Is stiff and usually fairly rough to the touch.
APPLICATIONS: Cutwork, some laces.
COMMENTS: Use hot, dry iron, and brush away residue. Use only on fabrics which will withstand the hot iron.

■ Clear & Melt™
DESCRIPTION: Looks like clear plastic wrap—is NOT cloudy in appearance like the water solubles.
APPLICATIONS: Suitable for all fabric types—even nylon. Excellent solution for problem fabrics which cannot be wet.
COMMENTS: Completely disappears with low to moderate heat.

PAPER STABILIZERS

■ Stitch 'n' Ditch™
DESCRIPTION: Looks like the paper on your doctor's examining table. Available in 2 widths: 3" and 8".
APPLICATIONS: Works well for small areas of very light stitching. Also great for long rows of stitch-building if the stitches aren't too dense.
COMMENTS: Tears away easily. Any tiny scraps which remain will disappear with first laundering.

OTHER STABILIZING MATERIALS

These materials were not developed specifically for machine embroidery stabilization.

Test to be sure that the product won't harm your machine or finished product.

▦ Armo-Weft™ Fusible Interfacing
DESCRIPTION: Looks somewhat like coarse cheesecloth.
APPLICATIONS: Works well on sweatshirt fleece and some heavier knits—fuse to wrong side of fabric. Hoop a layer of cut away, and use spray adhesive to adhere fabric for embroidery.
COMMENTS: Launder the garment or fabric before applying the fusible to prevent dimpling and wavy appearance after first washing.

▦ Fusible Tricot Interfacing
DESCRIPTION: Looks like loosely knit tricot—has heat activated adhesive on one side.
APPLICATIONS: Works well on knits. Fuse in place with lengthwise grain at right angles to grain of knit fabric. Can be used to cover back of work—especially nice on baby clothing. Test to ensure the end result will not be too stiff and tricot will not show through to right side of light colored knits.

▦ Adding Machine Tape
DESCRIPTION: Works best for rows of stitch building. Cheap and readily available.
COMMENTS: Use care when removing when stitches are light and airy—they are easily distorted. Lint has been a concern for some, but with frequent cleaning, there should be no problem.

▦ Freezer Paper
APPLICATIONS: Plastic coating on one side can be adhered to fabric with medium heat. Readily available. Can be used to replace iron-on tear away stabilizer in a pinch.
COMMENTS: May dull needles faster. Difficult to remove from open, airy stitching.

▦ Plastic Wrap
APPLICATIONS: Can be used as topping on napped fabrics—especially terry cloth. Even after laundering, it remains in place under the stitching, and prevents the stitches sinking into the nap.
COMMENTS: If design is full of small open areas, it must be picked out. A warm iron may melt it into the nap.

Remember that no advice about stabilizers can be complete. Your situation may be completely different; either the fabric, the application, threads, etc. NOTHING replaces doing a test on scraps of your fabric, or scraps that are as nearly identical to your garment as possible. Obviously, if you can hoop the stabilizer and fabric together, your work surface will be more stable. However, you must also take into consideration the marks left by hooping (these are called hoop burn).

*Fuse layers of gelatin type water soluble with Teflon pressing sheet and warm iron.
**Just because denim is fairly heavy, doesn't mean you don't need a stabilizer—denim is a twill, with a diagonal weave. This can cause a whole new set of problems with stretching and designs off grain.

Designed by Carol Lambeth, this stunning evening gown is fabricated in a soft, supple leather. (Photo courtesy of Carol Lambeth Couture.)

abutt To match edges or folds so they touch.

air-erasable pen Temporary pen.

all-purpose foot Zigzag foot with small indentation on the bottom.

appliqué (1) Design applied to the surface of another fabric; (2) to apply designs to the surface of another fabric.

assemble To sew the garment.

backing Same as underlining.

backstitch Technique for stitching backwards to secure threads at beginning and end of stitching.

band Strip at garment edge to finish or trim the garment.

baste To hold fabric layers together temporarily.

baste fuse Steam press only 3 to 5 seconds; then pat gently to fuse baste it in place.

bias Any cut which is not on the lengthwise or crossgrain. True bias is a line at a 45° angle to the lengthwise grain.

bias binding Binding made of bias fabric, used to finish the edge.

binding A strip of fabric that encases the edge of a piece of fabric.

bound pocket Set-in pocket with two welts. Looks like a large bound buttonhole.

butt Same as abutt.

casing Hem through which elastic or ties are inserted.

chain stitch To stitch from one fabric or garment section to another without cutting threads. Same as continuous stitching.

clapper Wooden tool used in pressing.

clearance above the eye Flattened area above eye of the needle. Same as needle scarf.

clip (1) A small cut made in the seam allowance, used for marking pleats, darts, garment centers, and notches. (2) During construction, clips are used on curves and corners to allow the fabric to lie flat.

coil Narrow, synthetic coil that secures a zipper. Same as zipper teeth.

cording Narrow, corded piping inserted into a seam.

course Horizontal rows on the back of single knit fabrics.

crimping Technique for easing fabric into the seamline. Same as ease-plus, staystitching plus, or crowding.

crock Dye color rubs off.

crooked straight stitch Narrow zigzag (W,.5).

crossgrain The filling threads which run from selvage to selvage; sometimes used to describe the course on knits.

crowding See crimping.

dart Stitched fabric fold, tapering at one or both ends. Used to shape flat fabric to contours of figure.

decenter To change the machine needle position to stitch at the extreme right or left.

demarcation line Ridge or shadow that shows on right side of fabric at the edge of interfacings, fusibles, or linings.

design ease Amount of ease allowed by the pattern designer to make the garment not only loose enough to wear, but fashionable.

directional stitching Same as stitch directionally.

ditch-stitch Technique of stitching inconspicuously from right side in the well of a seam or next to a seamline.

double/lay Two layers of fabric, spread for cutting.

double/ply Seams which have both the seam allowances stitched or finished together.

dropped shoulder Design with shoulder extended over the top of the arm.

duplicate pattern Pattern with pieces for both the right and left sides of the garment so the design can be cut in a single layer.

ease (1) The minimum ease in garment design that allows for movement. (2) The small amount of fullness on a longer section of fabric that is sewn to a shorter section.

ease basting A temporary stitch used to ease excess fullness into a seamline. Using a regular stitch length, loose upper tension, and a heavier thread on the bottom, stitch—right-side up—just inside the seamline and again midway between the raw edge and seamline. Pull both bobbin threads together to prevent breaking.

ease-plus Same as crimping.

edgestitch Topstitching ⅟₁₆" from the edge or seamline.

embroidery foot Sewing machine foot with a wide slot or V on the bottom, which allows the foot to move freely over satin stitching.

enclosed seam Seam enclosed between two layers of fabric, i.e. seams at garment edges.

even-feed foot Machine foot which feeds top layer of fabric at the same rate as the bottom. Same as walking foot.

extended facing Facing cut in one piece with garment section. To make an extended facing pattern, pin the facing pattern to the garment pattern, matching the stitching lines.

eyelet (1) Small round opening in fabric; (2) small metal ring.

face (1) Right side of the fabric; (2) to finish garment edge with a facing.

faced facing Same as interfaced facing.

facing Piece of self-fabric, lining or contrast fabric applied to finish the edge. Generally, it folds to the underside; but it can fold to the right side.

fadeaway pen Temporary marking pen which usually disappears within 48 hours. Same as air-erasable or 48-hour pen.

fashion fabric Face or outer fabric used for a garment. Same as garment or shell fabric.

fasteners Devices used at garment openings to close the garment.

feed dogs Pointed metal or rubber bars located under the presser foot on the sewing machine that move the fabric backward or forward.

fell To finish with a fell stitch.

filling Threads that run back and forth between the selvages. Same as weft.

findings Linings, underlinings, interfacings, zippers, buttons, thread, snaps, toggles, grommets, eyelets, etc. Same as haberdashery.

finish (1) Any method for neatening the edges of seams, hems, and facings; (2) to apply the appropriate finish to raw edges; (3) to complete the work.

flagging The clinging of the fabric to the needle as the needle moves up and down.

flat finish Finishes, i.e. overcast, zigzag multi-stitch zigzag, serged, raw edge, and seam tape, for seams and hems.

flat lining A method of underlining.

flounce Circular-shaped ruffle.

fly placket Placket which conceals the fasteners—zipper, hooks and eyes, or buttons and buttonholes.

fray retardant Lacquer-like liquid which retards fraying; discolors some fabrics. Same as seam sealant.

fuse To melt with heat.

fusible web A weblike material which melts when heat and moisture are applied, i.e., Stitch Witchery® and Wonder Under®.

garment fabric Same as fashion fabric.

garment shell Outermost layers of the main garment sections, excluding hems and facings.

gather To pull excess fullness into a seamline.

gathering rows Stitched lines used for gathering. Using a regular stitch length, a loose top thread and a heavier thread on the bobbin, stitch—right-side up—just inside the seamline; stitch again midway between the raw edge and seamline. Pull both bobbin threads up together to prevent breaking.

gauge stitch A line of machine stitching to help you gauge a distance accurately.

glover's needle Needle with a wedge point used for sewing leather and fur.

gore Garment section; usually larger at the bottom than the top.

gorge line Diagonal seamline which joins the collar and lapel.

grading Reducing bulk of enclosed seams by trimming the individual seam allowances different widths, clipping inward curves and corners, notching convex curves, and trimming away excess fabric at outward corners.

grainline Generally refers to the lengthwise grain.

grommets Large metal eyelets.

groove of the seam Well of the seam.

hem allowance Width of fabric between hemline and cutting line.

hemline The lower edge of the garment.

hera A wooden or molded plastic tool used for marking fabric.

inside Part of garment toward the body.

interfaced facing Interfacing applied to the facing; frequently seamed, right sides together, at the unnotched edge. Same as a faced facing.

interfacing Fabric placed between the garment and facing to add body, strength, or shape.

interlining Fabric layer applied to the wrong side of the garment or lining for warmth.

jeans foot Wide straight stitch foot which holds fabric firmly.

join (1) To stitch together; (2) a seamline.

key A guideline on two sections to facilitate matching them during the garment's construction.

knock-off Adaptation of a more expensive garment.

lapel Turned-back facing at garment edge between the first button and neckline.

lay Layer of fabric for layout.

layout The placement of pattern pieces on the fabric for cutting.

lengthwise grain The warp threads which run parallel to the selvage. Same as straight grain.

lining Fabric used on the inside of the garment to conceal the construction. Usually lightweight, a lining enhances the appearance, improves comfort and shape retention, and extends the life of the garment.

loft Batting or fabric thickness.

miter (1) To join two edges at an angle, frequently a 45° angle; (2) A diagonal seam at a corner.

mm Millimeters

mounting Same as underlining.

needle lubricant Silicone-like liquid which eliminates skipped stitches on fabrics, as well as eliminating sticking on leathers and vinyl. Sewers' Aid, Needle Glide, and Needle-Lube are popular brand names.

nonwoven fabric Fabric which is neither woven nor knit.

notches Matchpoints on cutting lines of paper pattern.

notions Sewing supplies and equipment needed to complete the garment.

off grain Seam or edge that is not on lengthwise grain.

on grain (1) On fabric, filling yarns perpendicular to warp. (2) On garment section, lengthwise grain parallel to marked grainline on pattern piece.

open lay Same as single, on grain lay.

outside (1) Right side of fabric; (2) part of garment seen when the garment is worn.

overcast or overedge foot Special machine foot which holds the fabric flat during zigzagging.

parallel Two lines evenly spaced.

pattern cloth Nonwoven fabric, plain or grid, used to make patterns.

pattern repeat The vertical distance required for one complete design on the fabric pattern.

perpendicular Two lines meeting at a right or 90° angle.

pick-up line Foldline at center of a dart or tuck.

piecing Joining two pieces together to make one piece wider or longer.

piping Decorative strip sewn into a seamline.

pivot To turn the fabric with machine needle inserted into it.

placket Any finished opening in a garment.

pocket sacks Portion of set-in pockets on the inside of the garment. Same as pocket bags.

ply Number of fabric layers or thread strands.

preshrink To treat fabric before cutting by laundering, steam pressing, or dry-cleaning to prevent shrinking later.

quarter To divide and mark seamline into quarters.

ravel Tendency of fabric to fray at cut edges. Same as unravel.

raw edge Unfinished or cut edges of garment.

reinforce To strengthen a section with short machine stitches, fabric scrap or tape.

release sheet A Teflon-like film which allows you to bond fusible web to a single layer of fabric.

rip To remove unwanted stitches. Using a small seam ripper, clip the needle thread every fifth stitch, then pull the bobbin thread out.

roller foot Special machine foot which grips top fabric and reduces underlayer creep.

rotary cutter and mat A cutting tool with a round cutting blade, to be used with a mat.

ruffle Decorative fabric band, gathered or pleated at one edge or in the center before sewn to the garment.

RTW Ready-to-wear.

sandwich stitch To stitch with seam sandwiched between two layers of stabilizer.

satin stitch Zigzag stitch of any width with a very short length (L,.5 or less).

seam allowance Width of fabric between stitching and cutting line.

seamline Stitching line.

secure To fasten threads permanently.

see-through ruler Plastic ruler with ⅛" grid, manufactured by C-Thru Ruler Co.

self-fabric Same as the fashion fabric.

selvage Finished edges on each side of a woven fabric; runs parallel to the lengthwise grain.

shim Leveling device to use when stitching layers of uneven thickness.

shrink To make smaller.

single/lay Single layer of fabric spread for cutting.

sleeve heads Narrow strips placed at the top of the sleeve cap to support the cap and make a smooth line.

spi Stitches per inch.

spottack Knot made by machine at the end of the stitching line by setting stitch length on 0 or by lowering the feed dogs.

stabilized seam Seam stabilized with lightweight selvage, seam tape, or elastic. Same as taped seams (see seams).

stabilizer Tissue paper, nonwoven materials, burn-away, or water-soluble materials which reduce stitching problems. See Appendix E.

stay Strip of lightweight selvage, seam tape, twill tape, tricot bias, bias tape, or elastic to prevent stretching.

staystitch To straight stitch through a single layer of fabric just inside the seamline.

steamer Pressing device with a plastic soleplate which only steams, such as a Steamstress.

stitch directionally Stitch with the grain; generally, stitching from wide to narrow.

stitching line Seamline.

stitch-in-the-ditch Same as ditch-stitch.

straight grain Same as lengthwise grain.

straight-stitch foot Foot used for straight stitching with a narrow space between the toes.

strike through Fusible seeps through to right side of fabric.

swatch Small fabric piece.

202 Temporary spray adhesive for patterns.

tack Stitches to hold fabric layers permanently or temporarily.

teeth Metal or nylon parts that hold the zipper together.

temporary marking pens Water-soluble and fadeaway pens designed to mark fabrics temporarily.

tension The amount of pressure on the needle and bobbin threads. Stitching tension is balanced when the threads lock at the center of the fabric layers.

test To try on fabric scraps.

thread trace Hand basting used to mark stitching lines, detail locations lines, grainlines, and garment centers on both the right and wrong sides of the fabric.

tissue-stitch To stitch with tissue or stabilizer between the fabric and feed dogs.

topstitch To stitch on right side of garment.

top weight Lighter weight fabrics suitable for blouses and dresses.

trim To cut away excess fabric.

turn of the cloth Amount of fabric which is "lost" because of the fabric thickness when a edge is folded or turned right-side out.

true bias A line at a 45° angle to the lengthwise grain.

underlap Part of garment which extends under another part.

underlining Fabric layer applied to the wrong side of the fashion fabric before the seams are sewn. Same as backing or mounting.

understitch Technique of stitching, by hand or machine, through the facing and seam allowances.

(W,2-L,2) Stitch width and stitch length in millimeters.

wales The lengthwise ribs on knits or corduroy.

walking foot Same as even-feed foot.

warp Threads parallel to the selvage.

water-soluble pen Temporary marking pen.

well of the seam The seamline on the right side of the fabric.

welt Visible part of a bound buttonhole, bound pocket, or welt pocket.

welt pocket Set-in pocket with band(s) on the outside of the pocket.

APPENDIX G – INTERFACING CHECKLIST

There are dozens of interfacings; this INTERFACING CHECKLIST includes those which are readily available at local fabric stores and mail-order sources. Each is listed by name, followed by the name of manufacturer or distributer.

FUSIBLE INTERFACINGS

Featherweight Fusible Interfacings/ Underlinings

Woven Fusibles

■ **Sheer Magic (HTC-2500)**
COLORS: Sand, mocha, dark, nude
NOTES: Very sheer, flexible support; 30", 100% poly; wash or dry-clean.

■ **Dream Weave Microfiber (Fabric Collections)**
COLORS: White
NOTES: Very sheer; 60", 100% poly; wash or dry-clean.

■ **Bi-Stretch Lite (Pellon-865F)**
COLORS: White
NOTES: Moderate two-way stretch, 22", 100%poly; machine wash/dry delicate or dry-clean.

Warp Insertion Fusibles

■ **So Sheer (HTC-1350,1355)**
COLORS: White, black, ivory
NOTES: Soft, crosswise stretch; 24" and 48", 100% poly; machine wash/dry.

■ **Nancy's Underlining (Fashion Sewing Group)**
COLORS: White, black
NOTES: Very sheer, 60", 100% poly; machine wash or dry-clean.

Tricot Knit Fusibles

■ **Fusi-Knit (HTC-1300, 1310)**
COLORS: White, black, ivory
NOTES: Soft, crosswise stretch; 20" & 60"; 100% nylon tricot, machine wash/dry, dry-clean.

Very Lightweight Fusible Interfacings/Underlinings

Woven Fusibles

■ **Touch o' Gold (HTC-1800)**
COLORS: White, black, ivory
NOTES: Low-temp, soft, lightweight; 36", 100% rayon, machine wash or dry-clean.

■ **Iron-on Cotton (Fabric Collections)**
COLORS: White, black
NOTES: Soft, 100% cotton; machine wash or dry-clean.

■ **Silk-weight interfacing (Prof. Sewing Supplies)**
COLORS: White, black, cream, beige
NOTES: Soft, 100% cotton or 100% poly; machine wash or dry-clean.

■ **Sewers Dream (Fabric Collections)**
COLORS: White
NOTES: Very sheer, give in width; 100% poly, 60"; machine wash or dry-clean.

Knit Fusibles

■ **Deep flesh (Fabric Collections)**
COLORS: Dark, nude
NOTES: Very sheer, 64", 100% poly.; wash or dry-clean.

■ **Sof-Knit (HTC-1725)**
COLORS: White, black
NOTES: Soft, "all bias" stretch, flexible support, 30"; 100% nylon; machine wash or dry-clean.

■ **Stylemaker Easy Knit (Fabric Collections)**
COLORS: Black
NOTES: Soft, "all bias" stretch, flexible support, 60"; 100% poly; machine wash or dry-clean.

■ **Fusible Tricot (Richard Brooks)**
COLORS: White, black, ivory
NOTES: Flexible, crosswise give; 60", 100% polyester; machine wash or dry-clean.

Weft Insertion Fusibles

■ **Feather Weft (HTC-7600)**
COLORS: White, black
NOTES: Light, flexible support; 29"; 100% poly; wash or dry-clean.

■ **Whisper Weft (HTC-88022, 88025)**
COLORS: White, black
NOTES: Soft tailoring, 24", 60% poly/40%rayon; machine wash/dry low or dry-clean.

■ **Perfect Fuse Sheer (Palmer/Pletsch)**
COLORS: White, black
NOTES: Crisp; 60", 100% polyester; wash or dry-clean.

■ **Stylemaker 601 (Fabric Collections)**
COLORS: White, black
NOTES: Soft, similar to Whisper Weft; 64" 62%/39%poly; dry-clean

Nonwoven Fusibles

■ **Designer's Sheer (Pellon-840F)**
COLORS: White, black
NOTES: Soft, gentle support; 22", 70%nylon/ 30%poly; machine wash/dry delicate or dry-clean.

■ **Designer's Lite (Pellon-845F)**
COLORS: White, black
NOTES: Shape, body without weight or stiffness; 22",70%nylon/ 30%poly; machine wash/dry delicate or dry-clean.

■ **Sew-Shape Featherweight (Sawyer Brook-IN/1200)**
COLORS: White
NOTES: 24", 100% polyester; machine wash or dry-clean.

Jiffy Flex
Super Lightweight (Staple-115)
COLORS: White
NOTES: Soft; crosswise stretch/bias give; 100% poly; machine wash.

Sheer D'Light Featherweight (HTC-2101)
COLORS: White, charcoal
NOTES: Soft, gentle support; 24", 100% poly; machine wash/dry.

Lightweight Fusible Interfacings/Underlinings

Woven Fusibles

Shape-Flex (Pellon-SF101)
COLORS: White, black
NOTES: Stable; crisp; 19", 100% cotton; machine wash/dry.

Woven Fusible (Staple-102,103, 122,123)
COLORS: White, black
NOTES: Lightweight

Knit Tricot Fusibles

Stacy Easy Knit (Pellon-EK130)
COLORS: White, black
NOTES: Medium crisp, crosswise stretch; 19", 100% nylon tricot; machine wash/dry or dry-clean.

French Fuse (Staple-188, 288)
COLORS: White, black, beige
NOTES: Medium crisp, crosswise stretch; 100% nylon tricot, 60"; machine wash/dry, dry-clean.

Poly Light (Staple)
COLORS: White, black, beige
NOTES: Crosswise stretch; 100% polyester; machine wash/dry or dry-clean.

Weft Insertion Fusibles

Perfect Fuse Light (Palmer/Pletsch)
COLORS: White, black
NOTES: Crisp; 60", 100% polyester; wash or dry-clean.

Stylemaker 602 (Fabric Collections)
COLORS: Ivory, charcoal
NOTES: Soft hand; 50", 78% viscose/22%poly. Wash or dry-clean.

Tailor's Weft (Fashion Sewing Group)
COLORS: White, black, grey
NOTES: Medium soft, stable; 48", 60%poly/40%rayon; machine wash or dry-clean.

Ultra Weft (Pellon-860F)
COLORS: Natural, black
NOTES: Soft tailoring, drape; 22", 85%nylon/ 15%poly; dry-clean only.

Nonwoven Fusibles

Pellon 906F (Pellon)
COLORS: White
NOTES: Soft; crosswise stretch; 22", 100% poly; machine wash/dry or dry-clean.

Pellon Fusible #911FF (Pellon)
COLORS: White, grey
NOTES: Medium soft, all-bias; 22", 80%nylon/20%poly; machine wash/dry or dry-clean.

Pellon Sof-Shape #880F (Pellon)
COLORS: White
NOTES: Soft, changes hand little, all-bias; 80% poly/20%nylon;machine wash/dry low or dry-clean.

Shaping Aid Featherweight Bias (Staple-207)
COLORS: White
NOTES: Soft; crosswise stretch;100% poly; machine wash.

Fusi-Form Lightweight (HTC-1140)
COLORS: White, charcoal
NOTES: Crosswise give; 24", 90% poly/ 10% rayon;machine wash/dry.

Sheer D'Light Lightweight (HTC-2102)
COLORS: White, charcoal
NOTES: Soft hand, supple shaping; 24", 100% poly; machine wash/dry.

Tailor's Elite (Pellon-855F)
COLORS: White, black
NOTES: Lengthwise control, crosswise elasticity; 22", 90%poly/10%nylon; Machine wash/Dry Delicate or dry-clean.

Jiffy Flex Lightweight (Staple-104,105)
COLORS: White, charcoal
NOTES: Soft; crosswise/bias stretch; 80% polyester/20% nylon; machine wash

Poly-O (Staple-120)
COLORS: White,charcoal, beige
NOTES: Soft; crosswise/bias stretch; 100% polyester; machine wash.

Pellon Fusible #906F (Pellon)
COLORS: White
NOTES: Soft; crosswise give; 100% poly; machine wash.

Medium-Weight Fusible Interfacings

Woven Fusibles

Form-Flex All Purpose (HTC-1010,1011)
COLORS: White, black
NOTES: Firm; durable press; 100% cotton; machine wash.

Japanese Womans (Fabric Collections)
COLORS: Light grey
NOTES: Soft, similar to fusible Hymo; 36", dry-clean.

Flex Weave (HTC-7800)
COLORS: White, charcoal
NOTES: Crosswise give; 29", 34%poly/ 33%modal/33%cotton; dry-clean.

Satin Weave (HTC-7700)
COLORS: White, charcoal
NOTES: Soft tailoring, 29", 78% Viscose/22%poly; dry-clean.

Weft Insertion Fusibles

■ Textured Weft (HTC-7900)
COLORS: White, charcoal
NOTES: Adds loft; 29", 100% poly; machine wash/dry or dry-clean.

■ Perfect Fuse Medium (Palmer/Pletsch)
COLORS: White, black
NOTES: Crisp; 60", 100% polyester; wash or dry-clean.

■ Suit Maker 660 (Fabric Collections)
COLORS: Ivory, charcoal
NOTES: Soft hand, slight crosswise stretch, similar to Satin Weave, 60", 66%poly/34% viscose; dry-clean.

■ Superior Soft Superior (Fabric Collections)
COLORS: White, charcoal
NOTES: Adds body, 60", dry-clean.

Nonwoven Fusibles

■ Shirt Shaper (HTC-1600)
COLORS: White
NOTES: Crisp, collars, cuffs, details; 22", 75% rayon/25% poly; machine wash.

■ Fusi-Form Suitweight (HTC-1160)
COLORS: White, charcoal
NOTES: Firm; crosswise give; durable press; 70% poly/30% rayon; machine wash/dry.

■ Sheer D'Light Medium-wt. (HTC-2103)
COLORS: White
NOTES: Soft hand, firm support; 24", 100% poly; machine wash/dry.

■ Tailor's Touch (Pellon-850F)
COLORS: White
NOTES: Shape, firm support; 22", 90%nylon/10%poly; machine wash/dry delicate or dry-clean.

■ Fusible Shirt Maker (Staple-610)
COLORS: White
NOTES: Crisp; detail areas; 100% polyester; machine wash

■ ShirTailor #950F (Pellon)
COLORS: White
NOTES: Crisp, stable; collars, cuffs; durable press; 100% poly; machine wash/dry.

<u>**Medium-Weight and Suiting Fusible Interfacings**</u>

Weft Insertion Fusibles

■ Armo® Weft (HTC-88001,
88002,88003,89001,89002,89003)
COLORS: White, black, grey
NOTES: Soft tailoring, 24" & 48", 60% poly/40%rayon; machine wash/dry low or dry-clean.

■ Suit Maker (Staple 108)
COLORS: Natural, charcoal
NOTES: Soft, stable; 24", 85%rayon/15%poly; machine wash or dry-clean

■ Perfect Fuse Tailor (Palmer/Pletsch)
COLORS: White, black
NOTES: Crisp; 60", 100% polyester; wash or dry-clean.

Nonwoven Fusibles

■ Pellon Fusible #931TD (Pellon)
COLORS: White
NOTES: Medium crisp, crosswise stretch; 50% poly/50% nylon; machine wash.

■ Pel-Aire (Pellon-881F)
COLORS: Natural, oxford, grey
NOTES: Crosswise stretch; tailoring, 22", 85%poly/15%nylon; machine wash or dry-clean.

■ Jiffy Flex Suit-weight (Staple-106,107)
COLORS: White, charcoal
NOTES: Medium crisp; tailoring; 50% polyester/50% nylon; machine wash or dry-clean.

■ Pellon Fusible #931TD (Pellon)
COLORS: White
NOTES: Medium crisp, crosswise stretch; 50% poly/50% nylon; machine wash.

Hair Canvas Fusibles

■ Fusible Acro (HTC-87002)
COLORS: Natural
NOTES: Crisp; 23", 54%poly/ 27%hair/12%cotton/7% wool; machine wash/dry.

SEW-IN INTERFACINGS

<u>**Feather-Weight Sew-In Interfacings/Underlinings**</u>

Woven Sew-Ins

■ Silk chiffon, Georgette, Crépe de chine
COLORS: Many
NOTES: Soft; use for same or similar fabrics; dry-clean.

■ Silk organza, Marquisette, Tulle
COLORS: Many
NOTES: Crisp; care depends on fabric, generally dry-clean.

■ Two-way stretch, Illusion (Fabric Collections)
COLORS: White, beige, flesh
NOTES: Soft; stretches in length and width. 60", 100% poly.; Wash or dry-clean.

<u>**Very Lightweight Sew-In Interfacing/Underlining**</u>

Woven Sew-Ins

■ Swiss Batiste, Sheath lining, Self-fabric, Voile
COLORS: Many
NOTES: Use in same fabric and sheers; various weights; 100% cotton or poly/cotton blend; wash/dry.

■ China silk
COLORS: Many, flesh
NOTES: Crisp; care depends on fabric, generally dry-clean.

■ Crépe de chine
COLORS: Many, flesh
NOTES: Soft, varies in weight; use in same fabric; generally dry-clean.

Handkerchief linen
COLORS: Many, flesh
NOTES: Crisp; washable, not durable press.

Nylon ninon
COLORS: Many, flesh
NOTES: Very crisp; machine wash/ dry.

Organdy
COLORS: Many, flesh
NOTES: Crisp; heavier than organza; 100% cotton or polyester/cotton blend; may not be durable press; washable

Polyester chiffon
COLORS: Many, flesh
NOTES: Crisper than silk chiffon, softer than silk organza; machine wash and dry.

Polyester organdy
COLORS: Many, flesh
NOTES: Varies in crispness; 100% polyester; machine wash and dry.

Miracle Cloth 2 (Greenberg & Hammer)
COLORS: White, black
NOTES: Stiff; 56" wide 100% nylon; machine wash.

Very Lightweight Sew-In Interfacings

Knit Sew-Ins

Sewin' Sheer (HTC-1360)
COLORS: White, black, cream
NOTES: Soft, stabilized tricot; does not ravel; 25", 100% nylon; machine wash/dry.

Net
COLORS: Many
NOTES: Varies from medium to very crisp; crosswise stretch; care depends on fiber.

Shaping Aid Featherweight Bias (Staple-207)
COLORS: White
NOTES: Soft; crosswise/bias stretch 100% poly; machine wash.

Souffle (Greenberg & Hammer)
COLORS: Nude, dark nude
NOTES: Soft, power net; crosswise stretch; 54", 100% nylon; machine wash.

Lightweight Sew-In Interfacings

Woven Sew-Ins

Batiste
COLORS: Many
NOTES: Soft; 45", 100% cotton or cotton/poly blend; machine wash/dry or dry-clean.

Percoline (Greenberg & Hammer)
COLORS: White, black
NOTES: Soft; 45"; 100% cotton; machine wash.

Armo Press Soft (HTC-84001, 84002, 84005)
COLORS: White, black
NOTES: Soft, durable press; 22", 45"; 50% poly/50% cotton; machine wash/dry.

Nonwoven Sew-Ins

Intra-face Lightweight (HTC-6000)
COLORS: White, black
NOTES: Firm, stable; 75% rayon/25% poly; machine wash;dry

Sheer D'Light Lightweight (HTC-2102)
COLORS: White, charcoal
NOTES: Soft; crosswise give; 100% poly; machine wash/dry.

Pellon Sew-In #905 (Pellon)
COLORS: White
NOTES: Soft; crosswise stretch; 22", 100% poly; machine wash/dry or dry-clean.

Pellon Sew-In #910 (Pellon)
COLORS: White
NOTES: Soft; all-bias; 100% poly; machine wash/dry or dry-clean.

Shaping Aid Lightweight Bias (Staple-208)
COLORS: White, charcoal
NOTES: Soft; crosswise/bias stretch; 22", 100% poly; machine wash.

Stretch & Bounce (Staple-210, 211)
COLORS: White, charcoal
NOTES: Crisp; crosswise/bias stretch; 50%poly/50% rayon; machine wash.

Shirt Maker Lightweight (Staple-600)
COLORS: White
NOTES: Crisp, stable; for details; 22", 100% poly; machine wash.

A favorite for all ages, a little spandex adds comfort to any fabric. (Photo courtesy of KWIK-SEW®.)

Medium-Weight Sew-In Interfacings

Woven Sew-Ins

■ Muslin, Broadcloth
COLORS: Natural
NOTES: Medium crisp; 100% cotton or cotton/poly blend; machine wash/dry.

■ Linen
COLORS: Many colors
NOTES: Crisp, 100% linen; dry-clean.

■ Armo Press Firm (HTC-84003, 84004)
COLORS: White, black
NOTES: Crisp, durable press; 22", 45", 50% poly/50% cotton; machine wash/dry.

■ Form Flex Woven (HTC-1060)
COLORS: White
NOTES: Crisp;100% cotton; machine wash.

■ Siri (Greenberg & Hammer)
COLORS: White, black
NOTES: Crisp; 44" wide; 50% poly/50% rayon; wash or dry-clean.

■ Wigan (Greenberg & Hammer)
COLORS: White, black, grey
NOTES: Soft, details; 100% cotton; machine wash or dry-clean.

■ Formite (Greenberg & Hammer)
COLORS: White
NOTES: Crisp; 45" wide; 100% cotton; machine wash or dry-clean.

■ Woven Durable Press (Staple-310,311)
COLORS: White, black
NOTES: Crisp; crease resistant; 45", 50%poly/50%rayon; machine wash.

■ 50/50 Durable Press (Staple-320,321)
COLORS: White, black
NOTES: Crisp; crease resistant; 22", 50%poly/50%rayon; machine wash.

Nonwoven Sew-Ins

■ Intra-Face Medium weight (HTC-6020)
COLORS: White
NOTES: Firm; crosswise give; 22",75% rayon/25%poly; machine wash/dry.

■ Shirt Maker Medium weight (Staple-601)
COLORS: White
NOTES: Crisp; for details; 22"; 100% poly; machine wash.

■ Shaping Aid Medium weight (Staple 203, 204)
COLORS: White, black
NOTES: Firm, stable; 22"; 100% polyester; machine wash.

Heavy-Weight Sew-In Interfacings

Woven Sew-Ins

■ Veri-Shape Durable Press (HTC-2030)
COLORS: White, black
NOTES: Crisp, firm support; 45", 50% poly/50%rayon; machine wash/dry.

■ Sta-Form Durable Press (HTC-7500)
COLORS: White, black
NOTES: Crisp; 50% poly/50% rayon; machine wash/dry.

■ Pellon Sew-in (Pellon-930)
COLORS: White
NOTES: All bias; 100%poly; machine wash/dry or dry-clean.

■ Intra-FaceTM Heavy weight (HTC-6040)
COLORS: White
NOTES: Stiff, details areas; 23"; 20% rayon/80% poly; machine wash/dry.

Hair Canvas Sew-Ins

■ Hair canvas (Richard Brooks, Lacy Lovelies, Cy Rudnick's)
COLORS: Lightweight Natural
NOTES: Crisp; 68", 60%wool/40%goat hair; dry-clean.

■ Hair canvas (Richard Brooks, Cy Rudnick's)
COLORS: Medium Natural
NOTES: Crisp; 72", 60%wool/40%goat hair; dry-clean.

■ Hair canvas (Richard Brooks, Cy Rudnick's)
COLORS: Medium White
NOTES: Crisp; 68", 35%wool/65%goat hair; dry-clean.

■ Hair canvas (Greenberg & Hammer)
COLORS: Medium Natural
NOTES: Crisp; 25", wool/goat hair; dry-clean.

■ Hymo (Greenberg & Hammer)
COLORS: Light, Med, Heavy Natural White, black
NOTES: Crisp; used in RTW; 66", quality depends on % wool/goat hair; dry-clean.

■ Women's Hymo (Fabric Collections)
COLORS: Grey
NOTES: Crisp; 74", rayon/poly blend; dry-clean.

■ Acro Medium weight (HTC-87001)
COLORS: Medium Natural
NOTES: Crisp; 25", 52%rayon; 43%poly/5%goat hair; washable.

■ Tailor's Pride (HTC-87003)
COLORS: Medium Natural
NOTES: Very crisp; 23"; 41%acrylic/19%goat hair/16%poly/15%viscose/9%cotton; dry-clean.

■ Haircloth (Greenberg & Hammer)
COLORS: Medium Natural
NOTES: Very stiff, wiry; 20", dry-clean.

Specialty Sew-In Interfacings: underlinings, ties, corsets, sleeve headers, hems, collars, cuffs, pockets.

Woven Sew-Ins

■ 714 (Fabric Collections)
COLORS: Ivory
NOTES: Soft underlinings. 25", 100% wool; dry-clean.

■ Collar linen (Greenberg & Hammer)
COLORS: Tan
NOTES: Medium crisp; 100% linen, tailored collars, dry-clean.

Armo® Rite (HTC-86001)
COLORS: Cream
NOTES: Soft; ties, underlinings, quilts, interfacing hems; 25", 100% poly; machine wash, dry-clean.

Coutil (Greenberg & Hammer)
COLORS: White, grey
NOTES: Heavy herringbone weave for corsets and underpinnings; 60"; 100% cotton; machine wash and dry-clean.

Baby flannel
COLORS: White, prints
NOTES: Napped on one side; 45", 100% cotton; machine wash/dry.

Double-napped flannel (Greenberg & Hammer)
COLORS: White
NOTES: Napped on both sides; 45", 100% cotton; machine wash/dry.

Knit Sew-Ins

Lamb's wool, Domette, Llama wool, Eskimo (Greenberg & Hammer)
COLORS: White, black
NOTES: Soft, loosely knitted with fleece on fabric face; sleeve heads, quilting, hems, shoulder pads; 45", 40%wool/60%rayon; dry-clean.

Buckram (Greenberg & Hammer)
COLORS: White, black
NOTES: Very stiff; millinery; 30", 100% cotton; Dry-clean.

Crinoline (Greenberg & Hammer)
NOTES: Very stiff; millinery and underskirts; 38", 100% cotton; dry-clean.

Above: Designed by Linda MacPhee, this jacket is simply cut to showcase the eyelash fabric. (Photo courtesy of MacPhee Workshop.)

Right: Crisp and cool, this linen top and skirt is ideal for warm weather dressing. (Burda pattern – 3005, courtesy of Burda.)

Left: A great surface for creative expression, this sampler jacket is fabricated in hemp. The embroidery designs are Bernina's Contemporary Motifs and Borders from Claire Shaeffer's Studio.

Resource List

A-1 Pleating Co.
1/2 West 3rd
Los Angeles, CA 90048
(323) 653-5557
(pleating; about 1 week)

Baer Fabrics
515 E. Market St.
Louisville, KY 40202
(502) 583-5521
www.baerfabrics.com

Banasch's Fabrics
Rookwood Pavilion
2692 Madison Rd.
Cincinnati, OH 45208
(513) 731-5757

Britex Fabrics
146 Geary
San Francisco, CA 94108
(415) 392-2910
www.britexfabrics.com

Burda Patterns-U.S.
c/o Simplicity Pattern Co., Inc.
Attn.: Sue Fleck
2 Park Ave., 12th floor
New York, NY 10016
Butterick Patterns
www.butterick.com

Buttons 'n' Bolts
1750 E. Ft. Lowell
Tucson, AZ 85719
(520) 795-1533
www.buttonsnboltsfabrics.com

Caledonia Fine Fabrics, Etc.
605 Americana Blvd.
Boise, ID 83702
(208) 338-0895
www.cff2@mindspring.com

Carol's Zoo
Carol Cruise
992 Coral Ridge Circle
Rodeo, CA 94572
(510) 245-2020
www.carolszoo.com

Casual Elegance Fabrics
2500 Durham Dayton Rd.
Durham, CA 95938
PO Box 6453
Chico, CA 95927
(530) 343-6838
www.casele@sunset.net

Claire Shaeffer's
Custom Couture Collection
Vogue Patterns
www.voguepatterns.com

Clotilde
B3000
Louisiana, MO 63353-3000
(800) 772-2891
www.clotilde.com

Couture Fabrics
7120 Indian School Rd.
Scottsdale, AZ 85251
(408) 949-8238
www.coutfab@msn.com

Cy Rudnick Fabrics
2450 Grand Ave.
Kansas City, MO 64108
(816) 842-7808

D'Leas Fabric & Button Studio
2719 E. Third St.
Denver, CO 80206
(303) 388-5665

East of Eden Leathers and
    Exotic Skins
1 Arthur Place
Yonkers, NY 10701
(888) 469-7238
www.eastofedenleathers.com

Eunice Farmer Fabrics
9814 Clayton Rd.
St. Louis, MO 63124
(314) 997-1531

Fabric Collections
900 S. Orlando Ave.
Winter Park, FL 32789
(407) 740-7737
www.fabriccollections.com

Fabric Gallery
l46 W. Grand River Ave.
Williamston, MI 48895
(517) 655-4573
www.fabricgallery.net

Fashion Affair
2828 E. 330 S.
Salt Lake City, UT 84109
(801) 486-7600
www.fashionaffair@aol.com

Frostline Kits
P. O. Box 3419
Grand Junction, CO 81502
(800) 548-7872
www.frostlinekitsllc.com

Gail K. Fabrics
2216 Cheshire Bridge Rd. NE
Atlanta, GA 30324
(404) 982-0366

Ghee's
2620 Centenary #2-250
Shreveport, LA 71104
(318) 226-1701
www.ghees.com

G Street Fabrics
11854 Rockville Pike
Rockville, MD 20852
(301) 231-8998
www.jschwartz@gstreetfabrics
    .com

Ginny's Fine Fabrics and
    Support Group
12 S. Broadway
Rochester, MN 55904
(507) 285-9134
www.ginnysfinefabrics.com

The Grapevine Collection
1009 Cheek-Sparger Rd. #106
Colleyville, TX 76034
(817) 514-6061
www.sewitup.com (coming)

Green Pepper
PO Box 42073
Eugene, OR 97404
800-767-5684
www.thegreenpepper.com

Greenberg & Hammer, Inc.
24 W. 57th St.
New York, NY 10019-3918
(800) 955-5135, (212) 246-2835
www.greenberg-hammer.com

Haberman's Fabrics
904 S. Main St.
Royal Oak, MI 48067
(248) 541-0010
www.habermanfabrics.com

Hidehouse.com
P.O. Box 509
Napa, CA 94559
(888) 443-3468
www.hidehouse.com

Joanne's Creative Notions
P. O. Box 44030
1 Wexford Rd., Unit #9
Brampton, Ontario L6Z 2W1
(800) 811-6611 Canada
(905) 453-1805 U.S.
www.joannescreativenotions.
    com

Karen's Kreations
Karen Rudman
6542 125th Ave. SE
Bellevue, WA 98006
(425) 643-9809

KWIK·SEW®
3000 Washington Ave. N.
Minneapolis, MN 55411
(888) 594-5739, (612) 521-7651
(patterns)
www.kwiksew.com

Lacy Lovelies Fashion Fabrics
35 Central Ave. NW
LeMars, Iowa 51031
(866) 322-7421
www.lacylovelies.com

La Fred
4200 Park Blvd., Suite 102
Oakland, CA 94602
(510) 893-6811
(patterns)
www.lafred.com

Linda Kubik
310 E. 8th Ave.
Ritzville, WA 99169
(509) 659-0209
www.kubikelements.com

LJ Designs
P. O. Box 18923
Reno, NV 89511
(775) 853-2207
(patterns)
www.LJDesignsOnline.com

Londa's Sewing Etc., Inc.
P.O. Box 267
Savoy, IL 61874
866-566-3211
www.Londas-Sewing.com

Lycra House, Inc.
263 W. 38th St., 2nd floor
New York, NY 10018
(212) 868-0944
lycrahouse.com

Make It Yourself With Wool
P.O. Box 175
Lavina, MT 59046
(406) 636-2731

Martha Pullen Co., Inc.
149 Old Big Cove Rd.
Brownsboro, AL 35741-9985
(800) 547-4176
www.marthapullen.com

Maryanne's Fabrics, Etc.
3965 Phelan #106
Beaumont, TX 77707
(409) 838-3965
www.maryannesfabrics.com

McCall Pattern Company
(McCall's, Butterick, Vogue)
11 Penn Plaza
New York, NY 10001
www.mccallpatterns.com

Mendel's Far Out Fabrics
1556 Haight St.
San Francisco, CA 94117
(415) 621-1287
www.mendels.com

Nancy's Notions
PO Box 683
Beaver Dam, WI 53916-0683
(800) 833-0690, (920) 887-0391
www.nancynotions.com

Newark Dressmaker Supply
P. O. Box 20730
Lehigh Valley, PA 18002-0730
(800) 736-6783
www.newarkdress.com
(notions)

Outdoors Wilderness Fabrics
16415 N. Midland Blvd.
Nampa, ID 83687
(800) 693-7467
www.owfinc.com
(outdoor fabrics)

Park Bench Pattern Co.
P. O. Box 191399
San Diego, CA 92159
(619) 269-9808
www.parkbenchpatterns.com

Peggy Sagers-Silhouette
    Patterns
305 Spring Creek Village #326
Dallas TX 75748
800-784-8245
www.silhouettepatterns.com

Professioal Sewing Supplies
P.O. Box 14272
Seattle, WA 98114-4272
(206) 324-8823
(notions)

Quest Outfitters
4919 Hubner Cir.
Sarasota, FL 34241
(800) 359-6931
www.questoutfitters.com
(outdoor fabrics)

Ragged Mountain Equipment, Inc.
Route 16-302, PO Box 130
Intervale, NH 03845
(603) 356-3042
www.raggedmountain.com
(outdoor fabrics)

The Rainshed
707 NW 11th
Corvallis, OR 97330
(541) 753-8900
(outdoor fabrics)

Richard Brooks Couture Fabrics
6131 Luther Ln., Suite 200
Dallas, TX 75225
(214) 739-2772

Rochelle Harper Patterns
www.rochelleharper.net

Rockywoods Outdoors Fabrics
3419 W. Eisenhower
Loveland, CO 80537
(970) 663-6163
www.rockywoods.com
(outdoor fabrics)

Rose City Textiles
2515 NW Nicolai
Portland, OR 97210
www.rosecitytextiles.com
(outdoor fabrics)

SAF-T-POCKETS
1385 NE 49th St.
Portland, OR 97213-2111
SAF-T-POCKETS.com

San Francisco Pleating Company
233 23rd Ave.
San Mateo, CA 94403
(415) 982-3003
(pleating; about 2 weeks)

Seattle Fabrics
8702 Aurora Ave. North
Seattle, WA 98103
(206) 525-0670
www.seattlefabrics.com
(outdoor fabrics)

Sew Baby
P. O. Box 721
Savoy, IL 61874
(800) 249-1907
www.sewbaby.com

The Sewing Place
18476 Prospect Rd.
Saratoga, CA 95070
(800) 587-3937, (408) 252-8444
www.thesewingplace.com

Sewing Workshop Collection
800-466-1599
www.sewingworkshop.com

Simplicity Pattern
2 Park Ave., 12th floor
New York, NY 10016
www.simplicity.com

Spandex House, Inc.
263 W. 38th St., 2nd floor
New York, NY 10018
(212) 354-6711
spandexhouse.com

Spiegelhoff's Stretch & Sew Fabrics
4901 Washington Ave.
Racine, WI 53406
(266) 632-2660
www.greatcopy.com

Stonemountain & Daughter
2518 Shattuck Ave.
Berkeley, CA 94704
(510) 845-6106

Tandy Leather
(800) 555-3130
www.tandyleather.com

Thai Silks
252 State St.
Los Altos, CA 94022
(800) 722-7455, (650) 948-8611
www.thaisilks.com

Things Japanese
9805 N.E. 116th St., Suite 7160
Kirkland, WA 98034
(425) 821-2287
www.silkthings.com

Timmel Fabrics
2635 Dublin Street
Halifax, Nova Scotia B3L 3J6
Canada
www.timmelfabrics.com

Vogue Fabrics
618 Hartrey Ave.
Evanston, IL 60202
(800) 433-4313, (708) 864-9600
www.voguefabricstore.com

Wild Ginger Software, Inc.
888-929-9453
www.wildginger.com

Foreign Suppliers:

Canada

Burda Patterns-Canada
H.A. Kidd & Co., Ltd.
5 Northline Rd.
Toronto, ON
M4B 3PS, Canada
416-364-6451

A Great Notion
108-19289 Langley ByPass
Surrey, B.C. V3S 6K3
604-575-9026
800-204-4117
www.agreatnotion.com

MacDonald Faber Ltd.
952 Queen St. West
Toronto, Ontario M6J 1G8
(416) 534-3940

MacPhee Workshop
Box 10, Site 16, R.R.8
Edmonton, AB T5L 4H8
Canada
(888) 622-7433
www.macpheeworkshop.com

Petite Plus Patterns
PO Box 81140, SBby PO
Burnaby, BC Canada V5H 4K2
1-877-909-8668
www.petitepluspatterns.com

United Kingdom
MacCulloch & Wallis Ltd.
25 Dering St.
London, W1R OBH, U.K.
171-629-0311

Burda Patterns–UK
Simplicity Ltd.
Attn.: Linda Saddler
PO Box 367
Stockport
SK 7WZ

Australia
Burda Patterns
Simplicity Patterns PTY Ltd.
Att.: Greg Penn
25 Violet St.
Revesby, NSW 2212

Bibliography

Aldrich, Winifred. Fabric, *Form and Flat Pattern Cutting*. Oxford: Blackwell Science, c. 1996.

Cornwell, Nancy. Nancy Cornwell's *Polar Magic: New Adventures With Fleece*. Krause Publications, c. 2001.

Harper, Rochelle. *Sewing Outdoor Gear: Easy Techniques for Outerwear that Works*. Newtown, CT: The Taunton Press, c. 2001.

Harper, Rochelle. *Sew the New Fleece: Techniques with Synthetic Fleece and Pile*. Newtown, CT: The Taunton Press, c. 1997.

Humphries, Mary. *Fabric Reference*. Upple Saddle River, NJ: Prentice Hall, c. 1996.

Humphries, Mary. *Fabric Glossary*. Upple Saddle River, NJ: Prentice Hall, c. 1996.

Parker, Julie. *All About Cotton*. Seattle: Rain City Publishing, c. 1993.

Parker, Julie. *All About Silk*. Seattle: Rain City Publishing, c. 1992.

Parker, Julie. *All About Wool*. Seattle: Rain City Publishing, c. 1996.

Shaeffer, Claire. *Couture Sewing Techniques*. Newtown, CT: The Taunton Press, c. 1993.

Shaeffer, Claire. *Claire Shaeffer's Fabric Sewing Guide-Updated Edition*. Iola, WI: Krause Publications, c. 1994.

Shaeffer, Claire. T*he Complete Book of Sewing Short Cuts*. New York: Sterling Publishing, c. 1981.

Tortora, Phyllis G. and Billie J. Collier. *Understanding Textiles, 5th, ed.* Upple Saddle River, NJ: Prentice Hall, c. 1997.

Tortora, Phyllis G. and Robert S. Merkel. F*airchild's Dictionary of Textiles, 7th ed.* New York: Fairchild Publications, c. 1996.

Index

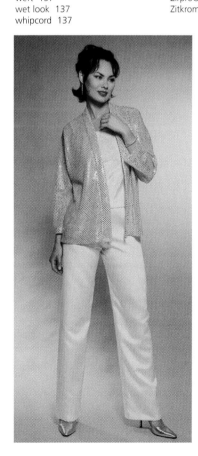

This smart evening ensemble features practical, easy-care polyesters topped by a stunning sequin jacket. (Photo courtesy of Simplicity — 7007.)

Hundreds of Tips, Techniques, and Project Ideas

Claire Shaeffer's Fabric Sewing Guide

by Claire Shaeffer
Learn the secrets of selection, wear, care, and sewing of all fabrics, including microfibers, stabilizers, and interfacings. Content and distinctive properties of each textile are detailed, as are appropriate designs and patterns. Plan and lay out a garment and learn where to obtain equipment and supplies.

Softcover • 8¼ x 10⅞ •
544 pages
24-page color section
Item# FSG • $32.95

Bridal Couture

Fine Sewing Techniques for Wedding Gowns and Evening Wear
by Susan Khalje,
Foreword by Claire Shaeffer
Create a fantasy! Susan Khalje guides readers through the principles and techniques of designing, constructing, and embellishing wedding gowns and evening wear. Ideal for the bride-to-be or seamstress, learn how to choose the right fabric, work with lace, or problem solve tricky construction issues.

Softcover • 8¼ x 10⅞ •160 pages
Color throughout
Item# BCWG • $29.95

Sewing With Nancy's Favorite Hints

20th Anniversary Edition
by Nancy Zieman
To celebrate the 20th anniversary of her popular PBS show, Nancy Zieman brings you a collection of her favorite tips, hints, and techniques from the past two decades. You'll find tips for keeping your sewing room organized, Nancy's favorite notions, helpful sewing solutions, embroidery hints, quilting tips, and more! Relive the memories of the longest-running sewing program on public television with the nation's leading sewing authority!

Softcover • 8¼ x 10⅞ • 144 pages
150 color photos
Item# NFTT • $19.95

Nancy Cornwell's Polar Magic

New Adventures With Fleece
by Nancy Cornwell
Join award-winning author Nancy Cornwell on another exciting and educational sewing adventure with fleece—one of today's hottest fabrics. Includes step-by-step instructions for 16 projects such as quilts, pillows, a jacket, vests, and much more, plus 15 different templates for stitch patterns used to embellish garments. You will love the versatility and the new twist Nancy puts on fleece.

Softcover • 8¼ x 10⅞ • 160 pages
200 color photos
Item# AWPF3 • $21.95

Sew Gifts With Love

by Nancy Zieman
Create gorgeous evening bags, picture frames, fleece throws, bathroom towels, jewelry baskets, and more. Give these wonderful creations away or keep them for yourself; either way, they will be treasured for years to come. Learn to incorporate unique designs, such as hearts, snowflakes, and pineapples, into everyday personal accessory and home décor items. Patterns, detailed illustrations, and step-by-step instructions ensure you complete projects successfully every time.

Softcover • 8¼ x 10⅞ • 144 pages
100 color photos
Item# SGWL • $21.99

Sewing With Nancy® 10-20-30 Minutes to Sew for Your Home

by Nancy Zieman
This exciting new book from the host of the top-rated PBS show Sewing With Nancy® offers more than 25 soft-furnishing projects for every room of the home that can be completed even by those who only have 10, 20, or 30 minutes to spare. You'll quickly learn to create a quilt for the bedroom, a table runner for the kitchen, a machine mat for the sewing room, crib sheets for baby's room, and much more! Expert author Nancy Zieman's step-by-step instructions will guide you through everything from choosing fabrics and supplies to a successful finished project.

Softcover • 8¼ x 10⅞ • 96 pages
50 color photos and step-by-step instructions
Item# MNSYH • $16.95

To order call 800-258-0929 Offer CRB3